DYNAMICS OF

Effective Teaching

DYNAMICS OF

Effective Teaching

Richard Kindsvatter
Kent State University

William Wilen
Kent State University

Margaret Ishler
Bowling Green State University

Longman

New York & London

Dynamics of Effective Teaching

Longman Inc., 95 Church Street, White Plains, N. Y. 10601

Associated companies:
Longman Group Ltd., London
Longman Cheshire Pty., Melbourne
Longman Paul Pty., Auckland
Copp Clark Pitman, Toronto
Pitman Publishing Inc., New York

Senior editor: Naomi Silverman
Production editor: Elsa van Bergen
Text design: Carole Basen
Cover design: Joseph DePinho
Production supervisor: Judith Stern

Library of Congress Cataloging-in-Publication Data

Kindsvatter, Richard.
    Dynamics of effective teaching.

    Bibliography: p.
    Includes index.
        1. Teaching.   2. Education, Secondary—United States.
3. Classroom management.   4. Motivation in education.
I. Ishler, Margaret F.   II. Wilen, William W.   III. Title.
LB1025.2.K5296 1987   373.11'02   87–4007
ISBN 0-582-28613-1

Compositor: Pine Tree Composition, Inc.
Printer: RR Donnelley & Sons Company

88 89 90 91 9 8 7 6 5 4 3 2 1

Contents

v

Preface

This is a book about teaching at the middle and high school levels. Its particular emphasis is on instruction as the focal point of teaching. Four of the ten chapters address instruction directly. The remaining chapters are complementary to that focus.

The book was conceived after realizing that current professional literature reveals new patterns of teacher behavior that are demonstrably more effective than common past practices. As a departure from the typical methods text, we produced a book that presents for the reader's consideration relevant research and theory. We encourage you, as preservice and beginning teachers, to acquire an informed belief system as the basis for your teaching decisions. Decision making, in fact, is a continuing theme throughout this book.

We also realized that, as instructors of professional education courses, teacher education is becoming increasingly more clinically oriented. Today preservice teachers engage in more simulated and practice teaching than in the past. They need a means for analyzing and assessing their performance, as do student teachers and beginning teachers. Therefore, we have incorporated numerous instruments that focus on discrete components of instruction and enable you to obtain selective data-based feedback. This is not simply a book about effective teaching. It is also a dynamic tool that will facilitate your growth in instructional competence.

We consider our audience to be teacher preparation students in a general secondary methods course, student or intern teachers who need a solid reference book and a comprehensive set of analysis instruments, and beginning teachers who intend to achieve their own level of optimum effectiveness. In a broad sense, any educator who engages in instruction or supervision will find something of value in this book.

The scope of the book must of necessity be limited. We included what we considered to be essential in a primer on general secondary instructional practice. We have not addressed many related topics which, while important to broadly conceived secondary education, are not central to the focus of this book. These topics include curriculum, exceptionality, learner characteristics, cultural diversity, and computers in the classroom.

It is true that in teaching, each of us must individually develop our own most effective style. It is a task that is made more difficult because there is no prior definition of that style or assurance of the task's completion. The most important purpose of this book is to encourage and support you in your personal quest.

Acknowledgments

We express thanks for kindly granted permission to include material from:

"Teachers' Thought Processes" by Clark and Peterson. In *Handbook of Research on Teaching*, Third Edition, edited by M. C. Wittrock. Copyright © 1986 by American Educational Research Association. Reprinted by permission of Macmillan Publishing Company.

A unit plan on aging by Nona Chambers, Anaconda, Montana. Adapted by permission.

"Questioning, Thinking and Effective Citizenship" by William W. Wilen, 1985, *Social Science Record*, 22, 1, pp. 5–6. Copyright 1985 by the New York Council for Social Science. Adapted by permission.

"Developing Effective Questioning Techniques" by William W. Wilen, 1983, *Southwestern Journal of Social Education*, 13, 1, pp. 23–26. Copyright 1983 by the Texas Council for the Social Sciences. Adapted by permission.

"Fry's Readability Graph" by Fry, 1968, *Journal of Reading*, April 1968. Copyright 1968 by the *Journal of Reading*. Reprinted by permission.

Rosenshine/Furst, "Research on Teacher Performance Criteria" in *Research in Teacher Education: A Symposium*, B. Othanel Smith ed., © 1971, p. 49. Adapted by permission of Prentice-Hall, Inc. Englewood Cliffs, New Jersey.

"Teacher Praise: A Functional Analysis" by Jere Brophy, 1981, *Review of Educational Research*, 51, 5–32. Copyright 1981 by the American Educational Research Association. Reprinted by permission.

"P Ratio Grid" by the Staff of the Reading Center, Omaha, Nebraska Board of Education. Copyright the Reading Center, Omaha Board of Education. Reprinted by permission.

Figure 6.1 is adapted from "The World Turned Upside Down" by Marta Norman and Richard Tringali, 1981, *Newsweek*, October 26, p. 38.

"Instructional Functions," reprinted with permission of Macmillan Publishing Company from *Handbook of Research on Teaching*, Third Edition, edited by M. C. Wittrock. Copyright © 1986 by the American Educational Research Association.

Model of and steps to implement cooperative learning, from *Circles of Learning* by Johnson and Johnson, 1984, pp. 27–28. Reprinted with permission of the Association for Supervision and Curriculum Development. Copyright © 1984 by the Association for Supervision and Curriculum Development. All rights reserved.

Kaleidoscope: Readings in Education (4th ed.) 1983, Houghton Mifflin; Dr. Benjamin Bloom's presentation of the structure of mastery learning presented by authors Kevin Ryan and James M. Cooper is included.

Adaptation of "Discipline Mystique and Discipline Practice." *The Clearing House,* 59, 9, pp. 406–407, May 1985. Reprinted with permission of the Helen Dwight Reid Educational Foundation. Published by Heldref Publications, 4000 Albemarle St., N.W., Washington, D.C., 20016, Copyright © 1985.

To the Instructor on Using This Book

In the preface, we have already described some of the ideas included in this book. A bit more explanation about the book may contribute to your understanding and effective use of it.

The particular sequence of chapters reflects what we consider to be a logical student approach to the study of teaching. Decision making, the most pervasive aspect of teaching, leads our presentation. The material that follows all has sound decision making as its basis.

All classroom teaching occurs within a social setting. Chapter 2 therefore addresses the teacher's role in providing for a productive climate and attending to students' motivation.

Planning is the first step in the 3-step process of teaching. Chapter 3 presents a fairly extensive description of planning because we feel that this is a topic that has not been thoroughly developed in other sources. We conceive of planning as a human process of decision making rather than the routine development of written plans.

Chapters 4, 5, 6, and 7 deal specifically with instruction as the second component in teaching. We begin with behaviors and techniques that are the basis for instruction, and show how they evolve into methods and strategies through the manipulation by the informed teacher. Meanwhile, we stress those elements of effective teaching that have the greatest impact on student achievement.

Chapter 8 deals with discipline, an ever-present factor in every classroom, and a concomitant of instruction. We have tried to describe an enlightened approach to discipline, keeping in mind that it is a supportive rather than a central topic of the book. Many helpful sources are readily available to instructors and students who wish to pursue the topic.

Evaluation, the third component of teaching, is addressed in Chapter 9. Like discipline, it is presented in a brief supportive chapter. The ideas in this chapter were selected carefully, and we believe we have included enough information to establish a reasonable foundation in this area. Again, any interested reader can find many excellent texts devoted entirely to the full development of this topic.

In the final chapter we describe the use of this book beyond the mere presentation of teaching ideas. As students become clinically involved with teaching through student teaching, internships, and finally in their first in-service year, the book will continue to be applicable. Use of the instruments at the end of most of the chapters will aid in the analysis of the various teaching components in clinical or field settings, and will promote improved performance.

We have purposely reserved one or more separate sections in each chapter for the research and theoretical base for discrete topics. This will aid the reader who wishes to refer directly to research/theory and is interested in its cumulative effect. However, reference is also made to research/theory in other parts of the text.

At the conclusion of each chapter and/or major section, we have included a Summary Point review of key points.

Activities are listed before the References section of each chapter and suggest useful ideas and activities to promote students' understanding and skill. Their inclusion at the end of each chapter will not interfere with the flow of ideas in the chapter. However, the instructor should determine when to refer students to the Activities section.

Instruments have been placed as appendices to each chapter rather than at the point in the chapter where the targeted performance is described. We feel that this is a smoother format. The instructor is encouraged to use his or her discretion as to the most effective application of the instruments within the course of instruction.

It is likely that more content is included in this book than can be fully covered in one semester of a general methods course. Some chapters may initially be given more attention than others, with the understanding that students may better utilize the other chapters at a later time, such as during student teaching or an internship. The instructor's wise judgment must determine this. We believe it is better for the instructor to have choices than to be too dependent on the authors' judgment and biases, as might be the case in a less comprehensive book.

We hope this book is of service to the instructor in teaching about teaching, and to the reader, as well, in learning about teaching.

An Approach to the Study of Teaching

ASSUMPTIONS AND BELIEFS

Assumptions and beliefs are the basis for much of our everyday behavior. Assumptions tend to be informal, while beliefs are more structured; however, one blends into the other so that, in many cases, distinguishing between them is impossible.

Teachers make assumptions and depend upon beliefs in their everyday teaching lives. For example, a teacher who lectures to a class about a particular topic assumes that the class will assimilate a sufficient understanding of that topic from the remarks. Or, the teacher who denies outside recess to a misbehaving child believes that punishment is a deterrent to future misbehavior. Some may not share the assumptions or beliefs of these teachers and would, therefore, use a different approach in these situations.

The role of beliefs and assumptions in decision making about teaching is addressed at greater length in Chapter 1, and serves as a thread throughout the book. At this point, we would like to share with the reader the assumptions and beliefs that underlie the approach to instruction in this book. These assumptions and beliefs reflect our particular preferences, perceptions, interpretations, and priorities and have been a guide in the development of this book. The reader must be aware of these assumptions and beliefs in order to understand the decision the authors have made about content, tone, and style in writing this guide to effective teaching.

Belief 1. The quality of teaching is directly contingent upon the quality of the decision making that precedes that teaching. In Chapter 1, decision making is fully described as a process, and as a cohesive concept that integrates various parts of teaching. In the following chapters decision making will be shown to be basic to establishing classroom climate, planning for teaching, interacting with students, and evaluating performance and achievement. It is the authors' intent to convince the reader that decision making deserves teachers' most professional attention.

Belief 2. Teaching is complex behavior. To attempt to interpret it in too-simple terms would surely lead to misunderstanding. This, in fact, is what occurs on the part of many non-educators, and results in distorted notions about the role of the teacher and the needs of schools. More tragically, some teachers are also guilty of such simplistic thinking, as reflected in classroom practices which disregard theory and research and rely on a "bag of tricks" approach.

Throughout the book, the authors are careful not to take for granted either teaching or their own collective experiences. They have attempted to identify the most pertinent theory and most useful research as the basis for the selection of content. The emphasis on effective teaching research is an example. Also, the reader will note a unique approach to planning as recommended in Chapter 3, presented after reviewing research findings which indicate that the most commonly recommended approach has serious limitations.

Belief 3.   Teaching is learned behavior. One often hears about the "born teacher," and that nobody had to teach Socrates or Christ how to teach. Because of a charismatic personality, personal sensitivity, and/or the gift of verbal dexterity, some people are better able to inform and influence others. These characteristics are, certainly, desirable traits in a teacher. However, pedagogy as the study of education is based on scientifically derived principles that have been established, especially over the past 100 years, through the work of thousands of scholars and practitioners. To assume that a teacher can be optimally effective without a reasonably sound grounding in this science is being naïve. One can draw the analogy of a kindly family doctor, a general practitioner, being called upon to perform quadruple bypass heart surgery, the task of a highly trained specialist. It is unthinkable; yet there are those who believe that it does not take extensive preparation to teach effectively.

In the latter section of the introduction, the discipline of pedagogy is retrieved from the academic dustbin and given the prominent place it deserves in academic thinking and decision making. The concept of pedagogy brings respectability and dignity to the science of the teaching profession. In fact, without pedagogy, teaching could not claim to be a profession. Throughout the book, the authors will emphasize the importance of pedagogy taking precedence over personal experience as a referent in effective teaching.

Belief 4.   Instruction should be based on the most effective strategies, methods, techniques, and behaviors as determined by current research and learning theory. Actually, this belief is an extension of the statements made under beliefs 2 and 3. A science of teaching, or pedagogy, is derived from research and learning t! ory, and is validated by practice. As professional practitioners, teachers must have faith in the science of the profession, for without it they approach it, essentially, as a craft. A totally personal approach hardly serves in guiding the development of the most complex entity known in the universe—the human mind.

In this book we have attempted to translate the most up-to-date, credible ideas from educational literature into practices teachers can integrate into their own teaching styles, especially in Chapters 4, 5, 6, and 7 dealing with instructional practices as such. In the final chapter on improving instruction, the authors provide teachers with the means for analyzing their own practice and creating their own unique versions of effective techniques.

Belief 5.   Students must be motivated. This is hardly a controversial statement. It is, in fact, so obvious and pervasive that it is regularly taken for granted. As this book was written, the concept of motivation could not be ignored, any more than any current or prospective teacher can afford to ignore it. Students must be motivated in the areas of emotional and academic needs, interests, and abilities in order for learning to occur. This is the cornerstone of instruction. The initial and essential responsibility of teachers is to arouse in students the desire to learn. To assume that students should want to learn, or will make the effort—especially if they already lack a personal sense of purpose—is naïve. The truest measure of teaching effectiveness is the extent to which a teacher creates conditions which promote student motivation.

Belief 6. The social setting in which instruction occurs is a major factor affecting that instruction. Admittedly, the possibility of tutorial teaching and independent learning exist, but when one thinks of schooling, one envisions teachers instructing a group of students in a classroom, laboratory, or on the athletic field. The nature of such interaction is termed "group process." A body of knowledge has been developed on the subject of group process, and principles related to its application have been established. Clearly, the classroom cannot be fully understood solely in terms of intellectual considerations. The quality of life in the classroom is also contingent upon social factors. Therefore, the classroom environment as it is affected by group process is the backdrop of productive learning.

In this book we do not focus specifically on theories dealing with the special area of study termed "group process." We have, however, attempted to employ some ideas that involve productive and cooperative interrelationships within the classroom. Discussions on classroom climate and classroom discipline draw heavily on these ideas, and throughout the chapters on instruction they are considered to be implicit.

Belief 7. Teaching is, in the final analysis, a personal invention. While pedagogy is the foundation of optimally effective teaching, it tends to be more suggestive than prescriptive. Individual teachers, meanwhile, are as different from one another as everyone else in the population. For example, a teacher who has a highly developed sense of humor may banter with students and use quips, the overall effect of which is quite positive. A more serious-minded teacher may conduct a more businesslike class, yet is equally effective in achieving student learning outcomes. Teachers will be most effective if they maintain their own personal identity and integrity while being guided by the tenets of pedagogy.

The observation has been made that effective teachers tend to be more diverse among themselves, while mediocre teachers tend to be more alike. We believe that teaching is a personal invention for each practitioner, and this book is intended to contribute to the personal inventing process. Throughout this book, the emphasis will be on helping teachers develop their own unique teaching styles within a framework of established principles.

PEDAGOGY—THE DISCIPLINE OF TEACHING

Pedagogy, like mathematics, music, or philosophy, is a discipline, that is, a recognized area of academic study and practice. The term *pedagogy* itself has Greek and Latin origins, and is a reminder of all that was excellent in classical education. In current use, it likewise connotes all that is best in modern education. While educators more commonly use the broader term *education*, *pedagogy* has the advantage of defining more precisely the opposite of anti-intellectualism. Pedagogy is understood to refer to the discipline of education, and not necessarily to all practices that in some way might be associated with teaching. Pedagogy, therefore, defined as an extensive body of knowledge that incorporates those principles and practices that have been validated by research and scholarly scrutiny, is a term that will be used often in this book to convey the ideal of enlightened teaching.

Pedagogy as a formal discipline is not always embraced enthusiastically by teachers. Attitudes range from unconcern through condescension to distrust. When teachers are suspicious of pedagogy, or associate it primarily with scholarly papers and textbooks, they consider the literature to have little relationship to what really happens in schools. Teachers sometimes remark that a particular idea "is okay in theory, but won't work in the classroom." Such a position reflects a misunderstanding of theory, or more precisely, pedagogy.

The authors do not maintain that pedagogy implies absolute certainty, but rather that it is currently the most accurate theory known about education. To reject it, or ignore it, and be guided primarily by individual personal experience is to assume a patently anti-intellectual posture. In doing so, one is in essence saying, "Don't confuse me with the facts."

If teaching is to reach its fullest potential, teacher decision making—the link between theory and practice—must be guided by pedagogy. Hunter (1979) has obseved that, "Now adequate preparation parallels that of medicine, for it requires the professional to learn, internalize and implement the contributions of science to increased productive human functioning" (p. 62).

GENERALIZATIONS

Two generalizations emerge from the previous commentary. First, teaching involves a high order of human functioning. The most effective teachers are well informed regarding modern pedagogical principles, and are able to translate those principles of teaching and learning into effective practice. Furthermore, teaching behaviors have many purposes: academic, social, personal, and behavioral. Teachers need a repertoire of skills and methods that will enable them to accommodate a host of instructional demands.

Second, the nature of teaching is best understood if it is conceived as a science that is implemented by artists. Automobile racing serves as an apt analogy. The sophisticated technology involved in modern automotive engineering achieves its potential only in the hands of a talented and skilled driver. Likewise, state-of-the-art pedagogy remains only a promise until it is made functional by competent teachers whose own personalities and perceptions provide the dynamic dimension of pedagogy.

This book uses as its point of departure the beliefs and generalizations presented in this section. The authors have attempted to collect and organize throughout the remainder of the book theories, principles, research findings, and practices which usefully elaborate these selected beliefs and generalizations. As previously stated, there is no possible prescription for effective teaching in a direct, one to one fashion. However, the authors believe that teachers and teacher education students—will benefit from giving careful consideration to the ideas and examples in this book, and translating them within the context of their respective teaching styles and settings.

ACTIVITIES

1. Consider the seven beliefs about teaching that are presented in this chapter.
   a. Arrange the beliefs as presented to reflect your own priorities.
   b. State those additonal beliefs you have, especially as they may relate to your own teaching area, that reflect your interpretation of the teacher role.
   c. Think of the most effective teacher you know as a student. How does that teacher ''measure up'' in terms of the factors suggested by the beliefs list you have developed?
2. In this book, pedagogy is defined as ''the science of education.''
   a. What are some possible reasons why pedagogy is considered suspect by some teachers?
   b. What conditions would have to exist in order for pedagogy to be universally held in high esteem by teachers?
3. Teaching is viewed in many different ways, dependent on the vantage point and values of the viewer.
   a. Rank the following professions from the highest to the lowest level of human functioning: architect, news correspondent, teacher, commercial pilot, surgeon, NBA player.
   b. What issues arise as you compare your list to those of others, including non-educators.
4. Assume you are filling in an application for a teaching position. One section asks you to state in no more than 200 words your position on what you consider to be the most important factor in teacher effectiveness. Write your statement.

REFERENCE

Hunter, Madeline. (1979). Teaching is decision making. *Educational Leadership, 37*(2), 62–67.

1 Teacher Decision Making

Why a chapter on decision making? Farr and Brown (1971) provide a persuasive rationale as they observe that "... most instructional decisions are made by forfeit; that is, by not recognizing that a decision can be made or by not being aware of possible alternatives. The usual forfeit 'decision' involves continuation of a practice whether or not it is the most appropriate procedure for the situation" (p. 341). This chapter attempts to guide teachers away from such forfeiting or decision making by default, toward purposeful decision making.

Furthermore, as Hunter (1984) points out, professional decision making and effective teaching are interrelated concepts.

> Education professionals need to move from the extremes of either intuitive or "recipe-based" behavior to deliberate professional decision making based on research plus experiential wisdom. There still remains plenty of room for intuition. Clearly, we desire educators who are inspired, empathetic, and sensitive to the needs of students and dedicated to the value of education. Those traits are more likely to emerge and be maintained, however, if educators see that students learn successfully as a resulting of effective teaching (pp. 189–190).

Finally, decision making is a thread that links all the topics in this book. Because it is pervasive, any improvement that is made in a teacher's decision-making skills will be reflected in every aspect of that teacher's practice. In this respect, any change in decision making has the possibility for a broad-based impact.

OVERVIEW

Decision making is very personal behavior. It does not lend itself to tightly designed prescriptions. Nevertheless, there are certain common aspects of the process that teachers should consider. The most important point that will be made in this chapter is that a well-informed belief system is the most credible basis for rational teacher decisions. As teachers develop particular attitudes and habits of practice (i.e., patterns of decision making) that define their personal teaching styles, they should examine each one carefully to assure its conformity to accepted educational principles. As they later plan their instruction, interact in the classroom, and evaluate instructional outcomes, the parameters of thinking they have established will be a safeguard against superficial reasoning.

SCENARIO

Ms. Knettel was listening as her 9th grade students read aloud from *The Rime of the Ancient Mariner*, one verse per student in succession. The reading was expressionless and halting. Students paid little attention as other classmates read. Squirming and fidgeting created a minor disruption.

In planning this lesson a few days earlier, Ms. Knettel speculated that this poem, in particular, was one to which students could relate. It involves a fierce storm at sea, the curse of a so-called Spirit, shipmates who become zombies, and other miraculous events. The poem has vivid imagery and a readily perceived moral. Although some feel it is not the best of Romantic poetry, it seemed well-suited to acquaint students with the Romantic style.

As she conducted the lesson, Ms. Knettel realized she had over-estimated the potential of the poem to capture the students' imagination. She occasionally interspersed questions like, "Why did Coleridge choose an albatross as the bird that was shot?", and "Why was the ancient Mariner telling this tale to the wedding guest, who was a complete stranger?", but the class sat dumbfounded. To continue, she realized, was pointless. Yet what could she do?

An actual crisis had not yet occurred. The students were not out of hand, even though they were restless. She could momentarily continue with the present activity and buy a little time to think about it.

One alternative, she thought, was for students to read silently, and write answers to questions she put on the board. Meanwhile she could circulate throughout the room helping students individually, because many hesitated to ask questions aloud. Another alternative might be to appoint the best readers as small group leaders, and each group could read through the assignment together. This would provide active involvement of a greater number of students. A third alternative was for students to act out scenes from the poem: shooting the albatross, the vehemence of the crew, zombies sailing the ship, and confronting the wedding guest. For the poor readers, this would be a particularly useful way of presenting the substance of the poem, and everyone would enjoy the poem more.

Ms. Knettel considered the likely consequence of each alternative, but none of them seemed quite right. Then a fourth alternative occurred to her that was even more appealing. Why not have a class meeting to give the students the opportunity to express their perceptions and opinions, and to help her think through the situation?

"Class," she said, "we seem to have gotten bogged down. Do you think it would help if we talked about it? Let's spend the 25 minutes we have remaining in a class meeting. Move your chairs into a circle, like we did the last time, but lift them so we're not too noisy."

Ms. Knettel sat in as a member of the circle, and asked Marge if she would chair the meeting. A lively discussion ensued. Some students felt that *The Rime of the Ancient Mariner* was not "the greatest thing since pizza parties" (their expression), and they didn't see the point in studying it. Other students said they enjoyed the poem, even though they had difficulty expressing a rationale for their position. Finally, Geri asked, "Do you really think this stuff does us any good, Ms. Knettel? How can we ever use it?"

Ms. Knettel had taken the opportunity to reflect and to formulate the outline of her response while the students discussed their views for nearly 20 minutes. Now Geri provided the opportunity to comment.

"As a matter of fact," Ms. Knettel said, "there are few things you learn in school that you use directly. Everything you learn becomes part of what you are, and contributes to broad understandings and appreciations. Remember, *The Rime of the Ancient Mariner* was written about 160 years ago. Many thousands of poems have been written since, yet few of them are known or read today. This poem is still popular, mainly because it tells us with beauty and grace something important about the human condition. For example, we now sometimes use the expression "a person has an albatross around his neck," and it has a useful meaning because of the legacy Coleridge left us in his poem. Along with other great literature, this poem has made our thinking and expression much richer."

The students were quiet for several moments. Then Geri and several others agreed that they hadn't thought of it that way before. Todd commented that he still didn't like poetry, in general, but that he could see how somebody might. The bell rang at that point and the students left the room still talking about the possible merits of good poetry.

Ms. Knettel now sensed more interest from the students. The likelihood existed that, for the moment, they were willing to give the poem the benefit of the doubt. She realized that her job was to try to get them to the point of making a reasonable commitment.

By tomorrow, she thought, I've got to use a little imagination, and come up with a plan that utilizes this apparent momentum. With that, further decision making was in progress.

RESEARCH AND THEORETICAL BASE

Ms. Knettel made a timely decision that redirected the activity in her class. She did, in fact, employ a systematic approach to decision making that may not be apparent to a person unfamiliar with the dynamics of the process. These dynamics have their basis, in part, in the knowledge base related to decision making.

Perhaps the single most significant statement in the literature related to decision making is that by Shavelson (1973) which pronounces decision making to be the basic teaching skill. It is a statement which stands unchallenged because it is self-evident. Support for the statement is founded in logic and experience, not in research. In this same vein, Hunter (1984) defines teaching as "the constant stream of professional decisions that affects the probability of learning: decisions that are made and implemented before, during, and after interaction with the student" (pp. 169–170).

This unquestioning, often unconscious acceptance of decision making as a tacit and pervasive aspect of teaching is one reason for the limited amount of research focused on it. Another reason is the intimate nature of decision making. Decision making is wholly internalized, and can be studied only by inference from observed behavior or personal reporting. A third reason for limited research is that decision making is a generic and many-faceted concept. Research has addressed such related matters as teacher beliefs (Sontag, 1968), categories which are used as the basis for teacher decisions (Clark & Peterson, 1976; Rubenstein & Fisher, 1974; Herbert, 1974), and the reliability of teacher decisions (Shavelson, Cadwell, & Iza, 1977). There is, however, no theory or concept which integrates all the parts into a cohesive whole.

Several models, flow charts, matrices, and lists reflecting the teacher decision-making process are presented in the literature (Cooper, 1982; Hurst, Kinney, & Weiss, 1983; Shavelson, 1973; Borko et al., 1979). Each has been included for a specific purpose, viz., to illustrate a sequence of steps in a problem-solving process, to show the relationship of the elements involved in decision making, or to represent a problem-solving style. Few of the paradigms have actually been associated with research per se, either as a means of investigation or as an outcome. One exception is the model for investigating teachers' decisions developed by Borko et al. (1979). That model posits three factors contributing to teachers' preinstructional decisions: (1) information or cues about students; (2) beliefs and attitudes about education; and (3) the nature of the instructional task. A conclusion from that study is that it tends to replicate what teachers already intuitively sense about teaching, and about the difficulty of making consistently effective decisions. Furthermore, investigators contend that the model might be most helpful to teachers by raising their awareness of their own decision-making strategies. As such, it contributes little guidance to the process.

Hunter (1979) has presented a useful set of categories for analyzing decisions made by teachers. In the first category, contents to be learned, she emphasizes that the teacher must sense where the students' knowledge leaves off, and focus instructional decisions accordingly. Regarding the second category, style of the learner, the teacher must design modalities on an as-needed basis to address the inevitable range of learning styles within any group. She suggests pairing of modes such as *see and say, diagram and describe, hear and indicate,* and *write and examine* to better accommodate the diversity of learning styles. The third category, behavior of the teacher, serves as a reminder to the teacher that students' needs, not the teacher's preferences, should determine the selection of content and mode. Berliner's (1984) review of research on teaching cites certain striking examples of teachers' self-serving decisions, possibly decisions made by default. As an example of faulty decision making he notes that teachers often devote time to teaching favorite subjects—at the expense of others.

Several limited reviews of the research on decision making are available in the literature. Borko et al. (1979) cited research on three factors (see above) to establish the credibility of those factors as the basis for their decision making model. Shavelson (1976) reported research which addressed, in particular, five features of decision making: (1) alternative acts; (2) states of nature (i.e., conditions not under direct teacher control); (3) outcomes; (4) utility for the teacher; and (5) goals. Shavelson contended that planning decisions may be the most important ones that teachers make, and that teacher understanding of the five features could contribute to an awareness of alternatives and consequences, especially in planning. He concluded that the fostering of this understanding should be a purpose of teacher education programs. Hurst, Kinney, and Weiss (1983) provide a research perspective on decision making in the social studies. This review organizes findings according to six stages of decision making: (1) problem awareness (2) problem definition (3) developing alternatives (4) evaluating alternatives (5) implementing a plan and (6) evaluating results. The conclusion reached in the review is that current theoretical models and related research should be considered as simply an initial, inadequate body of knowledge that needs extensive development.

Shavelson and Stern (1981) and Clark and Peterson (1986) both presented comprehensive reviews of the research on teachers' pedagogical thought processes. While these reviews took two somewhat different perspectives, and therefore complement each other, the general conclusion of each is the same. Both report that as researchers attempt to probe more deeply into teachers' thought processes, material on decision making at this stage is largely descriptive. Empirical and conceptual research relating more directly to teacher practice is needed. Meanwhile, the broadest conclusion that may be drawn from the

research as it relates to practice is that teachers must be clear about their pedagogical beliefs and must monitor their decisions in terms of those expressed
beliefs.

Decision making undoubtedly is a basic teaching skill, but educators are left
essentially to their own devices regarding its application. Evidence of the direct
impact of theory and research on teacher decision making is minimal. However,
each contribution to the literature on decision making expands our knowledge
of it. A critical mass of knowledge may one day exist, signifying a major break-
through in the skill and application of decision making.

APPLICATION TO PRACTICE

The Process of Decision Making

As cited, a persuasive argument has been made for designating decision making
as *the* basic teaching skill. Indeed, effective decisions inevitably precede effective
teaching. This is a compelling rationale for examining decision making and for
striving to become proficient in its essential skills. But decision making is a subtle concept, and involves skills that are not directly acquired. Instead, the teacher
must acquire certain predisposing awarenesses and attitudes, after which an
improved decision-making capability is possible and probable.

Impact of Belief System. Teachers accumulate teaching-related ideas over time.
Generalized information, attitudes, and assumptions are internalized, and constitute the teacher's belief system. In the classroom scenario, Ms. Knettel wanted
her students to be interested in lesson content, and was disturbed that her lesson was proceeding mechanically. She needed to make a decision. But the decision she ultimately made, like most thoughtful decisions, was not based on
one identifiable principle or idea, but was the product of a belief system consisting of many integrated ideas. If the ideas from which a belief system is developed are judiciously selected, the decisions that emanate from it will be generally sound. Unfortunately, the judicious selection of ideas is not an easily
monitored process, and it requires knowledge and experience.

Part of the skill of decision making, therefore, involves an astute selection
of ideas which will predispose subsequent decisions. One can assume that there
existed within Ms. Knettel's belief system regard for the democratic process and
respect for her students' perceptions and opinions.

Some teacher beliefs are fairly simple: that homework should be assigned
routinely, for example, or, conversely, that routine homework is an unproduc-
tive use of students' time. Other beliefs are more elaborate and far-reaching.
Some teachers subscribe to the proposition that learning occurs most effectively
when the teacher is authoritarian or, again conversely, that the best teaching
occurs when the teacher is minimally directive. Such beliefs—some soundly
conceived, some only superficially; some clearly defined, some vaguely—characterize individual teaching styles.

Figure 1.1 illustrates an interpretation of decision making that is especially pertinent to the concern raised above. The basic process as depicted in the model is familiar in the literature (Cooper, 1982; Hurst & Kinney, 1983). However, the personal belief system is an added feature which has been incorporated by the authors. It has its point of entry in the selection of an approach. Clearly, the belief system as the selection mechanism in decision making becomes a key variable in the process.

The belief system is itself informed from two bases, the intuitive and the rational. Each is comprised of several components. The intuitive components include:

> *Experience-based impressions*—teacher's personal judgment regarding what is appropriate or useful practice. Example: ''After ten years of teaching I know I must get students' total attention before I begin class.'' ''When I send a student to the office, I don't have any more trouble in that class the rest of the day.''

> *Traditional practices*—common strategies and techniques which are widely accepted in schools and which have a rationale rooted in conventional wisdom. Example: Friday is test day; students write out the

Figure 1.1 Process of Teacher Decision Making

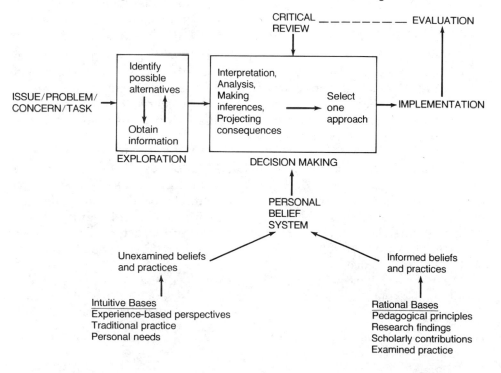

answers to the questions at the end of the chapter; reading is taught in the morning.

Personnel needs—personality-related and mental health-related factors that precondition the teacher's perception and behavior. Example: Students' desks are arranged in rows so that the teacher can control the noise level and direct lessons from the front of the room; all students in industrial arts lab work on the same project at the same time.

Rational components include:

Principles of education—those well-established and extensively documented tenets which often have a basis in related areas of study such as psychology, sociology, communications, leadership, organization, and group process. Example: positive reinforcement promotes the highest level of student achievement; students learn best when they perceive meaning and relevance in a topic.

Research findings—discoveries through systematic methods of research into content of education, instructional approaches, and learning effectiveness. Example: low ability students learn best from concrete approaches; task time correlates positively with student achievement.

Scholarly contributions—those essays, models, theories, and judgments of learned academicians which are an essential source of intellectual vigor and developmental thrust. Example: Bloom's (1956) *Taxonomy of Educational Objectives*; Report of the National Commission on Excellence in Education (1983) *A Nation at Risk.*

Examined practice—the strategies and techniques which have been determined through experience to be effective and consistent with professionally endorsed principles of pedagogy. Example: a variety of activities that show concern for students' span of attention result in effective teaching; treating students with respect and sensitivity contributes to the quality of classroom life.

Importance of Using Examined Beliefs and Practices. Even in our modern schools it is not unusual to find teachers whose practice is shaped primarily from their past experiences. Some teachers (also counselors and administrators) are unquestionably effective simply because of their ample intuitive grasp of what their role demands, and their talent for responding to students. These naturally gifted teachers are often referred to as "artist teachers." Less gifted teachers are obviously less effective.

To the extent that teachers operate primarily on the basis of experience, they perform analogously to the tribal medicine man. Through his use of both mystique and proficiency with primitive medicines, he may actually perform a valuable service for his fellow tribespeople. His practice, however, lacks a rationally developed base. Little change occurs in his practice from generation to generation because there is, essentially, no understanding of causes, and instead simply a recognition and treatment of symptoms. This is a casual analogy, and, in all fairness, should not be overstated. Changes have obviously occurred in education over any recent period of time one chooses to examine.

The fact remains that the gap between *what is* and *what might be* (real-ideal discrepancy) is a serious professional concern, evident by the 1980s' reports on the condition of schooling: *A Nation at Risk* (National Commission on Excellence in Education, 1983) as reported on by Goldberg and Harvey (1983) and A Study of Schooling (Goodlad, 1983). The former study states that inferior education is one reason for lack of competitiveness with other nations, and that even though mediocrity is the norm rather than the exception, we can—and must—do better. In a discussion of the latter study, Goodlad states, ''The most striking discovery to emerge from the data is what might be called sameness of form in the substance and design of the curriculum whether the subject is English/Language Arts, Mathematics, Science or Social Studies'' (p. 467).

There are many reasons for the real-ideal discrepancy in the schools, and teachers' use of unexamined beliefs and practices contributes to that discrepancy. If the recommendations in all of the studies of schooling were implemented, but some critical mass of teachers continued to use primarily experienced-based approaches, a real-ideal discrepancy would continue to exist.

Informed Decision Making

A science of education emerges from rational sources. Intuitive sources will inevitably remain as a factor in decision making, but practices based on rational sources should take precedence in any case in which they are available and applicable.

Intuitive sources are, in particular, inclined to reflect bias and self-service. Consider, for example, the case of a student in class who makes minimal efforts to perform assigned learning tasks. The teacher who makes a superficial evaluation of the student may consider that student to be lazy. That judgment places the fault—and therefore the responsibility—entirely on the student. The teacher may nag and occasionally reprimand the student, or simply ignore him except to assign low marks.

On the other hand, a teacher using a rational perspective is more likely to infer that the child lacks sufficient motivation, a factor for which the teacher shares responsibility, and may look for causes and solutions to the motivation problem. In Ms. Knettel's classroom scenario, she began searching for causes, rather than assuming that students would take an interest in Romantic poetry. A teacher who acknowledges his or her responsibility in a situation is more likely to take initiatives to improve the conditions for learning.

If educators were to relate their informed beliefs to their practice, changes would occur in their practice. Some possible areas of potential change are described below:

Discipline practices—The recent outpouring of professional literature on the management of student behavior signals a heightened awareness of past inadequacies and provides direction in the development of more enlightened approaches; approaches include the use of reasonable consequences, reality therapy, and behavior modification.

Individualization—New understanding through cognitive style studies and left brain/right brain experimentation raise expectations regarding the compatibility of teacher strategies with learner assimilation. A particular student's inclination towards intuitive (right hemisphere) or logical (left hemisphere) thinking has implications that are only beginning to be employed in classrooms in a systematic way.

Higher level thinking—Modern techniques of questioning can significantly raise the quality of students' thinking and increase the potential for a lasting impact. Bloom's Taxonomy (1956) stimulated efforts of scholars and practitioners to emphasize the use of information as a means to an end, not an end itself.

Instruction—Discriminating and imaginative use of a variety of strategies, such as those suggested in the *Models of Teaching* (Joyce & Weil, 1986) extends the purpose and range of instruction. Meaningful use of concepts such as time-on-task, direct teaching, instructional cues, and others popularized by research on effective teaching contribute to effective instruction.

Evaluation—Concepts such as non-graded classrooms, mastery level learning, contract grading, diagnosis and prescription, connoisseurship, and criterion/norm/person referenced considerations can help integrate evaluation with instruction.

The examples posed above include both some older, familiar ideas, as well as some recent ones. A teacher whose belief system, and, therefore, whose practice, is informed by such constructs is one for whom theory is—as Dewey (1929) insisted—the most practical of all things. Dewey meant simply that, as a practical matter in effective teaching, a sound conceptual framework (i.e., an informed belief system) is necessary. Without it, teaching is likely to be superficial and lacking in clear purpose.

Clark and Peterson (1986) have captured the spirit of informed decision making as it contributes to reflective teaching:

The maturing professional teacher is one who has taken some steps toward making explicit his or her implicit theories and beliefs about learners, curriculum, subject matter, and the teacher's role. This teacher has developed a style of planning for instruction that includes several interrelated types of planning and that has become more streamlined and automatic with experience. Much of this teacher's interactive thinking consists of routines familiar to the students, thus decreasing the collective information-processing load. During teaching, the teacher attends to and intently processes academic and nonacademic sociocog nitive events and cues. These experienced teachers have developed the confidence to depart from a planned course of action when they judge that to be appropriate. They reflect on and analyze the apparent effects of their own teaching and apply the results of these reflections to their future plans and actions. In short, they have become researchers on their own teaching effectiveness (pp. 292–293).

The remainder of this chapter essentially is an elaboration of this statement.

The Decision-Making Continuum

Virtually all teacher behavior involves choice, including the choice not to make a choice! By the idea of choice we mean that the possibility of alternatives exists, the simplest of which is whether or not to act. Some actions are characterized by the absence of any conscious choice; they represent unconscious behaviors on the part of the teacher. Other actions—and sometimes a complex sequence of actions—are preceded by deliberate reflection, such as the decision of Ms. Knettel to stage a classroom meeting. The range between these extremes represents a continuum of possibilities. Examples of behavior at each of the extremes and at the approximate midpoint will help to clarify different kinds of decision making.

Conditioned responses, and unconscious "knee-jerk" or habitual behaviors are at the absence-of-choice end of the continuum. The repeated use of certain words or phrases (especially *OK* and *you know*), rolling chalk in a hand, and raising the voice to talk over student noise are examples of this behavior. These examples and several other kinds of behavior from this end of the continuum are such a constant part of a teacher's pattern that they help define a teaching style, and in some cases are recognized as a teacher's idiosyncracies.

At the middle range of the continuum, behavior contains a conscious dimension, with some degree of spontaneity as well. Perhaps it is best described as conscious, non-reflective behavior. Examples of this sort of behavior often fall into the category of routine behavior. This behavior includes seating students in alphabetical rows, using the textbook as virtually the sole resource in a course, and starting lessons regularly by reading the answers to the homework.

At the deliberation end of the continuum, decision making is characterized by reflection. If one assumes that some degree of decision making has occurred all along the continuum—any teaching-related action is, by definition, preceded by a decision—the term "purposeful reflection" best describes the mental operation at this far end. Examples of this behavior are unit planning, offering enrichment or remediation to particular students, and using a balance of lower- and higher-order questions in classroom discussions.

Teachers make hundreds of conditioned responses and spontaneous choices in the course of a teaching day. For the sake of their sanity, they must. Practicing teachers may remember the mental fatigue they felt at the end of the day before they established a repertoire of effective responses and techniques.

On the other hand, teachers must not take their habitual choices for granted, and thereby engage in glib decision making. To do so inclines them toward the "mindlessness" syndrome observed by Silberman (1970) in so many classrooms in the late sixties, or the "monotonous sameness" reported by Goodlad (1983) in describing classrooms of the late seventies. These findings of mindlessness and monotony are, in part, due to superficial attention to decisions. Teachers should remain aware of the consequences of their decisions as reflected in their emerging teaching styles. A part of any teaching style, in fact, should be to give a full measure of reflection to decision making whenever it is due, as in planning a lesson.

Some situations arise that are unfamiliar and that present momentary uncertainty—even for an experienced teacher such as Ms. Knettel. Like Ms. Knettel, a teacher must consider the alternatives, weigh the likely outcomes, and select a course of action. This sequence of mental activities extends beyond spontaneous choice and requires decision making based on principles of education, research findings, and examined practice—the core of pedagogy.

A teacher may encounter the same situation in the future, and having previously made a personally acceptable response, may readily do it again. Therefore, the same teacher behavior (response) that once required reflective decision making may become, at a later date, a simpler matter of spontaneous choice.

In the process of teacher development, both of these types of teacher response—thoughtful and spontaneous—deserve consideration. If the teacher should develop a set of automatic behaviors that are counterproductive, then teacher effectiveness is diminished. For example, a teacher may habitually lecture as a means of covering content, and may exceed student attention span. Or a teacher may frequently threaten students whose behavior is considered inappropriate. These approaches may contribute to the teacher's momentary comfort as a means of responding to the immediate demands of teaching, but the long-term effects on students are contrary to the conditions of productive learning. Continual repetition of such practices can only result in mindless and monotonous teaching.

Since choice patterns or sets of responses result from prior decision making, reflective decision making as the basis for these patterns is an essential step toward successful teaching. Attention needs to be given to the sources from which these first-encounter decisions are made.

The Locus of Decisions

Decisions occur in three different aspects of teaching: planning and preparing for instruction; the interaction phase; and evaluating learning outcomes. Each of these aspects involves different kinds of considerations.

Planning Decisions. Decisions made prior to instruction can be made without haste or a sense of immediacy, and can be made after lengthy reflection. In the process, the teacher has time to pose some searching questions and make use of those educational principles, research findings and theories that relate to the intent of the instruction. Some of these broad questions are:

> Is this the topic or activity that is most worthwhile for these students at this time?
>
> Do the students have the knowledge and skills necessary to handle the content?
>
> What are students' attitudes about this topic, and what implications evolve from those attitudes?
>
> What broad approaches are likely to induce the greatest motivation within the students?
>
> How does this topic/activity relate to the objectives of this course?

Other more specific questions should also be posed, such as:

> What are some key questions that will direct students' thinking toward the lesson objectives?
>
> What arrangements and support must be provided?
>
> How can individual student differences be accommodated?
>
> What sort of entry will most effectively initiate learning?

Interactive Decisions. Teachers make an average of one interactive decision every two minutes (Clark & Peterson, 1986). Furthermore, decisions made during the interactive phase of instruction often must occur rapidly, for time is severely limited. Yet, one's success as a teacher clearly is contingent on the quality of these decisions. The seasoned teacher who has encountered a wide variety of conditions, and who has learned by some means—even trial and error—appropriate responses, is surely at an advantage. Ms. Knettel made the decision to use a classroom meeting based on prior experience with the activity.

A less experienced, but alert, teacher may speculate about possible situations which will require decisions and think them through beforehand. As situations arise, they won't be quite so strange or puzzling, and can be taken in stride. For example, a teacher may be planning small group activity for the following day's lesson. The class has not participated in small group activities as yet, so the teacher does not know how students will respond. Therefore, the teacher could make an alternate plan, such as an appropriate seatwork assignment, as a contingency.

But no amount of preparation can predict every situation that will occur. What then does the teacher do? Several nonspecific strategies can be kept in mind which apply in these cases.

Simply pause and take a moment to reflect, even at the risk of momentary awkwardness.

Admit honestly to the class that the situation requires some time to think through.

Make a decision, if the consequences are not irreversible, with the intent of reviewing it later.

Any teacher who has a well-informed belief system, and who is "in touch" with that belief system, has an important advantage in this interactive phase of instruction. When sound educational principles that can be quickly called to use populate the belief system, effective decisions are the probable outcome. Fewer "off-the-top-of-the-head" judgments will occur. The teacher whose belief system is more intuitively rather than rationally based, or who simply doesn't make a sufficient effort to act rationally, will make a large proportion of suspect decisions while teaching that can cause problems for both the teacher and the students.

Evaluation Decisions. Finally, decisions are made following instruction. The teacher must determine the extent to which students have performed according to some standard. The more explicit both the initial objectives for learning and the criteria for evaluation are, the more clear and valid are the decisions regarding students' performance. The teacher who has thoughtfully developed objectives and criteria beforehand will find the postinstruction evaluation decisions simpler to make. On the other hand, a teacher whose evaluation decisions are largely after-the-fact, fails initially to provide students with a clear idea of expectations, and is likely to engage in arbitrary, expedient means of assessing achievement. The consequences are predictable.

A second set of decisions should be made following instruction, although these are often ignored or done superficially. The teaching process, however, is not complete until the preceding instruction is critically reviewed—at the least casually and sometimes systematically—to provide an analysis. The obvious question is: How effective was this episode or unit of instruction? For the conscientious teacher, there are several sources which provide immediate answers to this question: student demeanor and initiative; demonstrated student achievement; and the teacher's own sense of how well the students complied with predetermined expectations. The more specific the teacher is regarding predetermined expectations, the more likely that evaluative decisions will be useful.

As the teacher moves toward greater specificity and objectivity, a more systematic means of analysis and data collection is required. Formal approaches, including audio and video recording, are useful for this purpose, and provide a reliable basis for decision making in the interest of improved teaching, and for developing a belief system.

SUMMARY POINT

Being aware of decision making as a process and understanding the dynamics of the process does not exhaust the potential of this concept to contribute to effective teaching. Decision making is the professional orientation and a pattern of thinking that undergirds one's instructional style and assures that teaching will be conducted as a thoughtful practice. To the extent that this occurs, a teacher cannot be comfortable employing unwitting, intuitive responses to the demands of teaching. Rather, rational sources become the only acceptable basis for decisions, and for subsequent related choices. Rational, reflective decision making is the basic teaching skill that, fully developed, is essential to optimally effective teaching.

REVIEW: CONSIDERATIONS IN DECISION MAKING

Optimal teacher decision making involves:

1. commitment to the proposition that decision making is the basic teaching skill;
2. the teacher's conscious desire to be a skilled decision maker;
3. acceptance of the science of education as the basis for enlightened instruction;
4. a belief system informed by the tenets of modern pedagogy; and
5. purposeful use of a systematic approach to decision making in planning, conducting, and evaluating instruction.

ACTIVITIES

In each of the following questions examine three important aspects of decision making: (1) those beliefs—priorities, values, principles—that are pertinent to the situation; (2) the feasible alternatives; (3) the approach finally selected.

ACTIVITY I: CLASSROOM MANAGEMENT DECISIONS

You are preparing for your first teaching position after recently graduating (you select the subject and/or grade level). One of your concerns is initiating effective classroom management. Decisions need to be made regarding the classroom furniture arrangement, establishing behavior expectations, use of the class library, use of the restroom, and other routine considerations. How will your beliefs enter into your decisions? What alternatives do you have? What approach will you finally use?

ACTIVITY II: PLANNING DECISIONS

You are planning a unit of study in a particular subject. Decisions must be made regarding concepts to be taught, the rationales that justify the unit, strategies that have promise of being especially effective, the most appropriate means of evaluation, and a provision for individualization. What beliefs may influence you in making decisions about planning a unit. How will you choose among a number of alternatives?

ACTIVITY III: CLASSROOM SITUATION DECISIONS

You are engaged in teaching, and the following situations occur. What will be your approach to decision making in each case? What decisions will you have to make? What will be the basis for your decisions?

1. Students lack any display of interest in the 1765 tax imposed on the American Colonists.
2. Students are having trouble with decimals in division.
3. Many of the students have not read the homework assignment.
4. The class is more restless and "hyper" than usual.
5. What are some other typical classroom occurrences that require teacher decisions?

ACTIVITY IV: DISCIPLINE DECISIONS

Certain discipline-related situations occasionally occur. Discuss these in terms of the decisions you would make and the basis for your decisions.

1. Jason frequently clowns and distracts others.
2. Permanent marker writing is found on several desks.
3. Sally has a habit of calling out.
4. Robbie is especially aggressive, often pushing and punching other children.
5. Jamie calls you an "old bitch" under her breath, but you hear her.
6. Sarah is caught cheating on a test.

ACTIVITY V: TESTING DECISIONS

You have just completed a unit of study which included some higher level objectives. You realize you should test students with essay-type questions, but you feel you have too little time to read them. Besides, many of the students write poorly, and are likely to be placed at a particular disadvantage. What decision can you make? What factors may influence your decision?

ACTIVITY VI: EVALUATION/INSTRUCTION DECISIONS

You have graded the papers from the unit you just completed. The students simply have not responded as you had wished, and obviously have not achieved the learning objectives on a sufficient level. What will you do? Why will you handle the situation in a particular way? How does your belief system influence your decision?

REFERENCES

Berliner, D. (1984). The half-full glass: a review of research on teaching [Review of P. L. Hosford (Ed.), *Using what we know about teaching*], Alexandria, VA: Association for Supervision and Curriculum Development, 51–77.

Bloom, B. (Ed.). (1956). *A taxonomy of educational objectives, Handbook I: Cognitive Domain.* New York: McKay.

Borko, H., Cone, R., Russo, N., & Shavelson, R. (1979). Teachers' decision making. In P. Peterson & H. Walberg (Eds.), *Research on teaching*. Berkeley, CA: McCutchan.

Clark, C., & Peterson, P. (1976). *Teacher stimulated recall of interactive decisions*. Paper presented at the annual meeting of the AERA, San Francisco.

Clark, C., & Peterson, P. (1986). Teachers' thought processes. In Merlin Wittrock (Ed.), *Handbook of research on teaching* (3rd ed.). New York: Macmillan.

Cooper, J. (1982). The teacher as decision maker. In *Classroom teaching skills*. Lexington, MA: Heath.

Dewey, J. (1929). *The sources of a science of education.* New York: Liveright.

Farr, R., & Brown, V. (1971). Evaluation and decision making. *Reading Teacher, 24.*

Goldberg, M., & Harvey, J. (1983). A nation at risk: The report of the National Commission on Excellence in Education. *Phi Delta Kappan, 65*, 14–18.

Goodlad, J. (1983). A study of schooling: Some findings and hypotheses. *Phi Delta Kappan, 64*, 465–470.

Herbert, G. W. (1974). Teachers' ratings of classroom behavior: factorial structure. *British Journal of Educational Psychology, 44*, 233–240.

Hunter, M. (1979). Teaching is decision making. *Educational Leadership, 37.*

Hunter, M. (1984). Knowing, teaching, and supervising. In Philip Hosford (Ed.), *Using what we know about teaching*. Alexandria, VA: Association for Supervision and Curriculum Development.

Hurst, J., Kinney, M., & Weiss, S. J. (1983). The decision making process. *Theory and Research in Social Education, 11*(19), 178–182.

Joyce, B., & Weil, M. (1986). *Models of Teaching* (3rd ed.). Englewood Cliffs, NJ: Prentice-Hall.

National Commission on Excellence in Education (1983). *A nation at risk.* Washington, D.C.: U.S. Department of Education.

Rubenstein, G., & Fisher, L. (1974). A measure of teachers observations of student behavior. *Journal of Consulting and Clinical Psychology, 42,* 310.

Shavelson, R. J. (1973). What is the basic teaching skill? *Journal of Teacher Education, 24,* 144–151.

Shavelson, R. J. (1976). Teacher decision making. In N. L. Gage (Ed.), *The psychology of teaching methods* (1st ed.). The seventy-fifth yearbook of the National Society for the Study of Education, Part I.

Shavelson, R. J., Cadwell, J., & Izu, T. (1977). Teacher's sensitivity to the reliability of information in making pedagogical decisions. *American Educational Research Journal, 14*(2), 83–97.

Shavelson, R. J., & Stern, P. (1981). Research on teachers' pedagogical thoughts, judgments, decisions, and behavior. *Review of Educational Research, 51*(4), 455–498.

Silberman, C. E. (1970). *Crisis in the classroom.* New York: Random House.

Sontag, M. (1968). Attitudes toward education and perception of teacher behaviors. *American Educational Research Journal, 5,* 385–402.

CHAPTER 2 Classroom Climate

Climate refers to the affective aspects of the classroom, such as the feelings generated by and about the teacher, the students, or the subject matter, along with aspects of the classroom itself that contribute positively or negatively to the learning atmosphere. Many teachers attempt to establish a supportive yet businesslike climate in their classrooms, knowing that this will facilitate learning and limit problems.

Environmental conditions can be influenced by factors over which teachers exercise control. Beginning teachers can learn to develop climate-related practices and analyze their effect on students. These practices must be considered in conjunction with motivation, because the desired outcome is to help students develop an intrinsic motivation to learn. Although the conditions of intrinsic motivation in the student are beyond direct teacher control, the effective teacher knows how to generate those particular conditions in the classroom that promote intrinsic motivation.

OVERVIEW

A classroom ''climate'' is the sum of all of the students' perceptions of and predispositions to their association with the classroom. An important part of the teacher's task is to affect these perceptions and predispositions in an advantageous way. Teachers as decision makers can work purposefully at effecting a productive learning climate by attending to the climate implications of four elements of effective teaching as identified in the research. These are academic climate, high standards, orderly environment, and expectations for success. (Other elements of effective teaching are presented at greater length in Chapter 5, where their relationship to instruction is described.) Finally, attribution theory, an aspect of motivation, is included as it affects classroom climate.

Environmental conditions can be produced by factors over which teachers exercise control. They are related to practices that beginning teachers can learn to develop and analyze in terms of their effect on students. These practices must be considered in conjunction with motivation because the intended end result is to help encourage all students' desire to learn. Although the conditions of intrinsic motivation in the student are beyond direct teacher control, an effective teacher knows how to promote conditions and rewards in the classroom that encourage intrinsic motivation development. Motivation practices will be examined in this chapter as part of climate conditions that affect student achievement.

The beginning teacher needs to understand that when making decisions about creating learning environments, the learner's particular needs and learning styles must be considered. In addition to generic practices, the characteristics of each student as a learner is important information for a teacher to know. Whenever possible, the teacher can match those characteristics to choices concerning teacher practice. Books such as Gage and Berliner's *Educational Psychology* (1984) and the work of Bernice McCarthy (1980) and the Dunns (1975) on learning styles are helpful because our understanding of what children and adolescents respond to in the environment has been increased by recent research and theory in developmental psychology. Because of space limitations, this book can only make reference to that important information, but we do recommend that beginning teachers become knowledgeable about the learners' cognitive and affective development and the variety of individual learning styles.

The following information is presented to help the teacher make decisions in planning and in instruction that build an effective climate for student achievement and promote student self-worth.

SCENARIO

In the first week of school, Tom Baldino was meeting his math class for the fourth time. The diagnostic tests he administered during the first days of class revealed that he had his work cut out for him. Basic skills seemed to be in place, but careless errors had affected test scores. Analytical reasoning skills registered low, as did problem-solving skills. Most of the class had obtained a 7th grade achievement level, putting them two years behind in math proficiency.

Mr. Baldino smiled at the students as they entered the room. He stood in front of the desks, seating chart in hand, trying to match names with faces. The halls emptied and became quiet as students found their seats.

Since he was standing in front of the class looking at the students, chatter subsided. He had explained on the first day that students could talk until he stood in front of the class, ready to start the lesson. Though still unfamiliar with him and with some of the other students, the class was following his rules. He had shared only three rules with them, and he intended to enforce them.

"I've been putting you through your paces the last few days so I could get an idea of your math skills and your knowledge." The class let out a subdued groan and waited expectantly.

"Now it's time to get started and use that ability you show to do well in math. How many of you want to do better in math this year? (About one-half of the class slowly raised their hands.) Well, you've come to the right place. All of you. Baldino-the-Wizard is going to start working his wonders on you ... even those of you who didn't raise your hands. Right here in this room, before your very eyes, and with considerable help from you, you are all going to become good math students. It won't happen overnight, but with some help from both you and the magic hat, it will happen."

Students giggled as Mr. Baldino reached under his desk and pulled out a magician's wand and a tall, black silk hat. Occasionally he had fun hamming it up for the classes, and being an amateur magician helped. All eyes were upon him as he postured in front of them, waving his wand over the hat as if he were going to pull out a rabbit. He couldn't help doing a few simple, sleight-of-hand tricks with chalk and pencils, like pulling a pencil out of the ear of the big boy sitting in the front row. Everyone laughed, and seemed to relax as math class took a turn toward the unexpected.

"Now that I've got your attention, let's see what mysteries the hat holds that are going to turn you into good math students. First, let me check again to make sure I know which students are going to use this magic this year." He peered carefully at the class, trying to contact every eye. "Let's see again those hands of people who want to become good math students this year." (This time more hands went up. Only about five remained down—a group of five boys in the back.) He made a mental note of their reluctance to get involved in the fun, and chose one of them to come forward to be an assistant. One of them reluctantly agreed and ambled to the front.

"Okay, now that I have some assistance, let's check the magic hat for ways to make our math powers stronger." He had the volunteer hold the hat and tap it with the wand as he pulled out a rubber chicken. The class laughed politely.

Baldino admitted to himself the act had gone over much better for the 7th grade, but he was determined to get them started on a higher note. After next instructing the aide to tap the hat twice, Mr. Baldino pulled out a slip of paper which, he explained, contained a magic, coded message. He went to the board and scribbled down some mathematical symbols, and then wrote on the board, "Math Magic. You become a math whiz by doing the following:" He did more hamming by chanting mysteriously and waving his arms, and then plunged into the hat for another magic message. This one read, "Homework papers turned in every day Monday through Thursday. Those who complete the week's assignments receive a magic award of no homework on Fridays." The proclamation was received with some groans and some cheers.

With a flourish, Mr. Baldino pulled out another slip. "All tests will be passed with a grade of 70% or higher. Student will continue to work on difficult material until able to pass a test." The list went on to include the following being written on the board:

"All students will bring magic tools to class: books, pencils and papers, and thinking caps."

"Students may move ahead to new material if teacher has gone over old material with them."

"Students may ask to work in small groups of two or three during weekly practice times."

"Students will be responsible for handing in work covered on days they are absent."

When he was finished, the class looked subdued, but they were all watching him. He described the magic fun corner of the room that would be filled with math games and math puzzles to be used for relaxation time after work was completed, or if a special award was given. (He hoped to add a computer to the room next year. It would be excellent for practice exercises and individual instruction.)

He ended with a pep talk on class attitude, saying that in order for the magic to work, everyone had to keep believing that they could handle the material. The tests showed that they had the ability; now they had to prove it to themselves and to everyone else by following the magic plan.

Mr. Baldino thought through his additional plans. He expected to give a quiz once a week and a bigger exam every two weeks. He would hold periodic review lessons and include items from past units in his tests. He would continually convey to the class and to each individual student his belief in everyone's ability to complete math successfully. He planned to have all students keep a chart on their quizzes and test scores so that their success profiles could be easily seen. This visible feedback about progress was to be an important part of the magic to make students feel successful. He explained aloud that his magic—along with the students' magic— would work together to achieve success.

After emptying the hat, he asked the class if they knew of any other magic formulas to promote success. One of the boys from the uncooperative five raised his hand and suggested that the teacher teach them how to pull money from people's ears. The class laughed, nodding approval. Mr. Baldino smiled. He located a quarter in his pocket, then seemingly pulled it from the ear of the girl in the front seat while, at the same time, he talked about the introduction to the lesson. "In math, as in magic, there are certain steps one must follow carefully in order to achieve the results one wants ... "

TOPIC 1: ESTABLISHING AN ACADEMIC CLIMATE

RESEARCH AND THEORETICAL BASE

The first element for building a productive learning climate comes from the effective school model (Lezotte, 1984), which emphasizes academics. This element impinges on decision making about curriculum and instruction, and encourages the teacher to focus class activities around the completion of academic objectives. The teacher presents the objectives to be met to the class, and helps each student reach those objectives to the best of everyone's ability.

Rutter's (1979) study of twelve inner-city London schools identified the characteristic of academic emphasis as one of the key traits of the effective schools. Brophy (1982), in a research summary of teacher effects on student achievement in urban schools, listed emphasis on cognitive objectives within a warm, supportive climate as key teacher behavior. In another study, Rosenshine (1979) cited a major focus on academic goals as a characteristic of teachers in effective classrooms. He indicated that students learn best in classrooms in which there is both academic emphasis and teacher-directed instruction. The direct teaching model he observed being employed in effective schools (see Chapter 7) included two practices related to emphasis on academics: (1) teachers placed a clear focus on academic goals; and (2) teachers made an effort to promote extensive content coverage and high levels of student involvement.

APPLICATION TO PRACTICE

The following practices are recommended to the teacher for generating an academic climate in the classroom:

1. Be task oriented.
2. Keep students on-task.
3. Encourage students to do homework.
4. Encourage students to master materials.
5. Give daily feedback.
6. Convey to students confidence in their ability to succeed.
7. Provide learning activities that offer academic challenges.
8. Be supportive of students' efforts.

A task-oriented teacher is aware of both the use of time spent on a lesson and the purpose of that lesson. A major effort is made to keep students productively involved throughout the lesson. The teacher starts class promptly by indicating to the class what is to be accomplished during a specific time period and the purpose for the day's learning activities. This "establishing set" technique is advocated by both Hunter (1967) and Rosenshine (1979). Rosenshine includes it as part of the first function, structuring the lesson, in his direct teaching strategy (see Chapter 7). With this introduction to the lesson's purpose, the students know what is expected of them and that the teacher will make sure that the tasks are accomplished. The instruction portion of the lesson will center on the planned objective(s) and the learning activities (including practice time) that will be used to accomplish the objective. The teacher monitors the students' progress in accomplishing the lesson's objective through feedback, circulating around the room to ascertain the progress, and collecting, checking, and recording their completed assignments.

The second practice for establishing an academic climate and keeping students on-task requires that the teacher be aware of the class's engagement time and of each student's academic learning time. Academic learning time is that high-quality time when the student is involved with the content and is succeeding. The teacher may have to use a variety of methods to help certain students increase their on-task time, such as calling on students by name, getting students busy with an activity, focusing on students by moving around the room and checking their papers, interacting with students about the content rather than other distracting topics, and spending little time on organizational and management tasks such as setting up equipment or handing out materials. Use of discipline measures is limited, and employed to maintain an orderly environment for learning. For example, we sense that Mr. Baldino in the scenario was task oriented even while maintaining a sense of humor, and that students would be kept productively occupied throughout the year in his class.

The third practice, the assignment of homework, is characteristic of the academic classroom. It received national attention when reports on schools in the early eighties revealed that little homework was being assigned in the nation's schools, and that less was being completed. The importance of homework was documented in a U.S. Education Department study entitled, *What Works*, which cited research showing the beneficial effects of homework on learning. In response, some city districts around the country passed mandatory homework laws that pressured the teacher to assign homework four or five times a week. For example, in 1986 the Chicago Board of Education adopted a policy across all grade levels that homework was to be assigned every night, from 15 minutes of work for kindergarten to two-and-a-half hours of work for high school students (Snider, 1986).

Such actions necessitate caution. Assigning homework will not in itself assure academic achievement. Homework activities must be carefully selected by the teacher to accomplish a specific purpose, and should be limited in quantity. The purposes for which homework is best suited are the following: to provide students with more practice, if needed, after a group practice session in class; to provide students more time to develop a paper or project over a period of several days; and to provide students time to become familiar with concepts or themes presented in reading material prior to discussion in class. Routine homework that has no purpose other than to keep students involved with twenty math problems or five pages of history every night will not increase achievement or encourage a climate for achievement. Such "busy work" homework will reap negative attitudes toward home practice.

When purposeful homework is assigned, the teacher makes decisions regarding the application of the assignment to the daily lesson and the weight of its evaluation. The teacher needs to go over the work in class in order to provide immediate feedback to students. Homework should be collected and checked to determine whether or not it is completed correctly. A teacher's cursory glance over a paper is enough to see if the homework is finished and to check on any problems that a student may have had with the assignment. A check mark in the grade book can indicate that the assignment has been accomplished. Those students who have not turned in homework should be notified that they are being held responsible for it. A student's handling of homework assignments should be an appropriately weighted part of the grade-period mark.

The fourth point in generating an academic climate, encouraging students to master the material, involves students' advancement at their own rate whenever possible. The teacher may have to reteach students until they can acquire the skill and the knowledge considered essential learning to pass the exam satisfactorily. Some content may have to be eliminated for those who fall behind the class in order to allow time for mastery of essential knowledge. Part of the class hour or day may be spent working in small group sessions of students on remediation activities. The important principle in this context is that students must know they are being held responsible to master the key information. They must sense that they have control over their school progress by meeting their responsibilities. Tom Baldino's "magic rules" conveyed to students the emphasis on standards, and his intention to monitor work in terms of students.

The fifth practice in establishing an academic climate, giving daily feedback, includes writing comments on corrected papers and holding conferences with students to discuss their progress and encourage their success. Optimally, the teacher should try to have some interaction with every student each day. The nature of this interaction should provide feedback related to progress, indications of teacher interest and concern for the student, and remediation suggestions. Displaying and sharing quality student work with the class is useful feedback because it reflects a high performance standard, student success, and a student product for peer comparison.

The sixth practice, the nurturing of each student's potential, must accompany the promotion of academic excellence. The teacher nurtures students, with the intent to encourage the students to keep trying, by making them aware of their individual progress and potential. Planning conference times during the school year or at the end of class several days a month are important ways to support students' feelings of success in the class by examining together information kept by the teacher that shows student progress. Results from pre- and posttesting can be shared, along with term grades and samples of student work. Conveying confidence to students was perhaps the most impressive aspect of Mr. Baldino's class. His so-called "magic" was his way of convincing students of their eventual success—the self-fulfilling prophecy.

The seventh practice that is essential to promoting an academic environment is providing students with learning activities that offer academic challenges. A teacher plans activities that involve students with application, analysis, and synthesis experiences as well as with practice with lower level knowledge and comprehension tasks. Learning activities should be examined to see if they encourage students to use higher-level thinking skills and problem-solving techniques. Extensive unit projects can be developed to provide students with opportunities to expand their thinking. For example, such activities might include planning and printing a grade level or room newspaper after studying a journalism unit, or developing a community survey form to focus the town's attention on the recreational needs of the youth and senior citizens. Any activity that creates excitement for learning encourages an academic climate.

All these practices for establishing an academic environment need to be employed within a warm, supportive learning climate (Brophy, 1982). Such a climate is characterized by teachers showing interest in each child, using those verbal behaviors specified by Flanders (1970) as indirect: accepting students' feelings, praising students, using student ideas, and asking questions. If the tone of the classroom created by the teacher's verbal behavior is cold, distant, and uncaring, the climate will adversely affect the students' motivation to learn.

TOPIC 2: PROMOTING HIGH STANDARDS

RESEARCH AND THEORETICAL BASE

Allied with creating an academic climate is promoting high standards. In the opening scenario Mr. Baldino addressed high standards in his classroom when he announced to the students that tests had to be passed at a 70% level or higher. If students failed, they would be retaught via programmed materials or through checks for understanding, controlled group practice, and independent practice (Hunter, 1976). He also stressed the importance of homework completion, bringing books to class, and paying attention. He believed that informing the class of the standards they had to meet was important.

The issue of establishing higher standards became a nationwide charge in 1983 following the publication of the findings of numerous national reports on the status of public education. The National Commission on Excellence in Education report, *A Nation at Risk* (1983), called for the upgrading of standards by increasing basic academic requirements for graduation. The Commission recommended that more rigorous and measurable standards and higher expectations for academic performance and student conduct be adopted by schools and colleges. One of the research studies that support the call for higher standards is the Rutter (1979) report which found that hallmarks of effective schools were that "high expectations were the order of the day." The Weber study (1971) on successful inner-city schools listed "high expectations" as a distinguishing characteristic. The Wellisch study (1978) showed that in schools where achievement was improving, principals were concerned about instruction and emphasized academic standards.

The Block study (1970) examined the impact that standards had on students' performance and attitudes, and found that higher standards resulted in higher cognitive achievement. This study also found that when required performance standards (that level at which student performance is considered acceptable) were too high, student attitudes were affected negatively. These results indicate the need to establish performance standards that will challenge students yet not discourage them.

Levin with Long (1981) point out that most researchers agree that a 100% mastery standard is neither realistic nor necessary in the classroom. A 70% to 80% performance level is acceptable if that score indicates a student has achieved the major objectives and is prepared to move ahead in the course. If students do not meet the acceptable performance level, then recycling through the content should occur.

To summarize the numerous research studies on effective teaching and effective schools, one can say that setting reasonable standards for performance in the classroom includes maintaining an acceptable level of performance on everything from conduct to homework and tests. The goal of these standards is to create a climate in the classroom that conveys the following: the business in the classroom is to learn; a student is expected to achieve; the teacher has high standards for herself and her students; school is concerned with achievement. Teachers and schools must relay these important messages in order to promote a climate for achievement.

APPLICATION TO PRACTICE

The following practices can convey to students that high standards are maintained in a classroom:

1. Setting an academic performance level that all students must meet
2. Establishing an organizational system for remediation
3. Maintaining a standard of performance
4. Rewarding excellent work and effort
5. Maintaining professional image in the classroom
6. Encouraging students to discover the excitement of learning
7. Requiring a level of work that challenges but does not frustrate
8. Emphasizing higher-level thinking as well as memory-level and comprehension-level cognitive functioning

The first point suggests to the teacher that a performance level be set for each key objective to indicate the level at which satisfactory completion of that objective has been met. For example, a teacher must decide that an objective can be considered mastered when students are able to pass a test on the information at the 70% level, or able to get eight out of ten problems correct, or write a paragraph with a minimum of two errors in sentence construction, spelling, and punctuation. The below-level student would continue to do remediation work and be retested on an objective until that achievement standard is met.

The level at which to set performance standards is a difficult decision for teachers to make, especially for a beginning teacher who cannot rely on past experiences. Research does not reveal appropriate performance levels for optimum learning. Each teacher must determine the level appropriate to challenge—but not frustrate—the class. Also, the teacher may decide to set individual performance levels. Performance levels may be raised or lowered during the year to improve the learning climate.

If a teacher defines a performance level for major objectives as recommended in point one, an organizational system for remediation will also need to be established. This means that the teacher builds a reserve of additional explanatory materials, practice activities, and tests on key objectives. If a student is unsuccessful in reaching the accepted level of performance, that student continues to study and practice until he reaches the level or until the teacher decides to move the student to the next phase. (This feature was emphasized in Tom Baldino's approach in the scenario.) A successful remediation program cannot be implemented until the teacher has a supply of materials from reference textbooks, sample texts, and, in those cases where skills and content have not changed, old textbooks from which to draw material and additional practice for the learner. If this remedial system is in place, the teacher has more time to reinstruct students not reaching the satisfactory performance level, and can repeat the instructional steps.

The remediation or recycling stage will be most effective if it involves the teacher's controlled practice with a small group or an individual. The teacher conducts the controlled practice to re-explain, model, and illustrate the material. Then the student proceeds to independent practice. When this step has been completed successfully, retesting occurs. During those times when the teacher is working with an individual or small group needing remediation, the rest of the class can be involved in independent practice to review the objective or to achieve a new objective. (These practices just described comprise part of the strategies of mastery learning explained in Chapter 7.)

Teachers who maintain an academic climate use certain pertinent practices in their instructional and management approach. Homework is collected and checked in order for students to know that homework is a required performance standard and that students will receive feedback on it either daily or intermittently. Not every homework paper must receive a grade. Other practices used by teachers to convey academic standards include assuring that work missed because of absences is made up; that most class time is spent on academic tasks; and that objectives for learning tasks are shared with students. Rewards are handled carefully. Marginal or wrong answers are not rewarded or criticized. Rather, corrective feedback is given. Excellent work and effort are rewarded.

The suggested practice for promoting high standards emphasizes rewards. The reward strategies the teacher chooses to use are important in maintaining the success climate in the classroom. Recognition for doing outstanding work can be given in a variety of forms such as displaying the work in the classroom or on the bulletin board, displaying student work in the school lobby in display cases or on hall walls, sharing the product with the class by reading it or passing it around for examination, giving special mention of the work to the class by allowing the creator to explain it. (Tom Baldino used no homework on Friday and the magic fun corner as rewards for his class.) Students can experience new rewards through help from teachers in submitting their written work for publication in student anthologies. For example, this author obtained literary recognition for several athletes, all football team members, by encouraging the class to send their poems composed for the poetry unit to the *National Student Anthology of Poetry*. All four of the athletes' poems were published. This recognition of the students' poetry caused quite a stir in the school. This example points out that the teacher can enter student work into local, state, and national arenas where it may receive recognition. Also, the school newspaper may accept written work of general interest in the school.

Another influence on the academic atmosphere in the classroom is certainly the tacit message communicated by the teacher's professional behavior. That behavior indicates acceptable standards for conduct, just as surely as written rules and procedures given to children. Brophy and Good (1985) reported that teachers who promoted the highest achievement in the classroom were businesslike and task oriented. Such professional teacher behavior evokes respect for the teacher's position.

Teacher behavior that reflects a professional attitude may include such practices as lessons prepared in advance, correct use of grammar, correct spelling and legible writing on board and papers, prompt return of student work, and good teacher attendance. A teacher's professional commitment to using class time to concentrate on academic tasks and conducting class in a supportive but businesslike manner impresses students. A professional teacher will also encourage students to provide feedback on how the class is functioning for them. In addition, the teacher conveys his or her interest in students' progress by supplying frequent feedback through quizzes, tests, comments on assignments, and daily comprehension checks.

Another practice that effective teachers employ to create enthusiasm for scholarly activity at any grade level is helping students enjoy the excitement of learning. A curious mind can lead to investigation that involves all of a student's higher thinking processes. Sharing the excitement for ideas can stimulate an environment that encourages students to share their ideas and interests, too. For example, after reading Barbara Brown's (1974) book on biofeedback, *New Mind, New Body,* a teacher shared some of the information with her science class. This sharing led to a lively discussion on the use of biofeedback and a visit from a guest speaker, a local psychologist who uses biofeedback in his practice. Encouraging students to share in a similar fashion can be contagious. One child may bring in all his books on snakes and display some of his pet snakes to the class. Another child may show her telescope to the class and explain the study of the evening sky she does with her father. A student's stamp collection can lead to a history lesson about famous people the class does not know. Spinoffs into and beyond the established course of study for a particular subject through the sharing of interests can be exciting.

The practice of requiring a level of work that challenges students but does not continually frustrate them is the seventh factor in promoting high standards. This practice necessitates that the teacher know the capabilities of each student so that expectations are realistic. This does not mean that less should be required of a slower achieving child, but rather that the requirements should be different. Consider the following example. Peter had been struggling with a paper examining the Puritan influence on Hawthorne's writing in *The Scarlet Letter.* The topic appeared too abstract for his thinking, even though the teacher had told him how to proceed. Peter was given a new assignment to investigate what Puritanism was, how Puritans lived, and how it would feel to live as a Puritan in that time period. He was better able to handle the latter, more specific task than the original analytical topic he was assigned.

Encouraging thinking at the higher levels of application, analysis, synthesis and evaluation based on Bloom's *Taxonomy of Educational Objectives* (1956) is a practice essential to promoting achievement and high academic standards. In their planning and questioning teachers need to remember that recalling information is a necessary, but not sufficient, condition for student success. In addition to the establishment of basic knowledge, opportunities for utilizing information through solving problems, generating hypotheses, analyzing alternatives, and creating imaginative solutions should be available. Bloom's Taxonomy can be helpful to teachers when developing objectives and learning activities on higher levels of the cognitive domain.

An academic climate with appropriately high standards can be maintained in any classroom. The climate is promoted by a teacher who conducts class in a businesslike manner; namely, someone who establishes objectives and helps students accomplish those objectives by using class time productively.

TOPIC 3: MAINTAINING AN ORDERLY ENVIRONMENT

RESEARCH AND THEORETICAL BASE

A beginning teacher makes many important decisions that influence order in the classroom. These decisions concern such factors as establishing rules and procedures, handling deviant behavior, organizing groups, and timing activities. Learning is dependent on students' being on-task, so much of a beginning teacher's time, typically, is devoted to planning and maintaining order in the classroom. The third important climate condition, therefore, is the existence of an orderly environment. This condition relates to the classroom as a social group and refers to the maintenance of a climate in the classroom that encourages cooperation and productivity within the group. To maintain an orderly environment teachers must learn how to manage groups and structure the classroom around specified goals so that they spend a minimal amount of time on classroom disruptions.

In addition to a number of research studies that provide verification of the importance of a well-managed classroom, Soar and Soar's (1976) research study on elementary teaching found that students learned more in classrooms where teachers established limits on student freedom and choice, unnecessary movements about the room, and disruptive behavior. Effective teachers talked more than others as they provided information, feedback and support, and controlled pupils' task behavior. Another study done by Evertson, Anderson et al. (1980), of seventh and eighth grade students, reported that misbehavior was uncommon in classrooms with higher achieving students.

Characteristics of the orderly classroom is a recurring topic for research. Classroom order is best initiated very early in the school year by establishing class routines, procedures, and rules. Anderson and Evertson (1978) studied teachers during the first three weeks of school. Effective teachers who managed high engagement rates with their students spent the first few days emphasizing management and organizational planning. They taught students procedures for the use of the room and management routines. They gave students guided practice in class procedures such as the timing of how long it took the class to move into reading groups, and they gave students feedback on the results. They taught management of the classroom as they would any other unit content. Classroom rules were included in lesson plans, and practice and feedback were given to students on their progress in learning and following rules.

Establishment of rules and procedures enabled the students to learn teacher expectations and to practice fulfilling them during the first weeks of school. This pro-active approach to classroom management yielded excellent results. After the initial training period, management problems remained at a minimum. Although this study was conducted with elementary teachers, implications for secondary level teachers in stressing class organization, routines, and management during early class meetings are obvious.

Rules and procedures may be formulated with the class if the teacher wants to develop a democratic atmosphere in the room. In the Anderson and Evertson (1978) studies, this factor did not make a significant difference in student respect for the rules. However, less effective teachers simply told students the rules, and did not give practice and feedback on their execution.

Research on the rules and procedures that teachers maintain in orderly classrooms reveals that all phases of group activity within each class session should be considered in planning procedures. Researchers Bremme and Erickson (1977), and Erickson and Shietz (1981) reported that teachers' rules and operations were related to the phases of entry, preparation for lesson, lesson proper, close of lesson, and exit. Teachers had procedures for students to follow in each of these segments. This information alerts beginning teachers to the importance of considering these different phases when planning order-securing procedures for the classroom.

APPLICATION TO PRACTICE

Some of the practice used by effective managers in maintaining an orderly environment and in making the initial decisions on establishing order are:

1. Promoting an orderly classroom by establishing class routines, procedures, and rules
2. Letting students know what they are to accomplish and how they are progressing
3. Being well prepared for each lesson
4. Using instruction time purposefully
5. Keeping students on-task
6. Smoothing transition times
7. Handling interruptions and disruptions promptly with a minimum of turmoil, and
8. Handling management problems promptly

Since students are social, interactive beings, rules and procedures that pertain to appropriate behavior during each phase of the period should be established on the first day. These rules need not be lengthy or rigidly prescriptive. However, they should provide clear direction to the students on teacher expectations for order.

The teacher needs to decide on procedures for such actions as entry into the room, attention to the start of the lesson, participation in discussion, attending to the lesson, sharpening pencils, going to the restroom, asking questions, handing in work, handing out papers and books, closing books, and leaving the classroom. Procedures then need to be continually monitored and reinforced. Being consistent in carrying out these classroom procedures is important to the establishment of an effective classroom. In the scenario, by the fourth day of class, Mr. Baldino's rule that students prepare to go to work when he stands in front of the class was operating well.

Just as the students should know what is expected of them in terms of their behavior, they should also know what standards and goals are set for each learning experience. Students need to know the direction in which they are going and how they are progressing toward classroom goals. Objectives shared with the students for each learning activity give the class a sense of purpose and order in their learning.

Teacher preparedness is a vital contributing factor to an orderly classroom. The ability to orchestrate interaction among thirty students for either 1 hour or

6 hours necessitates hundreds of decisions, many of which can be made prior to teaching, in order to ensure smooth operation of classes. (Tom Baldino's preparation with his "magic" approach is a prime example.) As any student teacher can attest, finding oneself confused in the middle of a lesson because of not knowing what questions to ask or how to explain a difficult concept can cause frustration, disruption, and a considerable loss of academic learning time. Rutter's study (1979) of secondary classrooms identified teacher preparation of lessons in advance as an essential characteristic.

Careful preparation will include thorough planning of instruction to obtain optimum student involvement. Each learning activity will be conducted for a purpose. Films will be viewed as visual representations of curriculum content. Games will be used to illustrate concepts or to practice skills. A time filler such as routinely using the last fifteen minutes of a period for unsupervised or unmonitored study wastes learning time and can add up to as much as a week of unengaged time by the end of the year.

On-task study behavior is an essential factor for student achievement and is accomplished only in an ordered classroom. The goal of the effective teacher is to increase students' engagement time in order to provide them with maximum opportunities for learning. If students are concentrating on learning activities, behavior problems will be minimized. To encourage on-task behaviors, the teacher continually monitors students when not immediately interacting with them.

Smoothing transition times for the least amount of disruption and loss of time is another important technique in maintaining an ordered classroom. Transition times occur as students change from one activity to another, from one subject to another, finish a test and move into another activity, or complete one assignment and wait for the next. The handling of transition time should be planned, along with the rest of the lesson. A teacher should give procedural directions prior to transition time. Directions are given clearly at the start of a learning activity so the teacher does not interrupt those who are working with information for those who have completed the activity on what to do next. Also, essential materials and equipment need to be available so that activities can proceed smoothly. A well-planned transition will tie activities together, and will tie together different subjects in a logical manner.

The following are three examples of such transitions, the first from a middle school, the second from a high school, the third not identified with a particular level.

When you are finished with your math exercises, read "The Puzzle" on page 57 in your language arts book. Since you have been working on solving word problems in math, see if you can solve Wert's problem in the story. Only read to page 61 then stop. We'll talk about your solutions, then read the author's ending.

Earlier today we were examining the plate tectonics theory of the continents. Now let's take that theory and apply it to the continental drift theory. Does the information on page 156 support one or the other of these ideas? Write a short paragraph, no more than 60 words, giving your reasoning.

(Before the test starts.) When you have finished the test bring your papers up to the desk, then read Chapter 4 in your text and identify three main points from the chapter. Write them on a piece of paper to turn in at the end of class or tomorrow.

Some of the more vexing problems that challenge an ordered classroom as identified by experienced teachers involve students being absent, tardy, or misbehaving (Stallings, 1976). Effective teachers develop a system to deal with returning students who have been absent or tardy so that these students can be updated quickly and made ready for the day's activities. Teachers should keep copies of each day's worksheets and/or handouts in a file cabinet. Returning students can go to the file themselves to find out what they have missed and need to make up.

The teacher's system for dealing with misbehaving students must be put in place early and be made known to the students along with the reward system for appropriate behavior. Interruptions from the public address system or people coming to the door for students can take the class off-task. Other disruptions may be caused by external stimuli such as lessons held after a pep rally or class party, or before vacation. Teachers should focus student attention on the lesson promptly after an interruption by calling on individuals and continuing the lesson while moving around the room and using nonverbal behavior to control students, or by discussing the disruption for several minutes to satisfy students' curiosity before getting back on-task. The teacher needs to plan differently for these disruptive times. For example, a lesson with high motivation and activity should be planned on a day before vacation. Story time or quiet seat work can bring students' attention back to the classroom after a pep rally. The pertinent principle is that teachers must plan the methods they will use to accommodate anticipated departures from regular classroom activities.

When management problems occur, they need to be handled promptly. There should be recognized and accepted standards of discipline which are uniformly enforced as well as a reward system in place that recognizes student effort. Fewer management problems will occur if previously established teacher behavior is made part of the teacher's decision bank on an orderly climate.

As noted previously, an orderly classroom is a structured classroom in which students know the expectations the teacher holds for them. An orderly, structured classroom does not mean a classroom that allows no opportunity for creativity, student input, or spontaneity. Rather, an orderly classroom provides a framework in which the class functions smoothly. Students may be encouraged to share ideas, lesson plans may be changed or discarded, individual needs may be addressed, and group processes may be considered in decision making.

The classroom should not become so rigidly ordered that individual needs are ignored. For example, an insecure student who craves the teacher's attention will have to be handled individually until the student has acquired confidence.

Individual attention can be given after the rest of the class is at work on an activity.

Room for spontaneity must also exist within the order. Unexpected events can ease tensions and relieve fatigue. Consider the book title, *The Geranium on the Window Sill Just Died But Teacher You Went Right On* (Cullum, 1971). It projects the image of a teacher so committed to order and structure as to be wholly insensitive to the perceptions and feelings of students. The indictment made in this book warns us against ignoring the climate in the room in order to maintain a rigid schedule. Order itself is a necessary but insufficient condition for effective teaching; understanding is just as necessary.

Research literature is full of studies that substantiate the effect of teacher expectations on student achievement. Good (1981) reviewed ten years of research on teacher expectations and concluded that teachers behave differently toward different students, and affect student achievement. Over time, student achievement and behavior will conform more and more closely to the teacher's expectations. One finding from a Brophy and Good study (1970) reported that students for whom teachers held high expectations gave more correct answers in reading groups and achieved higher average scores on a year-end standard test than did students for whom the teacher held low expectations. Again, a study conducted in an elementary classroom has clear implications for secondary classrooms as well.

This self-fulfilling prophecy (Rosenthal & Jacobson, 1968; Rosenthal, Baratz, & Hall, 1974) illustrates the need for teachers to be aware of the effect their expectations may have on student behavior. Students may behave in a particular way because the teacher conveys the expectation that they behave in that manner. Thus, a student who is considered slow by his teacher might consider himself a poor student regardless of his ability. Good and Brophy (1984) note that teachers' expectations for student success may be changed when teachers realize that a student's ability is comparable to that of his classmates.

The effective schools research conducted by Edmonds (1979), Brookover, and Lezotte (1977), and others discovered that raising expectations for success among both teachers and students improved the achievement level of that school. An apparent cause of poor achievement in urban schools is directly related to the low academic expectations teachers tend to hold for pupils in those schools.

The research cited has examined the effect teacher attitudes have on students. The classic Coleman study (1966) upset the educational world because it reported that school-related factors contribute much less to variability in student achievement than do environmental factors. However, student attitudes, whatever their source, have the strongest relationship to achievement. Children who have a sense of control over their environment have a better opportunity to achieve. This means that if children feel that their efforts will produce results in schools and that the teacher and school are supportive of their efforts, they are more likely to succeed. Coleman has helped us understand that we must work as hard to develop positive attitudes in pupils as to deliver subject matter.

TOPIC 4: EXPECTATION FOR SUCCESS

RESEARCH AND THEORETICAL BASE

In the opening scenario, Mr. Baldino was well aware that by the time many students reach 9th grade, they have poor self-images in mathematics. He knew that in order to improve their achievement he needed to promote a successful image for them all. His expectations for students were positive. He had assessed their potential through diagnostic tests, and knew that they were capable, even though they had been mediocre achievers in the past. He had formulated plans about the methods he would use to improve their math images.

As was attested by the classic but controversial ''Pygmalion in the Classroom'' study by Rosenthal and Jacobson (1968), teachers' attitudes toward students do influence student performance. Those students in the study who were identified as supposedly having a high potential for success achieved higher than would otherwise be predicted. Purkey (1978) relates a student's story concerning his inability to sing: ''When I was in the 3rd grade, a choral teacher said that I was a good listener (implying a poor singer). Everyone laughed except me. I've never uttered a musical note in public from that day to this.'' Purkey's book goes on to emphasize the importance of sending students verbal and nonverbal supportive messages that invite them to learn and to succeed.

APPLICATION TO PRACTICE

Effective teachers like Mr. Baldino develop a climate for success in the classroom by doing some or all of the following practices:

1. Develop positive attitudes concerning students' abilities.
2. Develop positive attitudes in students toward their success in the subject.
3. Help students to understand that success can be reached through their efforts.
4. Demonstrate that the teacher and the school are supportive of student success.
5. Adapt learning activities and materials to fit students' abilities for success.
6. Provide all students with opportunities to be successful.
7. Give effective feedback.
8. Become aware of messages being communicated to students—both verbally and nonverbally.
9. Show interest in all students.
10. Check for each student's understanding.
11. Encourage students to compete with themselves.

A personal experience illustrating the effect of teacher attitudes on a class was recounted to one of the authors by a friend who was a secondary English teacher. She explained that her third period class had been giving her headaches because they were not doing their work, talked throughout the class period, and conveyed to her that they did not like English—or her. At her wits' end in trying to cope with the situation, she decided to try a positive approach. She began to smile a lot at the class, made positive remarks to individuals, dropped her negative approach to classroom management, praised them for their efforts, and explained that she had been frustrated with them because she knew this class had a high potential but was not reaching it. The effect was that the class slowly began to turn around, and within a month she was amazed to find that it was one of her favorite classes. Students were achieving considerably better than in the past. She acknowledged that the experience taught her a valuable lesson in building positive expectations.

Teachers need to have positive attitudes concerning students' abilities. Teachers need to believe in their students regardless of their ability level, their background, or their previous records, because students look to them for cues about how the teachers assess their abilities. A teacher can trap students in poor achievement if little is expected of them because of their ethnic group, academic labeling, or family background. Therefore, teachers must try to keep an open mind and encourage positive behavior in each child.

Helping students not only to feel good about themselves but to believe in their ability to be successful in a school subject is important, too. The current state of low math achievement in the country as reflected in national testing results may be directly linked to a nation's poor self-concept concerning the ability to do well in that subject. Consider how frequently one hears intelligent, successful people admitting in conversations or on late night talk shows that they were terrible in math. Teachers must help students develop a positive attitude by convincing them of their potential for success through supportive comments, reinforcement, and individual help as needed. Such supportive communications with students may sound like this:

Your questions during class today were important ones. You asked about key points that were causing others trouble, too. You had over 70% of your homework correct yesterday. Keep up the good work. Remember, I'll be available to answer your questions if you get confused again.

Building expectations for student success means encouraging students to understand that success can be reached through their own efforts. The importance of students recognizing that they are in control of their academic successes and failures is discussed in a later section of this chapter. Helping students realize that they control their fortunes in school by the amount of time and effort they are willing to expend on their work is an important task. This control principle can be impressed upon students by having them keep track of the time they put into a unit or project, as well as by encouraging them to self-evaluate their work using the criteria previously developed by the teacher and/or the class. Showing students through charts and graphs the progress they are making helps them become aware that they have control over their achievement. They realize that the grades they receive are not given by the teacher, but rather result from their own purposeful efforts.

As was revealed by the Coleman study (1966), a student needs to feel that the school as well as the teacher supports students and encourages their success. Such conditions as public telephones for student use, an attractive cafeteria setting where students have access to hot and cold drinks during study hours, and attractively decorated classrooms are all examples of messages sent to students about the concern of the school for their welfare. Display cases filled with academic and extracurricular awards and athletic trophies are important. Displays of student pictures and work convey positive messages. Guidance counselors with doors open to students, a student and teacher tutoring system within the school, and teachers with hours available to help students are important for establishing a support network.

In the opening scenario Mr. Baldino let all his students know that during his seventh hour planning period every day he was available to tutor anyone needing help. He would also arrange tutoring sessions before or after school upon request. This type of teacher behavior conveys to students that teachers are concerned about them and are trying to help them.

Such teacher concern can be introduced by learning activities and materials usage that fits student needs. For example, a student who may not be able to write an exam, for whatever reasons, can take the test orally. A student who has poor reading ability in junior high may use a different textbook or do different assignments with fewer pages involved. These are straightforward, even obvious, examples. In other, particular cases, imaginative, concerned teachers will find many ways to individualize tasks. The point is that teachers must be flexible, and willing to adapt to individual needs if all students are going to be successful in the classroom.

In order to promote success, the teacher needs to structure success experiences so that all students can feel positive about themselves as learners. Students need opportunities to succeed frequently on learning tasks. Crawford (1978) noted that college students who were identified as having low motivation for achievement and high fear of failure did best when their success rate was over 90% and did poorly when their success rate was under 60%. Students with high motivation for success and low fear of failure achieved best at a 60% success rate and poorest at a 93% rate. This information reinforces the recommendation to vary testing measures for different students. Therefore, teachers need to individualize learning tasks whenever necessary so that students are engaged with tasks and materials in their success rate. Also, each student's success rate should be monitored and used as a basis for decision making about that student.

Other suggestions teachers may consider for establishing a success climate in the classroom include giving feedback that informs students how to become more proficient in those areas that have not been successfully learned. The importance of feedback that tells students how and where they need to improve and gives opportunities for additional practice and relearning needs to be understood by all teachers.

Teachers need to become aware of the messages they send to students through their verbal and nonverbal behavior. These messages may reinforce the more able academically and ignore or criticize the weaker students (Good, 1981). Examples of such debilitating behaviors are:

1. Good students are seated across the front and down the middle of the room.
2. Teacher eye contact is mainly with good students.
3. Teacher calls on good students much more frequently than slower students.
4. Teacher punishes off-task behavior in slower students and more frequently ignores it in good students.
5. Teacher communication with slower students is mainly negative and critical.
6. Teacher gives little wait time to slower students to answer questions.
7. Teacher praises better students more.
8. Teacher displays work of only the good students.
9. Teacher gives good students more cues with which to respond to questions.
10. Teacher requires less effort and work from slower students.

By changing the seating pattern to meet students' needs, teachers can convey an interest in students. Those who have difficulty paying attention or seeing the board may sit in the front; talkative students can be mixed with quiet students to encourage better attention. Regardless of the seating pattern, teacher eye contact with students—even those in the back of the room and in the far rows by the windows or the doors—needs to include all students so that the teacher can send and receive nonverbal feedback.

Verbal and nonverbal behavior that expresses teacher interest, such as speaking to each student at least once in a period and trying to have some individual communication daily, is important for positive classroom climate. Weaker academic students or quiet students may sit in class without recognition for a week or more at a time. Part of the communication should be positive feedback given at the appropriate time.

Point ten in suggestions for building a success climate in the classroom, checking for understanding, reminds the teacher to monitor a student's progress by constant checks on comprehension of the material. Group comprehension checks can be taken as suggested by Hunter (1967), by having the class raise a finger to indicate their answers to a multiple choice or true-false oral question. With this method the teacher can quickly determine whether the class understands a part of the lesson.

Encouraging students to compete with themselves requires that the teacher give students frequent feedback about their progress by checking homework, giving quizzes and tests, and writing comments on papers. Through extensive feedback, students can be encouraged to consider their personal progress in regard to objectives rather than to their ranking in respect to the rest of the class.

An effective teacher does not have to be a magician, although Tom Baldino used this ploy. However, an effective teacher does need to be able to make those purposeful decisions that help establish a climate for success in the classroom. The decisions Mr. Baldino made in approaching his class through one of his hobbies were based on his knowledge that students work harder if the climate in the room is interesting to and supportive of students, and if students know what is expected of them. He understood that in achievement, reinforcement can bring results. He planned to use the puzzles and math games for reinforcement as well as for teaching interested students a bit of magic. He would see that students received frequent feedback so that they would know the results of their efforts and the skills they needed to learn. Many exercises would be available for group and individual practice. Through practice and self-checking, students would learn at their individual rates.

Those students who fell behind would either become a separate group that Mr. Baldino would teach ten or fifteen minutes of each day, or they would be introduced to new material while still being held responsible for learning the material of the past unit. Promoting student feelings of responsibility to learn the course material was an important goal set by Mr. Baldino. Holding them accountable for practice exercises or for taking tests that would be self-checked encouraged their feelings of responsibility.

Mr. Baldino had decided to use much of his class time for working with individuals and small groups on remediation problems as necessary, as well as on enrichment experiences. The beginning of most classes would consist of large group instruction in which review and introduction of lesson content would occur. Explanation and demonstration would follow, after which groups would work on exercises to demonstrate their understanding. Individual practice would then follow. An important part of the yearly curriculum would be working on problem-solving and analysis skills. He would give unit and review tests so that he could monitor class progress. Much feedback and reinforcement would be used to encourage positive feelings toward the subject and to emphasize the standards students should meet.

Mr. Baldino looked forward to the effect his plan would have on the class. His success rate had been high before. He knew he could encourage success for everyone again, but he knew that for this class, he would have to learn a few new magic tricks himself.

SUMMARY POINT

One of the important roles teachers play is that of shaping the classroom learning environment. Teachers create the classroom environment by verbal and non-verbal behavior displayed toward the students, and by their professional execution of teaching responsibilities. The decisions teachers make regarding the treatment of students and the standards of the classroom—including behavior and academic standards—contribute to the classroom climate. Within this climate each student's self-image is influenced positively or negatively toward learning.

This section of the chapter on climate has included many practices that teachers may use to promote a positive learning environment. These practices were detailed to enable beginning teachers to recognize the choices available to them when making decisions about their teaching behaviors. Classroom practices need to be considered in light of the effect they have on creating a favorable learning climate.

REVIEW: IMPORTANT PRACTICES FOR ESTABLISHING A PRODUCTIVE
        LEARNING CLIMATE

1. Establish an academic atmosphere in which academic goals are emphasized.
2. Promote high standards, then monitor and reward achievement.
3. Maintain an orderly environment.
4. Build expectations for success by convincing students of their ability to succeed and providing them with success experiences.

TOPIC 5: MOTIVATION AS IT RELATES TO CLIMATE

Climate refers especially to the stimuli that emerge from the social interactions throughout a group. Motivation, on the other hand, refers to stimuli that are internal to the student, and so must be personally defined. In practice, the line between these two constructs is not clearly drawn. One cannot be fully understood in the absence of the other; they are inseparable and mutually reinforcing. One might even take the position that they are different perspectives on the phenomenon of behavior.

Previous commentary in the chapter focused on the findings from effective teaching research concerning climate. Mr. Baldino served as an example of a teacher who translated four aspects of effective teaching—emphasis on academics, orderly environment, success expectations, and high standards—into classroom practices. The most important construct underlying the effect of each aspect of a positive learning climate is the student's motivation. If a teacher is to be an autonomous, fully functioning decision maker, an understanding of motivation theory is necessary; otherwise, the teacher is in a position of selecting motivating methods indiscriminately rather than purposefully to achieve desired educational goals for the student.

The literature on motivation is extensive, much of it derived from social psychology theory. Psychologists describe motivational factors as those influences on behavior that direct action, select action, and energize behavior. Motivation in this context is considered to be a state of need or desire that impels a person to do something to satisfy that need or desire. A motivated student in the teacher's perspective is one in whom there is the desire and intention to achieve the class learning objectives.

A perspective on motivation is presented by Hunter (1967b) and reinforced through research on attribution using extrinsic and intrinsic rewards (Cohen, 1986). Hunter has identified through her study and practice six factors that affect motivation. She states that "motivation is a state of unresolved need or desire existing within the child." Therefore, the teacher cannot directly motivate the child but can manipulate environmental variables that reflexively change the child's motivation. With an understanding of those environmental variables that may be manipulated to encourage student learning, the teacher can make more effective decisions. Those variably include such factors as rewards, teacher interest, peer pressure and support, and control issues.

Lepper's (1983) recent research in the area of intrinsic motivation suggests that students' motivation to accomplish a task tends to be diminished if they feel they are being overly controlled—for example, being too carefully monitored regarding on- and off-task behavior. This aspect of control in shaping students' motivation is important for teachers to consider in their motivation decision making.

A theory derived from the work of Deci and Poroc (1978) suggests that rewards may be perceived by the student either as controlling them or giving them useful information about their performance. If students perceive the rewards as information about their progress and success, then the rewards increase motivation; if students perceive rewards as controlling their behavior then the rewards are ineffective. Therefore, the teacher should avoid using rewards as bribes or threats. For example, the teacher may point out that students who can pass a test on factoring equations with 100% accuracy will be rewarded with a "math whiz" certificate that acknowledges their ability to factor mathematical expressions accurately. A controlling approach to the reward would threaten that if they did not work hard they would not receive the special certificate which the rest of the class probably would receive.

How the students perceive themselves in regard to the learning task and the amount of control they have over the outcome is a key to understanding and influencing students' behavior. The internal perceptions that determine students' motivation is called attribution theory (Heider, 1958; Rutter, 1966; and Weiner, 1984). This theory maintains that the quality of a person's motivation can be analyzed in terms of three factors:

1. Location of cause—emerges from within a person or stimulated by external factors.

2. Constancy—enduring causes such as personal abilities and talents or variable and controllable causes such as effort or conditions that vary over time or situation.
3. Responsibility—extent of control persons have over the event and whether their actions are intentional

Cohen's (1986) research review relating this theory to the classroom indicates that people perceive their successes or failures in different ways depending upon their analysis of the three attributing factors. People with high achievement needs assume responsibility for both their successes and failures and acknowledge that some outside causes over which they had no control may have been operating. People with low achievement needs feel they have little control over their failures, which they attribute to their own inadequacies. They view success as unattainable through their own efforts because it is based on luck or ''connections.'' Teachers who understand motivation theory and research can use practices that encourage the student to feel more control over his or her destiny in the classroom.

Attribution theory can be helpful in enabling the teacher to understand how certain unsuccessful students view themselves. The teacher can then attempt to help a student change his or her success perception from one determined by uncontrollable factors to controllable ones. For example, Jesse, a low-achiever 9th grader, believes he is failing because his teacher doesn't like him. If Jesse can be helped to see that he will receive points for attending class and turning in his work—two areas of deficiency for Jesse—and that a certain accumulation of points will enable him to reach the passing level for that term, he may change his defeatist attitude and begin to work toward passing. Jesse needs to realize that passing or failing are within his ability to control. The teacher's feedback to Jesse can transmit that message to him. As suggested by the effective teaching research on appropriate feedback, the feedback the student receives shapes the student's perception of whether he or she has control over the situation. Such feedback moves the student from internal causes to external causes: ''This paper needs to have the main ideas of your paragraphs supported with examples and elaboration; then the paper will be a stronger one. Let me show you what I mean.'' Now the student knows that a low grade on the composition is based on some specific writing factors that can be improved—not on congenitally poor writing skills.

The teacher needs to convince the low achiever that he or she can experience success through applying certain practices that include using appropriate study skills and time management. The teacher can provide the student with the appropriate feedback that lets the student know what needs to be done. An example of appropriate feedback to encourage a student's feeling of control is to suggest the student outline the chapter and look for the main ideas, rather than ''to study hard'' for the next test. A student may not know how to study productively. The student may feel that passing a test with a high grade is beyond his or her ability; hence, the student lacks motivation due to a poor academic self-concept.

The importance of helping students realize that they are in control of their academic progress and that they can do what is needed to succeed is essential to teachers' motivation strategies. Giving effective feedback that explains what students need to do and how they are to do it is a key step in building students' intrinsic motivation and paving the way for higher achievement.

The factors which affect motivation are diverse social and psychological ones that include students' internal perceptions of educational goals in relation to their needs, perceptions of their abilities to meet those goals, perceptions of the desire to meet goals, and perceptions of their own power in meeting goals and succeeding in the classroom. All of these factors need to be considered in the teacher's structuring of the classroom climate.

In the interest of fostering motivation teachers make sincere efforts to establish clear and relevant goals, and to present learning in a way that is interesting and enjoyable. To the extent that they are successful, students undoubtedly benefit. But there are immediate and obvious limitations to this approach because it is not possible to make all academic topics interesting and learning activities enjoyable for all students. As an expedient, teachers may be inclined to resort to students' aversion to pain. They threaten or inflict consequences that are more painful than engaging in learning, thus providing students with the choice of the "lesser of evils." This approach is so firmly rooted in conventional wisdom and popular practice that it is rarely questioned. There is, however, a broader perspective to motivation that includes insights into understanding student motivation through theoretical information such as the attribution theory that will enable the teacher to translate more knowledgeably and competently the four aspects of effective teaching into pertinent classroom practices. Without such an expanded view, the teacher relies on conventional wisdom as the basis for instructional decisions rather than sound pedagogy. Therefore, it becomes important for the beginning teacher to understand psychological theory and research on motivation including attribution theory in order to provide a basis for informed decision making.

SUMMARY POINT

The climate in a classroom is influenced by the quality of the students' motivation, i.e., their inclination to learn, that exists collectively within them. Teachers cannot affect student motivation directly, but through a variety of approaches they can manipulate classroom conditions that, in turn, affect students' feelings and perceptions. Attribution theory, which helps teachers understand students' motivation, provides a basis for making motivation-related decisions.

REVIEW: IMPORTANT PRACTICES FOR AFFECTING STUDENT MOTIVATION

1. Analyze the way the student perceives himself or herself as a learner.
2. Discern the causes for that student's perception.
3. Help the student gain confidence in his or her ability to control and be responsible for the learning situation and its outcome.

ACTIVITIES

I. ORDERLY ENVIRONMENT

1. Interview two teachers to get information about the following:
   a. What are established classroom rules?
   b. What are ways to promote student success?
   c. What are the established classroom standards for performance in academics and behavior?

   Information analysis: How do the teachers' responses to the questions compare? Is the information you gathered consistent with that generated from research reported in this chapter on effective schools practices?

2. Develop a lesson plan that could be used during the first few days of school to help establish an orderly environment, high standards, and success emphasis in the room. (Decide what content and learning activities you would use.)

II. CHECKLIST FOR CLIMATE CONDITIONS

Observe a teacher in a school for an extended period of time. Check the descriptor that most nearly describes that teacher's practice. If no descriptor fits, write your own for the element. If two descriptors fit, check both.

1. Use of Class Time
   a. Teacher records amount of time to be spent in instructional activities. _____
   b. Teacher is able to report orally actual amount of class instruction time used, and indicates those parts of the period that are not used for instruction. _____
   c. Teacher knows amount of time allotted for lesson but has not checked on amount of time spent on actual instructional activities. _____
   d. Other _____

2. Monitoring On-Task Behavior
   a. Teacher keeps records of on-task behavior time for students with learning problems. _____
   b. Teacher supervises students during individual practice times. _____
   c. Teacher occasionally monitors off-task behaviors from behind teacher's desk. _____
   d. Other _____
3. Homework
   a. Teacher assigns homework at least three times a week, collects it, and records it, using it as a basis for providing rewards when appropriate. _____
   b. Teacher assigns homework occasionally and collects it. _____
   c. Teacher seldom assigns homework and does not collect it. _____
   d. Other _____
4. Instruction Pace
   a. Teacher retains students on materials until they can pass content test. _____
   b. Teacher disregards failing on tests and moves on to next unit. _____
   c. Teacher holds re-learning sessions with students having difficulty but moves along to next unit. _____
   d. Other _____
5. Feedback
   a. Teacher gives oral feedback to each student every day. _____
   b. Teacher praises students having difficulties, and encourages all students with positive comments. _____
   c. Teacher displays student work. _____
   d. Teacher writes comments on papers. _____
   e. Teacher sends communications home to parents. _____
   f. Teacher conducts individual conferences. _____
   g. Teacher encourages students to keep charts on their progress. _____
   h. Teacher returns student papers promptly. _____
   i. Other _____
6. Learning Activities
   a. Teacher plans a variety of learning activities during a unit that includes analysis and synthesis level experiences. _____
   b. Teacher classifies learning activities regarding level of thinking involved to accomplish the task. _____
   c. Teacher is familiar with Bloom's Taxonomy but does not overtly use it in classifying learning activities. _____
   d. Teacher does not know Bloom's Taxonomy but plans "thinking" activities for students. _____
   e. Teacher does not consider the level of thinking involved in class activities. _____
   f. Other _____
7. Instruction Practice
   a. Teacher shares with students the lesson objectives and their rationale. _____

b. Teacher plans instruction so that students receive feedback during each lesson.   _____

c. Teacher starts lesson with directions and/or lecture on new materials.   _____

d. Teacher feedback is given mainly through tests.   _____

e. Other _____

8. Management Rules

a. Teacher, possibly with input from students, establishes classroom rules and procedures.   _____

b. Teacher has strict classroom routine which is followed throughout the week.   _____

c. Teacher provides rules when necessary.   _____

d. Teacher has no specific classroom rules or procedures; plays each day "by ear."   _____

e. Other _____

III. TEACHER BEHAVIORS FOR EFFECTIVE CLASSROOM CLIMATE

Directions:

This climate checklist can be used for self-evaluation or to provide observation data to another teacher. The observer marks the far right column to check off a climate-producing behavior the teacher uses during that observation period. The self-evaluating teacher uses the rating scale to evaluate, and may request evaluation information from the observer.

	Teacher's Effectiveness Scale (from Very Effective to Not Effective)					Observer's Checklist: Yes or No
1. Academic atmosphere	5	4	3	2	1	
a. Teacher is task-oriented; has objectives to accomplish.	___	___	___	___	___	_____
b. Teacher fills class time with instructional activity.	___	___	___	___	___	_____
c. Teacher keeps students on-task.	___	___	___	___	___	_____
d. Teacher plans a variety of challenging learning activities using higher thinking skills.	___	___	___	___	___	_____
e. Teacher encourges high standards in quality of student work.	___	___	___	___	___	_____
2. Orderly environment						
a. Teacher has established class routines, procedures, and rules.	___	___	___	___	___	_____
b. Teacher lets students know what they are to accomplish.	___	___	___	___	___	_____

	Teacher's Effectiveness Scale (from Very Effective to Not Effective)					Observer's Checklist: Yes or No
	5	4	3	2	1	
c. Teacher keeps students on task during instructional periods.	___	___	___	___	___	_____
d. Teacher personally handles management problems promptly.	___	___	___	___	___	_____
e. Teacher is well prepared for each lesson.	___	___	___	___	___	_____
f. Teacher returns student papers promptly.	___	___	___	___	___	_____
g. Teacher plans smooth transition from one subject to another or one activity to another.	___	___	___	___	___	_____
h. Teacher handles interruptions and disruptions competently during instruction.	___	___	___	___	___	_____

3. Success Expectations

	5	4	3	2	1	
a. Teacher displays positive attitude concerning all students' ability to succeed.	___	___	___	___	___	_____
b. Teacher provides all students with an opportunity to be successful by adapting activities and materials to fit students' abilities and needs.	___	___	___	___	___	_____
c. Teacher uses verbal and non-verbal behavior that demonstrates teacher interest in all students.	___	___	___	___	___	_____
d. Teacher monitors each child's daily success and gives feedback.	___	___	___	___	___	_____
e. Teacher gives much feedback through homework check, tests and discussion.	___	___	___	___	___	_____
f. Teacher encourages child to compete against himself rather than against the class.	___	___	___	___	___	_____

4. High Standards

	5	4	3	2	1	
a. Teacher maintains high standards of performance within the classroom including policies on homework, class absences, use of class time.	___	___	___	___	___	_____
b. Teacher maintains an academic performance level that students must meet or be reinstructed.	___	___	___	___	___	_____

	Teacher's Effectiveness Scale (from Very Effective to Not Effective)					Observer's Checklist: Yes or No
	5	4	3	2	1	
c. Teacher rewards excellent work and effort.	——	——	——	——	——	————
d. Teacher exhibits professional behavior.	——	——	——	——	——	————
e. Teacher requires a level of performance that challenges but does not frustrate.	——	——	——	——	——	————

IV. Self-Evaluation for Producing a Climate for Success

Audio- or videotape a class session, review the tape and evaluate it on the following, using this scale: 1 = Unsatisfactory Practice; 2 = Fair; 3 = Average; 4 = Good Practice; 5 = Excellent Practice.

	5	4	3	2	1
a. Shared objectives with students	——	——	——	——	——
b. Established procedures and standards	——	——	——	——	——
c. Developed on-task climate	——	——	——	——	——
d. Showed support for students' efforts	——	——	——	——	——
e. Made adaptations to encourage individual success	——	——	——	——	——
f. Communicated with all students	——	——	——	——	——
g. Maintained eye contact with all students	——	——	——	——	——
h. Gave feedback to students concerning their success and remediation procedures	——	——	——	——	——
i. Exhibited a businesslike manner	——	——	——	——	——

V. MOTIVATION ACTIVITIES: GUIDED PRACTICE

Plan and deliver a mini-lesson of 5 to 10 minutes in length in which you emphasize as many motivational teachings as you can within the context of the lesson. Consider the following components of a motivational lesson:

1. Create interest in topic at beginning of lesson
2. Explain topic's relevancy or application to other knowledge or life experiences
3. Use novel or different approach to the lesson to maintain student attention
4. Use stimulus variation to change the instructional approach (from oral instruction to visual aid, etc.)
5. Use positive, informative feedback in guided practice
6. Provide a reward for students in some manner

Allow your peer group and your instructor to critique your performance based on the above practices.

REFERENCES

Anderson, L. M. & Evertson, C. M. (1978). Classroom organization at the beginning of school: Two case studies. Austin, TX: University of Texas.

Berliner, D. (1984). The half-full glass: A review of research on teaching. [Review of P. L. Hosford (Ed.) *Using what we know about teaching*], Alexandria, VA: Association for Supervision and Curriculum Development, 51–77.

Block, J. (1970). The effects of various levels of performance on selected cognitive, affective, and time variables. Unpublished doctoral dissertation, University of Chicago.

Bloom, B. (Ed.). (1956). *A taxonomy of educational objectives. Handbook I: Cognitive Domain.* New York: McKay.

Bremme, O., & Erickson, O. (1977). Relationships among verbal and non-verbal classroom behaviors. *Theory Into Practice 5*, 153–161.

Brookover, W. & Lezotte, L. (1977). Changes in school characteristics coincident with changes in student achievement. East Lansing: Michigan State University, College of Urban Development.

Brophy, J. (1982). Successful teaching strategies for the inner-city child. *Phi Delta Kappan, 63,* 527–530.

Brophy, J. & Good, T. (1970). Teacher communication of differential expectation for children's classroom performance: Some behavioral data. *Journal of Educational Psychology, 61,* 365–374.

Brophy, J. & Good, T. (1985). Teacher behavior and student achievement. In M. Wittrock (Ed.), *Handbook of research on teaching.* New York: Macmillan.

Brown, B. (1974). *New mind, new body.* New York: Harper & Row.

Cohen, M. (1986). Research on motivation: New content for teacher preparation curriculum. *Journal of Teacher Education, 37*(3), 23–28.

Coleman, J., Campbell, E., Hobrau, C., McPartland, J., Mood, A., Weinfield, F., & York, R. (1966). Equality of educational opportunity. Washington, D.C.: U.S. Government Printing Office.

Crawford, J. (1978). Interactions of learning characteristics with the difficulty level of instruction. *Journal of Educational Psychology, 70*(4), 523–531.

Cullum, A. (1971). *The geranium on the window sill just died but teacher you went right on.* New York: Harlan Quist.

Deci, E. & Porac, J. (1978). Cognitive evaluation theory and the study of human motivation. In M. R. Lepper & D. Green (Eds.), *The hidden costs of reward* (pp. 149–176). Hillsdale, NJ: Erlbaum.

Dunn, R. & Dunn, K. (1975). *Educator's self teaching guide to individualizing instructional programs.* West Nyack, NY: Parker.

Edmonds, E. (1979). Effective schools for the urban poor. *Educational Leadership, 37*, 15–24.

Erickson, F. & Shultz, J. (1981). When is a context? Some issues and methods in the analysis of social competence. In J. L. Green & C. Wallat (Eds.), *Ethnography and language in educational settings*. Norwood, NJ: Ablex.

Evertson, C., Anderson, C., Anderson, L., & Brophy, J. (1980). Relationship between classroom behaviors and student outcomes in junior high mathematics and English classes. *American Educational Research Journal 17*, 43–60.

Flanders, N. (1970). *Analyzing teaching behavior*. Reading, MA: Addison-Wesley.

Gage, N. & Berliner, D. (1984). *Educational Psychology*, 3rd ed. Boston: Houghton Mifflin.

Good, T. (1981). Teacher expectations and student perceptions: A decade of research. *Educational Leadership, 38*, 415–422.

Good, T. & Brophy, J. (1978). *Looking in classrooms*. New York: Harper & Row.

Heider, F. (1958). *The psychology of interpersonal relations*. New York: Wiley.

Hill, K. T. (1984). Debilitating motivation and testing: A major educational problem—possible solutions and policy applications. In R. E. Ames & C. Ames (Eds.), *Research on motivation in education: Student motivation* (pp. 245–274). New York: Academic Press.

Hunter, M. (1967a). *Improved instruction*. El Segundo, CA: TIP Publications.

Hunter, M. (1967b). *Motivation theory for teachers*. El Segundo, CA: TIP Publications.

Johnston, R. (1976). The relationship between cooperation and inquiry in science classrooms. *Journal of Research in Science Teaching, 13*, 55–63.

Johnson, R. & Johnson, D. (1985). Student-student interaction: Ignored but powerful. *Journal of Teacher Education, 36*(4), 22–26.

Lepper, M. (1983). Extrinsic reward and intrinsic motivation: Implications for the classroom. In J. Levine and M. Wang (Eds.), *Teacher and student perceptions: Implications for learning* (pp. 281–317). Hillsdale, NJ: Erlbaum.

Levin, T., with Long, R. (1981). *Effective instruction*. Alexandria, VA: Association for Supervision and Curriculum Development.

Lezotte, L. (Ed.). (1984). Conducting an effective school program. *The effective school report, 2*, 10, 1.

McCarthy, B. (1980). The 4 MAT system: Teaching to learning style with right/left mode techniques. Arlington Heights, IL: Excel, Inc.

National Commission on Excellence in Education. (1983). *A nation at risk*. Washington, D.C.: U.S. Department of Education.

Purkey, W. (1978). *Inviting school success*. Belmont, CA: Wadsworth.

Rosenshine, B. (1979). Content, time, and direct instruction. In P. Peterson & H. Walberg (Eds.) *Research on teaching: Concepts, findings, and implications*. Berkeley, CA: McCutchan.

Rosenthal, R., Baratz, S., & Hall, C. (1974). Teacher behavior, teacher expectation, and gains in pupils' rated creativity. *Journal of Genetic Psychology, 124*, 115–122.

Rosenthal, R. & Jacobson, L. (1968). *Pygmalion in the classroom: Teacher expectation and pupils' intellectual development*. New York: Holt, Rinehart and Winston.

Rutter, J. (1966). Generalized expectancies for internal versus external control of reinforcement. *Psychological Monographs, 80.*

Rutter, M., Maugham, B., Mortimore, P., & Ouster, J. (1979). *Fifteen thousand hours.* Cambridge, MA: Harvard University Press.

Snider, W. (1986, June 11). Chicago board adopts strict homework policy. *Education Week, 38,* 3.

Soar, R. & Soar, R. (1976). An attempt to identify measures of teacher affectiveness from four studies. *Journal of Teacher Education, 27,* 261–267.

Squires, D., Huitt, W. & Segars, I. (1984). *Effective schools and classrooms: A research-based perspective.* Alexandria, VA: Association for Supervision and Curriculum Development.

Stallings, J. (1976). How instructional processes relate to child outcome in a national study of follow-through. *Journal of Teacher Education, 27,* 43–47.

U.S. Department of Education. What works. Washington, DC: Government Printing Office.

Weber, G. (1971). Inner-city children can be taught to read: Four successful schools. (CBE Occasional Papers No. 18). Washington, DC: Council for Basic Education.

Weiner, B. (1984). Principles for a theory of student motivation and their application within an attributional framework. In R. Ames & C. Ames (Eds.) *Research on motivation in education: Student motivation: Vol. 1* (pp. 15–38). New York: Academic Press.

Wellisch, J., MacQueen, A., Carriere, R. & Duck, F. (1978). School management and organization in successful schools. *Sociology of Education, 51,* 211–266.

3 Planning For Teaching

All teachers plan. No teacher enters the classroom without having an idea of what to present (except perhaps those unfortunate substitute teachers who arrive at the school and find that no plans are available for their use). However, the nature of plans differs widely from teacher to teacher. Some plans may be quite structured and comprehensive. Others might exist only as vague intentions in the mind of the teacher. For teachers who are particularly glib, "winging it" without benefit of much deliberate planning may be considered by them to be a sufficient practice. Few conscientious educators would agree.

Sound planning contributes to good teaching. Claims to the contrary are likely to involve self-serving rationalizing, if not outright naiveté. The issue is not whether one *should* plan, but *how* one should plan. No single answer fits all cases. Some teachers, especially inexperienced teachers, are likely to find rather detailed plans to be beneficial. Other teachers may find that less specific plans, but plans which nevertheless contribute to purpose and direction in the lesson or unit, are more useful.

To some extent, plans are the extension of the teacher's personality and instructional style. As Hoover (1972) observes, they are, in that sense, a personal invention on the part of each teacher. The teacher who is basically a structured person will take a different approach to planning than a "free spirit." One could hardly use the plans of the other effectively even while covering the same topic. The approach taken in this book attempts to accommodate a wide range of personalities, teaching styles, grade levels, subject areas, and teacher experience, while stressing the necessity for conscientious, soundly conceived planning.

Because there are so many different approaches to planning being practiced by teachers, Clark and Yinger's (1980) definition of planning seems appropriate because of its broadness: ". . . any activity of a teacher that is concerned with organizing his or her school-related activities, or the activities of students. . . ." A general definition such as this takes into account the diversity of teachers' personalities and styles: formal, detailed planning for highly structured teachers and more informal approaches for those less structured. From this perspective, it is relatively easy to adapt a broad definition of planning to the more specific task of instructional planning. Within this context, plans are designs for guiding students' involvement in learning activities.

As a framework, consideration should be given to the (1) objectives of the lesson, (2) sequence of methods and strategies to be employed by the teacher, and (3) the extent to which the students have achieved the objectives. These three major aspects are a part of every teacher's preparation for instruction, although they may not be accorded equal importance or receive equal attention. The unit and daily plans designed as preparation for instruction are dependent on the intuitive and rational decisions made by the teacher about his or her students, the content and skills to be taught, and the instructional style and situation.

OVERVIEW

Starting with the premise that effective teaching, in large part, reflects careful planning, this chapter endeavors to describe the three major components of plans—objectives, instructional approaches and evaluation—and to explain the different types of long- and short-range planning. Emphasis is given to how teachers can use this information to make reflective decisions about the plans they design to guide instructional efforts. An instrument designed to facilitate the analysis of the major components of a daily lesson plan is provided in the Appendix of this chapter.

SCENARIO

Virginia Grove is a 5th-year social studies teacher at a large suburban high school. It is the last period of the school day. Virginia's study hall is small and the students are occupying themselves with completing homework assignments. The two students in the back of the room talking quietly are not a disruption, so she has some time to reflect on how she can wrap up the Civil War unit the class has been studying for the past 2 weeks. For the past several years she has done this by reviewing the major battles and discussing the surrender of Lee to Grant at Appomattox Courthouse in 1865. Last year she had enough time to show a short film of the War based on original Matthew Brady photographs.

As Virginia reflects on the class's activities up to this point, she is concerned that most of the time has been spent on political and military aspects of the War such as the causes, elections, comparisons of the North and South, and the battles. She recalls that in a Civil War history course she had in graduate school last year, the instructor, in his lecture on the final campaign, aroused her feelings about the tragedy and futility of war. Her students, she felt, should understand war in its most basic human terms. Would the school library have a copy of Grant's *Memoirs* and another source documenting common soldiers' experiences and attitudes? Grant's perceptions of the surrender and the soldiers' feelings would help her communicate to students the emotional dimension of war. She makes note of several questions that might serve as the basis of a discussion to stimulate some feelings and higher level thinking. Could she use a small group activity? A small group activity might be useful as a means for students to share feelings. Why not have the students assume the role of a Southern or Northern soldier as he thinks about returning home after the surrender is announced. The small groups could compose hypothetical letters, and share them with the whole class.

At this point, Virginia worries whether there will be enough time to review the major battles of the War. Is it necessary? Because of the high interest generated by the War, the students had been particularly conscientious in completing their reading assignments on time. They seemed to be conversant with the major battles and perhaps only needed a quick review. Why not challenge the students with the concept teaching game she had successfully used to introduce the westward movement and Manifest Destiny last month. Would the students be able to identify as the target concept the battles in which Grant participated, after he assumed command of the Union armies? Why not try it? The students would enjoy the game-like quality of the method and would benefit from a quick review.

As the period drew to a close she recalled that the public library had a large history section. Surely she could find some primary sources there if the school library did not have them. Virginia started toward the library. Better check whether Monday would be okay to have her students in the library to do a short research project comparing the Civil War with civil wars in other countries during recent times. Virginia smiled at the thought of this assignment because the in-service day social studies speaker had stressed the importance of relating the past to the present to help students find relevance in U.S. History. Perhaps this could be an opportunity to involve the students in inquiry. As she said hello to the principal in the hall, it occurred to her that she should check the newly revised U.S. History course of study to be certain that she had fulfilled all of the objectives listed for the Civil War. She began to feel good about the upcoming lesson.

RESEARCH AND THEORETICAL BASE

Virginia Grove used a systematic approach to planning the end of the Civil War unit. She carefully considered what the students had learned during the unit and instructional methods used in the past to design lessons based on students' needs and interests. Decisions related to planning were made reflectively. In addition, several characteristics of Virginia's approach to planning can be supported by current principles and research on planning.

The precept that effective planning is essential for effective teaching is a familiar one to teachers. In the past, so little research was done on planning that this was a statement of faith rather than certainty. Although a substantial body of research currently exists relating teacher behaviors and techniques to achievement, it has only been within the last ten years that significant research has been conducted on planning. Most of it has been descriptive, and has been conducted at the elementary level. Generalizations based on this research must be considered tentative, but they do have implications for teachers preparing unit and daily lessons on the secondary level.

Methods texts have, historically, consistently recommended a remarkably similar format for planning unit and daily lesson plans. This consensus on the major principles of planning has led to their uncritical acceptance. Little impetus has emerged for conducting research challenging those principles. One universally accepted principle has been that objectives must be specified first in order to provide direction for the teacher and students as learning activities are implemented. Decisions then need to be made about which instructional approaches should be used to achieve the objectives. Finally, evaluation means must be conducted to determine the extent to which students learned what was intended. Implicitly, the teacher's effectiveness was also indicated by this outcome.

What does research say about teachers' actual planning practices? In a review of research on planning, Clark and Yinger (1979) found that teachers generally have not faithfully applied the principles advocated by teacher educators. In general, the studies conducted by Peterson, Marx, and Clark (1978), and Morine (1976) in a variety of settings with a range of pupils showed that teachers considered content and instructional strategies before objectives as they planned for classes. Most of the time teachers spent on planning was used making decisions about the instructional context; far less time was spent on objectives and evaluation. Clearly, teachers generally do not consider objectives to be an essential part of the planning process. Some do not even consider them to be useful.

Such findings bear careful scrutiny in light of the research on effective teaching that has identified a focused approach to instruction as a characteristic of effective teachers. Levin with Long (1981) analyzed a substantial number of studies relating students' knowledge of instructional goals to achievement. Although some disagreement occurs, generally it was found that students achieve more if the teacher has informed them of the objectives in specific terms. It was concluded that instructional objectives facilitate learning when communicated to students through helping them determine what is to be accomplished and indicating how they are to do it. Objectives in these studies apparently served to provide students with a sense of direction and security.

Some other interesting conclusions have been made based on research about teachers' planning practices. Clark and Yinger (1980) found that teachers spend approximately 12 hours per week engaged in instructional planning. Teachers consider unit planning the most important form, and the process begins with a general idea that moves through phases of continual modification and elaboration. Teachers' written plans reflect only a small portion of the total plan. Most remains in the teacher's mind. Clark and Peterson (1986) concluded, ''. . . substantial teacher energy is devoted to structuring, organizing information, and managing limited instructional time.''

It has also been found that the development of routines in planning practices increases teacher efficiency and flexibility. To a great degree, routine helps reduce the complexity and unpredictability of teaching, thereby allowing teachers more time and energy to devote to other activities. Another finding of particular value to beginning teachers is that long-term benefits can be derived from concentrated planning during the first weeks of the school year. During this time teachers develop a workable system of procedures, time allocations, group ings, schedules and outlines. For the most part, their established systems remain in effect for the entire school year.

One of the major thrusts of educational research today is determining which teacher-controlled learning environment variables have an impact on students' achievement. A considerable number of studies have yielded findings that have significant implications for teachers' planning. Weil and Murphy (1982) reviewed teacher effectiveness research and found that students tend to achieve more in teacher-directed and controlled learning environments. Within these environments a strong academic focus is evident, students are actively involved in learning with minimal off-task behavior, and the teacher holds students accountable for their work. In order for teachers to involve students continually and consistently in direct teaching modes, planning is essential. Brophy and Good's (1986) very recent review of research on teacher behaviors and student achievement supports this finding: the teacher who produced students who achieved most planned and organized themselves on a daily basis *prior to instruction.*

Cooper (1982) defines an effective teacher as ''. . . one who is able to bring about intended learning outcomes.'' Given the current findings from research, the complexity of decisions that must be made anticipating and reacting to the immediate classroom situation, it is extremely difficult to visualize an effective teacher at work in the classroom who has not made careful decisions about objectives, methods and strategies, and evaluation procedures.

APPLICATION TO PRACTICE

Decision Making as the Basis for Planning

In one sense, as was implied in Chapter 1, life is inevitably a series of decisions. Every conscious behavior one engages in follows a decision to perform that behavior. But most decisions occur as habit, conditioning, or simple response. In teaching, examples of such habit decisions include calling for order when the bell rings, taking attendance, recognizing a student who raises his or her hand to ask a question, and watching the clock to make sure the lesson is completed in time. None of these decisions requires reflection.

At a somewhat higher order, decisions require some reflection, and involve making fairly straightforward choices. Some examples of reflective decisions are choosing whom to call upon to answer a particular question; determining the point at which a source of disruption requires overt attention; and deciding whether a particular item should be included on the unit test.

At the highest order, decisions require extensive reflection, often involving synthesis and evaluative thinking. The decisions made at lower levels might generally be characterized as *process oriented*. At the highest level, the decisions are more likely to be *purpose oriented*. Some examples of this type are determining what seating arrangement best facilitates instruction, choosing the appropriate referent to evaluate particular episodes of learning, and selecting certain remediation activities for children with particular learning difficulties. This level of decision making was evident in Virginia Grove's approach to planning the culmination of the unit in the scenario.

Planning requires attention at the highest order of decision making. When planning is ineffective or marginally effective, the reason very likely is that planning has received perfunctory attention rather than serious reflection. The "mindlessness" that Silberman (1970) recognized in classrooms and that Goodlad (1983) implicitly reaffirmed, could be due, in large measure, to the lack of thoughtfulness that teachers have given planning. Therefore, teachers should give deliberate attention to the following questions as they develop their plans.

What concept, topic, or skill is most important for the students to learn at this time in this class? It is quite possible, given a particular textbook, syllabus, or past practice, to proceed to the next unit of work without any serious consideration of whether it is *the* most appropriate one. What then is the rationale for each particular unit and the sequences that are planned? Is this the most defensible unit, given all feasible alternatives? Furthermore, do students have the appropriate entering ability and knowledge to achieve the goals of the unit?

How can the teacher ensure students' motivation for studying this topic or unit? Motivation is arguably the most basic factor in students' learning. Ultimately, students choose what they learn, and the extent to which they learn it. Their values and priorities are inevitably involved. To take students for granted, to predicate their interest or intent, is a self-deception of which teachers are occasionally guilty. Thus, how can the teacher initiate momentum in studying and learning, given a particular group of students (each unique in his or her own right), with their background, interests, and predispositions?

What methods and strategies should be employed in teaching this topic or unit? This question is, in large measure, complementary to the motivation question, but does deserve separate consideration. If the most effective long-term learning results when students find personal meaning in the outcomes, then what approaches are likely to result in achieving personal meaning? Those methods which only expose students to ideas are efficient in terms of time, but unlikely to make a strong impact. For example, Virginia Grove could have concluded the Civil War with a lecture reviewing the important facts related to the War.

At the other end of the continuum, those methods which involve the students experientially require large expenditures of time, but are more likely to be "peak experiences" that will affect students in significant ways. This theory is the reason Virginia chose to expose her students to primary accounts of soldiers' feelings and experiences. Given time considerations and importance of outcomes, what should be the balance among strategies? Furthermore, given students' different learning styles and spans of attention, what variety of methods will optimize outcomes?

How should students' progress in achieving the goals of the unit and lesson objectives be determined? Teachers need to know the extent to which students are learning the content, knowledge, skills, and attitudes being taught. Without this feedback on a regular basis, planning lacks specific direction. How often should the students be evaluated? What means might be used to informally and formally assess students' effort and progress?

Planning Act
Planning begins as the teacher initiates thinking about possible learning activities for subsequent classes. The procedure for such planning appears to be straightforward, systematic, and logical. It involves developing objectives, selecting subject matter and associated materials, choosing strategies and methods to be employed, and deciding how to evaluate the achievement of intended outcomes. This approach is typically recommended in textbooks on instruction and by methods course instructors. Preservice students and student teachers, in particular, are pressured to comply with this rational model.

Ultimately, the plan actually written by the teacher may reflect a format somewhat similar to that described above. But planning is essentially the intellectual process that occurs in the mind of the teacher, more so than the mechanical process of writing it. As previously mentioned, research indicates that teachers rarely plan according to this approach. Objectives, as such, play a very little part in planning (although they are subsequently useful for communicating learning intentions to students). However, they can be a valuable focus for the lesson, particularly for the beginning teacher.

Although textbooks and instructors apparently subscribe to the assumption that planning is self-evidently a logical process, in actual practice planning is more psychological and intuitive. It is more analogous to developing one's own original cocktail sauce than baking a cake from a recipe. Therefore, as one engages in serious planning, it should be done in a natural way, while considering knowledge to be taught, ability and interest of students, time constraints, and materials available.

Consider Virginia Grove's situation described at the opening of this chapter. Virginia had reason to believe that her past teaching of the final campaign of the Civil War had proceeded fairly well. Students had been nominally interested, more so even than with some of the earlier lessons within the unit dealing with the causes, battles and other aspects of the War. She speculated that with the inclusion of the concept teaching game in this year's lesson to provide a brief review of battles, students' interest and involvement would be stimulated even more.

Nevertheless, Virginia had the nagging sense that somehow this was not enough. The unit had taken on the form of a dispassionate narrative of political and military events rather than a dramatic and dynamic conflict of values. The students had too little realization of the bitterness and agony that had gripped a young, uncertain nation. Unfortunate as the ugly episode was, there are useful insights that the students may acquire from studying it. As high school students, they are capable of perceiving the Civil War—and as an extension, any war—in its tragic human terms. The Civil War may serve better than any for this purpose for it placed Americans in the position of methodically killing other Americans—an unthinkable and outrageous act in conditions other than war.

With this new perspective in mind regarding the potential the Civil War unit could serve, Virginia realized that the instructional methods she had used previously, primarily involved reading, lecture, recitation, discussion, and films, were inadequate to stimulate students' expression of feelings. Students needed to become involved with more than the simple processing of knowledge which had characterized most of the unit. A vicarious association with one who suffered the most from the consequences of war—the common Northern or Southern soldier—had to be established. The small group method was selected as a promising approach through which students could express and share feelings elicited by composing a soldier's letter.

The chapter began with the statement that "all teachers plan." By now it should be apparent that a major requisite for effective teaching is a consistently conscientious effort toward planning. This effort was quite evident in Virginia's preparation for wrapping up the Civil War unit. The decisions she made regarding content and instructional approach for the lesson were based on her judgments about students' progress and the balance of the kinds of learning and experiences they had to date. The result was a dynamic and innovative plan.

Long- and Short-Range Planning

It is time now to examine more closely the structure of a typical lesson plan. The format is easily recognized by teachers. Following it as one plans will greatly increase the probability of a beneficial learning experience for students.

A useful way of analyzing teacher plans is to initially separate them into three broad categories: long-range plans, unit plans, and daily lessons. Each has a different purpose, a different level of generality, and covers a different time span.

Long-range plans are generally developed for a semester, a year or perhaps longer. They are called by various names such as *course of study, syllabus,* or *curriculum guide.* They usually include global course or program goals, a content or topic outline, major concepts and generalizations, and a proposed weekly time schedule. In Virginia Grove's case, the curriculum guide is for 11th grade United States History.

Unit Plans. Unit plans are the intermediate stage of planning. They reflect several long-range course goals, and are the means of organizing a discrete aspect of the course of study. Unit plans serve as a basis for developing a set of related daily teaching plans, and may extend from 1 to 6 weeks, or longer. Unit plans can include general goals, a rationale, major generalizations and concepts, diagnostic tests, instructional methods and strategies, evaluation procedures and learning resources. At the middle or junior high school level an example unit is, "Uses of Fractions"; in high school, "The Legacy of the Transcendentalists." The title of Virginia Grove's unit is "The Civil War."

Some teachers plan simply on a day-to-day basis without first developing a unit plan. Often the textbook is the only source for these plans. Without the unit plan to aid in organizing ideas and approaches, teaching is likely to lack cohesiveness, continuity and relevance. A unit plan is essential to maximize a teacher's influence as a facilitator of students' learning and experiencing. Table 3.1 shows a sample unit plan, adapted from one developed by Nona Chambers, Anaconda, Montana.

Daily Plans. The daily teaching plan takes as its point of departure the general goals and broadly defined instructional strategies of the unit plan. In effect it is a schedule of teacher approaches and student learning activities described in some detail. The lesson plan provides the teacher with organization and specific direction on a daily basis. The daily teaching plan includes as essential components one or more specific objectives, a sequential arrangement of instructional methods and strategies, and a procedure for evaluation.

Table 3.1 Example Unit Plan

Unit Focus: Aging

Grade: 6

Subject: Multidisciplinary with emphasis on reading

Unit Duration: 2 weeks

I. GOALS

The students will:

become familiar with the variety of personalities of the elderly;

infer the importance of art as a means to bring together the older and younger generations;

Table 3.1   Continued

understand the role advertisements play in stereotyping the elderly;

determine how current music has depicted the elderly;

analyze the ways in which the elderly interact with other members of the family;

realize the possibilities for a productive life in old age;

understand the contributions of the elderly from a historical perspective

realize how young and old people can relate socially;

become aware of how people deal with the death of a loved one and one's own dying;

speculate how people in their homes and community can help and learn from the elderly.

II. TOPICS

Different kinds of grandparents

Art as a bridge to understanding being old

Stereotyping of the elderly through advertising

Elderly in today's music

Elderly in family settings

Creativity in old age

Famous oldsters

Relating to the elderly

Death and dying

Helping the elderly

III. INSTRUCTIONAL PROCEDURES

A. Discussion based on the book, *Grandpa*.
B. Students create their own self-portraits using a variety of art mediums and draw pictures of what they expect to look like when they are about 70 years of age. Individual discussions with students on differences between portraits.
C. Students locate advertisements that show how society depicts the elderly, share with the group, make judgments about stereotyping, and speculate how the advertisements could be changed to a more positive view of the elderly.
D. A variety of songs will be played related to the elderly ("When I'm

Table 3.1   Continued

64''—Beatles; ''Old Folks''—from Jacques Brel; ''It Was a Very Good Year''—Sinatra, etc.). Students will share their opinions through discussion about the meanings of the words and how the elderly are depicted.

E. Role playing will be used to depict the elderly and analyze how the elderly interact with members of the family. Several reenactments will take place based on students' impressions, opinions, positive and negative stereotypes, and perceptions of reality.

F. Individual student reports on famous oldsters including inferences about their motivations to be productive and creative beyond 70 years of age. Optional activity is student sharing of reports to class.

G. Students will view the film *Peege* about an elderly woman experiencing isolation in a nursing home. After students respond individually to questions in written form about the film, small groups will be formed for students to share responses, experiences, and attitudes.

H. Students read the book, *About Dying*. Discussion on the feelings about the characters, their opinion about the book, and their own personal experiences with death such as with a relative, friend, or pet.

I. Unit culmination: review of students' learnings and appeal to students to become actively involved in activities and programs related to the elderly in the community. Perhaps the inquiry method can be used if the class perceives an issue that they care to investigate formally or a problem they wish to attempt to solve.

IV. EVALUATION

Informal observation of students within large and small group discussions and during listening (records), viewing (film) and doing (art) activities.

Formal evaluation of students' written reports on famous oldsters. Students' advertisements brought to school will also be graded.

V. RESOURCES

A. Books. *Grandpa*, Barbara Borack; *About Dying*, Sara Bonnett Stein; *The Family at Sunday Dinner*, Marcia Cameron; *Age and Youth in Action*, Gray Panthers; *Growing Old; Getting Beyond Stereotypes*, George Maddox

B. Records. ''When I'm 64,'' Beatles; ''Old Folks,'' from *Jacques Brel Is Alive and Well and Living in Paris*; ''Hello in There,'' Bette Midler; ''Old Friends,'' Simon and Garfunkel; ''No Time at All,'' from *Pippin*; ''And When I Die,'' Blood, Sweat, and Tears; ''It Was a Very Good Year,'' Frank Sinatra

C. Film. *Peege*, Phoenix Films

Widespread differences occur among teachers regarding the exact form and degree of detail in daily planning. Experienced teachers generally do not need to prepare extensive daily lessons because they have taught similar lessons previously. Their daily plans may be concise outlines of objectives, methods, and evaluation and can be recorded in a typical lesson plan book. The beginning teacher, however, has very little experience upon which to draw for effective instructional approaches. For this teacher, thorough planning must compensate for experience, suggesting that the beginning teacher needs more than a brief outline. Plans developed in some detail—and this will vary from teacher to teacher—are necessary to increase the probability of effectiveness. Daily lesson plan format examples are included in Table 3.2, and two illustrative secondary lesson plans are included in Table 3.3.

Goals and Objectives in Planning

As has been stated, goals and objectives tend to come after the fact, even though they are usually incorporated as the first section of a formally written plan. As investigation of teachers' planning habits reveals, if objectives are not usually used as a basis for developing learning activities, they are helpful later in making explicit what otherwise are only implicit intended outcomes from studying a given topic or unit. Writing objectives after determining what subject matter is to be dealt with helps the teacher clarify in his or her own mind the most appropriate outcomes of a unit or lesson. When these objectives are, in turn, communicated to the students, they provide a focus for their learning. Research on effective teaching verifies that incisively stated and clearly communicated objectives function as useful cues for students.

Program Goals. Those broad and general objectives written to cover units of instruction are often termed ''goals.'' Very often they incorporate verbs such as *understand, comprehend, know, realize, appreciate,* and *create.* Goals often deal with the intended learning at the level of concepts and values to be acquired. For example:

The students will know the parts and operation of five power woodworking machines (Industrial Arts).

The students will realize the purpose for conducting lab experiments using a systematic-analytical approach (Science).

The students will understand how values are formed (Social Studies).

The students will perceive how the concept of *role* is used to create credible and consistent characterization in a story (English).

Although there is no research that supports one preferable style of expressing goals, the convention adopted by most authors writing in professional literature is useful. If nothing else, it tends to lend credibility to the objectives as they are reviewed by other knowledgeable educators (e.g., the principal or supervisor who has occasion to examine the teacher's plans).

Table 3.2   Example Daily Lesson Plan Formats

These formats are designed particularly for planning the use of the three primary instructional methods presented in Chapter 6

FORM 1 (LECTURE):

    I. Objectives
    II. Instructional Approach
       A. Entry: Preparation for Learning
       B. Presentation
       C. Closure: Review of Learnings
    III. Evaluation

FORM 2 (INQUIRY):

    I. Objectives
    II. Instructional Approach
       A. Entry: Presentation and
          Clarification of a Problem, Issue, or Query
       B. Formation of Hypotheses
       C. Collection of Data
       D. Test Hypotheses
       E. Closure: Drawing Conclusions
    III. Evaluation

FORM 3 (DISCUSSION):

    I. Objectives
    II. Instructional Approach
       A. Entry: Identification of Problem, Issue, or Topic
       B. Clarification
       C. Investigation
       D. Closure: Summary; Integration; Application
    III. Evaluation

The convention involves simply (1) using "students" as the subject of the statement, that is, posing the students as the actors rather than those acted upon; (2) having each goal statement express just one broad outcome or learning task; and (3) keeping this statement as brief and precise as possible. Although this may seem simple enough upon initial consideration, some practice will be necessary to master the skill. A friendly, knowledgeable critic can be very helpful in this regard. The following is a list of several social studies goals that might

Table 3.3   Example Lesson Plan (Discussion—Secondary Science)

I. OBJECTIVES

1. The students will suggest solutions to a hypothetical community pollution problem.
2. The students will appraise the proposed solutions and select the most feasible one.

II. INSTRUCTIONAL METHODS AND LEARNING ACTIVITIES

Entry: Identification of Problem, Issue, or Topic

1. Students read a hypothetical account of a local gas station owner who knowingly pollutes the stream flowing behind the station by emptying gas and oil wastes into it on a daily basis.

Clarification

2. Ask questions to have students review the facts of the hypothetical account. What wastes were dumped into the stream? How much was beng dumped on a daily basis? What was the noticeable effect on water life? How did the owner rationalize his actions?

Investigation

3. Ask questions to have students speculate about possible solutions to the problem: If you were a member of the community and knew the owner was violating the law, what could you do about it? What are the alternatives? What might be some consequences of the alternatives? Do the consequences conflict with your values? What might be some legal implications?

Closure: Summary; Integration; Application

4. Have students appraise the suggested alternative solutions and decide on one approach: Which do you consider the best and why?

III. EVALUATION

Each student writes a brief paragraph summarizing his or her selection of a problem solution and provides support.

Table 3.3   Example Lesson Plan (Discussion—Middle School Reading)

I. OBJECTIVES

1. The students will explain why moral issues are difficult to resolve.
2. The students will evaluate Joey's circumstances and decide whether they would keep the $1.00 or return it to the stranger.

Table 3.3   Continued

II. INSTRUCTIONAL METHODS AND LEARNING ACTIVITIES

Entry: Identification of Problem, Issue, or Topic

1. Students read the short story (or teacher reads the story), *Finders Keepers?*

Clarification

2. Ask questions to have students review the facts of the hypothetical account of a stranger who unknowingly drops a $5.00 bill out of his pocket. Joey notices. Does he have a dilemma; If so, what is it?

Investigation

3. Ask questons to have the students determine alternatives open to Joey: What could Joey do? What might the man say to Joey if he returned the $5.00? What could Joey buy with it?

Closure: Summary; Integration; Application

4. Ask questions to have students decide what they would have done in the same situation: What would you do? Why do you feel that way? Has this ever happened to you?

III. EVALUATION

The thoughtfulness of the students' answers will indicate the extent to which they can deal effectively with the moral issue.

---

have been presented in Virginia Grove's U.S. History course of study for the Civil War:

The students will experience the feelings soldiers have about war.

The students will create a compromise proposal for resolving conflicts.

The students will know the major events that led the U.S. into specific wars.

The students will become familiar with the major historical schools of thought and their interpretations related to the causes of wars in which the United States participated.

The students will know the strategies, leaders, and outcomes of major battles of wars.

Goals are a generally accepted part of a unit plan. No particular controversy exists over whether or not they should be used or how they should be stated. The situation is not so placid with objectives, which are more explicit statements of outcomes of particular lessons. For years a major controversy has existed over whether objectives must be stated behaviorally. The argument is made that learning is defined as a change in behavior, and objectives, therefore, should describe the expected change in observable terms. Only when this approach occurs can teacher accountability be straightforwardly assessed. Opponents of behavioral objectives contend that many important learning outcomes cannot feasibly be measured, that many learning outcomes cannot even be anticipated, and that, in any event, learning is highly individual.

The authors have no final resolution for this long-standing controversy, and research provides no definitive answer. Any answers, it seems, are likely to be more related to individual choice than to general consensus. Nevertheless, the authors offer some suggestions for consideration in the matter of writing objectives.

Subject Objectives. Objectives at higher levels of thinking are more difficult to specify in precise form. Making overly precise statements in these instances is a forced, artificial task for the teacher. Furthermore, learning at these levels becomes more individualized. Working routine mathematics problems produces a similar skill in each of the students involved; deriving meaning from a story has as many outcomes as there are students reading it. Therefore, where the learning experience provides for a range of outcomes or variability based on the perceptions of the learners, *subject objectives* are most appropriate. The term means their use is predicated on the assumption that the act of engaging in certain learning experiences is important even though the outcome is not specifically predictable. The degree of achievement of these objectives is difficult to measure, as has been pointed out by proponents of behavioral objectives. However, the value of an objective is not so much whether it can be measured as whether it guides students toward worthwhile learning and informs students of the teacher's intent for their learning. The subject objective is specific and relates to singular subjects and grade levels. It includes the following parts:

1. *Audience*—who is to do the task?
2. *Behavior*—what is the task to be completed?

The parts can easily be identified in an example subject objective:

(Audience)   (Behavior)

Students will *write their own ending to the story "The Lady and the Tiger."*

Some additional examples of these objectives are listed below:

Students will summarize the meaning of *"The Fox and the Grapes"* in two or three sentences.

Each student will state one example different from any previously given about how he or she has applied math in an important way for personal purposes.

Students will defend a position they take on dealing with illegal aliens in the United States.

Virginia Grove might have used the following subject objectives in her planning:

Students will compare the role of women in new fields during the Civil War with their role during World War II.

Students will write a hypothetical letter home after Lee's surrender to Grant based on accounts of the Civil War recorded by common soldiers.

Students will explain why the Civil War strengthened the national government.

It may be noted that subject objectives often may be read as activities as much as outcomes. There is less precision, and even the possibility of ambiguity, in such statements. However, some kinds of activities may be considered ends in themselves. To have simply attempted to find a personal meaning or develop a sound position on an issue are worthwhile intellectual activities.

Pupil Performance Objectives. In instructional instances in which the outcomes are clearly observable and quantifiable, objectives written in terms of pupil performance provide the clearest possible learning cues for students. When the learning involves, for example, working mathematics problems correctly, identifying direct objects, placing living organisms in appropriate taxonomic categories, or typing some average number of words per minute, specific statements of competency levels are especially useful. Pupil performance objectives include the following parts:

1. *Audience*—who is to accomplish the task?
2. *Behavior*—what is the task to be accomplished?
3. *Condition*—what are the circumstances for performing the task?
4. *Degree*—at what level of proficiency is the task to be accomplished?

The parts can easily be identified in an example objective:

(Audience)   (Behavior & Degree)

Students will correctly *complete eight addition problems*

        (Condition)

on a quiz that includes ten problems.

The following are several other examples of specific pupil performance objectives:

Given a news item from their *Scholastic Magazine,* students will correctly identify at least four direct objects in context.

Given a list of five living organisms, students will key them into the appropriate family.

Students will type copy in standard form at 40 w.p.m. with a minimum of two errors per minute of typing.

Virginia Grove might have used these if she had been using the pupil performance format for objectives:

Students will identify four of the five major provisions of the Compromise of 1850.

Students will write a 500-word essay comparing the Civil War with one civil war in a foreign country since 1945, incorporating within the narrative at least four similarities.

Domains and Levels

As teachers devise goals and objectives for their unit and daily teaching plans, another fundamental consideration must be addressed. What level of student learning will be targeted? In other words, will the information, attitudes or skills to be learned be offered at introductory and basic levels, at more advanced and abstract levels, or, more likely, somewhere in between? Goals and objectives can be classified by areas or domains. Each domain reflects a particular set of beliefs and assumptions about how students learn and behave:

Cognitive Domain—objectives which have as their purpose the development of students' intellectual abilities and skills.

Affective Domain—objectives which have as their purpose the development of students' emotional growth and values development and clarification.

Psychomotor Domain—objectives which have as their purpose the development of students' motor and coordination abilities and skills.

Each domain consists of a hierarchy of levels that reflect a range of student behaviors from simple to complex. As objectives are devised, knowledge of the domains and levels are useful in providing students with opportunities to engage in a wide variety of behaviors to accommodate their diverse interests, needs and abilities. Knowledge of the levels also assists teachers in making decisions about individualizing instruction. The three domains and their hierarchies of levels will be presented with an emphasis on the cognitive domain because of its wide acceptance and application. Examples of educational goals and objectives will be provided.

Cognitive Domain. Bloom (1956) has provided teachers with a taxonomy, or hierarchy, of objectives appropriate for classifying behaviors in the cognitive domain. The Taxonomy consists of six levels ranging from Knowledge, with a focus on eliciting facts-oriented reproductive thinking, to Evaluation, which represents sophisticated, high-level productive thinking. All the levels relate to developing students' intellectual abilities and skills:

1. *Knowledge*—emphasis on remembering information. Characteristic student behaviors include: define, state, name, recall, identify. Examples:

   The students will know the characteristics of Impressionistic paintings (program goal).

   The students will correctly identify 45 out of the 50 state capitols (subject objective).

2. *Comprehension*—emphasis on understanding and organizing previously learned information. Characteristic student behaviors include: relate, describe, rephrase, compare, summarize, interpret, translate, explain. Examples:

The students will understand the rules of soccer (program goal).

The students will translate the given paragraph from English into French with 90% accuracy (subject objective).

3. *Application*—emphasis on using information in pertinent situations. Characteristic student behaviors include: give an example, apply, solve, demonstrate, compute, prepare, classify, use. Examples:

The students will solve two-digit by three-digit addition problems (program goal).

The students will write a 200-word essay on the topic of the role of the modern woman, applying the pertinent rules of grammar and logical sentence structure (subject objective).

4. *Analysis*—emphasis on thinking critically about information by studying its parts. Characteristic student behaviors include: reason, analyze, conclude, infer, generalize, identify causes and motives, support, provide evidence. Examples:

The students will distinguish between the use of melody and harmony in musical pieces (program goal).

The students will analyze the Secretary of the Interior's two motives in leasing federal government lands to the oil companies from the documents presented to show their understanding of the influence of the business community (pupil performance objective).

5. *Synthesis*—emphasis on original thinking about information by putting its parts into a new whole. Characteristic student behaviors include: develop, predict, create, synthesize, compose, devise, build, solve, write, paint, produce, speculate, hypothesize. Examples:

The students will propose a plan to support the development of a new recycling center in the community (program goal).

The students will design a solar home that includes the three essential factors in order to demonstrate their understanding of the application of passive solar energy principles (pupil performance objective).

6. *Evaluation*—emphasis on making judgments about information based on identified standards. Characteristic student behaviors include: decide, opine, evaluate, appraise, judge, assess, select, agree/disagree, take a position for/against. Examples:

The students will judge the contribution of selected books to the development of American fictional literature (program goal).

The students will express reasons for their choice of a favorite color from the chart to demonstrate the range of preferences (subject objective).

Affective Domain. Although the primary emphasis in the schools has traditionally been on the development of students' cognitive learnings, attempts have been made to balance intellectual learnings with affective learnings. David Krathwohl and his associates (1964) have classified students' attitudes, feelings, interests and values into five levels of affectivity. The range of behaviors is from simple awareness or perception of something to internalizing a phenomenon so that it becomes a part of one's life-style. All the levels relate to developing students' emotional learning. Only the first three levels will be presented because of their potential to be practically applied in planning for classroom instruction.

1. *Receiving*—emphasis on becoming aware of some communication or phenomenon from the environment. Characteristic student behaviors include: attend, listen, describe, identify. Examples:

   The students will acquire an awareness of different artistic expressions ranging from realism to surrealism (program goal).

   The students will listen for the different sounds characteristic of the season of spring in order to develop an awareness of sound as a form of communication (pupil performance objective).

2. *Responding*—emphasis on reacting to a communication or phenomenon. Characteristic student behaviors include: read, write, tell, practice. Examples:

   The students will show interest in mystery stories (program goal).

   The students will participate in a community action project to demonstrate their commitment to active citizenship (pupil performance objective).

3. *Valuing*—emphasis on attaching worth to something from the environment. Characteristic student behaviors include: appreciate, follow, form, justify, choose, demonstrate, show, value. Examples:

   The students will demonstrate respect for other students' property in school (program goal).

   The students will police their own and others' laboratory behaviors in order to show they value safety (pupil performance objective).

The remaining two levels of the affective domain are generally not associated with realistic goals and objectives in the secondary classroom. They involve very high-level affective structure and internalization: Organization, or emphasis on organizing values into a system, and characterization, or emphasis on developing an internally consistent system by which one lives.

Psychomotor Domain. Classification of goals and objectives in the Psycho-motor Domain is especially appropriate for the objectives generally associated with motor and muscular skill development at the elementary and secondary levels: art, music, physical education, business, industrial arts. Specific units within language arts (writing skills), mathematics (calculators), and science (microscopes) also might emphasize the development of student behaviors in this domain.

There have been several approaches developed to classify goals and objec-tives in the Psychomotor Domain. One taxonomy has been developed by the American Alliance of Health, Physical Education, and Recreation (Jewett & Mul-lan, 1977). The three major levels are (1) Generic Movement—emphasis on be-coming aware of and displaying basic movements; (2) Ordinative Movement—emphasis on organizing perceptual-motor abilities to accomplish particular physical tasks; and (3) Creative Movement—emphasis on creating physical movement in personally unique ways. Another taxonomy was developed by Harrow (1972) that focuses on observable behaviors ranging from simple to com-plex: Reflex Movement, Basic Fundamental Movement, Perceptual Abilities, Physical Abilities, Skilled Movements, Non-Discursive Communication.

Applying a taxonomical and hierarchical approach to classifying goals and objectives when preparing units and daily lessons enhances teacher decision making. The very nature of three different but related domains, each with many levels, suggests alternatives from which teachers can choose. Choice also in-creases the probability of variety in teaching and thereby the accommodation of a wide range of students' abilities, interests and needs. Meeting individual dif-ferences in the classroom results in more effective teaching.

Sequencing of Instruction

The instructional sequence is closely related to the student learning level to be targeted during the planning stage. At this stage the teacher's concern is how the content and methods should be optimally organized in order to achieve the objectives established for the lesson. Another concern is arranging the objectives themselves to increase the probability that the unit goals will be attained.

Designing a logical sequence of instruction involves an analysis of the con-tent to be taught, whether it be representative of the cognitive, affective, or psychomotor domains. The process for the teacher in teaching a generalization, for example, is to build the simpler facts and concepts into more complex re-lationships in order to enhance students' comprehension. The same process would also apply to a skill. As an illustration, social studies students would not be expected to engage in decision making that might lead to social action with-out first understanding and practicing the skills associated with the decision-making process. Those skills would include defining the decision to be made, identifying alternatives, examining their possible outcomes, evaluating alter-native decisions, selecting the best alternative, implementing the decision and assessing results of the action. In summary, the skill of effective decision making is complex, and in order for students to learn it, the teacher needs to determine the subskills involved and to sequence them in a logical order.

SUMMARY POINT

Effective teachers approach planning systematically using rational decision making. Research supports the relationship of student achievement and teachers who have planned and were organized. Selecting and devising goals and objectives is an important part of planning. Goals and objectives serve as student learning outcomes necessary to provide instructional direction for the teacher.

REVIEW: IMPORTANT PRACTICES IN PLANNING

Plans

1. Develop long-range plans (courses of study, syllabi, or curriculum guides) to cover a period of a semester or a year.
2. Develop unit plans to cover a period of one to six weeks or more.
3. Develop daily plans for a period of one to several days. Include specific objectives, methods and strategies, and evaluation.

Objectives

4. Incorporate within written program goals an audience (who is to accomplish the goals?) and a broad outcome (what is to be accomplished?)
5. Incorporate within subject objectives an audience, behavior (what is the task to be accomplished?), condition (what are the circumstances for performing the task?) and degree (at what level of proficiency is the task to be accomplished?)
6. Incorporate within pupil performance objectives an audience, behavior and purpose (what is the reason for the task?)

Domains

7. Consider the level of student learning to be targeted when planning goals and objectives.

Sequencing

8. Use a systematic approach to planning for sequencing instruction.

The Instructional Component in Planning

The primary role of teachers in the schools is instructional, whatever form it may take. What is instruction? In its broadest definition, it is the systematic use of selected techniques, methods, and strategies to create a dynamic interface between the curriculum and the students.

Research has demonstrated that teachers generally think of the content of the lesson and the learning activities before forming objectives when making decisions about lesson planning. In general, they consider the instructional context the most important part of planning. Therefore, the examination of planning decisions related to instruction will begin with a focus on content.

Content

The curriculum in any content area is that which is to be taught. It is usually prescribed in course syllabi, curriculum guides, or course outlines. The approach to classifying content can take many forms representing the major cognitive, affective, and psychomotor domains of learning. The application of these three domains in the formation of goals and behavioral and performance objectives was previously discussed. Facts, concepts, ideas, generalizations and theories, or, in short, the intellectual content of communication, are representative of cognitive learning. In our introductory scenario, Virginia Grove selected several levels of content to be taught. The cognitive aspect of her lesson was focused on a brief review of the facts associated with the major battles of the Civil War. She intended to accomplish this by having the students identify more specifically those battles in which General Grant participated after assuming command of the Union armies. Another aspect of the cognitive content was analysis of information students would gather in the library related to 20th-century civil wars. Generalizations from their analyses would help them understand the concept of civil war. She is intending to engage students in low and high level thinking.

The affective content consists of those learnings related to the development of values, attitudes, and feelings. Generally referred to as the emotional content of communication, affective domain learnings help provide balance to the curriculum by focusing on students' needs and interests. This content balance was a very real concern to Virginia as she planned her final lessons of the unit. The major learning activity she devised focused on the emotional dimension of war. She intended to have students express the feelings they may have developed about the end of the Civil War, and war in general, using letters written home by northern and southern soldiers as the means to reveal feelings.

The content in the psychomotor domain focuses primarily on displaying skills associated with muscle coordination and on integrating physical performances with the outcomes of the other two domains. Skills of this nature are quite evident in performance-related areas such as industrial arts, physical education, music, art, and driver education. For her final lessons in the unit, Virginia had not planned to involve students in activities that required the display of skills associated with the psychomotor domain. If balancing the cognitive and affective domains with the psychomotor was important for Virginia to achieve her goals, she might have involved the students in drawing maps of the final Civil War campaign. Balancing the content representative of the major domains needs not be a goal of every daily lesson, but teachers should consider the extent to which students will be involved in the major areas of learning, especially at the unit planning level.

Consideration of the major domains of learning is important during the planning stage in order to provide students with a variety of learning experiences. Teachers should attempt to incorporate objectives representative of at least two of the domains to provide balance in the content taught during the implementation of a unit. Some questions to consider when selecting content are:

> *Cognitive Domain*—what are the important facts, concepts, and generalizations to be learned?
>
> *Affective Domain*—what beliefs, attitudes, feelings, and values should be clarified and emphasized?
>
> *Psychomotor Domain*—what physical skills need to be learned and practiced?

Techniques, Methods, and Strategies

The other major component of the instructional context is the act of instructing. The curriculum component answers the question, What shall be taught? The instructional component answers the question, How shall it be taught? They are complementary; teaching would not be possible without both of these components. To illustrate this relationship, imagine a large group lecture to high school science students. The guest speaker is using both facial expressions to communicate feeling about a topic of deep concern and gestures to emphasize major points. Overhead transparencies are used extensively to clarify and illustrate ideas. It seems to be a very interesting presentation. But no words are heard and the transparencies are blank. This is instruction without content.

Now imagine a 6th grade teacher sitting with a small group of remedial students in a circle. Each has a book of readings and a specific story has been assigned to be read. When the reading has been completed the teacher collects the readers and passes out mathematics books. No questions are asked by the teacher to determine the extent to which students understood the plot, nor are comments made to clarify characters' actions. Students' comments and questions are not entertained. This is content without instruction. Instruction and content are, self-evidently, inseparable.

Decisions about the instructional approach involve a consideration of three major closely related components: techniques, methods, and strategies. As a teacher plans a lesson, these components are generally considered together. Instructional techniques are a part of every method, and methods are combined to form strategies. The question confronting every teacher planning a lesson is which technique(s), method(s), and/or strategy will enable me to achieve my instructional objectives?

Techniques. Instructional techniques are combinations of teacher behaviors and skills essential for the implementation of methods and strategies. The teacher behaviors comprising techniques are relatively specific in that each one can generally be observed and analyzed in the classroom setting. Behaviors are the focus if the teacher intends to engage in a self- or shared-analysis of performance so as to gather systematic information to use as a basis for improving instruction. Examples of the more widely applied techniques include:

1. *Information-giving*—the teacher verbally provides students with explanations and directions necessary to conduct the activities of the lesson. Skills include clarifying, providing student feedback, and using audio-visual aids.
2. *Motivating*—those verbal and nonverbal teacher behaviors that stimulate students' attention, interaction and participation. Skills include physical movement, voice, pacing and body language, i.e., gestures, posture, facial expression and eye contact.
3. *Supporting*—teacher uses verbal and nonverbal reinforcement and encouragement of acceptable student behaviors. Skills include the use of praise, words of courtesy, acceptance and use of feelings and ideas.
4. *Listening*—teacher uses primarily nonverbal behaviors that communicate to students that the teacher is attending to what is being said. Skills include physical distance, eye contact, silence and facial expressions.
5. *Questioning*—teacher use of verbal statements that have an interrogative function generally requiring students to engage in specific levels of thinking. Skills include formulating convergent and divergent questions, probing, wait time and phrasing. (These are explained more fully in Chapter 4.)
6. *Managing*—teacher uses verbal and nonverbal behaviors to control student behavior and ultimately to encourage students to control their own behaviors. Skills include physical position and movement, eye contact and facial expressions.

Although these techniques as applied by teachers as instructional methods are implemented in the classroom, not all needs to be directly considered each time a lesson is planned. The extent to which techniques need to be planned will depend on the objectives of the lesson.

Methods. An instructional method is an organized arrangement of instructional techniques that is intended to achieve a discrete learning outcome. Examples of primary methods used by many teachers at all levels include:

Formal lecture
Interactive lecture
Demonstration
Recitation
Guided discussion
Reflective discussion
Small group discussion
Guided inquiry
Open inquiry
Individualized inquiry

Other methods include:

Role playing
Computer-assisted instruction
Simulation
Game
Panel and debate
Laboratory
Field trip

Although instructional methods are presented in more depth in Chapter 6, several implications for planning will be noted. Methods are the backbone of instruction because they are the most basic way students have traditionally been taught. Teachers understand the nature of methods and can anticipate their positive and negative impact on students. Each teacher has a preference for a method(s) most suited for his or her classroom situation and personality. Although teachers have specific preferences for particular methods, the variety of students' interests and needs within any one class suggest very strongly that teachers should plan to utilize a variety of methods. This will increase the probability of holding students' interest and attention. Another factor to be considered in planning is that different methods can be used to attain the same objective.

Strategies. An instructional strategy is a sequential combination of methods designed to accomplish learning objectives. The methods Virginia employed to achieve the objectives associated with expressing and sharing feelings are activities that could also be considered part of a strategy. This relationship of methods and strategies is illustrated in the introductory scenario. For the past several years, Virginia Grove employed a general strategy consisting of a combination of several methods to review the final phase of the Civil War. From what can be inferred, recitation was used to review the major battles, followed by discussion to involve students in higher level thinking about the surrender at the Appomattox Courthouse. This strategy incorporated a film which probably served the purposes of information-giving and enrichment.

This year Virginia is planning to alter her approach because her objectives have changed, partially as a result of the above-average level of the students. She has tentatively decided to employ another strategy to achieve her goal of helping students to understand war in its most basic terms. First she intended to read selections from several primary Civil War sources and this was to be followed by a discussion to stimulate students' feelings about war. An alternative she was considering was to have the students form small groups in which to conduct their discussions. As a follow-up, she also thought of having each small group write a hypothetical letter that they would then share and discuss.

As she employs the discussion method, we can envision a natural emphasis on the use of the techniques of questioning and listening. If she decides to form the students into small groups, we can envision her relying on the techniques of information-giving to provide students with structure and direction for the small group task in an effort to keep students on-task. In summary, the strategy Virginia was planning to use consists of several methods sequentially arranged to achieve her objective: teacher reading, large or small group discussion, student group writing, student reporting, and discussion.

Virginia also had another objective in mind she had hoped to achieve during this lesson, but we get the impression she did not consider it as important as the first. She decided to use a concept teaching game to review the battles of the War. This method involves the teacher in presenting positive and negative examples of a concept (battles in which Grant participated, in Virginia's lesson), students generating and testing hypotheses (guesses about the concept), and the final identification of the concept. This method is quite effective in stimulating student involvement and student inductive thinking. We can also envision her mainly using questioning and managing techniques to successfully implement the "game."

Although most strategies are devised by teachers in this manner, a number of strategies have been formally designed and labelled by educators. Joyce and Weil (1986) have identified 20 teaching "models" drawn from the work of educators, sociologists, psychologists, and curriculum specialists. They have assigned the models into different groups characterized by a different genre of learning goals.

This book will focus on another group of more formal strategies that have evolved from the effective teaching research and emphasize as their purpose higher student achievement. They are:

1. *Direct Teaching*—academically focused teacher-directed classroom instruction using sequenced and structured materials.
2. *Mastery Learning*—an individualized diagnostic approach to instruction in which students proceed with studying and testing at their own rate in order to achieve the prescribed level of success.
3. *Cooperative Learning*—the use of peer tutoring, group instruction, and cooperation to encourage student learning.

The implication for teachers involved in planning on a daily and long-term basis is that they need to be aware that a variety of instructional strategies exists from which to draw to meet their objectives, classroom situations, and students' abilities, interests and needs. These strategies can be informal or formal. (Additional commentary on techniques, methods, and strategies and their relationship can be found in Chapters 4, 6, and 7.)

Given the wide variety of techniques, methods, and strategies from which to choose when planning a unit or daily lesson, beginning and experienced teachers should be able to understand why decision making is so important. A systematic approach to decision making becomes more valuable as the choices in a situation increase. Some of the questions a teacher needs to consider when planning the instructional approach to be utilized are:

1. Which combination of methods and/or strategy is best to achieve the objectives of the lesson?
2. How much time is available during class for implementation of a particular method and/or strategy?
3. To what extent should the methods and/or strategy be adapted to individual students or small groups of students?
4. How can transitions between the use of methods and strategies be made smoothly and beneficially to enhance students' understanding?
5. To what extent will students be actively and passively involved during the implementation of a particular method and/or strategy?

Lesson Presentation

Planning for instruction—the implementation of specific techniques, methods and strategies—also involves consideration of several other generic or basic teaching concerns. The preparation of objectives for the purpose of specifying learning outcomes, which provides direction for instruction, has already been discussed previously in this chapter. Similarly, content within the major domains of learning has been discussed. Other considerations, referred to as lesson presentation skills by Shostak (1982), include entry into the lesson and closure. Entry and closure generally occupy the first and last 5 minutes of a lesson, respectively, and are potentially the most powerful influences on students' learning. Each of these important factors should be accounted for when decisions are made about how the lesson should be presented in class.

The intent of a lesson entry is to focus students' attention on the lesson.

This can be accomplished in several ways. The teacher can inform students of the goals and of what is expected of them within the lesson. In this sense the entry serves as an organizer to prepare students for an upcoming activity. Another way a teacher can focus students' attention on the lesson is to stimulate their interest as a means of getting them involved. This can often be accomplished by attracting students' attention with something puzzling, an artifact, or a problematic situation naturally related to the lesson. The entry is usually associated with the beginning of the lesson, but it can also be used to introduce a new topic within a lesson.

We can now imagine how the concept teaching game Virginia Grove has selected could be used as a pertinent entry into the review segment of her lesson. With this method, a list of Civil War battles is presented, perhaps on a transparency. Virginia tells the students she has a concept in mind that she would like the students to guess. She then tells the students which battles are "yes" examples and which are "no" examples. The students are expected to search for a commonality among the "yes" examples and inductively arrive at the concept. In this lesson the concept is the battles in which Grant participated after he assumed command of the Union armies. The puzzling nature of this problem will hold students' attention. The students could be informed of the goals of the lesson after the "game."

Closure also needs to be considered when planning a daily lesson. It is the wrap-up to the lesson. The teacher's intention in the closing stage of the lesson is to reinforce the key learnings of the lesson and to help students transfer learnings to the next lesson. In many respects, the closure is the complement to the entry. The closure to Virginia Grove's lesson after students have shared their hypothetical letters written by Northern and Southern soldiers might be for the students to generalize the major feelings expressed in the letters. Perhaps she could leave them with a question to think about for the next day's lesson: To what extent would the feelings Civil War soldiers had in 1865 be similar to those today of Lebanese fighters from the different warring factions as they return to their homes? This closure would help bridge the lesson to the upcoming library assignment Virginia was planning in which students would be examining civil wars in other lands. (For a more detailed explanation of the skills, see Chapter 4.)

SUMMARY POINT

Planning for instruction involves making decisions about the selection of an appropriate variety of techniques, methods and strategies to achieve the goals and objectives of units and lessons. Research reveals that teachers actually consider instructional approaches and content before objectives when planning lessons. An appropriate sequence of planning events is: (1) establish the content to be taught and the methods to be employed; (2) devise or select the strategy(ies) within which the methods are subsumed; (3) consider the techniques that are necessary to implement the methods/strategies; and (4) prepare an entry to initiate learning and a closure to reinforce the impact of the lesson.

REVIEW: IMPORTANT PRACTICES IN PLANNING FOR INSTRUCTION

Content

1. Select content to be taught with careful consideration given to balancing the domains of learning: cognitive (facts, concepts, ideas, generalizations), affective (values, attitudes, feelings) and psychomotor (skills).

Techniques

2. Plan to utilize instructional techniques to help create the cognitive "climate" of the classroom.

Methods

3. Plan to incorporate a variety of instructional methods in order to increase students' interest and attention while striving to achieve objectives.

Strategies

4. Build a variety of instructional strategies into unit plans in order to meet the needs of a generally diverse student population.

Lesson Presentation

5. Decide how to focus students' attention on the lesson (entry) and how to wrap up the lesson (closure) during the planning stage.

Planning for Evaluation

The third major planning component is evaluation. Teachers need to give as careful consideration to this area as to the formation of objectives and selection of instructional approaches. Evaluation is the process of forming judgments about student progress. These judgments collectively serve as a basis for making decisions. The question facing teachers on a daily basis in the classroom that reflects this concern about student progress is the extent to which students attained the objectives set for the lesson. Over a longer period of time, teachers are concerned with achieving broader unit goals. Evaluative data gathered in response to these questions are determined by the appropriateness and specificity of the objectives, and the quality of instructional methods and strategies employed. In many respects, the outcomes of student evaluation can be a direct reflection on the teacher's effectiveness in the classroom. The implication for planning is that the evaluation component deserves considerable attention.

Evaluation involves making judgments in the form of reflective decisions about instruction. In order to make decisions to redirect instruction, data need to be gathered. The major part of the evaluation process, and the most time consuming element, is gathering information about student performance and progress. The decisions a teacher makes based on the data gathered are reflected in both short- and long-term planning.

Planning for evaluation is primarily conducted at the unit plan and daily lesson levels. The major concerns teachers have while planning units are determining the time when assessments of student progress should take place, the nature of the evaluation instruments, and how to interpret and represent student progress. At the daily lesson level, teachers are primarily concerned with how data regarding student progress should be collected.

Unit Evaluation. One of the first concerns teachers have while planning for evaluation at the unit level is incorporating diagnostic and summative evaluation. Diagnostic evaluation is the formation of judgments about a student's learning potential prior to instruction. The data gathered at this preinstructional stage can be very useful in helping a teacher individualize instruction.

Summative evaluation is the most common approach to assessing students' performance used by teachers. It is generally conducted when the students have completed an instructional unit. The most common form of summative evaluation is a written test. We can imagine Virginia Grove's 2-week unit test on the Civil War. Typically unit tests at the secondary level consist of a mixture of objective and subjective (essay) items. (Diagnostic and summative evaluation are further explained in Chapter 9.)

Judgments resulting from summative evaluation assess the degree to which students have attained the learning objectives of the unit. Postinstructional decisions have a direct bearing on the objectives and instructional approaches to be used in the next unit. Other important decisions relate to how this same unit will be taught even more effectively in the future.

Another major concern teachers have about the evaluation process when designing a unit plan is interpreting and representing the information gathered about student performance. Interpretation is necessary in order to make judgments about the assignment of values, generally in the form of grades, representative of students' levels of progress over a specified period of time or unit of study. The teacher's responsibility is basically to decide whether to assign marks based on a comparison of individual student performance to group performance, or a comparison of progress to a predetermined standard, or a comparison to past individual performance. Although the first approach has deeper historical roots and is better known, the other two approaches have had important applications over the years. (These approaches—norm-, criterion-, and self-referenced, respectively—are described more fully in Chapter 9.)

Daily Evaluation. Judgments made by the teacher on a daily basis during instruction are part of formative evaluation. These judgments serve as a basis to make decisions about the objectives and instructional approach guiding students' learning. Evaluation conducted during the midinstructional phase on a daily basis is important so that modifications can be made in the program to increase the probability that the objectives will be achieved by the students. The major concerns teachers have while planning for evaluation on a daily basis is how the data regarding student progress should be collected.

Appropriate techniques must be selected or devised to determine whether students have achieved lesson objectives. A wide range of techniques are available for teachers to use formally or informally. When engaging in lesson planning on a daily basis, evaluation can be formal or informal, depending on the means used to gather data. Informal approaches might include observations of student behavior, analysis of students' contributions to group discussions, conferences with individual students, brief reviews of written homework assignments, and impressions of performance. Formal techniques might range from a test to a checklist used to judge students' contributions in a class debate. Other formal approaches might include quizzes, rating scales, and attitude measuring instruments. The important consideration when evaluating students' progress is that the technique employed needs to provide data directly related to the objective that is being evaluated. The important point to be made here is that evaluation, like instruction, must be planned.

SUMMARY POINT

The decisions teachers make about planning for the evaluation of students' progress are important and require thoughtful consideration. The evaluation component of planning exists as a means to determine if the goals of the unit or the objectives of the lesson were achieved. As such, the outcomes of student evaluation are a direct reflection on the effectiveness of teachers. Decisions need to be made about the timing of evaluation, the techniques used to gather information on student progress, and how to interpret and represent student progress. Each component needs considerable thought and expression in sufficient detail to be beneficial to students and teachers.

REVIEW: IMPORTANT PRACTICES IN PLANNING FOR EVALUATION

1. Give attention to planning for evaluation along with planning for goals and objectives and instructional approaches.
2. At the unit level, plans need to be made for gathering information about students' learning potential prior to instruction and assessing students' performance at the completion of the unit.
3. At the unit planning level, decisions also need to be made about interpreting and communicating the information about student performance.

4. At the daily lesson level, decisions need to be made regarding which formal and informal techniques will be used to gather information regarding students' progress.

ACTIVITIES

ACTIVITY I: GOALS AND OBJECTIVES

Classify the following as a G (goal), SO (subject objective), or PPO (pupil performance objective).

1. Students will underline the subjects and verbs within example sentences with 80% accuracy after reading the assigned chapter in the text.   _____
2. Students will measure the amount of sunlight available over a given period of time.   _____
3. Students will correctly identify ten foods representative of the four food groups after viewing the filmstrip.   _____
4. Students will enjoy the story about a cub scout who becomes a hero by leading his baby sister to safety from a fire in their home.   _____
5. Students will identify the politically motivated reasons behind the President's decision to postpone the major decisions on the budget until after the election.   _____
6. Students will realize the need to be conscientious in their cleanup of the lab.   _____
7. Students will create a watercolor painting of their own design using the three primary and three secondary colors after listening to a presentation by a local community artist.   _____
8. Students will be able to bow the violin straight before the sixth scheduled lesson.   _____
9. Students will critique their essays on the meaning of an environmental crisis.   _____
10. Students will correctly compute price/earnings ratios for five stocks based on earnings per share and current market prices of the stocks.   _____

ACTIVITY II: DOMAINS OF LEARNING

Classify the following *goals* as representative of the C (cognitive), A (affective), or P (psychomotor) domains:

1. The students will perform a one-act play.   _____
2. The students will evaluate the effectiveness of their experiment.   _____
3. The students will provide an example of how their families cooperate to solve problems at home.   _____

4. The students will enjoy playing an ancient African tribal game.   _____
5. The students will know what prejudice means.   _____
6. The students will be able to properly use a putter.   _____
7. The students will be able to operate a sewing machine.   _____
8. The students will show their awareness of current events.   _____
9. The students will figure out a reason why the narrator of the television show provided misleading information.   _____
10. The students will express an interest in visiting the art museum.   _____
11. The students will volunteer for the community environmental beautification project.   _____
12. The students will learn how to shift a four-speed manual transmission.   _____
13. The students will demonstrate their ability to use a protractor.   _____
14. The students will recognize Emily Dickinson's style of writing poetry.   _____
15. The students will understand the differences between facts and opinions.   _____
16. The students will analyze the Tonkin Gulf Resolution.   _____
17. The students will demonstrate how to purchase food items in a grocery store simulation.   _____
18. The students will evaluate the President's State of the Union address.   _____
19. The students will write about their experiences during summer vacation.   _____
20. The students will listen to classical works to learn more about their composers.   _____

ACTIVITY III: COGNITIVE LEVELS

Classify the following student behaviors, appropriate for the statement of subject objectives, in terms of their cognitive levels: K (knowledge), C (comprehension), AP (application), AN (analysis), S (synthesis), E (evaluation):

1. compute the problem's answer   _____
2. choose from several alternatives   _____
3. interpret the graph   _____
4. name the seasons   _____
5. compose a short musical score   _____
6. define photosynthesis   _____
7. judge the statesman's decision   _____
8. describe the events leading up to the surrender   _____
9. support your point of view   _____
10. take a stand on the issue   _____

11. generalize a solution to the "problem" from data gathered   _____
12. predict the GNP   _____
13. translate this paragraph into English   _____
14. classify the leaves   _____
15. recall the parts of the lathe   _____
16. design a hairstyle   _____
17. compare the actions of the story characters   _____
18. reason his motive   _____
19. provide an example of your idea   _____
20. determine a cause for the discrepancy   _____

ACTIVITY IV: OBJECTIVES

The following is a list of four improperly written objectives. Read each, decide why it is incorrect and rewrite it in the proper form.

1. Show how the students are to react to strangers that might approach them on the way to and from school.

2. The students will locate appropriate materials and equipment prior to beginning the laboratory experiment.

3. The students will see the importance of setting up a proof to prove problems in geometry.

4. The students will be given a demonstration of Charles' Laws of Gases.

ACTIVITY V: GOALS AND OBJECTIVES

Devise one unit goal, subject objective, and pupil performance objective for the hypothetical teaching situation presented below:

> Mrs. Vaughn is teaching an interdisciplinary unit on American families to her rural junior high social studies class. She wants her students to learn about the lives of four urban families with different national origins. Specifically, she wants them to get a good look at similarities and differences in the kinds of homes, work and interests of people from different social, religious, economic and racial backgrounds. She also wants to involve students in a cultural fair at the school where they will have an opportunity to meet people representing a variety of nationalities and cultures.

1. *Goal* _____

   _____

2. *Subject Objective* _____

   _____

3. *Pupil Performance Objective* _____

ACTIVITY VI: LESSON PLAN DESIGN

Select either the subject or pupil performance objective you devised in Activity V and design a brief 30-minute lesson for a group of students at the grade level of your choice. Modify the objective to suit a content area of your choice. Specifically, you need to select instructional techniques and methods that will be appropriate to achieve the objective. Be sure to sequence the instructional approaches to form a strategy. Remember to include a means for determining the extent to which your objective has been achieved.

Objective:

Instructional Procedure:

Evaluation:

ACTIVITY VII: SHARING LESSON DESIGNS

Share the plans developed for Activity VI orally within the large group in order to demonstrate the wide range of approaches that can be used to teach similar content.

ACTIVITY VIII: FORMATIVE EVALUATION

Select two of the goals from Activity II and devise a related and logical performance objective for each one.

ACTIVITY IX: SHARING LESSON SEQUENCES

Exchange the sequence of instructional approaches you developed (for Activity VI) with your neighbor and note any differences in sequencing. When you return papers give your neighbor a reason why you think he or she sequenced instruction the way it was done.

ACTIVITY X: LESSON PLAN DESIGN

As a group, observe a short film or read a newspaper article related to a current issue or problem. Devise a brief lesson plan including the general areas of objective, instructional procedure and evaluation. Once completed, share orally plans to show the variety of approaches that can be used to teach one topic.

RESPONSES TO ACTIVITIES I–V

ACTIVITY I: GOALS AND OBJECTIVES	ACTIVITY II: DOMAINS OF LEARNING	ACTIVITY III: COGNITIVE LEVELS
1. PPO	1. C	1. Ap
2. SO	2. C	2. E
3. PPO	3. C	3. C
4. G	4. A	4. K
5. SO	5. C	5. S
6. G	6. P	6. K
7. PPO	7. P	7. E
8. SO	8. A	8. C
9. G	9. C	9. An
10. SO	10. A	10. E
	11. A	11. An
	12. C	12. S
	13. P	13. C
	14. C	14. Ap
	15. C	15. K
	16. C	16. S
	17. C	17. C
	18. C	18. An
	19. C	19. Ap
	20. C	20. An

ACTIVITY IV: OBJECTIVES

1. Students will demonstrate one of the two proper ways to react to strangers as presented in class.
2. Students will calculate the amperage of the full wave bridge rectifier, to the nearest tenth, provided for in the electronics laboratory.
3. Students will provide three reasons why proofs are needed to prove a problem.

4. Students will hypothesize why the volume of a fixed mass of gas held at a constant pressure varies directly with the absolute temperature after Charles's Law is demonstrated.

ACTIVITY V: GOALS AND OBJECTIVES

1. Students will appreciate their family backgrounds after studying the lives of four families with different national origins.
2. Students will compare the recreational activities enjoyed by teenagers representative of the four families.
3. Students will summarize in 50 to 75 words two current event articles selected from weekly news magazines and/or daily newspapers over the past 2 months that relate to the countries of the four families.

APPENDIX

ANALYSIS FORM   *DAILY LESSON PLAN*

TEACHER _____   *ANALYSIS SCALE* _____

OBSERVER _____   OCCURRENCE

CLASS _____   1. Not evident   4. Quite evident
2. Slightly evident   5. Not applicable
3. Moderately evident

DATE _____

	OCCURRENCE AND COMMENTS
OBJECTIVES:	
1.The objective(s) is stated in specific subject or performance terms.	
2. The objective, if more than one, reflects a variety of levels within the cognitive, affective, or psychomotor domains.	
3. The objective(s) is expressed in terms of student learning outcomes.	
4. The objective(s) is related to the unit goals.	
INSTRUCTIONAL APPROACH:	
5. A variety of techniques and methods have been incorporated into the plan.	
6. Questions that have been included accommodate a variety of student cognitive thinking levels.	
7. The techniques and methods have been sequenced.	
8. An entry has been planned.	
9. A closure has been planned.	
10. The learning activities provide for students' active involvement.	

continued

Analysis Form: Daily Lesson Plan, *continued*

11. Students' varied interests, needs, and abilities have been accommodated within the instructional approach.	
12. Information that is to be presented is outlined.	
13. Print and nonprint media have been incorporated to supplement the instructional approach.	
EVALUATION: 14. Means of evaluation relates to the objectives.	

REFERENCES

Bloom, B. (Ed.) (1956). *A taxonomy of educational objectives. Handbook I: Cognitive domain.* New York: McKay.

Brophy, J., & Good, T. L. (1986). Teacher behavior and student achievement. In M. C. Wittrock (Ed.), *Handbook of research on teaching.* New York: Macmillan.

Clark, C. M. and Peterson, P. L. (1986). Teachers' thought processes. In M. C. Wittrock (Ed.), *Handbook of research on teaching.* New York: Macmillan.

Clark, C. M., & Yinger, R. J. (1980). *The hidden world of teaching: Implications of research on teacher planning.* Research Series No. 77. East Lansing, MI: Institute for Research on Teaching.

Clark, C. M., & Yinger, R. J. (1979). Teachers' thinking. In P. L. Peterson & H. J. Walberg (Eds.), *Research on teaching: Concepts, findings, and implications.* Berkeley, CA: McCutchan Publishing.

Cooper, J. M. (1982). The teacher as a decision maker. In J. M. Cooper (Ed.), *Classroom teaching skills.* Lexington, MA: Heath.

Gagne, R. M. (1965). *The conditions of learning.* New York: Holt, Rinehart and Winston.

Goodlad, J. I. (1983). A study of schooling: Some findings and hypotheses. *Phi Delta Kappan, 64,* 465–470.

Harrow, A. J. (1972). *A taxonomy of the psychomotor domain: A guide for developing behavior objectives.* New York: McKay.

Hoover, K. H. (1972). *Learning and teaching in secondary school.* Boston: Allyn and Bacon.

Jewett, A. E., & Mullan, M. R. (1977). Movement process categories in physical education in teaching-learning. In *Curriculum design: Purposes and process in physical education teaching-learning.* Washington, DC: American Alliance for Health, Physical Education and Recreation.

Joyce, B., & Weil, M. (1986). *Models of teaching.* (3rd ed.) Englewood Cliffs, NJ: Prentice-Hall.

Krathwohl, D. R., Bloom, B. S., & Masia, B. B. (1964). *A taxonomy of educational objectives. Handbook II: Affective domain.* New York: McKay.

Levin, T. with Long, R. (1981). *Effective instruction.* Washington, DC: Association for Supervision and Curriculum Development.

Morine, G. (1976). *A study of teacher planning: Beginning teacher evaluation study* (Technical Report 76-3-1). San Francisco: Far West Laboratory for Educational Research and Development.

Peterson, P. L., Marx, R. W., & Clark, C. M. (1978). Teacher planning, teacher behavior, and student achievement. *American Educational Research Journal, 15,* 413–432.

Shostak, R. (1982). Lesson presentation skills. In J. M. Cooper (Ed.), *Classroom teaching skills.* Lexington, MA: Heath.

Silberman, C. E. (1970). *Crisis in the classroom.* New York: Random House.

Weil, M., & Murphy, J. (1982). Instructional processes. In H. E. Mitzel (Ed.), *Encyclopedia of educational research* (5th ed.). New York: American Educational Research Association.

CHAPTER 4 Basic Instructional Techniques

The following four chapters comprise the central focus of the book, instruction. The first several chapters have provided ideas, information, and practice related to those components that are considered the foundation of instruction. Decision making is the most pervasive component of instruction, so much so that effective teaching is inevitably the outcome of effective decision making. Consideration of classroom climate is critical within the instructional process because optimal learning occurs only in a setting of optimal conditions. Planning is essentially a description of the instructional decisions intended to be implemented in the classroom. Instruction, as a logical consequence, is the direct application and testing of the decisions made about students, environment, content, and method.

Instruction has generally been defined as ''a process by which knowledge and skills are developed in learners by teachers'' (Hawes & Hawes, 1982). Clearly the person responsible for initiating, maintaining and evaluating the instructional process in the school is the teacher. As a process, instruction can be depicted as consisting of teacher behaviors, techniques, methods and strategies. Basic physical teacher behaviors comprise the primary instructional techniques of informing, motivating, supporting, questioning, managing and listening. A sampling of these behaviors includes gestures, voice volume, divergent questions, physical movement and eye contact. Varying degrees of all these techniques are a part of every instructional method teachers employ in classroom settings. Guided discussion, demonstration, recitation, interactive lectures, guided inquiry and small groups are among the most commonly used today. Methods are selected and sequenced by teachers during planning to form strategies which are the most comprehensive forms of instruction. Strategies can be informal and formal. Informal strategies are the most common, and are extemporaneously devised during the planning phase of a lesson. Formal strategies are research-based and are more highly structured. An example of a formal strategy is Direct Teaching. Entry and closure are the two critical lesson presentation components to be considered when implementing methods and strategies. The relationship of these instructional components is depicted in Figure 4.1. Notice the indication of which chapters in this book provide analyses of each element.

Figure 4.1 Instructional Model

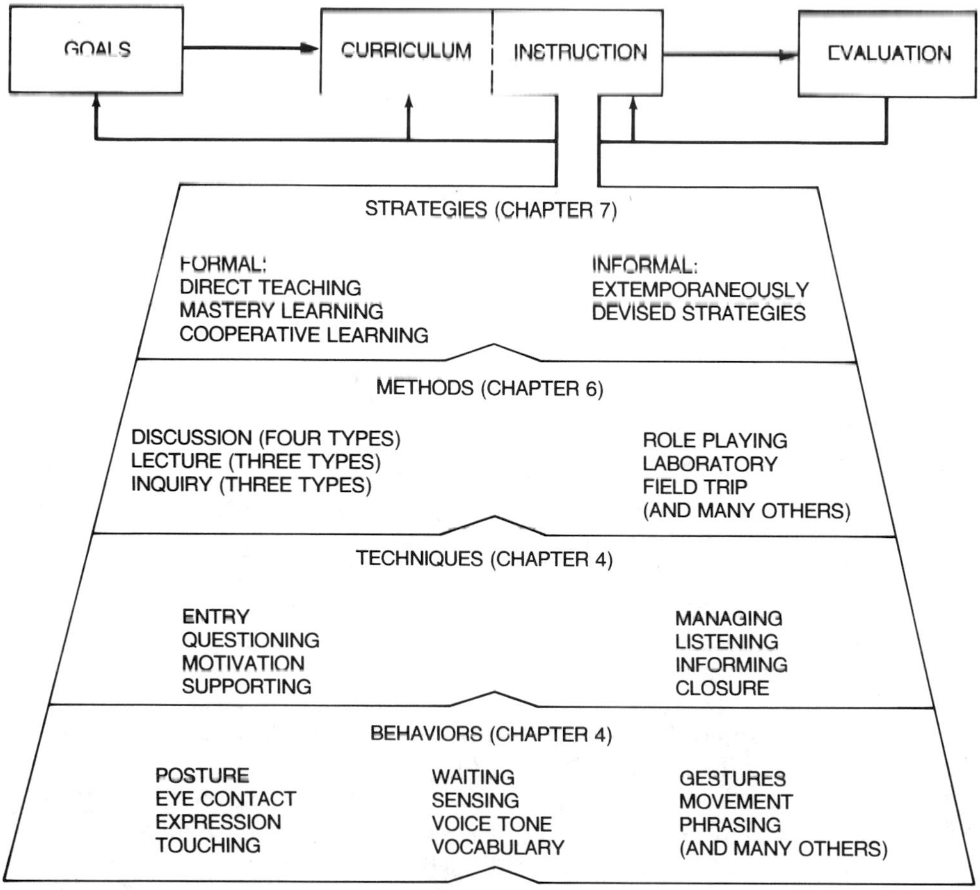

| GOALS | → | CURRICULUM | INSTRUCTION | → | EVALUATION |

STRATEGIES (CHAPTER 7)

FORMAL:
DIRECT TEACHING
MASTERY LEARNING
COOPERATIVE LEARNING

INFORMAL:
EXTEMPORANEOUSLY
DEVISED STRATEGIES

METHODS (CHAPTER 6)

DISCUSSION (FOUR TYPES)
LECTURE (THREE TYPES)
INQUIRY (THREE TYPES)

ROLE PLAYING
LABORATORY
FIELD TRIP
(AND MANY OTHERS)

TECHNIQUES (CHAPTER 4)

ENTRY
QUESTIONING
MOTIVATION
SUPPORTING

MANAGING
LISTENING
INFORMING
CLOSURE

BEHAVIORS (CHAPTER 4)

POSTURE
EYE CONTACT
EXPRESSION
TOUCHING

WAITING
SENSING
VOICE TONE
VOCABULARY

GESTURES
MOVEMENT
PHRASING
(AND MANY OTHERS)

OVERVIEW

This chapter focuses on instructional techniques and lesson presentation components. The research reviewed is drawn, in large part, from the so-called process-product research conducted during the past 20 years. This research has focused on determining the effect of specific teacher behaviors and instructional techniques (process variables) on students' learning outcomes (product variables). Most of the research has been concentrated on academic achievement because it is the most obvious and readily measured aspect of learning. The result of researchers' efforts has been the identification of a series of teacher behaviors that positively correlate with students' achievement. The findings of several major reviews of research and other specific research studies will be reported here, supporting the contention that effective teaching consists of, in part, the purposeful and consistent display of specific instructional behaviors and techniques, and presentation skills.

A series of teaching analysis instruments is included in this chapter, and in Chapters 6 and 7 on effective teaching elements and methods and strategies. These data-gathering forms are intended to be used by teachers and their support personnel (colleagues, team leaders, departmental chairs, and supervisors) as they begin to formally inquire into the nature of their teaching. The purpose of this inquiry is for teachers to become more informed about their instructional behaviors and approaches. Ultimately the data gathered can be used effectively to make decisions about improving instruction.

SCENARIO

Richard Taylor wondered how his students would react to the lesson he had planned for the day as they drifted into his 7th period Earth Science class. For the past 3 weeks they have been studying the earth's environment, particularly its renewable and nonrenewable resources and energy. The focus has been on learning how people depend on the environment and how they can influence it. As a major goal, though, he wanted his students to participate in identifying environmental problems in Norwood, their local community. Wouldn't it be wonderful if the students actually wanted to make an effort at solving one of the problems they identified? As the bell signaled the beginning of class his thoughts drifted to the state science teachers' conference he attended the month before and the session on encouraging high school-age students to become actively involved in resolving local community environmental problems. Two boys continued talking in loud voices as the period began, and several others still had not taken their seats. Generalizing from this capricious behavior, he realized that his students were probably still too immature to be interested in dealing with community problems.

"Dave and Todd, I would appreciate your attention so we can get started." Once he was sure everyone was ready, he told the students, with excitement in his voice, to close their eyes and imagine an environmental crisis taking place in Norwood. After about 20 seconds he asked several who volunteered to describe their imagined catastrophes. Barbara described their family getting a letter from the EPA informing them that their immediate neighborhood was likely to have been built on a toxic waste dump left from an old paint manufacturing plant that had gone bankrupt 30 years ago. Jim graphically described an imagined killer smog that enveloped their community for 5 days, killing several older people and a number of animals, and making many people sick. It had been caused by an air inversion that created a pocket of trapped waste gasses from the steel mill down the river. Shawn talked about not being able to swim in the nearby lake this summer because of the high level of pollution, and Judy thought a crisis for Norwood might be a monstrous trash and garbage accumulation due to a prolonged strike by sanitation workers. Two other students volunteered to share their crises.

As Mr. Taylor slowly moved around the room maintaining eye contact with the participants, he noticed that for several students interest was beginning to wane. He commented about the participants' vivid imaginations, thanked them for their contributions, and mentioned that they were going to be focusing on Norwood's environmental problems. "Yesterday we finished with our discussion of the dangers of nuclear energy and the problems faced by that industry. Now we need to bring our focus down to the community level. Let's leave our imagined crises for the moment and get back to reality by thinking about the present environmental situation in Norwood." He told the students their objective over the next two days was to identify at least three environmental problems Norwood was currently facing. "I would like you to get out your notebooks and take two minutes to write down either one environmental problem you think Norwood is experiencing right now or one that Norwood could realistically be facing in the near future." When the students began the assignment, Mr. Taylor circulated among them to assist individual students and keep others on-task.

"What are some of the problems you think we have?" One cited several abandoned houses in the south section of town that look like they are ready to collapse. Another student added that they were also dangerous since they weren't boarded up. Mary thought Norwood needed to do more to promote solar energy conservation. "Using solar energy makes so much sense, but we only have one solar home in town," she said. Harold said that he thought there was too much trash on the streets and that maybe the street cleaners were not doing their job. After some further encouragement, several other students volunteerd contributions related to the lack of parks, the foul-tasting tap water, and the need for more trees and flowers downtown. Mr. Taylor wrote the last of the students' ideas on the board.

Mr. Taylor complimented the students on how observant they were of the community. "I didn't think you would have come up with the number of problems you did. Well done!" He then asked, "How do we know if these are really problems that Norwood should do something about?" After a sufficiently long pause he called on Jim, who seemed to be deep in thought. Jim commented that he thought many people in the community would have to consider something a real problem before the city government would do anything about it. "In other words, a problem to one person may not be a problem to others. Would you agree?" Jim agreed and Lynn quickly opined that she didn't think a majority of people needed to consider something a problem before the city government did something about it. After all, she couldn't remember Norwood voting on an environmental problem, yet changes seemed to have come about.

Mr. Taylor could hardly contain his enthusiasm for Lynn's insight. "You have just hit on one of the major things I wanted you to learn by the end of the unit! That is, the responsibility city government has in dealing with environmental problems." Moving to the side of the room, he then took some time to describe why the city council passed legislation creating the recycling plant last year. The point was that the decision was made without initiation from the people and without a vote, because the city council, after gathering information from a consultant, was convinced that it was environmentally beneficial to the community. Both individuals and government are responsible for the condition of the environment.

Realizing that several students were either glancing at the clock or gazing out the windows, and that there were 20 minutes left in the period, Mr. Taylor decided to quicken the pace of the lesson. "How many remember the definition of a scientist's hypothesis?" Several hands went up and, after pausing, he called on Julie. She replied that it was a solution to a problem. Jim quickly added that it was a guess or proposed solution that needed checking. "How are your ideas about Norwood's environmental problems and hypotheses related?" After getting no responses, Mr. Taylor asked Chris if he had an idea.

Chris, a capable student but mentally lazy at times, responded with, "I don't know."

Mr. Taylor attempted to lead him to the idea he had in mind. "Could the class's thoughts about Norwood's environmental problems be considered hypotheses?"

"I guess so," was the reticent student's response.

Mr. Taylor confirmed his minimal response and asked the class for an explanation. David responded that the problems the class proposed were only guesses at this point because more information and opinions were needed. "Thanks, David."

"For homework tonight I would like you to find out if your parents agree with you." Mr. Taylor explained that the students were going to investigate a problem just like scientists, gathering data to support or refute their hypothesized environmental problems. He passed out a survey rating form for students to write down the proposed environmental problems and record parents' responses. "Tomorrow, with your help, we'll know a little more about our community's environmental condition."

During the remaining 10 minutes, Mr. Taylor had the students read a short article from the *Journal of Environmental Education* on a western community's successful attempt to make their environment safe for its citizens. He thought the article would be appealing to the students because of the dramatic confrontation between the mayor and the representatives of several self-serving special interest groups at one of the town council meetings.

With one minute left before the bell was to ring, Mr. Taylor asked the students to pass their copies of the article to the front of the room. "Christine, which of the problems we identified do you think your parents will consider the most critical?" She thought the lack of parks and recreation areas was a real concern. Mr. Taylor was able to direct the question to two other students before the bell rang. "I think tomorrow's class will be very interesting because of the information you will be bringing in. See you then."

RESEARCH AND THEORETICAL BASE

The growing research related to instructional techniques, teacher behaviors and presentation skills is becoming increasingly influential. Attempts to discover those factors that constitute effective schools and effective teaching have provided the major impetus for this developing body of research. School districts and university teacher education programs are becoming increasingly aware of these research findings. They are incorporating the findings into in-service and preservice programs to disseminate effective teaching skills that enhance students' learning.

Presentation skills are displayed in one form or another in every lesson taught. Based on his review of the literature, Shostock (1982) found that the entry into the lesson and lesson closure are among the most frequently researched lesson presentation skills. The entry is the students' first contact with the content and the method(s) to be used by the teacher. Teachers, though, infrequently introduce lessons with students' motivation in mind. The majority of teachers' task-presentation statements are neutral, and many are negative (Brophy et al. 1983). Brophy and Good (1986), in their extensive review of the research, concluded that students learn more efficiently and their achievement is maximized when the teacher structures the new information by relating it to what they already know. This form of entry has been termed set induction (Allen & Ryan, 1969). In a series of studies conducted by Schuck (1985), it was found that students achieved and retained more knowledge when their teacher used set induction techniques. Another consideration in the entry is novelty. Based on his review, DeCecco (1968) suggested teachers should incorporate discrepancies, and the element of surprise into lessons to attract and stimulate students' attention and interest. The decisions teachers need to make about the entry to a lesson center on structuring the lesson to relate new information to previous learning and introducing topics and lessons in atypical and interesting ways.

All lessons achieve closure by virtue of the fact that finite periods of time govern lesson length. Although logic suggests that a lesson needs a closure to complement the entry, little research has been conducted on the impact of closure on student learning. Based on their review of research, Gage and Berliner (1984) concluded that closure is an important part of an instructional repertoire and effective teachers use it regularly, especially in lecture situations. Closure requires teachers to make decisions regarding how the lesson will be brought to a close and how the bridge to the next lesson will be made.

Of all the major techniques the teacher uses to teach in a classroom setting, the skills associated with motivation are the most important in terms of encouraging and stimulating students to attain lesson objectives. Research literature has primarily focused on teacher enthusiasm as a major factor contributing to motivation. The other aspect of motivation that will be discussed is the use of a variety of instructional approaches in teaching lessons. Good and Brophy (1984) identified two major aspects of enthusiasm: interest in the subject matter and dynamics in presenting the material. Both contribute toward maximizing student achievement, especially for older students (Brophy & Good, 1986). Gage and Berliner (1984) reviewed several major studies that demonstrated that student learning is affected positively as teachers employ a variety of expressive behaviors they labeled the ''teacher's style.'' In another review of research on enthusiasm, Larkins and McKinney (1984) did not find conclusive evidence relating enthusiasm to achievement, but did find a positive correlation between student ratings of the teacher and the teachers' level of enthusiasm. They also found that teachers can be trained to increase their levels of enthusiasm. Decisions about motivation primarily center around which verbal and nonverbal behaviors to employ in the classroom to convey enthusiasm for the subject matter being taught, and those behaviors necessary to maintain student interest and attentiveness throughout the lesson.

Motivation can also be gained by varying the instructional approach. Research supports teachers' use of instructional variety and flexibility as a means of maintaining students' attention and increasing achievement (Gage & Berliner, 1984). Based on their review, Good and Brophy (1984) found that in terms of sustaining students' interest, a variety of methods is better than the extended use of one method. Furthermore, the most current research suggests that the decisions a teacher makes that are related to instructional ''activity structures'' or methods also influence students' attitudes and behavior because each limits or enhances factors that have an impact on instruction (Berliner, 1984). Teachers need to decide how their lessons will vary in terms of the number and kind of instructional methods and strategies to be used and the time necessary to effectively employ them within and between each class session.

Information-giving is another technique that teachers regularly employ in the classroom. Teachers generally give information informally over short spans of time, such as when directions are given for an assignment. More formal information-giving is used, for example, in the lecture method. Information-giving as a technique focuses on short-term purposes—the emphasis in this section.

The sparse amount of research on information-giving that is available centers on the value of structuring new information for students. One of the 14 major findings from the Beginning Teacher Evaluation Study was that structuring lessons for the students and giving directions on task procedures were positively correlated with high student success (Fisher et al., 1980). Brophy and Good (1986), in their more recent review of research, found that students learn more efficiently when teachers structure new information for students. The decisions teachers make about the information they will be presenting should address the provision of an appropriate form of structure in order to enhance students' understanding.

The most basic way teachers stimulate thinking and learning in the classroom is through the use of questions. The research literature on questions and questioning is growing, primarily because of the movement to identify those teacher behaviors and techniques that contribute to students' learning gains. One major research conclusion consistently supported over the years is that teachers' questions primarily require students to engage in low cognitive-level thinking in which the emphasis is on recall of information. This contrasts to theorists' point of view that higher level questions are more valuable for students' learning and preparation for life beyond the classroom (Gall, 1984). Another finding is that teachers can be trained to raise the cognitive levels of their questions and to effectively apply a variety of questioning techniques (Dillon, 1984; Wilen, 1984).

In a more recent review Wilen and Clegg (1986) identified questioning practices of teachers that correlated positively with student achievement. The practices were synthesized from four major reviews of research on effective teaching practices that had questions and questioning as part of their focus: Berliner, 1984; Brophy and Good (1986); Levin with Long (1981); and Weil and Murphy (1982). These practices are: academic questions, phrasing, lower cognitive-level questions with elementary students, higher cognitive-level questions with intermediate and secondary students, encouragement of student responses, wait time, acknowledgment of correct responses, balancing responses from volunteering and non volunteering students, student call-outs, encouragement of correct responses, and probing. Wilen (1987) illustrates these practices in a hypothetical classroom application. Because of the potential impact teachers' questions and questioning techniques have on students, teachers need to carefully develop those questions intended to achieve objectives, and to select the techniques that are most certain to ensure their effectiveness in stimulating thinking and learning.

Research supports the important role teachers' listening behaviors play in interactive learning situations with students in the classroom. Flanders (1970) found that teacher verbalizations that indicated acceptance of students' feelings and use of their ideas contributed significantly to a positive social-emotional classroom climate. In order for teachers to genuinely express empathy or paraphrase students' ideas, for example, effective listening behaviors are essential. Garrett, Sadker, and Sadker (1982) further substantiated the need for teachers to regularly display such attending behaviors as eye contact and facial expressions as teachers listen to and communicate with students in group discussions and individual conversations. Furthermore, if teachers expect students to be aware of and regularly display good listening skills, they must also model careful listening behaviors in the classroom (Good & Brophy, 1984).

Teachers' display of support for students' responses and activities is primarily noticed in the form of feedback encouraging them to continue their efforts. Support usually takes the form of reinforcement such as praise, acknowledgement of correct responses, and assistance with incorrect answers. Teachers are also supportive when they accept students' feelings and use students' ideas. Flanders' (1970) research indicating a positive relationship between these behaviors and a supportive classroom climate was previously cited. Brophy (1981), found in his review that praise was not always effective in stimulating students' learning gains. A high rate of praise defeats its purpose and therefore does not always serve as reinforcement. On the other hand, Gage and Berliner (1984) found in their review that the discriminating use of praise, use of corrective feedback, and a teacher's use of student ideas showed a positive relationship with students' achievement and attitudes. In one survey, students ranked teacher praise 10th out of 15 forms of recognition indicating that it is not a very influential reinforcer (Ware, 1978). Simple use of acknowledgment can often be used to communicate acceptance of students' contributions in place of praise. Good and Brophy (1984) found that the most effective form of praise is that which specifies to the student the reason for the praise. Teachers should provide feedback to students regarding their performance in order to encourage them to achieve goals.

The research indicates that the effective classroom teacher is also an effective classroom manager. In his review of the effective teaching research, Berliner (1984) found that effective classroom management begins with decisions made prior to instruction. Decisions related to time allocation, lesson pacing, student grouping patterns, and instructional approach affect students' attitudes, behavior, and achievement. Also, if students have been taught management skills they are more likely to display less deviant behavior. In their review, Emmer and Evertson (1981) found that good classroom management leads to increased academic learning time. They also found that the best classroom managers practiced preventive maintenance in that they planned ahead to prevent classroom problems. In their review of the effective schools research, Purkey and Smith (1983) concluded that a school's behavior problems can be reduced and feelings of pride and responsibility can be promoted if "clear, reasonable rules, fairly and consistently enforced" are in effect. This conclusion can be extended to individual classrooms as well.

APPLICATION TO PRACTICE

Entry

The first few minutes of a class are the most crucial times in relation to teacher impact. The entry to a lesson is generally recognized as the first instructional phase implemented immediately after the teacher has gained the attention of the students. This usually commences at the beginning of the class period. An entry can also occur several times during a lesson as the teacher makes transitions and introductions to discrete segments of any single lesson. The commonality of the two forms of an instructional entry is that it serves the purpose of setting the learning process in motion.

The primary purposes of the entry are to focus students' attention on the learning activity, prepare them for what they are going to learn and encourage them to get involved. Classes too often begin with statements such as, "Okay, take out your homework," or "I'm going to pass out some material I want you to read now," or "C'mon class, let's get going. We've got a lot of material to cover before the end of the period." Although these statements may accurately inform and direct the students, they quickly become routine and boring to those who may not have a high level of intrinsic motivation. One way to capture students' attention is for the teacher to make casual or personal comments that indicate respect for students or interest in them. A comment of this type contributes toward a positive social-emotional climate and enhances student-teacher relationships. Examples are: "Weren't Chris and Jenny great in the Thanksgiving play yesterday?" or "I understand that the Vocational Electronics class needs some broken radios and televisions to repair. How many have one at home they can contribute?"

Another approach to focus students' attention is to use a springboard to induce them to get involved with the objectives of the lesson. This can be accomplished by relating the content to their lives and experiences. Examples include: "How many have seen at least one of the Rocky films and would like to describe a major fight scene?" (springboard for a Sociology lesson on violence) or "Who would like to tell about a book you read over Christmas vacation?" (springboard for lesson on reading skills). Using springboards such as these serve the purpose of focusing students' attention and also stimulating them to get involved.

A more sensational, and perhaps more effective way to get students involved with the learning activity is to do something unexpected. This entry can take many forms such as starting off the class by solving a challenging puzzle related to a math concept to be taught during the lesson. Another approach is to play a discovery game such as having students guess what lesson-related object the teacher has in his or her possession (perhaps ration stamps as an introduction to the home front during World War II). Occasionally a shock statement can be used, such as "If you are an average group of students in this school, then two girls in here have had abortions" (as an introduction to a health class unit on birth control). Anything that stimulates students' curiosity, suspense, or creativity is a possible means to get students directly or indirectly involved with the content to be taught.

One approach to lesson entry that many teachers use fairly consistently is preparing students for the upcoming learning activity. The extent to which students are prepared for the ensuing activity directly affects an entry's effectiveness in orienting them and setting the learning process in motion. Ideally this phase of the entry would include a review and preview to prepare students for new learning. The review consists of the important facts, concepts, and skills learned from the previous lesson. In this way the immediate lesson would be placed into context and cumulative learning would be encouraged. For example, "In the last several lessons we have tried to show how some great thinkers, in speaking to the men of their times, were in fact speaking to people of all times. Today we shall begin to try to discern that much of their wisdom is still pertinent for us over a century later."

During the preview, the teacher describes what the class will be engaged in during the period, the objectives pertinent to the lesson, and a rationale. Although it seems the preview involves extensive teacher commentary, it can actually be effectively accomplished in a short period of time. For example: "Today if we get through the vocabulary drill and reading section, we can spend the last part of the period playing French Bingo . . . Our primary objective is that you will be able to pronounce correctly the 20 new vocabulary words from the story, "Jeanne D'Arc." Although the story is historical, the key words that we will focus on are ones you will find in everyday conversational usage."

An important point to keep in mind about the entry to a lesson is that it is a means to an end, not an end in itself. The effectiveness of the entry is directly dependent on how well the students have been prepared for the upcoming learning activity and how highly they are motivated to pursue the objectives. The decisions a teacher makes during the planning stage are crucial because the impact of the entry will directly affect students' attitude. Their attitude, to a large degree, determines how interested they are in attaining the objectives and how conscientiously they engage in the planned learning activities.

Mr. Taylor, in the illustrative scenario, implemented an interesting and relatively thorough lesson entry. Approximately 10 minutes was consumed in the entry from the time he gained the attention of the students at the beginning of the class session to when he stated the objective. The students certainly did not expect to close their eyes at the beginning of the lesson as Mr. Taylor directed them to do. The effectiveness of this approach was enhanced as the students thought about something quite unusual—a hypothetical environmental crisis in Norwood. Judging from student involvement, the springboard succeeded. After a very brief review to link the previous lesson to the new one, Mr. Taylor mentioned what they would be doing during the day in class. The entry culminated with his stating the objective: "Over the next two class sessions I would like for us to identify at least three environmental problems Norwood is experiencing." The only phase of the entry lacking in Mr. Taylor's lesson, when comparing his approach to the ideal, is a rationale for the objective. Perhaps he could have mentioned that responsible citizens are aware of current issues and problems and many become actively involved in resolving them for the betterment of the community.

The entry is the initial contact students have with the teacher and the planned learning activity. During these first few minutes teachers have the opportunity to focus students' attention on the learning task in an interesting—and perhaps exciting—way, and to adequately prepare them for new learning. In many respects, the entry to a lesson sets the tone for the entire lesson and, because of this, it is important for teachers to take extra care during the planning stage.

Closure

The closure to a lesson is self-evidently the counterpart to its entry. With a closure, the instructional cycle of a lesson is completed. Whereas the goal of the entry is to focus, prepare, and stimulate the students, the closure serves to reinforce learning outcomes, integrate what has been taught, and make the transition to the next lesson. Unfortunately, classes sometimes simply stop abruptly rather than end appropriately. Teachers who have not planned for closure may abruptly quit teaching when the material runs out, then make lame, time-filling comments or inform students that they may have the rest of the class to study. Occasionally the bell rings and this cuts activities short. Either way, the students are left to make of the class what they will. This implicit faith in the students' ability or inclination to synthesize information from a presentation meaningfully is largely unfounded.

Usually the closure occurs at the end of the lesson. Yet often several "mini" closures are used to terminate segments of a lesson. Just as there can be several entries within any one lesson, there should be complementary closures. The extent to which closure is used will more than likely depend on the ability and interest level of students, the complexity of the content to be covered and the objectives to be achieved, and the time limitations.

One of the major purposes of closure is to reinforce the important learning outcomes that have occurred during the lesson. This can be accomplished by organizing student learning through the use of summary and review. The teacher uses review to reinforce major terms, facts, and concepts. There may be reference to notes on the chalkboard, overhead transparencies, or handouts. Questions are often asked in order to determine the extent of student knowledge and understanding. Higher-level information and ideas from the lesson are summarized by the teacher or students. During this phase of the closure, the teacher begins to determine if his or her objectives have been attained.

Learning is further reinforced as ideas are integrated within students' cognitive structures. Higher-level ideas are synthesized to clarify relationships, to illustrate concepts and generalizations or to lead students to insights or self-realizations. New learning also needs to be integrated within the unit. The teacher refers to the overall unit goals in an effort to make the link. For example, "Today we have studied the conditions under which conifers develop. This, then, should help you understand one more factor of the overall ecological development of a free-growth region. We have another factor, deciduous growth, to cover for a complete understanding." The most influential form of integration occurs when students attempt to apply learning. In this case, the teacher provides an incentive by referring to some practical and immediate use of the information or skills learned. For example, "Now that you know the long-range effects of marijuana on your mental and physical well-being, you have evidence for formulating your own attitude about its use," or "Within a week you should be able to tune up your own car."

The closure to a lesson should also facilitate the transition from one lesson to another. The transition helps students understand the larger picture within which the immediate lesson fits. In terms of lectures, Gage and Berliner (1984) referred to this aspect of closure as "interlecture structuring." The teacher attempts to build a bridge from one lesson to the next by giving a preview of the next lesson, by asking the students to think over a pertinent issue or problem, or by suggesting an assignment using divergent thinking that will prepare the student for involvement in the next class. This aspect of closure implies more than the routine assignment of homework. For example, "By the next class period, make a note of as many causes of inflation as you can think of, and suggest a way that each might be controlled. We can consolidate our ideas, and decide what the government should be doing. Then maybe we'll write our Congressman if you like."

Reference to the accomplishments made by the students during a lesson should also be part of the closure, particularly if the lesson was a good one. Comments such as this contribute significantly in producing a positive social-emotional climate in the classroom. The teacher indicates to the class the extent to which the objectives have been achieved or the amount of material that has been covered, especially as this is determined relative to some predetermined guideline. For example, "You people have done nicely to have already gotten through the fourth step of the experiment, and we should have no problem completing the final two steps during the next lab period."

Mr. Taylor used formal and informal approaches to bring closure to the lesson. He began his closure approximately 10 minutes before the end of the period by informing students of the homework assignment which required them to apply what they learned in the home setting. In addition, the assignment helped serve as a bridge to the next day's lesson because of the continuing nature of the students' inquiry. More directly, he indicated that they will know more about their community as a result of the data they gather. Mr. Taylor had the students write the proposed environmental problems on the survey rating form he distributed. This activity seemed to serve as a very informal review of major learnings. In this case it was the tentative identification of Norwood's environmental problems which related directly to his goal for the lesson. Students' thinking might have been extended with the reading of the article, but there is no evidence that it will be pursued further.

His culminating activity which involved students in making the transition from class to the home was particularly effective. Asking them to form judgments about how their parents might react to their tentative list of environmental problems was an excellent way to stimulate higher level thinking. Mr. Taylor also indicated that he thought the class was interested and that he was looking forward to the next day.

SUMMARY POINT

The lesson presentation skills of entry and closure are important instructional components. With the entry, momentum is established with a purposely designed lesson component. With the closure, students are provided with a "kicker" to reinforce the learning that has occurred. Continuity with previous and upcoming lessons is also made during the entry and closure. Research suggests that students learn and achieve more when teachers plan and use entries to lessons. Teachers are also more effective when closures are used. Reflective decisions about each lesson's entry and closure need to be made by the teacher during the planning stage in order to enhance the learning of their students.

REVIEW: IMPORTANT PRACTICES IN LESSON ENTRY AND CLOSURE

Entry

—purpose is to focus students' attention on the learning activity, prepare them for what they are going to learn, and encourage them to get involved.

1. Casual or Personal Comments—assists in establishing a comfortable climate for learning.
2. Springboard—focuses student attention on objectives by relating the content to students' lives.
3. Attention-Getter—stimulates students' curiosity, suspense or creativity.
4. Review—relates past learnings to current lesson.
5. Preview—lesson objectives and rationale are presented.

Closure

—purpose is to reinforce learning outcomes, integrate what has been taught, and make the transition to the next lesson.

1. Summary—review of important lesson learnings.
2. Integration—lesson is related to previous learnings and unit goals.
3. Application—learnings are applied to the real world of the student.

4. Transition—preview of next lesson.
5. Reference to Accomplishment—reinforcement of students' contribution to attaining lesson objectives.

Motivating Skills

The conscious attempt by teachers to stimulate students in the classroom to achieve learning goals is a complex process. The major reasons for this complexity are the diversity of students' attitudes and needs within any one class, and the varying effect of any teacher's attitude and personality. It is self-evident that all students are motivated in some way. For the teacher facing 25 to 35 students in 5 or 6 classes each day, the question quickly becomes, "Motivated to do what?" It should be obvious that teacher frustration quickly develops when students are motivated to actively pursue interests unrelated to the lesson's objectives. The enthusiastic teacher who demonstrates his or her enjoyment of the subject and teaching has a considerable advantage in commanding student attention and stimulating their involvement. Likewise, the teacher whose behavior is complacent will probably have problems in encouraging students to get mentally and physically involved.

From an instructional point of view, the effect of the teacher's motivation-related behavior is reflected in the students' inclination to attain the lesson objectives. Motivating behaviors may take many forms. A teacher's instructional style determines the motivational techniques that are characteristic of him or her. The most pervasive form of teacher motivational behavior is the use of a variety of verbal and nonverbal behaviors to create a dynamic presence in the classroom. The teacher who purposely utilizes a wide range of behaviors to display interest in the subject and the students is displaying a certain presence that contributes to enthusiasm.

The range of motivating behaviors displayed by a teacher is influenced considerably by his or her personality and attitude. Another major approach teachers can use to stimulate student interest and involvement is the use of a variety of teaching strategies, methods, and techniques. Although sensitivity to the instructional flow influences the extent to which teachers "shift gears" within and between lessons, other factors such as knowledge of instructional practices and time for preparation play an important part.

A highly motivating teacher consistently displays dynamic personal behaviors in the classroom. Students and fellow teachers describing him or her would probably use descriptors such as *enthusiastic, energetic, exciting*, and *stimulating*. The teacher with a high degree of presence is visually and auditorally dynamic. Four major areas that contribute to presence are: physical movement, nonverbal behaviors, lesson pace, and voice quality.

A motivating teacher moves about the classroom. The teacher avoids patterned pacing, but moves purposefully about the front and, when possible, to the sides, rear, and through the rows in order to give students a "moving target.'' The teacher attempts to position himself or herself at a distance from a reciting student in order to encourage the student to speak loudly. This often requires retreating from a student who is responding. The teacher refrains from sitting on the desk for more than a few minutes at a time, and avoids sitting at or standing behind the desk or demonstration table except as necessary. A spatial mapping category system has been devised recently to help chart patterns of observed teacher classroom travel (Susi, 1985; Susi, 1986).

A motivating teacher uses nonverbal behavior to create presence. Research has indicated that nonverbal behaviors have a powerful impact in the classroom. Besides moving about the classroom, this also includes using a variety of facial expressions, maintaining eye contact, using a variety of gestures, using body movements such as nods and head shakes, and placing a hand on a student's shoulder or moving into close proximity to students. The teacher's mode of dress and grooming also send nonverbal messages to students. A neatly dressed and clean teacher will command more respect than one who does not seem to care about appearance. There is an overall impact, a cumulative effect, of the teacher's nonverbal behaviors which will hopefully leave students with the impression that their teacher is an enthusiastic and dynamic person who enjoys immensely both the subject and the work.

A motivating teacher uses his or her voice effectively. The voice is the most obvious instrument with which the teacher conducts the business of teaching. Ideally, the teacher's voice should be strong (not just loud), and have pleasant tonal qualities. The use of inflection should complement the meaning of words being spoken. The voice should not have shrill or strained qualities, or obvious impediments, which cause the listener to experience discomfort or difficulty. A teacher's vocabulary should be appropriate for the students. The teacher's mode of delivery should be smooth and mature, without the annoying repetition of particular words or phrases, or the use of adolescent speech habits (e.g., ''like,'' ''you know,'' ''stuff,'' and ''kind of''). And, it should go without saying, the use of correct pronunciation and grammar is absolutely essential.

A motivating teacher controls the pace of the lesson. Controlling the pace helps to maintain student attention and to accomplish objectives. Pacing in the classroom results from the teacher's sensitivity to the tenor of student behavior. Although changing mode is a means to control pace, pacing occurs intramodally as well. In a foreign language drill, for example, students are pushed to the limit they can tolerate; in a discussion in science, patience is exhibited while students reflect on responses. Stepping to the board to write important information is an effective means of adjusting pace, because it ''freezes'' student thought on a point for a few deliberate moments. The teacher moderates the students' excessive exuberance, but makes deliberate efforts to provide stimulation when the class lags. The teacher's actual behaviors in the interest of pacing may take many forms; it is important that the teacher behaves deliberately to maintain that optimum learning pace.

A teacher also motivates students by varying the instructional mode. Instructional mode refers to the techniques, methods, and strategies used. Just as a teacher commands student attention through personal behaviors, a teacher also sustains attention through instructional behaviors. Attention span is an important consideration, and changing the instructional mode is one means of coping with it. This is most often accomplished by using a particular teaching mode for only a limited period of time, then moving to another mode. There should be at least one major shift during any given class period, and possibly as many as three or four depending on the nature and level of the class.

The most effective shifts are those which vary the learning stimulus of the students. For example, students in a high school government class might listen to a lecture on the concept "compromise" and how the process plays a crucial role in government and the formation of laws today. In order to demonstrate a historical application of the concept, the teacher might then organize students into small groups to read about, discuss and report on several of the specific compromises of the Constitutional Convention of 1787. A shift from a lecture to small-group interaction is better than a shift from a lecture to a film on the Constitutional Convention, for example, because students move from passive to active involvement. The occasional rearrangement of chairs in the classroom to fit the nature of the learning activity is also involved in changing mode.

As best we can tell from a written transcript as the only data source, Mr. Taylor seemed to create a relatively stimulating teaching environment through his use of personal and instructional behaviors. At the beginning of the period he entered the lesson by telling the students "with excitement in his voice" to close their eyes and imagine a crisis taking place in their community. With some imagination we can almost visualize the altered facial expressions and inflection in his voice on the word "crisis," as one way to depict excitement. Later in the lesson he "sincerely" complimented the students on their speculations about community problems. Perhaps we can imagine a lowering of the voice for most of the compliment and a louder and inflected voice as he said "Well done!" We do have a strong indication, though, that Mr. Taylor was concerned about contributing to the students' motivation through varying the pace of the lesson and his physical position in the classroom. He was aware that several students were losing interest at two points during the lesson and in response to the last observation, purposely quickened the pace of the lesson to finish what he had planned in the remaining 20 minutes.

A major strength of Mr. Taylor's lesson in terms of the students' motivation that we can determine from the transcript was the significant variety of instructional shifts he employed to sustain students' attention and interest. The lesson was initiated with a brief discussion followed by an equally brief individually oriented writing exercise that shifted senses. He then continued with discussion involving considerable interaction related to the environmental problems Norwood was facing. At one point he incorporated information-giving in the form of an extended explanation and then shifted again to discussion. Senses were shifted once more after he presented the assignment and students had to write on their forms. During the closure he had students read a short article and then wrapped up the lesson with a brief interchange of viewpoints. All told, there were three major instructional shifts: discussion-writing-discussion, explanation-writing-explanation, quickly followed by a reading-discussion shift. Minor shifts also occurred.

Questions and Questioning Skills

Question Levels. Since the time of Socrates the questions a teacher asks in the classroom and the techniques used to stimulate interaction have been considered essential components of the instructional process. Questions are essential because teachers can conveniently and effectively use them to engage students' thinking about issues, problems, and topics under discussion. Although research has shown that the congruency of the thought level of teachers' questions to students' responses is only approximately 50% (Dillon, 1982; Mills, 1980), teachers still have considerable impact in their ability to control the thought levels of students in the classroom. Because of this teachers need to pay attention to the questions they ask and the way they ask them.

Once the teacher realizes that there are different cognitive levels of questions and that a relationship between questions and student thinking exists, decisions need to be made about the proportion of time students will spend engaged in lower and higher level thinking. These decisions will take into account the objectives of the lesson and the method(s) employed to achieve these objectives. Practically every method and strategy that a teacher can employ with individuals or groups of students involves questioning. Two of the most common methods are recitations involving primarily low-level convergent questions to get students to recall important facts and concepts related to an issue or topic, and discussions which are designed to encourage students to think at divergent levels as they analyze and evaluate issues and problems. As teachers plan lesson objectives and methods and strategies to achieve them, decisions will necessarily be made about the balance of thinking levels and the corresponding kinds of questions needed to be asked.

The following classification scheme for identifying and devising cognitive levels of questions is based on Gallagher and Aschner's (1963) well-known adaptation of Guilford's (1956) "structure of intellect" model. The levels have been initially categorized as convergent and divergent to correspond to narrow and broad student thinking, and then subdivided into two additional levels that reflect the hierarchy of thinking levels. Convergent questions serve the important purpose of determining students' basic knowledge and understandings, and are the basis for subsequent higher level thinking. Therefore, lower level questions should rarely become ends in themselves; they should serve as a means to achieve higher level thinking. Divergent questions serve the purpose of requiring students to process what they have learned by thinking critically and creatively. Students need opportunities to practice higher forms of thought if they are expected to become independent and reflective thinkers. Each of the four cognitive levels is accompanied with a definition, example student behaviors and illustrative questions.[1] In addition, corresponding levels to Bloom's Taxonomy (1956) are identified because of teachers' familiarity with this system. Bloom's Taxonomy was used as the basis for devising instructional objectives and goals in Chapter 3 on planning.

Level I - Low Order Convergent: questions requiring students to engage in reproductive thinking. The teacher's intention is to have students recall or recognize information. Because emphasis is on memorization and observation, students' responses can easily be anticipated. Level I corresponds to the knowledge level of Bloom's taxonomy.

Example student behaviors: define, recognize, recount, quote, identify, list, recall, answer "yes" or "no."

Example questions: Who invented the sewing machine? How many colors are on the chart? What is the definition of photosynthesis?

Level II - High Order Convergent: questions requiring students to engage in the first levels of productive thinking. The teacher's intention is to have students go beyond recall and demonstrate understanding of information by organizing material mentally. Students also apply learned information. Although more thinking is involved at this level, student responses still generally can be anticipated. Level II corresponds to Bloom's comprehension and application levels.

Example student behaviors: describe, compare, contrast, rephrase, summarize, explain, translate, interpret, relate, apply, use, provide an example, solve.

Example questions: What is an example of cooperation in your home? How are these numbers related? How would you solve this problem using the accounting procedure we just discussed? In your own words, according to the story, how did the dog get loose?

Level III - Low Order Divergent: questions requiring students to think critically about information. The teacher's intention is to have students analyze information to discover reasons or causes, draw conclusions or generalizations, or to find evidence in support of opinions. Because higher level productive thinking is involved, students' responses may or may not be anticipated. Level III corresponds to Bloom's analysis level.

Example student behaviors: identify motives, reasons, or causes; draw conclusions, inferences, or generalizations; provide evidence, support ideas, analyze information.

Example questions: Now that you have completed the experiment, what is your conclusion about why the substance became denser? Why do you think the girl ran away from home? What evidence can you provide to support your view that the Constitutional power of the President has diminished over the years?

Level IV - High Order Divergent: higher order questions requiring students to perform original and evaluative thinking. The teacher's intention is to have students make predictions, solve lifelike problems, produce original communications, and judge ideas, information, actions, and aesthetic expressions based on internal or external criteria. Because this level represents the highest level of productive thinking, students' responses generally cannot be anticipated. Level IV corresponds to Bloom's synthesis and evaluation levels.

Example student behaviors: produce original communications, predict, propose solutions, create, speculate, hypothesize, synthesize, construct, devise, write, design, develop, judge, value, choose, opine.

Example questions: How would you rate the effectiveness of the Environmental Protection Agency? What is a good title for this story? How can we raise money to support the recycling center? What is your favorite orchestral instrument and why?

Questioning Skills. The formation of questions appropriate to desired objectives is extremely important, but no more so than the questioning process. The teacher's effectiveness as a questioner depends not only on devising good questions, but also on the way questions are asked. The skillful application of questioning techniques is essential if the questions are to serve the purposes for which they are intended. Effective application of a series of questioning techniques can make the difference between a class of students who are passive, confused, frustrated and mentally unchallenged, and a class of students who are active, stimulated, and reflective.

Following is a list of questioning techniques synthesized from the major literature on questioning (Good & Brophy, 1984; Groisser, 1964; Hyman, 1974; Cunningham, 1971; Carin & Sund, 1971; Wilen, 1986).[2] In addition, a growing body of research on effective teaching practices supports a variety of teacher questioning techniques as positive correlates with student achievement (Wilen & Clegg, 1986; Wilen, 1987).

Question Phrasing. Questions need to be phrased clearly to precisely communicate response expectations to students. Vague or ambiguous questions self-evidently lead to student confusion and prolonged frustration if the practice becomes a regular occurrence. A vague question such as "What about the law Congress passed?" forces students to try to guess what the teacher wants rather than thinking of and formulating a direct response to the question. Another source of ambiguity is the run-on question. This occurs as two or more uninterrupted and often incomplete questions are asked in a series. Frustration develops as students try to guess which question to answer. One major implication for teachers is that key questions need to be planned because these are often on a higher cognitive level. Divergent questions need more planning because of their difficulty. Another implication is that teachers may need to acquaint students with the different levels of questions to increase the probability that expectations might be communicated more clearly.

Adapting Questions. Questions need to be adapted to the language and ability level of the class and, in many cases, individual students within the class. Since most classes are heterogeneously grouped, questions need to be phrased in natural, simple language to increase the probability that they will be understood by all. Within classes, language will need to be simplified for slower or certain mainstreamed students and made more thought-provoking for gifted students. A question for a lower ability student might be, ''From the article you have just read, how does the demand for a product affect its supply?'' To higher ability students, the question might become, ''Going beyond the article a little, how does price affect supply and demand and at what point is market equilibrium reached?'' An important implication for teachers is the need to get to know their students in order to adjust their questions and thereby increase comprehension.

Question Sequence. Asking questions in a planned and patterned sequence will enhance student thinking, comprehension, and learning. Random questioning rarely communicates a clear focus or intent. The primary factors influencing the choice of question sequence include the objective of the lesson, ability level of the students, and prior knowledge and understanding students have of the content being discussed. Some sequences will begin with lower level questions and will progress to stimulating, higher level thinking. Others will start with higher level questions and stay there. With this approach, adjustments may need to be made if students do not have a good command of the content under discussion.

Asking lower level questions will quickly determine the extent to which they understand the content. For example, consider the following episode. After having the students read an article on proposed changes in immigration laws, the teacher asks the question, ''Should the United States permit the immigration of unlimited numbers of refugees from war-torn countries?'' Students give minimal support for the opinions they express. The teacher then asks these review-oriented questions: ''What is the number one problem the author associates with immigration?'' ''What do the current immigration laws say about refugees from nations involved in war?'' The implication for the teacher is that the intention to ask questions should involve planning the pattern of those questions.

Balancing Cognitive Levels of Questions. Balancing questions designed to stimulate convergent and divergent thinking will enhance the possibility that a greater range of student cognitive abilities will be developed. Research has demonstrated that teachers at all levels tend to ask predominantly convergent questions with an emphasis on Level I convergent questions. Convergent questions should serve the purpose of determining students' basic understandings so they can apply their knowledge by engaging in subsequent higher level thinking. Critical and creative thinking is stimulated with divergent questions. Four levels of convergent and divergent questions have been previously presented. The implication for the teacher is that unit and lesson objectives should require a variety of levels of student thinking, and that this in turn will provide direction in devising an appropriate balance of questions.

Student Participation. Student involvement in classroom interaction can be increased by balancing responses from volunteering and nonvolunteering students, redirecting initially unanswered questions to other students, and encouraging student-student interaction. Too often, only a few students participate in class discussions and recitations, and therefore dominate the interaction. Every student can make a contribution to class interaction, and teacher alertness is necessary to perceive verbal and nonverbal cues from reticent students such as a perplexed look or partially raised hand. Discretion should be used regarding the difficulty level and intimacy of the questions when calling on nonvolunteering students.

Another useful approach to stimulate a response and thinking is to direct a question to other students. The redirection could be prompted by an unanswered question, an incorrect response, or a desire to get additional responses to the same question. Redirection can involve volunteering and nonvolunteering students. Participation during discussions, particularly, can be stimulated by encouraging students to interact with each other. Sometimes there is a delicate balance between teacher intervention and teacher facilitation. ''Jim, how do you react to Mary's point of view that *Catcher in the Rye* is an example of pornography?'' is one way to stimulate student-student interaction. Most interaction is of the teacher-student-teacher type. Student-student interaction involves more students, increasing the probability of a greater diversity of ideas, perspectives and judgments that are very appropriate during a discussion. The implication for the teacher is that the way interaction is encouraged and conducted communicates expectations to the students. More students will get involved in interaction if encouraged by the teacher.

Probing Responses. During discussions in which the emphasis is on stimulating more complex student thinking, students sometimes lack skill and confidence in expressing themselves at the higher cognitive levels. Resulting responses to questions are then ambiguous, incomplete, or superficial. In these cases teachers need to follow up with probing questions or comments to encourage students to complete, clarify, expand, or support their answers. Probes to encourage students to complete and clarify responses are often necessary with younger learners as they begin articulating the basics of reflective thinking, or with older learners at the upper grades who have not been sufficiently exposed to higher level questions. Probes are often useful to encourage students to elevate thinking to higher cognitive levels. Comments such as ''What if . . .'' ''Suppose . . .'' ''How about . . .'' are common during discussions in which teachers are challenging students' thinking. Probably the most common probes during discussion are those that request learners to support their points of view, opinions or judgments with evidence from internal or external sources. Comments such as ''Why?'' ''What evidence do you have?'' and ''How can you support your view?'' are common in reflective discussions. The implication for the teacher is that learners' initial responses to questions must be heard before probes can be used. Listening skills are very important. Also, to be effective, probes must be used in a supportive manner.

Wait Time. Because of the complexity of thinking required by teachers' divergent questions, particularly during discussions, students require more time to formulate thoughtful responses. Although students need more time to think, research shows that teachers wait only approximately 1 second after asking a question before calling on a student and 1 second after a student responds before probing the response, rephrasing the question, redirecting to another student, or providing the answer (Rowe, 1974).

Teachers can use wait time two different ways to increase the probability that students' responses will be more acceptable. The first, postquestion wait time, is the pause after a teacher asks a question and before a student responds, and the second, postresponse wait time, is the pause after a student responds and before the teacher reacts. Research has shown that a 3- to 5-second pause is particularly effective in stimulating a greater quantity and quality of student thinking (Rowe, 1974). The implication for the teacher is that higher level questions will be minimally effective in stimulating thinking unless students are allowed time to think. A conscientious effort needs to be made to pause after asking a question and after a student responds, particularly during reflective discussions.

Student Questions. Students generally expect to answer questions in most classes, not to have to ask them. Except when they do not understand something or need more information, students rarely ask questions. Students should be encouraged to formulate questions because they become more actively involved in the learning process. Just as importantly, as students ask questions at higher cognitive levels, it can be reasonably assumed that corresponding levels of thought are stimulated. For example, suppose students in a Spanish III class have been studying the culture of Latin America. The teacher requests that each student devise two questions to ask a hypothetical visitor from Mexico in the class in order to acquire a deeper understanding of the lifestyle of Latin Americans. The questions are shared and answered cooperatively by the teacher and students. The implication for teachers is that they may have underestimated students' ability to generate thoughtful questions and that they need to plan ways for students to get more involved in this manner (Wilen & Clegg, 1986).

Scenario Analysis

Mr. Taylor involved his students in several mini-reflective discussions during the course of the period in the illustrative scenario. The discussions were interspersed with learning activities designed to structure students' critical thinking about their community's environmental problems. The vast majority of questions he asked were at the divergent level, and the questioning techniques he employed were realistic and conducive to a reflective discussion. He initiated a discussion at the beginning of the period after having the students imagine an environmental crisis taking place in their community. The question—it is actually an implied question—is classified at Level IV because original thinking was required as students engaged in speculation. Several students responded with their predictions. Asking students what problems they think their community is facing now requires analytical and evaluative thinking. Students are making generalizations based on observations of their surroundings, and making a judgment as to which observation is most important. This question could be categorized at Level III, although there is no indication that all students supported their responses with evidence.

During the next questioning sequence, Mr. Taylor used several questioning techniques. It was initiated with a Level III question, "How do we know if these are really problems that Norwood should do something about?" This requires students to draw conclusions, a characteristic of analytical thinking. After using wait time he called on a nonvolunteer who appeared "deep in thought." Mr. Taylor proceeded to probe Jim's response to expand his thinking on the issue by requiring that he make a judgment. Several other students then offered their points of view. Approximately half way through the period, Mr. Taylor asked students to recall the definition of "hypothesis." Defining is a characteristic of Level I thinking. There was also an indication he purposely used wait time. In attempting to get the students to relate the definition to their guesses about their community's environmental problems, he called on another nonvolunteer with little success. Even with a probe, the student responded minimally. The question was then redirected to another student who gave a more complete response. After assigning homework and having the students read a brief article, Mr. Taylor directed a level IV divergent question to a student. She was asked to make a judgment about her parents' perception of the most critical environmental problem.

In regard to the other questioning techniques, there was evidence that the questions were phrased well and adapted to this average group of students. Although all the questions stimulated primarily divergent thinking, a sequence of questions is evident based on logical thinking about solving problems. Because of the capabilities of the students, Mr. Taylor needed to spend only a minimal amount of time reviewing facts. Therefore, a balance of questions was not necessary. He did not consider it pertinent to have the students devise questions during this lesson.

Supporting Skills

The extent to which a teacher provides cognitive and emotional support to students in the classroom is primarily based on the kind of climate that has been created. Climate is generally perceived as ". . . the generalized attitudes, feelings, and actions that prevail in a class" resulting from a variety of physical, psychological, social, and intellectual stimuli. A classroom's climate is, in many

ways, its character or personality, and climate has an impact on learning in significant ways (Levin with Long, 1981).

The teacher is primarily responsible for establishing the classroom climate.
If a positive social-emotional climate has been created, the students feel supported by their teacher. For example, if the teacher regularly displays behaviors
suggestive of a positive attitude toward learning and school in comments to
students, promotes cooperation among the students, and is accepting of students' feelings and ideas, students will feel a sense of belonging and will develop respect for the teacher and for each other. In addition, they will be stimulated to participate in class activities.

There is some research evidence, based primarily on the work of Flanders
(1970), that suggests a teacher's "indirect influence," as Flanders described this
form of climate, is more conducive to students' learning and to the development
of a positive attitude in the classroom. Conversely, a teacher's "direct influence" established by directing students' actions, using criticism, and generally
projecting an authoritarian image is characteristic of a negative social-emotional
climate. Needless to say, students feel minimal support within this atmosphere
(Silvernail, 1983).

Several supportive teacher behaviors contribute to the creation of a positive
climate. They have been identified by Flanders (1970) as acceptance of students'
feelings, praise, encouragement, and use of students' ideas. An additional area
of support is the use of courtesy. Teachers can demonstrate to students acceptance of their feelings by making those feelings explicit, be they positive or negative. Teachers can do this with individual students or with the entire class. For
example, imagine a group of excited 6th-grade students returning from a special
assembly. In order to get them focused on the task the teacher might say with
facial expressions depicting enthusiasm, "You must have really enjoyed the
presentation. I would like to hear your thoughts before we go back to our work."
The teacher has been supportive by displaying acceptance of students' feelings.

Verbal praise is probably the most commonly and frequently used form of
reinforcement and support by teachers in classrooms at all levels. Praise can be
expressed as comments ranging from brief expressions such as "okay" and
"right" to extended judgments including the specifics of the accomplishment.
An example of the latter situation is, "That was an outstanding report, Jimmy.
You not only organized it well and presented it neatly, but also you drew some
very interesting conclusions about acid rain that we will discuss in class."

Students' contributions and achievements are often taken for granted. Because of the influence of praise on student behavior, teachers should remain
constantly aware of opportunities to praise students in a genuine manner. An
important consideration to keep in mind based on current research findings is
that the focus must be on the quality of praise. When quantity is the major
emphasis, praise does not always have the effect of reinforcement, thereby defeating the teacher's intent. Several rules of thumb have been offered: deliver
praise simply and directly in a natural tone of voice; specify the accomplish-

ment; make sure nonverbal behaviors are congruent with the verbal praise; and use a variety of expressions (Good & Brophy, 1984).

Encouragement of student behaviors is similar to the use of praise in that it may have the same supportive effect. The difference is that praise is an expression of a teacher's value judgment. The intent of expressions of encouragement is to stimulate a student to initiate or continue with a learning activity or task related to the objectives. Examples include continuing with a response to a question, further pursuit of an investigation in the library, attempting a new skill, and considering a different approach to solve a problem. Expressions such as, "You're on the right track," "Keep going," "You almost have it," "O.K. How about a little more?" are relatively common. Using wait time (pausing) after a student has made a response might encourage some to continue their responses with a new perspective at a higher level of cognition. Expressions of encouragement such as eye contact and a hand on a shoulder communicate support for students' efforts and motivate them further.

Another approach a teacher can use quite readily to demonstrate a supportive climate is to use students' ideas. The expression of ideas by students is an inevitable occurrence in the classroom and, when feasible, the teacher should capitalize on these ideas. Repeating a student's answer serves to give emphasis to it. When a student has given a somewhat lengthy answer, the teacher may respond with paraphrasing for both clarification and emphasis, for example, "Am I correct that you mean . . . ?" On the occasion that a student has introduced a pertinent idea in the classroom, the teacher may further elaborate, even at some length, as is appropriate. Finally, the teacher may recall students' ideas introduced earlier in the class, giving credit by name when possible, as they pull together ideas into meaningful generalizations.

A teacher's display of courtesy also contributes to creating a positive social-emotional climate in the classroom. It is a very natural way to support students' participation in learning activities and other contributions. The idea is simple: teachers should be courteous to students because they expect courtesy from them. Research reveals that modeling has the potential to markedly influence students. Thanking a student for his or her point of view during a discussion might be more appropriate than using praise, particularly if the teacher did not want to express a judgment on the opinion. Telling a small group of students their conscientious effort on a project is appreciated is supportive, and encourages students to repeat the behavior.

Mr. Taylor displayed a variety of supportive behaviors that were conducive to the creation of a positive social-emotional climate. Early in the lesson there was an indication that he maintained eye contact with students as he listened to and reinforced their contributions. He wrote students' opinions about community environmental problems on the board, a demonstration of support for students' ideas. At one point he expressed considerable enthusiasm for a student's insight, and one can imagine the animated behaviors accompanying the supportive comment, "You have just hit on the one thing I wanted you to learn by the end of the unit!'' The remaining supportive comments were basically expressions of courtesy. He complimented students on how observant they were of the community, and toward the end of the lesson he thanked David for the opinion he contributed. The only praise we can find in the scenario occurred at the end of the lesson when he commented that he thought the lesson had been an interesting one and that he expected more of the same the next day.

SUMMARY POINT

The instructional process consists of techniques, methods, and strategies that teachers have at their disposal as they make decisions about how to plan to meet unit goals and daily objectives in their classrooms. The most basic elements in this process are teacher physical behaviors that, for the most part, can be observed, analyzed and evaluated. Instructional techniques consist of a series of skills that, in a sense, represents groups of teacher behaviors. Six major techniques have been identified. Varying degrees of all these techniques are used in each method and strategy teachers employ in the classroom.

The first three of these techniques are motivating skills, questions and questioning skills, and supporting skills. Research confirms the importance of these techniques as part of a teacher's instructional repertoire. Student motivation is influenced by the teacher's display of verbal and nonverbal behaviors related to enthusiasm and the use of instructional variety. A teacher's application of a variety of question levels and techniques directly influence the degree of student thinking and participation in the classroom. Support, primarily noticed through the teacher's use of praise, has a significant impact on the classroom's social-emotional climate and student learning.

REVIEW: IMPORTANT MOTIVATING SKILLS, QUESTIONS AND QUESTIONING SKILLS, AND SUPPORTING SKILLS

Motivating Skills

—purpose is to stimulate students to attend and get involved in a lesson in order to achieve its objectives. Components include:

1. Physical Movement—teacher varies positions to heighten student attention.
2. Nonverbal Behaviors—teacher uses body language to create a dynamic presence.
3. Voice—teacher varies volume and inflection to stimulate student attention.
4. Lesson Pace—teacher changes pace in response to student reaction.
5. Instructional Mode—teacher employs variety to stimulate learning.

Question Levels

—purpose is to encourage students to engage in a balanced variety of thinking levels. Components include:

I. Low Order Convergent   students recall or recognize information
II. High Order Convergent—students demonstrate understanding.
III. Low Order Divergent—students think critically about information.
IV. High Order Divergent—students perform creative and evaluative thinking.

Questioning Skills

—purpose is to encourage students to participate and think by engaging in group interaction. Components include:

1. Phrasing—teacher asks clear questions.
2. Adapting Questions—teacher adjusts questions to language and ability of students.
3. Sequence—teacher asks questions in a planned and patterned order.
4. Balance—teacher asks convergent and divergent questions.
5. Participation—teacher stimulates a wide range of student involvement.
6. Probing—teacher follows up initial questions to encourage students to complete, clarify, expand, or support responses.
7. Wait Time—teacher pauses after asking questions and student responses.
8. Student Questions—teacher encourages students to ask questions.

Supporting Skills

—purpose is to create a positive social-emotional classroom climate. Components include:

1. Acceptance of Feelings—teacher recognizes and accepts students' feelings.
2. Praise—teacher verbally and nonverbally reinforces students' contributions.
3. Encouragement—teacher verbally encourages student participation.
4. Use of Ideas—teacher accepts and uses students' ideas.
5. Courtesy—teacher expresses thanks or appreciation for students' help or contributions.

Information-Giving Skills

Information-giving, as a technique teachers regularly display in the classroom, is basically a shortened and informal form of the lecture. Teachers frequently give information spontaneously, for example, in response to student questions and comments, when presenting an assignment, explaining something, giving short directions, and introducing a film or speaker. Information-giving can also be more formal and involve more planning, such as when introducing a lesson or summarizing learnings, demonstrating a skill or process, giving involved and extended directions, or presenting a formal explanation. Information-giving might last from a brief moment to as long as 10 minutes. The lecture, in contrast to information-giving, is generally more highly structured, more formal, and may last from approximately 10 to 45 minutes in a middle school or secondary classroom, depending on the situation.

Although most information-giving takes place in unanticipated situations and therefore opportunities for planning are almost nonexistent, several considerations will increase the effectiveness of the communication. Spontaneous responses to questions, explanations, directions, and introductions need to be clearly understood by the students. Approaches to increase the probability of clarity include defining difficult terms and concepts as part of the commentary and providing examples and illustrations to aid comprehension. Feedback should also be solicited from the students. This can be accomplished by simply asking students if they have questions regarding the information given, requesting students to summarize key points, or asking students specific questions as part of a review. Much depends on the ability level of the students, the complexity of the content being presented, and time limitations.

Preparation for more formal information-giving is similar to preparing for a lecture. The primary differences are the length of time of the information-giving, and therefore, ostensibly, the time necessary for planning the presentation. This form of information-giving might properly be termed a "mini-lecture" involving approximately 5 to 10 minutes. In addition to clarifying the lesson content and obtaining feedback characteristic of spontaneous information-giving, additional considerations for formal information-giving include providing for an introduction, organizing the content, and wrapping up with a brief closure.

The introduction to a mini-lecture should precisely communicate to students what content will be covered, why it is important to know it and how it fits into the lesson or unit currently being studied. This need not take any more than 1 to 2 minutes within a brief 10-minute information-giving session.

Organization refers to the presentation of the content in a logical way, moving from simple facts, concepts, skills, or ideas to more complex ones. Starting with what the students know is a logical basis for presenting new information. This is the body of the mini-lecture.

The intention of closure is to review what has been presented, determine the extent to which students understood what was covered, and make a tie-in to the next learning activity. Clearly the more time devoted to information-giving, the more structured and formal the presentation must become in order to increase the probability that the students will understand what is being taught. Suggestions for conducting effective lectures are presented in Chapter 6.

In addition to the above-mentioned skills, other more personally related behaviors and skills influence the effectiveness of information-giving. These behaviors have been previously presented and discussed as part of the technique of motivation in this chapter. The inference is that a teacher presenting infor mation, even for a short period of time, must be concerned with providing an enthusiastic image in order to focus and sustain students' attention and interest. Of course, the display of motivating skills becomes more essential as information-giving turns into a lecture. Physical movement, use of nonverbal behaviors, and voice are among the most important motivating skills. If the teacher has the freedom to move during a short information-giving session, the probability for student attention to be maintained is increased. Nonverbal behaviors contribute to creating a dynamic presence, and are, therefore, an interesting and appealing focus for student attention. Naturally, voice volume and inflection are critical when presenting information.

Because Mr. Taylor's lesson was primarily discussion and activity-oriented, he engaged in only two instances of information-giving. The first time he reacted spontaneously to a student's insightful comment by providing reasons why their community initiated environmental legislation and how it was done. It took less than 5 minutes. The second time he explained their homework assignment. The assignment explanation, including passing out and clarifying the use of the survey form, took no longer than 3 to 4 minutes. Minimal information-giving was required primarily because the majority of Mr. Taylor's students had prior knowledge and experiences with their community's environmental problems, and they were interested in the topic.

Listening Skills

Another essential component of classroom interpersonal communication is the regular display of a teacher's listening behaviors. Primarily nonverbal in nature, they influence all forms of teacher-student interaction and contribute to the so-cial-emotional climate of the classroom. As a result of their impact on communication, it is important that teachers are aware of their use of listening behaviors and model them for students in class. Teacher modeling will also serve to indirectly encourage students to display appropriate listening skills.

The display of effective listening behaviors is dependent on the implementation of a series of skills. Seven behaviors have been identified by Garrett, Sadker, and Sadker (1986): eye contact, facial expressions, body posture, physical space, silence, brief verbal acknowledgments, and subsummaries. Maintaining eye contact with a student who responds to a teacher's question tacitly communicates the teacher's interest in what is being said. Having a personal knowledge of the respondent is important because some are uncomfortable with direct eye contact. A teacher's facial expressions provides the student with feedback about the teacher's reaction to what is being said. A smile as compared to a frown, for example, communicates a very different mood and reaction to students. Overdoing facial expressions could also be distracting and hinder communication. Body posture can determine the formality the teacher intends for the situation, and body gestures communicate meaning. Gestures include the position of the arms, hands, and fingers, and touching. Communication can be quite varied, depending how gestures are used, in what classroom situation and with whom. The physical distance between the teacher and student(s) is also influential in communicating quite literally how close a teacher wants to be to the students. Close proximity communicates intimacy, whereas distance communicates separateness. All of these nonverbal behaviors need to be closely monitored when working with groups and individual students because of their implicit positive and negative messages.

The display of verbal behaviors, particularly in conjunction with the above-mentioned nonverbal behaviors, are effective in communicating to students that a teacher wants to hear what is being said and encourages continuance. The behavior most often associated with teacher listening is silence. Silence, or wait time, has been discussed previously in this chapter as an effective teacher questioning technique. It communicates interest and respect for what is being said and it stimulates reflection. Too much silence can be awkward, and can hinder communication. Brief verbal acknowledgments uttered by the listener during discourse can communicate interest and concern to the speaker. Essential for the effective use of verbal acknowledgments is that they be brief and infrequent. Examples include "Hmmmm," "I understand," and "O.K." A brief verbal summary of what has been said may also be useful. Subsummaries are the least used of the listening skills, but occasionally summarizing for the speaker what has been said clarifies the message and supports the speaker (Garrett, Sadker, & Sadker, 1986).

Although we can readily imagine Mr. Taylor engaging in a variety of listening behaviors during the lesson depicted in the scenario, there was no direct indication that he used any specific listening skill. Indirect clues are the success he had in stimulating responses to his questions, many at the divergent level, and the respect students apparently had for him as indicated by the lack of classroom management problems. Mr. Taylor has established a positive climate for learning. One major characteristic of such a climate is the mutual respect between teacher and students. The congruence of the willingness to listen to one another and the display of listening skills is a contributing factor in the development of respect between teacher and students.

Managing Skills

A major requisite to effective instruction is good classroom management. A well-managed classroom is one in which the students are actively engaged in learning and discipline problems are minimal. As experienced teachers know, a well-managed classroom does not just happen; it depends on how much a teacher is willing to work to create the necessary conditions for a productive learning environment. Although the extent to which a classroom is well managed also depends on the nature of the students in the class and other variables such as the size of the group, the teacher is ultimately responsible for establishing the classroom environment. The inference is that a teacher will need to be more diligent in creating the conditions necessary for good management with more immature and less motivated students. One of the conclusions drawn by the Northwest Regional Educational Laboratory (1984) upon its review of the research on effective schooling practices is, as one would expect, that positive classroom management increases the probability that learning will occur.

Successful classroom management primarily depends on prevention of those conditions and situations that lead to discipline problems. The managing behaviors a teacher engages in are in essence a combination of instructing and controlling behaviors. Figure 4.2 depicts management as a roughly defined area in the middle of a continuum between instruction and discipline. One inference is that a classroom can be managed using strong, authoritarian discipline, much as we would expect in the military. Control problems are minimal and are handled quickly and efficiently.

Another inference is that a classroom can be managed using instructional practices. We can envision an industrial arts laboratory where all the students are busy working on their individual projects at their stations while the teacher confers with a small group of students needing assistance. In the real world of the classroom, though, students are managed through a combination of a teachers' instructional and discipline-related behaviors. According to the research, effective teachers rely more on instructional behaviors to manage the classroom. This can be accomplished by creating the conditions for a good learning environment and thereby increasing the probability that discipline problems will be prevented. Effective teachers are effective managers; effective managers prevent potential problems.

If the researchers and theorists on classroom management had to describe the basis for a well-managed classroom with one word, it would probably be *organization*. A teacher who purposely organizes instruction diminishes the likelihood of noncompliant behavior problems regardless of the nature of the students. The effective classroom manager is prepared for class, structures the learning environment, teaches with direction and variation, keeps students on-task, and closely monitors their learning. ''All teachers plan'' is a statement that introduces the planning chapter. At the secondary level this generally means

Figure 4.2 Classroom Management as a Function of Instruction and Discipline

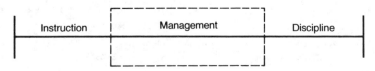

that the teacher has an outline of the content that he or she expects to cover, and notations related to the intended instructional approach. The effective classroom manager has organized the lesson by taking into account such considerations as shifts of instructional approaches to hold students' interest, varied seating arrangements appropriate for the methods being used, and particular individualized learning activities to accommodate different learning styles. The teacher may have also anticipated discipline problems with certain students and planned specific control techniques.

Closely related to preparation is the structuring of the learning environment. The effective manager physically organizes the classroom to efficiently implement learning activities. For example, desks are arranged appropriately for discussion, lectures and small group work. The learning environment can also be structured psychologically by setting expectations for student learning and behavioral conduct. As an illustration, "Today we are going to do some role playing to try to understand how teenagers make decisions about their social lives. In order to be able to accomplish this, I will need your cooperation. Role playing is a very effective method to learn and feel the values others are experiencing—only if everyone is listening and paying attention." Rules can be set and routines can be established to help guide students as they go about their learning tasks.

The effective managing teacher has planned to vary instruction to achieve learning objectives in different ways and for the purpose of stimulating students' interest and involvement. When students are faced with the same instructional method or strategy each day in one class, they become bored. Boredom provides opportunities for students' minds to wander and become preoccupied with other students and nonacademic activities. Teachers need to maintain command of a repertoire of methods and strategies in order to provide a stimulating instructional environment. The great variety of techniques, methods, and strategies presented in Chapters 4 through 7 should contribute significantly to a teacher's repertoire of instructional approaches. Teaching must also be focused to maintain students' attention and involvement. Preplanned specific objectives are essential to provide instructional direction and focus.

While instruction is under way, the teacher continues to manage the classroom by attempting to maintain student task orientation and continually monitoring their learning and personal behaviors. Experienced teachers know that if students are off-task for any length of time, the probability that noncompliant behavior will occur increases. The managing teacher encourages students to be constructively occupied throughout each class period with attempts to achieve the preplanned objectives. Active student mental and physical participation is essential. Monitoring students' behaviors is the means by which teachers increase the probability that they will remain on-task. More than simply being aware of what students are doing at any given moment, monitoring involves teachers directly in individual and group activities. Management is enhanced as teachers intervene indirectly into the affairs of students for instructional purposes. Use of eye contact or gestures assists the teacher in guiding students' behavior. Physical positioning, verbal directives, and touching are also often necessary to keep them on-task. As one can readily infer, depending on the nature of the students and situation, effective classroom management requires highly polished organizational skills and the full-time involvement of the teacher during the class period.

Judging from the variety of instructional approaches, the involvement of the students in learning activities, and the lack of control problems, it is clear that Mr. Taylor displayed several key and effective management skills. As was pointed out in the section on "Motivation," one of Mr. Taylor's major strengths was the implementation of a variety of instructional approaches that continually shifted students' senses. With three major shifts, it was obvious his preparation was considerable. More direct indications of his preparation were the survey form he had prepared and passed out for students to record their parents' viewpoints on their community's environmental problems and the article he distributed for students to read. On three occasions, Mr. Taylor monitored students' behaviors. At the beginning of class he handled two boys' talking quickly and effectively. Shortly into the period he noticed several students were beginning to drift off, so he moved to another phase of the lesson. Approximately 20 minutes into the period he noticed several students gazing out the window, and decided to quicken the pace of the lesson to attempt to hold students' interest more effectively. There was little immediate evidence of his structuring the learning environment since this was a longer range management consideration and cumulative in its effect. Generally we can say that Mr. Taylor was successful in establishing a well-managed learning environment, the evidence of which was in how effectively students were involved in learning activities.

SUMMARY POINT

In addition to motivating skills, questions and questioning skills, and supporting skills, there are three other major instructional techniques found in every teacher's instructional repertoire: information-giving skills, listening skills, and managing skills. Varying degrees of all these techniques can be found in each method and strategy teachers employ in the classroom. The research literature supports these techniques as effective teaching practices, and because of this, teachers need to carefully consider these techniques while making decisions about instructional variety during the planning stage. Skills associated with information-giving have been positively related to students' learning efficiency and success. Listening skills contribute significantly to classroom communication and to a positive classroom climate. Managing skills affect students' attitudes, behaviors, and achievement. The decisions a teacher makes regarding the use of instructional techniques are critical because of their resulting impact on classroom climate, learning activities, and student outcomes.

REVIEW: IMPORTANT PRACTICES: INFORMATION-GIVING SKILLS,
      LISTENING SKILLS, AND MANAGING SKILLS

Information-Giving Skills

—purpose is to provide students with limited amounts of information spontaneously or, more formally, assist in attaining lesson objectives. Components include:

1. Clarity—teacher delineates content precisely, relates it to objectives, avoids irrelevant discourse.
2. Feedback—teacher obtains feedback from students during or after information-giving.
3. Introduction—teacher prefaces mini-lecture with an introduction.
4. Organization—teacher presents content in a logical and purposeful manner.
5. Closure—teacher concludes or causes students to wrap up the lesson with reference to primary learnings.

Listening Skills

—purpose is to communicate to students that a teacher is interested in what a student is saying and that what is being said is important. Components include:

1. Eye Contact—teacher maintains eye contact with students.
2. Facial Expressions—teacher uses a variety of positive facial expressions in response to students' communications.
3. Body Posture—teacher uses positive posture and a variety of gestures.
4. Physical Distance—teacher adjusts position vis-à-vis students according to the conditions of instruction.
5. Silence—teacher maintains silence while the student is the active communicator.
6. Verbal Acknowledgments—teacher uses brief appropriate verbal acknowledgments while listening to students.
7. Subsummaries—teacher interjects brief mini-summaries while listening to students during lengthy communications.

Managing Skills

—purpose is to create appropriate physical and psychological conditions in the classroom in order for learning to occur. Components include:

1. Preparation—teacher is well organized and prepared for class.

2. Learning Environment Structure—teacher establishes expectations for students' learning and conduct.
3. Instruction—teacher uses instructional approach to assist in the management of students' learning and behavior.
4. Task Orientation—teacher keeps students oriented toward achieving objectives.
5. Monitoring—teacher is aware of students' learning and conduct behaviors.

NOTES

1. From W. Wilen, "Questioning, Thinking and Effective Citizenship," *Social Science Record,* 22 (Spring, 1985), 4–6.
2. From W. Wilen, "Developing Effective Questioning Strategies," *Southwestern Journal of Social Education,* 13 (Winter/Spring, 1983), 21–27.

ACTIVITIES (ANALYSIS FORMS FOLLOW)

ACTIVITY I: ENTRY SKILLS

Devise an appropriate lesson entry that includes all three elements (focus students' attention, review, and preview) to introduce the two teaching situations presented below:

A. 10th grade geometry class: the class has been studying geometric proofs of parallel lines. At the beginning of class the teacher has five students put the homework problems on the board. The students at their seats are told to check their homework against the problems on the board while the teacher circulates to determine who has completed the assignment.

B. 6th grade language arts lesson: The teacher has the students read the first paragraph of the short story, "Escape Across the Wall."

ACTIVITY II: ENTRY SKILLS

Observe either a videotape or a live performance of a teacher entering a lesson. Use the teaching analysis form for "Entry" provided in the Appendix of this chapter to identify the extent that aspects of the entry are present and to appraise the teacher's performance. Share and compare the data you have collected with your peers and discuss how the lesson's entry might be improved.

ACTIVITY III: CLOSURE SKILLS

Contact two teachers and get their views about the most effective approach to closing a lesson. Compare their views with the ideas presented here and begin to form a judgment about the role closure will play in your future classroom.

ACTIVITY IV: CLOSURE SKILLS

Apply the teaching analysis guide for "Closure" to a videotaped teaching episode in which the end of the lesson is included. Determine the extent to which the elements of an effective closure are evident, and appraise the teacher's performance.

ACTIVITY V: MOTIVATING SKILLS

Watch a television game show and record all those personal and "instructional" behaviors in which the emcee engages that suggest an enthusiastic presence. Compare with the behaviors listed on the teaching analysis form for "Motivation" and suggest additional behaviors.

ACTIVITY VI: MOTIVATING SKILLS

Observe a teacher in the classroom or on videotape and analyze and evaluate his or her performance in creating a stimulating environment through the application of motivating behaviors. Write a brief reaction statement indicating those motivating behaviors that seem to need the most attention and improvement. Also indicate which motivating behaviors you believe you possess and how they might have an impact on the climate of the classroom.

ACTIVITY VII: QUESTIONS AND QUESTIONING SKILLS

Analyze an interview on television or radio conducted by a person such as Barbara Walters, Ted Koppel, or Phil Donahue. Categorize the questions asked using the Levels I–IV categories. List the variety of questioning techniques used.

ACTIVITY VIII: QUESTIONS AND QUESTIONING SKILLS

Plan for a discussion of about 20 minutes appropriate for the classroom setting. Incorporate in your outline at least two examples of each of the four levels of questions into the interaction. Trade with your neighbor and categorize the questions according to the thought levels being stimulated. Discuss differences in categorization.

ACTIVITY IX: QUESTIONS AND QUESTIONING SKILLS

View a videotape or listen to an audiotape of classroom interaction depicting a discussion or recitation. Use the questions and questioning analysis form to categorize the questions and evaluate the techniques used to guide the interaction. List several areas needing improvement that a supervisor might review in a conference with the teacher. Make suggestions about how the teacher might improve in those areas.

ACTIVITY X: QUESTIONS AND QUESTIONING SKILLS

Assume you are a teacher. Select a topic, issue, or problem and devise a sequence of questions from low to high cognitive emphasis that you might ask in class during a discussion of about 20 minutes.

ACTIVITY XI: SUPPORTING SKILLS

Observe three 15-minute videotaped segments from different grade levels of secondary school classes. Use the "Supporting Skills" analysis form and analyze and evaluate the three teachers in terms of their display of supportive behaviors. Compare the data from the three settings and draw conclusions about the effectiveness of the respective teachers in creating positive social-emotional climates. Focus on the teachers' display of nonverbal behaviors and draw conclusions regarding the impact of these behaviors on students in the three different settings.

ACTIVITY XII: INFORMATION-GIVING SKILLS

Carefully listen to a 5- to 10-minute episode of information-giving on radio, television, or live. The person may be explaining a point of view (perhaps on a current event), giving directions on how to do something (preparing a dinner dish or repairing something), or describing an experience (vacation trip or an accomplishment). Analyze the "mini-lecture" in terms of the criteria specified on the analysis form. Although the narrator might not have an introduction or closure as would be expected of a teacher, analyzing the organization of the presentation will be useful. Did the person define or explain terms or procedures? Were examples and illustrations given to enhance understanding? To what extent did the narrator move from simple to complex understandings?

ACTIVITY XIII: LISTENING SKILLS:

Develop awareness of the importance and use of listening behaviors by observing them in practice in social conversations with friends in informal settings. Make mental notes of the extent of your friends' use of verbal and nonverbal listening skills. Draw conclusions about the use and effectiveness of the application of listening skills in pairs.

ACTIVITY XIV: LISTENING SKILLS

Observe a class discussion in which extended interaction is apparent. Use the analysis form to analyze and evaluate the teacher's application of listening skills. Note also the students' listening behaviors.

ACTIVITY XV: MANAGING SKILLS

Using the analysis form for Managing, gather data regarding how teachers and leaders in other group settings display effective management behaviors. Record data from live or videotaped class sessions. Nonschool-setting data can be gathered from church, adult evening, college, or other classes, and from a variety of meetings (city council, club, community, business). Compare the school and nonschool data to arrive at conclusions regarding how you would improve the use of management skills if you were the leader in either a school or nonschool situation.

ANALYSIS FORM

ENTRY

TEACHER _____

OBSERVER _____

CLASS _____

DATE _____

ANALYSIS SCALES _____

OCCURRENCE	EFFECTIVENESS
1. Not evident	1. Not effective
2. Slightly evident	2. Slightly effective
3. Moderately evident	3. Moderately effective
4. Quite evident	4. Quite effective
N Not applicable	N Not applicable

CATEGORIES (Parts A–B Correspond to Occurrence and Effectiveness in the Analysis Scale)	A. OCCURRENCE	B. EFFECTIVENESS
1. CASUAL OR PERSONAL COMMENTS: A. Teacher makes casual or personal comments intended to affect the lesson entry. B. Teacher establishes a friendly, comfortable climate for learning.		
2. SPRINGBOARD: A. Teacher uses a springboard in the entry. B. Teacher establishes relevance of the content to arouse interest in the current lesson.		
3. ATTENTION-GETTER: A. Teacher does something unexpected or sensational in the entry. B. Teacher stimulates students' curiosity, suspense, or creativity to focus attention.		
4. REVIEW: A. Teacher reviews learnings from previous lesson. B. Teacher presents a well-organized, succinct review of pertinent learnings that provides momentum for the new lesson; or teacher asks incisive review questions to begin the new lesson.		
5. PREVIEW: A. Teacher previews upcoming lesson. B. Teacher states the objectives pertinent to the lesson, presents the rationale, and describes enthusiastically the learning activities which are imminent.		

continued

Analysis Form: Entry Skills, *continued*

CONSIDERATIONS

Describe the entry used.

How much time was devoted to the entry?

What was the student response to the entry?

ANALYSIS FORM   *CLOSURE*

TEACHER _____

OBSERVER _____

CLASS _____

DATE _____

	OCCURRENCE	EFFECTIVENESS
	1. Not evident	1. Not effective
	2. Slightly evident	2. Slightly effective
	3. Moderately evident	3. Moderately effective
	4. Quite evident	4. Quite effective
	N Not applicable	N Not applicable

CATEGORIES (Parts A-B Correspond to Occurrence and Effectiveness in the Analysis Scale)	A. OCCURRENCE	B. EFFECTIVENESS
1. SUMMARY: A. Teacher summarizes or causes the lesson to be summarized. B. Teacher and/or students synthesize important points from the lesson; this includes more than only repeating the information in the lesson.		
2. INTEGRATION: A. Teacher cites the broad context within which the lesson is a part. B. Teacher meaningfully relates the lesson to the goals of the unit and to students' previous learnings.		
3. APPLICATION: A. Teacher mentions possible uses of the topic/skill learned. B. Teacher makes convincing suggestions regarding the intended immediate or long-range application of the learning outcomes.		
4. TRANSITION: A. Teacher builds a bridge to the next lesson with comments or an assignment. B. Teacher previews coming learnings/activities in a manner that piques student interest; teacher makes a thought-provoking assignment in anticipation of the next class meeting.		
5. REFERENCE TO ACCOMPLISHMENT: A. Teacher comments on accomplishment(s). B. Teacher analyzes the class's progress in terms of the learning objectives; teacher gives specific praise as deserved or encouragement as appropriate.		

continued

Analysis Form: Closure Skills, *continued*

CONSIDERATIONS

Describe the closure used.

How much time was devoted to the closure?

What was the student response to the closure?

ANALYSIS FORM

MOTIVATING SKILLS

TEACHER _____

OBSERVER _____

CLASS _____

DATE _____

OCCURRENCE	EFFECTIVENESS
1. Not evident	1. Not effective
2. Slightly evident	2. Slightly effective
3. Moderately evident	3. Moderately effective
4. Quite evident	4. Quite effective
N Not applicable	N Not applicable

CATEGORIES (Parts A–B Correspond to Occurrence and Effectiveness in the Analysis Scale)	A. OCCURRENCE	B. EFFECTIVENESS
1. PHYSICAL MOVEMENT: A. Teacher uses movement purposely. B. Teacher successively repositions self in a manner that heightens students' attention and serves the monitoring function; doesn't pace nervously.		
2. NONVERBAL BEHAVIOR: A. Teacher uses a variety of nonverbal behaviors to create a presence. B. Teacher uses facial expression (laughs, smiles, frowns, scowls, looks inquisitive) for effect and emphasis; gestures, nods, points, touches; creates a dynamic presence.		
3. VOICE: A. Teacher uses his or her voice to attract students' attention. B. Teacher has a pleasant voice with a meaningful tone which expresses confidence and competence; easily heard; inflection evident; speech pattern is appropriate for the level of class.		
4. LESSON PACE: A. Teacher varies the lesson pace. B. Teacher moderates or stimulates the flow of activity for optimum learning; adjusts pace in response to evidence of boredom, confusion or frustration.		
5. INSTRUCTIONAL MODE: A. Teacher varies the instructional approach during the lesson. B. Teacher changes methods and learning activities with appropriate frequency; varies nature of student participation.		

continued

Analysis Form: Motivating Skills, *continued*

6. ENTHUSIASM: A. Teacher embodies the qualities of liveliness and personal interest. B. Teacher employs a combination of verbal and nonverbal behaviors, lesson pacing, and lesson modes that visibly affect students' attention and participation.		

CONSIDERATION

What aspect of the lesson created the most motivation within the students?

TEACHER _____

OBSERVER _____

CLASS _____

DATE _____

COGNITIVE LEVELS—	NUMBER OF QUESTIONS ASKED	PERCENTAGE OF TOTAL	ESTIMATED % OF TIME DEVOTED TO EACH LEVEL
LEVEL I—LOW ORDER CONVERGENT: Requires students to recall or recognize information. Emphasis on memorization and observation. Responses can easily be anticipated. Students define, recognize, quote, identify, recall, and answer "yes" or "no." Corresponds to Bloom's Knowledge Level.		%	%
LEVEL II—HIGH ORDER CONVERGENT: Requires student to demonstrate understanding and apply information. Students describe, compare, contrast, rephrase, summarize, explain, translate, interpret, relate, apply, use, provide an example, and solve. Corresponds to Bloom's Comprehension and Application Levels.		%	%

continued

139

Analysis Form: Question Levels, *continued*

LEVEL III—LOW ORDER DIVERGENT: Requires student to critically think about information, ideas, and opinions. Students discover motives, reasons or causes; draw conclusions, inferences or generalizations; provide evidence or support for conclusions, inferences or generalizations. Corresponds to Bloom's Analysis Level.		%	%
LEVEL IV—HIGH ORDER DIVERGENT: Requires students to perform original, creative and evaluative thinking. Students produce original communications, make predictions, propose solutions, create, solve lifelike problems, speculate, construct, devise, write, design, hypothesize, synthesize, develop/judge ideas and problem solutions, express opinions, and make choices and decisions. Corresponds to Bloom's Synthesis and Evaluation Levels.		%	%
Totals		%	

ANALYSIS FORM   QUESTIONING SKILLS

ANALYSIS SCALES

TEACHER _____

OBSERVER _____

CLASS _____

DATE _____

ANALYSIS SCALES

OCCURRENCE	EFFECTIVENESS
1. Not evident	1. Not effective
2. Slightly evident	2. Slightly effective
3. Moderately evident	3. Moderately effective
4. Quite evident	4. Quite effective
N Not applicable	N Not applicable

CATEGORIES (Parts A–B Correspond to Occurrence and Effectiveness in the Analysis Scale)	A. OCCURRENCE	B. EFFECTIVENESS
1. PHRASING: A. Teacher uses questions. B. Teacher phrases questions so that response expectations are clearly communicated to students; no run-on questions.		
2. ADAPTING QUESTIONS: A. Teacher adapts questions to the class. B. Teacher adjusts questions to the language and ability level of the students.		
3. SEQUENCE: A. Teacher asks questions sequentially. B. Teacher asks questions in a patterned order indicating a purposeful questioning strategy.		
4. BALANCE: A. Teacher balances convergent and divergent questions. B. Teacher uses questions at appropriate levels to achieve the objectives of the lesson.		
5. PARTICIPATION: A. Teacher uses questions to stimulate a wide range of student participation. B. Teacher encourages student involvement by balancing responses from voluntering and nonvolunteering students; redirects initially answered questions to other students; encourages student-student interaction particularly appropriate during a discussion		

continued

Analysis Form: Questioning Skills, *continued*

6. PROBING: A. Teacher probes initial student responses to questions particularly during discussions. B. Teacher follows up initial student responses with questions that encourage students to complete, clarify, expand, or support their responses.		
7. WAIT TIME: A. Teacher uses wait time after asking questions and after students' responses, particularly during discussions. B. Teacher pauses a minimum of 3 seconds after asking divergent questions in order to allow student thinking; teacher also pauses after students' initial responses to questions to encourage continued commentary.		
8. STUDENT QUESTIONS: A. Teacher requests students to ask questions. B. Teacher encourages students to devise pertinent questions to stimulate thinking at the divergent level; students ask thoughtful questions.		

CONSIDERATIONS

Did the questions asked elicit that quality of thinking intended?

How would you describe the questioning strategy (or pattern) used by the teacher?

ANALYSIS SCALES

TEACHER _____

OBSERVER _____

CLASS _____

DATE _____

OCCURRENCE	EFFECTIVENESS
1. Not evident	1. Not effective
2. Slightly evident	2. Slightly effective
3. Moderately evident	3. Moderately effective
4. Quite evident	4. Quite effective
N Not applicable	N Not applicable

CATEGORIES (Parts A–B Correspond to Occurrence and Effectiveness in the Analysis Scale)	A. OCCURRENCE	B. EFFECTIVENESS
1. ACCEPTANCE OF FEELINGS: A. Teacher recognizes and accepts students' feelings. B. Teacher responds to students' expression of feelings with sensitivity, possibly empathy.		
2. PRAISE: A. Teacher expresses approval of students' efforts. B. Teacher uses a variety of verbal and nonverbal praise; praise is stated simply and genuinely; accomplishment is specified.		
3. ENCOURAGEMENT: A. Teacher requests students to participate. B. Teacher uses expressions of encouragement to stimulate students to initiate or continue with a task or learning activity.		
4. USE OF IDEAS: A. Teacher acknowledges students' ideas. B. Teacher repeats or paraphrases students' comments; elaborates on students' ideas; refers back to previous ideas of students.		
5. COURTESY: A. Teacher thanks students for help or contributions. B. Teacher uses expressions indicating appreciation for students' assistance, ideas, and efforts; teacher contributes to students' feelings of belonging and having worth and dignity.		

CONSIDERATION

What evidence is available of the effect of the teacher's supportive behavior on students?

ANALYSIS FORM   INFORMATION-GIVING SKILLS

ANALYSIS SCALES

TEACHER _____   OCCURRENCE   EFFECTIVENESS

OBSERVER _____   1. Not evident   1. Not effective
                            2. Slightly evident   2. Slightly effective
CLASS _____   3. Moderately evident 3. Moderately effective
                            4. Quite evident   4. Quite effective
DATE _____   N Not applicable   N Not applicable

CATEGORIES (Parts A–B Correspond to Occurrence and Effectiveness in the Analysis Scale)	A. OCCURRENCE	B. EFFECTIVENESS
SPONTANEOUS		
1. CLARITY: A. Teacher presents information clearly to the students. B. Teacher defines difficult terms and concepts; examples and illustrations are used to aid comprehension.		
2. FEEDBACK: A. Teacher obtains feedback from students during or after information-giving. B. Teacher asks students if they have questions, requests they summarize key points, or directly asks review questions.		
MINI-LECTURE		
3. INTRODUCTION: A. Teacher prefaces mini-lecture with an introduction. B. Teacher communicates to students what content will be covered, why it is important, and how it relates to the lesson/unit being studied.		
4. ORGANIZATION: A. Teacher presents a cohesive body of information/content to the students. B. Teacher's presentation is logically organized; teacher moves from simple to complex ideas, skills, concepts; teaching aids are employed; new content is related to students' current knowledge.		

continued

Analysis Form: Information-Giving Skills, *continued*

5. CLOSURE: A. Teacher makes a discrete closure to the mini-lecture. B. Teacher reviews, or has students review, what was presented; bridge to the next learning activity is made.		

CONSIDERATION

How would you describe the students' behaviors during the presentation?

ANALYSIS FORM   LISTENING SKILLS

ANALYSIS SCALES

	OCCURRENCE	EFFECTIVENESS
TEACHER _____	1. Not evident	1. Not effective
OBSERVER _____	2. Slightly evident	2. Slightly effective
CLASS _____	3. Moderately evident	3. Moderately effective
	4. Quite evident	4. Quite effective
DATE _____	N Not applicable	N Not applicable

CATEGORIES (Parts A–B Correspond to Occurrence and Effectiveness in the Analysis Scale)	A. OCCURRENCE	B. EFFECTIVENESS
NONVERBAL		
1. EYE CONTACT: A. Teacher maintains eye contact with the students. B. Teacher uses continuous eye contact as the students respond to questions, initiated comments, etc.; eye contact is accompanied with positive facial expressions; teacher does not create discomfort by staring.		
2. FACIAL EXPRESSIONS: A. Teacher facial expression in response to students' comments is evident. B. Teacher shows interest in what the students are saying by smiling, nodding, and changing expressions as appropriate.		
3. BODY POSTURE: A. Teacher "body language" in response to students' comments is evident. B. Teacher uses postures indicating attention and interest; gestures using body, hands, fingers are appropriate and not distracting.		
4. PHYSICAL DISTANCE: A. Teacher moves with apparent purpose regarding student-teacher communication. B. Teacher establishes and maintains close proximity in order to hear when working with individual students and small discussion groups.		

continued

Analysis Form: Listening Skills, *continued*

VERBAL 5. SILENCE. A. Teacher maintains silence as students speak responsibly. B. Teacher uses congruent nonverbal behaviors including eye contact and body posture while listening; does not interrupt except to use brief verbal acknowledgments, paraphrases, or subsummaries.		
6. VERBAL ACKNOWLEDGMENTS: A. Teacher uses verbal acknowledgments while listening to students' extended communications. B. Teacher interjects brief comments communicating interest, concern and encouragement.		
7. SUBSUMMARIES: A. Teacher responds with mini-summaries during lengthy communciations. B. Teacher displays congruent and appropriate nonverbal behaviors while using subsummaries.		

CONSIDERATIONS

Describe the general demeanor of the teacher as a listener.

What is the apparent effect of the teacher's listening behavior on students?

ANALYSIS FORM

MANAGING SKILLS

TEACHER _____

OBSERVER _____

CLASS _____

DATE _____

	OCCURRENCE	EFFECTIVENESS
	1. Not evident	1. Not effective
	2. Slightly evident	2. Slightly effective
	3. Moderately evident	3. Moderately effective
	4. Quite evident	4. Quite effective
	N Not applicable	N Not applicable

CATEGORIES (Parts A–B Correspond to Occurrence and Effectiveness in the Analysis Scale)	A. OCCURRENCE	B. EFFECTIVENESS
1. PREPARATION: A. Teacher is well prepared for class. B. Teacher's lesson is well organized; written lesson plan is evident; materials and audiovisual aids are prepared in advance.		
2. LEARNING ENVIRONMENT STRUCTURE: A. Teacher establishes expectations for students' learning and conduct. B. Teacher establishes a routine to guide students' actions; physical environment is organized appropriately for learning activities.		
3. INSTRUCTION: A. Teacher's instructional approach assists in managing students' learning and behavior. B. Teacher's use of methods and strategies is varied; instruction is clear and focused.		
4. TASK ORIENTATION: A. Teacher keeps students oriented toward the learning task(s). B. Teacher directly and indirectly encourages students to attain objectives by using verbal and nonverbal prompts; students are constructively occupied.		
5. MONITORING: A. Teacher monitors students' behaviors during the lesson. B. Teacher uses eye contact and physical position to maintain awareness of the learning and personal behaviors of students; teacher awareness of students in varied instructional groupings is apparent.		

continued

Analysis Form: Managing Skills, *continued*

CONSIDERATIONS

What pattern or general management approach does the teacher effect?

What was the demeanor of the students during the presentation?

What instances of noncompliant behavior occurred?

REFERENCES

Allen, D. & Ryan, K. (1969) *Microteaching*. Reading, MA: Addison-Wesley.

Berliner, D. C. (1984). The half-full glass: A review of research on teaching. In P. L. Hosford (Ed.). *Using what we know about teaching*. Alexandria, VA: Association for Supervision and Curriculum Development.

Bloom, B. (Ed.). (1956). *A taxonomy of educational objectives. Handbook I: Cognitive domain*. New York: McKay.

Brophy, J. (1981). Teacher praise: A functional analysis. *Review of educational research, 51*, 5–32.

Brophy, J. & Good, T. L. (1986). Teacher behavior and student achievement. In M. Wittrock (Ed.), *Handbook of research on teaching*. New York: Macmillan.

Brophy, J., Rohrkemper, M., Rasid, H., & Goldberger, M. (1983). Relationships between teachers' presentations of classroom tasks and students' engagement in those tasks. *Journal of Educational Psychology, 75*, 544–552.

Carin, A. A. & Sund, R. B. (1971). *Developing questioning techniques*. Columbus, OH: Charles E. Merrill.

Cunningham, R. T. (1971). Developing question-asking skills. In J. Weigand (Ed.), *Developing teacher competencies*. Englewood Cliffs, NJ: Prentice-Hall.

DeCecco, J. P. (1968). *The psychology of learning and instruction: Educational psychology*. Englewood Cliffs, NJ: Prentice-Hall.

Dillon, J. T. (1982). Cognitive correspondence between question/statement and response. *American Education Research Journal, 19*, 540–551.

Dillon, J. T. (1984). Research on questioning and discussion. *Educational leadership, 42*, 50–56.

Emmer, E. & Evertson, C. (1981). Synthesis of research on classroom management. *Educational leadership*, 342–347.

Fisher, C. W., Berliner, D. C., Filby, N. N., Marliave, R. S., Cahen, L. S. & Dishaw,

M. M. (1980). Teaching behaviors, academic learning time and student achievement: An overview. In C. Denham & A. Lieberman (Eds.) *Time to learn*. Washington, DC.: NIE.

Flanders, N. A. (1970). *Analyzing teacher behavior*. Reading, MA: Addison-Wesley.

Gage, N. L. & Berliner, D. C. (1984). *Educational psychology* (3rd ed.). Boston: Houghton Mifflin.

Gall, M. (1984). Synthesis of research on teachers' questioning. *Educational leadership, 42,* 40–47.

Gallagher, J. J. & Aschner, M. J. (1963). A preliminary report on analyses of classroom interaction. *Merrill-Palmer Quarterly, 9,* 183–194.

Garrett, S. S., Sadker, M., & Sadker, D. (1986). Interpersonal communication skills. In J. M. Cooper (Ed.), *Classroom teaching skills* (3rd ed.). Lexington, MA: Heath.

Good, T. L. & Brophy, J. E. (1984). *Looking in classrooms* (3rd ed.). New York: Harper & Row.

Groisser, P. (1964). *How to use the fine art of questioning*. Englewood Cliffs, NJ: Prentice-Hall.

Guilford, J. P. (1956). The structure of intellect. *Psychological Bulletin, 53,* 267–293.

Hawes, G. R. & Hawes, L. S. (1982). *The concise dictionary of education*. New York: Van Nostrand Reinhold.

Hyman, R. T. (1974). *Ways of teaching*. Englewood Cliffs, NJ: Prentice-Hall.

Larkins, A. G., McKinney, C. W., & Gilmore, A. C. (1984, November). *Are enthusiastic social studies teachers better teachers? A critical review of research.* Paper presented at the annual meeting of the NCSS, Washington, D.C.

Levin, T. with Long, R. (1981). *Effective instruction*. Washington, D.C.: ASCD.

Mills, S. R., Rice, C. T., Berliner, D. C., & Rousseau, E. W. (1980). Correspondence between teacher questions and student answers in classroom discourse. *Journal of Experimental Education,* 194–204.

Northwest Regional Educational Laboratory (1984). *Effective schooling practices: A research synthesis*. Portland, OR: NWREL.

Purkey, S. C. & Smith, M. C. (1983). Effective schools: A review, *Elementary School Journal, 93,* 428–452.

Rowe, M. B. (1974). Wait time and reward as instructional variables, their influence on language, logic and fate control: Part one—wait time. *Journal of Research on Science Teaching, 11,* 81–94.

Schuck, R. F. (1985). An empirical analysis of the power of set induction and systematic questioning as instructional strategies. *Journal of Teacher Education, 36,* 38–43.

Shostock, R. (1982). Lesson presentation skills. In J. M. Cooper (Ed.), *Classroom teaching skills*. Lexington, MA: Heath.

Silvernail, D. L. (1984). Teaching styles as related to student achievement. *What research says to the teacher series*. Washington, D.C.: NEA.

Susi, F. D. (1985). Spatial mapping as a method for observing classroom art instruction. *Studies in Art, 26,* 163–168.

Susi, F. D. (1986). Physical space and the teaching art. *Art Education, 39* (2), 6–9.

Ware, B. (1978). What rewards do students want? *Phi Delta Kappan, 59,* 355–356.

Weil, M. & Murphy, J. (1982). Instructional processes. *Encylopedia of educational research* (5th ed.). (pp. 890–917). New York: The Free Press.

Wilen, W. W. (1983). Developing effective questioning techniques. *Southwestern journal of social education, 13,* 21–27.

Wilen, W. W. (1984). Implications of research on questioning for the teacher educator. *Journal of research and development in education, 17,* 31–35.

Wilen, W. W. (1985). Questioning, thinking and effective citizenship. *Social science record, 22,* 4–6.

Wilen, W. W. (1986). *Questioning skills, for teachers* (2nd ed.). What research says to the teacher series. Washington, D.C.: NEA.

Wilen, W. W. (1987). Effective questions and questioning: A classroom application. In W. W. Wilen (Ed.), *Questions, questioning techniques and effective teaching.* Washington, D.C.: National Education Association.

Wilen, W. W. & Clegg, A. A. (1986). Effective questions and questioning: A research review. *Theory and research in social education, 14,* 153–161.

CHAPTER 5 Elements of Effective Teaching

The elements of effective teaching practice are a recent addition to the traditional content of methods texts. Their inclusion is witness to the growth of knowledge from educational research since the early 1970s on the characteristics and practices of effective schools and effective classrooms, and the impact that research is having on school curriculum and teaching practices. They call to the attention of teacher educators a substantial body of knowledge which confirms that certain generic teacher practices common to instruction in all subjects are positively correlated with certain student achievements and attitudinal outcomes (Smith, 1984).

A disclaimer is in order at the onset. Although identified instructional processes make a difference, these research studies do indicate that complex instructional problems cannot be solved with sure-fire prescriptions (Brophy & Good, 1986). The key to instructional effectiveness is, as ever, wise and informed teacher decision making within the context of a particular class in a certain school. The complexities of the instructional process are such that no teacher can "plug in" certain practices and achieve instant success. Rather, the practices presented in this chapter emphasize the importance of understanding the interaction between teachers and students and the influence that instruction has on student success. As the effective teaching and effective schools research of the 1970s and 1980s reaffirms, what the teacher says and does in the classroom makes a difference in students' achievement (Brophy & Good, 1986).

The latest correlational studies show that effective practice differs little from elementary to secondary teaching (McGreal, 1983). Teacher performance common to instruction in all subjects has been identified as positively correlated with student outcomes (Smith, 1984). Certain practices, regardless of grade level, encourage student achievement, especially in basic skill acquisition. The literature relating to the general area of classroom management and to the subject areas of elementary reading and mathematics instruction in particular has a well-established knowledge base that is pertinent for teacher decision making (Brophy & Good, 1986). The practices presented here are selected so that beginning teachers can include them in their teaching repertoire as well as develop an understanding of the reasons why these groups of techniques can promote students' academic success. Experienced teachers can examine these practices to confirm that they are part of teachers' instructional skills or that they need to be added or emphasized because of their strong validation by research and learning theory.

OVERVIEW

Research over the past 15 years has identified several key areas of teacher influence that significantly affect student achievement. This chapter examines four
elements within the instructional area: time on task, content coverage, academic
success, and effective feedback. This chapter presents a summary of the research
that validates each of these elements and describes applications of the pertinent
practices associated with each.

The findings of effective teaching research reported in this chapter are not
unusual or surprising. Rather than bringing entirely new information to teachers, they tend to verify what the most competent teachers already do. The research findings are compelling. Teachers who might have ignored instructional
approaches associated with effective teaching in favor of other personally preferred practices are no longer immune from demands to expand their instructional repertoire.

In 1986 the National Institute of Education awarded federal funds to teacher
training institutes to implement teaching effectiveness knowledge into teacher
training programs. All signs indicate that the knowledge gained from effective
teaching research will be dominating training, practice, and evaluation through
the rest of this century. Therefore, it is essential that the teacher is familiar with
the key findings from that research, since it informs us that more effective instruction can result in higher student achievement.

SCENARIO

Laura Trilby glanced at the clock—10:55 a.m. She had 20 minutes
left for this practice phase of the lesson. She had decided to allow
20 minutes for practice today because she wanted time to work with
Bill, Cindy, and Mark to see if she could help them resolve their
problems with the unit while the rest of the class reviewed in order
to synthesize the learning of the current unit.

Laura wondered if she could start moving around the room to
do a quick overview to determine whether students were working
and/or encountering problems before she pulled the three aside to
work with them.

Yes, she decided she needed to travel. Joe and Tom in the back
had stopped pushing each other when she looked back at them and
were settling down to work. She walked slowly down the aisle between their two rows and surveyed the class as she stopped beside
their desks. The class seemed to be engaged in the practice activity. Her directions must have been clear because she had been
asked to repeat them only once. Tom was working on the second
question already. He had answered the first one with an appropriate

response. "You're working well today, Tom. I'll be back to see how you do on the seventh question. That's a tricky one."

As she moved up the rows she reinforced selected students. (Had she spoken to Scott yet today?) "Good response to that question, Scott. You've got the point."

A glance at Susan made her shove her book back under the desk and return to her writing. Must remember to check on her in a few minutes after I see what's happening to Bill, Cindy, and Mark, Mrs. Trilby thought to herself.

Bill thumbed through the book and appeared to be looking for answers. His paper was blank. "Did you finish the chapter, Bill?" Bill reads very slowly, Mrs. Trilby remembered. He probably never finished reading the material. He would have difficulty with the questions in the book. "Keep on reading, Bill. When you finish the chapter write out the answers to these questions, rather than those in your book." Mrs. Trilby wrote out two questions on his paper, then she moved on to Cindy.

The class remained quiet except for a few exchanges among the "super-star four," the students with the best grades. Could they be done already?

"Joan, Charlie, Dan, and Steve, when you are finished, please exchange papers and check each other's answers. Check them for the following points: (She walked to the board and wrote on it) (1) Correct? (2) Good form—complete sentences and paragraphs? (3) Spelling and punctuation correct? (4) Grade you would give paper. The group exchanged papers. "Please give papers back to their owners after they are corrected. Then you have free time."

Mrs. Trilby checked the rest of the class. Those four had been the first ones finished. Everyone else appeared to be working. She called Bill, Cindy, and Mark to bring their work over to the table where she could work with them individually.

A brief thought about her bridge party that night passed through Mrs. Trilby's head. Should she serve dessert; would they like chocolate pie? She let the decision go and moved over to Cindy, who had copied the questions onto her paper. Cindy was always staying busy—bless her heart—but composing answers was difficult for her. "What does that first question ask you to do, Cindy?" Cindy went back to the first question while Mrs. Trilby helped her pick out the key words. "Now tell me what you want to write down."

Cindy responded while Mrs. Trilby turned her head to look at Tommy. He saw her glance. He made an exaggerated move to appear as though he were writing very diligently. Joe, beside him, smirked. Cindy finished her explanation. Mrs. Trilby patted her shoulder while saying, "Have you gotten to the seventh one yet,

Tom? I'll be back to check it in a minute—and yours too, Joe." It takes a lot of attention to keep Joe and Tommy on-task, she noted.

She turned back to Cindy. "You answered the questions well, Cindy. Now see if you can put that on paper. Use your book to help with the spelling." She moved on down the table to give individual feedback to Bill and Mark and to check their papers.

Five minutes to go. The class was stirring. Most seemed to be done. What to do now? "Which of you has finished the assignment and thinks you have it correct?" About eight people raised their hands. "Okay. Joan, Charlie, Matthew and Christie, please bring your papers here for a check. Then, if you have them correct, you can move around the room and check people who have their hands up. When the bell rings, everyone please put your papers on the desk. Remember the quiz tomorrow on this chapter."

The practice period seemed to have gone smoothly. Only her usual three appeared to have difficulty. Tomorrow she'd make out a different test for them with fewer questions. She'd skip the synthesis question for them, perhaps limit theirs to memory, application, and evaluation.

She moved toward the front of the room. "Look at Number 4 again, Mary Beth. Charlie just told you that wasn't correct. Check that second line of the question." Silence. "Read that part over again. See if the information is there."

She noted that almost every book was closed now. Her desk had a pile of papers on it. Only 30 seconds until the bell. "Good job today class. You worked well. Papers look good. Remember the quiz tomorrow."

The bell rings. The room becomes filled with voices, shuffling feet and desk sounds. Mrs. Trilby smiles at students as they pass her. "All finished, Jeff? Good work today, Tom. Is Northwood going to win on Saturday?" Three students respond to that question as they leave. What was she going to do about the difficulties Cindy, Bill, and Mark were having in analyzing reading material? She would talk to the reading specialist about that.

Strawberry tart or chocolate pie? Decisions!

Mrs. Trilby had many decisions to make during that 20-minute practice session in her classroom. Her decisions were related to the questions of how to keep students on-task; how to provide adequate coverage of content for them; how to encourage students' performance; and how to give students effective feedback and praise.

Her decisions on these questions were made on the basis of her knowledge of her students and her past experiences with them; her knowledge of research on teaching; her knowledge of the content; and her knowledge of herself. With 30 students, it is obvious that she did not have time to think through all the implications that might emerge from the above sources, but rather behaved according to her understanding of effective teaching practice with this class. The decisions were made and would be reviewed in light of the effects they had on the children.

Both Mrs. Trilby's and her students' behavior illustrate key elements identified in effective teaching research concerning performance and achievement: namely that both student and teacher behaviors are significantly related to students' academic achievement in the following ways (Squires, Huitt, & Segars, 1983):

1. Student achievement is directly related to the use of time, i.e., the amount of on-task time the student spends being successfully involved with learning.
2. Student achievement is directly related to coverage of the appropriate material on which the student is to be tested.
3. Student achievement is related to the amount of academic success the student experiences.
4. Student achievement is related to the student's processing of the teacher's effective feedback.

The above behaviors are significant in determining student achievement. Those behaviors that enable the student to be actively involved with materials that the student can understand and that bring success experiences within ready reach will promote good performance. It is the teacher's responsibility to help students practice those behaviors that will encourage their success.

This chapter will examine the above four key instructional points that Mrs. Trilby was involved with in the scenario and study them for their implications on improving practive.

TOPIC 1: TIME ON-TASK

RESEARCH AND THEORETICAL BASE

The first important process behavior that affects achievement is that of student involvement, or the amount of time the student spends thinking about and working with the content. The teacher must consider three aspects of the involvement behavior: (1) how much time is provided by the teacher (allocated time); (2) to what degree students are engaged during the time provided (engagement rate or time on task); and (3) how successfully students are engaged (academic learning time, that high-quality time in which students devote themselves to and succeed in meaningful tasks) (Fisher et al., 1978). Teacher allocated time for a subject can vary considerably. The amount of time a teacher spends on teaching in a day may be less than the teacher realizes (Alschuler et al., 1975; Conant, 1973; Cusick, 1973). In secondary high schools, within a 50-minute class period teachers may allocate only 30 to 35 minutes for instruction. In many classrooms observed by the researchers, the first and last 5 minutes of the period are noninstruction time. Many high school teachers use the last 15 minutes of the period for student study time and/or homework completion. This practice time is often unsupervised and not efficiently used by the students. Therefore, allocated time for instruction in a secondary classroom could differ as much as from 15 to 20 minutes up to the complete utilization of the 50-minute period. In elementary classrooms, Dishaw (1977) reported a wide variance in the allocation of time citing ranges in daily second grade reading and language arts from 34 to 127 minutes and for math, 30 minutes to 59 minutes.

The implication for practice from this information is that teachers need to consider the amount of time they have designated for teacher and student involvement in the lesson and the amount of time *actually used* for that involvement. Beginning education student observers in classrooms regularly report on the amount of time they observe being wasted in any number of noninstructional activities or in off-task behaviors by the students.

A powerful argument in reaction to the idea of extending the school year to improve student learning is that teachers should increase first the amount of student and teacher engagement time within the already allocated class period day. The amount of time allocated by the teacher or the system for instruction is important, but not sufficient to ensure learning. Stallings' (1983) work in elementary and secondary schools did not indicate greater student achievement in longer school days or class periods. Longer instruction time will not increase learning unless student engagement time increases also. The Beginning Teacher Evaluation Study also confirmed the importance of effective use of time. The largest increment in achievement occurred in classes of teachers who maximized the time devoted to instruction and minimized time devoted to preparation, procedures, or discipline, and who spent most of their time actively instructing the students and monitoring their work.

Research shows that the average engagement rates range from 60% to 75% at any given time. Students in some classrooms are on task an average of 30% of the time while in others, 90% (Squires, Huitt, & Segars, 1981; Brady et al., 1977; Fisher et al., 1978).

The importance of on-task time for student achievement is supported consistently in the literature. Brophy and Good (1986), in their review of research on teacher behavior and student achievement, state that cutting across all the findings is that academic learning is influenced by the amount of time students spend engaged in appropriate academic tasks. Research studies comparing the amount of time low-achieving students and high-achieving students spend actively working with content have revealed that students with the higher involvement time also have the higher achievement level (Good & Beckerman, 1978; Perkins, 1965).

Correlation between academic learning time and affective measures such as attitudes toward self, self-concept, and attitudes toward school have been noted (Anderson, 1973; Block, 1970; Lahaderne, 1968; Hecht, 1977). Since these are achievement variables teachers can affect to some extent, it appears important for the teacher to consider increasing the use of affective techniques such as rewards, reinforcement, and showing concern and interest in order to encourage students to improve on-task time.

The importance of close supervision to encourage improved academic learning time has been emphasized in many studies. These studies show that small study groups without supervisors have lower levels of student involvement than study groups supervised by teachers (Anderson & Scott, 1978; Good & Beckerman, 1978; Kounin & Gump, 1974; Stallings & Kaskowitz, 1974).

Motivation theory research emphasizes the importance of supportive as well as informational feedback from the teacher. Studies in motivation theory identify the teacher as an external stimulus who can encourage students to increase academic learning time through teachers' use of reinforcement and feedback (Bushnell et al., 1968; Chadwick & Day, 1971; Hops & Cobb, 1972).

An important study that gives direction for teacher practice is that of Stallings and Mohlman (1981) which found that effective teachers use their time differently from other teachers. They found that effective teachers spent 15% or less time in management and organization tasks; 50% *more* time in interactive activities and 35% less time monitoring student activities. They attempted to divide their time so that they could spend some time with the total group, and some with small groups and with individuals.

Other studies with similar direction for teacher practice include the summary findings on use of pupil time (Mitzel, 1982). This source states that the more effective teachers (more effective being described as having classes that achieve higher than classes with similar demographics) spent more time in academic involvement and more time organized in a single large group with the teacher in charge. When students were doing seatwork, they were supervised closely.

More time is not always better. Research cautions the teacher concerning the use of time. More time does not automatically result in improved student achievement. The teacher as decision maker must determine how much time is productive given the makeup of the students involved and their ability to increase their own on-task time.

SUMMARY POINT

Academic Learning Time—the time spent involved with learning and succeeding—is the most important variable that affects student achievement. Change the degree and quality of student involvement and changes will occur in student learning results (Levin with Long, 1981).

APPLICATION TO PRACTICE

Keeping students on-task requires the teacher to be constantly involved with the lesson and the students. Think back to the opening scenario, to Mrs. Trilby who was busy moving around the room, providing verbal or nonverbal direction to keep students working, helping students who were having difficulties, re-assigning students who were finished to another task, and ascertaining who was or was not handling the assignment successfully. She was in perpetual motion, maintaining a positive leadership posture throughout the practice session. Her teacher involvement was 100% and her students, for the most part, were close to that level.

Experienced teachers will acknowledge the accuracy of the above description but point out that Mrs. Trilby's practice session was only a 20-minute segment in a long day. Beginning teachers should not be expected to handle a class as effectively as Mrs. Trilby; however, beginning teachers need to be aware of how they are using time. In order to clearly establish appropriate practice for this important external variable related to teacher and student behavior, practice suggestions are discussed in the next section on the effective use of time. The suggestions are based on the implications from research and learning principles and are recommended for teachers who want to improve their use of time.

Analyzing Use of Time

Teachers need to become aware of their use of time during the instructional day. Through conscious clock watching for several days, or by using a student observer, a fellow teacher, or the principal, they will be able to gather information that informs them about how time is being used in that room. How much time is spent on the opening of class? When do students stop working? Is the time spent on a task in proportion to the importance of the task? How much time during a week is spent on classroom management? Does it take 15 minutes every day after lunch to get students back to work? How much time do the students spend on teacher materials in contrast to working with the teacher? How much time does a student receive each week for individual attention from the teacher? How much time during each class period does the teacher spend interacting with the class? How much time does the class actually spend actively involved with the lesson?

Trying to find the answers to these questions through the analysis of the instructional pattern of one's own teaching will develop a time awareness sense for the teacher. Teacher and classroom observers can determine the amount of students' engagement time by using uncomplicated observational instruments. Percentages can be determined for students' time-on-task during the observation period. Student engagement time—another term used to describe student on-task time—takes into consideration both teacher allocated time and the amount of time the students actually spend working on content during that period. Other methods that can be used to gather time-related information could include use of Flanders Interaction Analysis for quantitative time analysis of classroom interaction, time-on-task instruments, teacher notation of time at beginning and ending of instruction segments, student notation of time, teacher noting in plan book amount of time for each phase of instruction or time spent with certain students for several class periods. Observing academic learning time (high quality involvement) is more difficult unless the observer moves around the room and examines the students' output.

Beginning Class Efficiently

Developing a time sense will help teachers to engage in those practices that will encourage greater student involvement. For example, the practice of starting class promptly is an important one. Much time can be lost at the beginning of the class period or the beginning of a day in housekeeping tasks. The teacher should develop an efficient system in order to complete the housekeeping tasks in a few minutes. Roll must be checked quickly; perhaps a student can help. All materials should be ready to be handed out. Audiovisual equipment should be ready to turn on. All transparencies should be in order ready to be used. All demonstration and lab equipment should be prepared. The chalkboard can be used for information such as assignments, main points, diagrams. No time is taken up by organizational tasks that could have been accomplished prior to class.

Ending Class With Bell

The final minutes of class are susceptible to being a segment of wasted time. The on-task teacher reserves the right to signal the conclusion of the lesson, and establishes the expectation that students will remain on task until then. If left unsupervised, many students will close books 5 minutes prior to the end of class. With supervision, such as that demonstrated by Mrs. Trilby in which she was moving around the class interacting with students even as they left the room, the students are more likely to stay on task until class is over. To paraphrase a saying from baseball's Casey Stengel, the effective teacher makes sure that the class is not over until the class is over.

Supervising Practice

Close supervision during the practice part of the lesson when students are working on the material by themselves or starting their homework is important. Notice that Mrs. Trilby was modeling the behaviors needed to keep students on task during a practice time by moving around the room, checking on students who might have problems, and interacting with individuals and groups.

Noting Off-Task Behavior

Becoming a keen observer in the classroom is important in order to be able to pick up those signals that indicate off-task behaviors. Teachers need to recognize both verbal and nonverbal feedback from students that signal off-task behavior and call for teacher intervention with either control or instruction. Teachers need to remain aware of conditions throughout the room as they work with a group or an individual student. They need to move around the class so that they can observe carefully how and what students are doing. Notice in the scenario how Mrs. Trilby checked Tommy's behavior. She asked him a question about his progress to help him get back on track. She used nonverbal behavior by moving around the room and glancing over students' papers to keep them working while she monitored their progress.

Expressing Interest

Letting the student know that the teacher is interested in their progress can help motivate the child to work. The teacher can indicate that he or she will return later to examine a student's work. Note in the scenario that Mrs. Trilby communicated to certain students that she would be back to check on them. Stress applied to the appropriate students can encourage them to keep working. In the case of a student who does not work well under stress, this practice should not be used.

Increasing Teacher Interaction

Increasing teacher and student interaction is an important part of improving student involvement. Teachers need to engage in many instructional techniques such as directing, probing, testing, listening, inquiring, and giving feedback. Reducing the amount of time students spend with seatwork and increasing the teacher-student interaction should have an effect on student involvement. When working with the total class, the teacher can survey the entire class rapidly and frequently. Seating patterns need to be changed occasionally to provide the largest number of students the benefit of being in the front of the room. An attempt should be made to call on every student at least once a period. A student's question or answer can be referred to another student to maintain attention and encourage good listening. Enthusiasm demonstrated with voice and body movements will promote attention, as well. Using a variety of reinforcement techniques, the teacher will reward students for their participation. Indicating that material is important by writing it on the board or on a transparency helps the student attend to the important ideas of the lesson.

Controlling Transitions

Controlling transition times is important for maintaining a high level of on-task behavior. Transition times are those times between lessons or between passing out the papers and the next activity, those in-between times during which class attention wanders. By thinking ahead, beginning teachers can plan how they will handle these times. Will the students pass back the papers while the teacher moves around answering questions? Will the assignment for the math lesson be written on the board so that students can turn to the proper page while others are still getting books? These periods of time need careful consideration because much time can be lost moving from large group to small group, from reading to math activity, from concept development to concept practice. Transitions can be accomplished more smoothly by such activities as the teacher's writing directions for the day on the board; letting students know what objectives are to be accomplished for the class period or the day; and establishing rules and routines for transition activities such as passing out books, moving to different groups, and passing papers forward. Teachers also need to plan the use of students' free time to ensure that students have a variety of options such as reading books, going to the library, or playing a game.

Good directions can help teachers with transition times as well as other times when they are trying to maintain on-task behavior. Writing directions on the board whenever possible keeps the assignment in front of the students, enabling all students to know what is expected of them. Another key practice for giving good directions that every beginning teacher must learn is to wait to give directions until all eyes in the class are on the teacher, thus signaling the class's attention.

Using Affect

Using the affective domain to develop improved on-task behavior is important. Students will not cooperate readily if they do not respect the teacher. The teacher must have established within the room that climate that lets each child feel that the teacher is interested in him or her as a learner and as a person. This point was graphically brought home to one of the authors when she did a stint of practice teaching in a local high school to renew her teaching skills with teenagers. Replacing a favorite teacher with a stranger did not sit well with the students, nor did the author's attempts to keep the class of average general English students on-task throughout the period. Some of the students who resented the new teacher's constant prodding for on-task behaviors became hostile. This hostile climate encouraged more disruptions and frustrated the visiting "expert," to say the least. Only through attempts to get to know individual students and to have personal communication with them along with positive reinforcement of class contributions did the situation improve. The importance of developing a positive feeling between teacher and student in order to obtain the cooperation of the reluctant teenage students was brought home directly through this first-hand experience.

The teacher needs to develop a positive feeling within the student that he or she is responsible and capable of accomplishing the task. If a student must constantly be raising his or her hand to seek reassurance that the work is progressing correctly, both the teacher's and student's time is being wasted. The student must be made aware that the teacher will be available to help, as will the student's classmates, but the learner needs to accept responsibility for accomplishing the task.

To encourage the independent learner attitude toward productive use of time, teacher support of students' efforts is essential. The teacher can support positive feelings that increase student self-assurance with statements such as, "You have spent more time working in class today, Joe. Since you are becoming such a good worker, I have a fun activity for you to do near the end of the period tomorrow. I think you will like it." Or, "Since you have worked so well today, tomorrow you might like to work with your friends. I think you have proven that you can handle that situation."

Despite the use of all the above practices, some students may continue to have trouble staying on-task. The teacher needs to study those students to determine possible intervention measures (see Chapter 8). The teacher may check past rewards used with the student. An interview with the student, parents, or former teachers will help the teacher learn about the concentration problems and lead to possible solutions. The student may need different materials, different assignments, or different teacher techniques to help improve the proportion of on-task behaviors.

The above practices are described to emphasize the importance of keeping students on-task with meaningful learning experiences. The practices do not signify that a story cannot be read, a song sung, or laughter enjoyed. There is always room for fun and spontaneity in every learning situation. Such happenings can increase the students' sense of comfort and pleasure in a businesslike classroom environment. These practices are described to show a teacher who is in control and purposefully generating effective conditions for learning.

SUMMARY POINT

Increasing student and teacher on-task time is a complicated but important venture. The child's success rate with learning is dependent on it. Teachers need to examine the use of time to determine how much of the class period is spent in high quality, academic learning, and also to determine the point at which emphasis on on-task behaviors produces diminishing returns. Teachers' reflective, data-based decisions are needed to optimize the use of class time.

REVIEW: IMPORTANT PRACTICES TO INCREASE STUDENT INVOLVEMENT

Teacher Control of Time

1. Plan the allocation of time carefully for each part of the lesson.
2. Gather data on how much time is spent on each part of the lesson.
3. Start class promptly.
4. Plan effective closure to the lesson and keep students involved up to the end.
5. Increase the amount of time used in class for teacher-directed activities such as explaining, demonstrating, and giving feedback.
6. Plan smooth transitions from one activity to another.

Teacher Control of Student Involvement

1. Assess the amount of time each student is actively engaged in the lesson.
2. Supervise the practice part of lesson.
3. Encourage on-task behavior by becoming a keen classroom observer.
4. Work to increase student participation.
5. Encourage students to feel good about themselves as workers.

TOPIC 2: CONTENT COVERAGE

RESEARCH AND THEORETICAL BASE

The second effective teaching practice that influences student achievement is content coverage. It refers to the topics studied in terms of the appropriateness of the learning task for the learner, the curriculum, and the assessment. Given the background and prior learning of the student, the teacher must know if the materials are appropriate. The teacher must decide whether the student has the cognitive prerequisites necessary to learn the new materials. Students having the necessary prerequisite learnings are better able to learn new content and become more involved (Levin with Long, 1981; Bloom, 1976). The teacher often assumes that because a student has reached a certain grade level, the student has acquired the knowledge and skills necessary for learning content at that level. However, as any experienced teacher can attest, student test results and cumulative records provide ample evidence that shows that students differ considerably in their acquisition of content. Thus teachers need to know the extent of their students' prior learning in order to prepare them for present learning. Bloom (1976) emphasizes the importance of teachers' assessment of students' prior learning by citing that 80% of the variance in posttest scores may be accounted for by pretest scores alone. This means that a low-scoring student will continue to be unsuccessful unless the teacher bases instruction on what the student knows and can do now, regardless of grade level. The teacher must help the student break the habit of failure.

The second point the teacher must consider is the appropriateness of content to the tests to be administered. Obviously, students will experience greater gains in achievement if they have covered the content of the test (Brady et al., 1977). The Canterbury Studies (Wright & Nuthall, 1970) of elementary science teaching conducted over a decade indicated that content coverage is more important to achievement than particular teacher behaviors.

The amount of overlap between the content and the criterion-referenced testing instruments is closely linked to achievement gains. Research studies indicate that there can be considerable variance in overlap between what is taught and what is tested. Students in some classrooms covered an average of only 4% of content tested, while students in other classrooms covered an average of 95%.

Investigating the knowledge and skills students need in order to be suc cessful with the content is an important step to take in working toward more student success in learning, as is testing for objectives taught. Structuring and content with overviews, stating objectives, outlining content, and calling atten- tion to main ideas are important factors to consider in enhancing student learn- ings (Squires, Huitt, & Segars, 1983).

APPLICATION TO PRACTICE

Coverage involves decision making, particularly in the planning and evaluation stages. Questions the teacher must answer in planning in order to promote stu- dent success include: What must my students know in order to handle this material? What instructional level is this material on? What prerequisite skills must my students have? What are my students' present cognitive thinking abil- ity levels and skill development levels? What adjustments must be made to ac- commodate student differences? In order to answer these questions, the teacher can implement certain practices such as those described in the remainder of this section on coverage.

Learning Students' Needs

An effective teacher gathers information on these questions during the unit planning stage in order to arrive at that match of learner and content that can produce the best results. This means that at the beginning of the year the teacher takes time to gather important diagnostic information on the students beyond the achievement test scores and grade card reports available. Examination of their skill levels in reading, writing, and mathematics can be undertaken by informal tests such as listening to each one read aloud from books to be used in the course, asking comprehension questions after a reading, having students write a short one-to-three paragraph essay on a topic, and presenting students with basic mathematical function problems. Also the teacher can involve chil- dren in some basic thinking skills operations from categorizing to hypothesizing and problem solving in order to learn about their cognitive development. Al- though this process may take several days of instructional time, the knowledge gained concerning each student's level of acquisition of skills is essential for planning appropriate learning activities for that student.

Assessing Level of Materials

The teacher needs to know the instruction level of the materials being used. It is important to know the readability level of the textbook. This can be deter- mined by running a readability check with an instrument such as Fry's Read- ability Graph. Having students turn to a certain page in the text and list all the words they do not understand can provide a rough estimate of the appropri-

Figure 5.1 Fry's Readability Graph

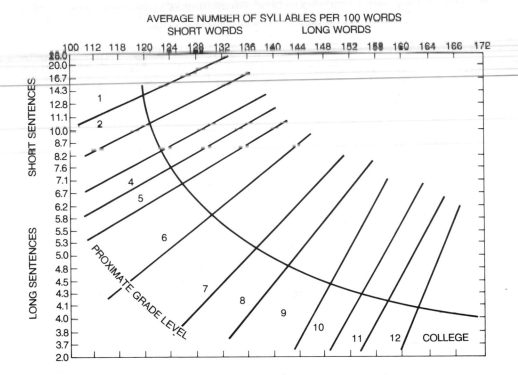

DIRECTIONS: Randomly select three 100-word passages from a book or an article. Plot the average number of syllables and the average number of sentences per 100 words on the graph to determine the grade level of the material. Choose more passages per book if great variability is observed to determine whether the book has uneven readability. Few books will fall in the gray area, but when they do, grade level scores are invalid.

EXAMPLE:

	SYLLABLES	SENTENCES
1st Hundred Words	124	6.6
2nd Hundred Words	141	5.5
3rd Hundred Words	158	6.8
AVERAGE	141	6.3

READABILITY 7th GRADE (see dot plotted on graph)

For further information and validity data, see the April, 1968 *Journal of Reading* and the March, 1969 *Reading Teacher*.

ateness of the book for that grade level also. More than five unknown words on a page may indicate the text is too difficult for that reader unless they are new terms specific to that area of study.

Analyzing Prerequisite Knowledge

When the teacher plans the beginning of the unit, he or she must take time to analyze the content regarding the skills and information the students must already have in order to be successful with the subsequent content. For example, for the purpose of introducing paragraphing, the teacher has to consider the information the student should have in order to be able to write paragraphs. An analysis would identify the following necessary prerequisites:

> Understanding the concept of a *sentence*
>
> Ability to write a complete sentence
>
> Ability to group common ideas together
>
> Ability to use punctuation and capitalization properly

If students can already perform these functions, they can learn to identify main ideas and provide supporting information to develop a paragraph.

Breaking down the content into the essential skills and information needed can be helpful in remediation to pinpoint the place where the student may be having the problem and what information must be learned before progress can take place.

After the teacher has analyzed the content concerning essential knowledge to know and perform, he or she checks on students' prior learning in this area to see if it is sufficient to learn the new skills and information. Again, a simple diagnostic test can be devised to check on acquisition of background knowledge. For example, taking the above unit on paragraphing, the teacher can give students lists of main ideas and supporting ideas and determine whether they can group them correctly. Also, students can be asked to write some sentences on a particular topic. From this information the teacher knows where to begin instructions, which students will need special attention and in which areas.

Some simple rules to follow in putting together a diagnostic instrument include the following: (1) keep the instrument brief—requiring no more than 30 minutes response time; (2) make it easy to administer with clear, simple directions and minimal equipment; (3) make it easy to score so that the teacher can see quickly by the student's answer that the student does or does not have the information or skill; (4) include a range of questions from simple to complex; (5) build in success by including at least one item that everyone can answer.

Individualizing Coverage

Although whole group instruction is being identified as the effective instructional approach to basic skill teaching, this does not mean that grouping should be abandoned. Rather it stresses that students achieve more in classes in which they spend more of their time being taught or supervised by their teachers than working on their own much of the class day or period (Brophy & Good, 1986). It emphasizes that the most efficient approach is to conduct a group lesson on the content with the teacher interacting with the whole class; later in the practice section of the lesson, different materials may be used with certain students, small groups may be brought together for further instruction, or peer teaching may take place. McGreal (1983) recommends that grouping to develop the basic skills of reading and mathematics is still essential. However, he suggests that teachers do not tie themselves up all morning in small group instruction that will keep them away from the whole group and from interaction with more individual students. Individualizing can be done at the practice level with materials and activities geared to the level of the student.

Remember Mrs. Trilby, who made a decision concerning coverage as she moved around the room during the practice period? She knew that Bill's reading and comprehension skills with the lesson would cause problems for him. Therefore, she modified the assignment to accommodate his problem by giving him more time to read, fewer questions to answer, and questions on the comprehension and application levels rather than higher cognitive level questions. She recognized that in order for Bill to experience some success in this assignment she would have to make some coverage changes.

Evaluating Coverage

The evaluation phase of coverage requires that the teacher test on the content that was taught. Tests should be composed from lesson and unit objectives. Certainly there should be a close fit between test content and lesson content.

If teachers are concerned about increasing student achievement on standardized tests, they must be familiar with the content assessed so that knowledge and skills can be covered in the curriculum. Teaching for a test is not heresy. If the knowledge examined in a standardized test is considered the appropriate knowledge for students in a district to learn, then teachers should cover much of that content. Certainly the competencies evaluated on basic competency tests must be carefully taught and retaught. If the school system demands that certain tests be taken, the system is indicating that the content of the tests is important and should be covered. (One would hope that each system devises its own testing program to evaluate the progress of its students toward meeting the designated goals and objectives of the school district.)

School districts can help teachers with coverage if curriculum guides are developed for each grade level and subject. These guides can indicate the content which is to be taught at that level and serve as the reference for the content of districtwide achievement tests. Furthermore, when textbook committees select a text they can choose that book which covers most of the content identified in the curriculum guide.

Individualizing tests to reflect a student's learning style and level is also important for student achievement. When assessment of a student's background knowledge reveals that he was not prepared to move into the next math unit, the student's math lessons could be different from those who have the necessary knowledge to handle the materials. The student should be given opportunities to learn the essential knowledge and then be retested until the results indicate that he has the knowledge to handle the new information. Without individual consideration, he would be doomed to failure.

SUMMARY POINT

Student achievement is related to teachers' ability to match the content taught with the content tested. The coverage of material—its appropriateness for the knowledge and skills of the learner and its appropriateness for testing instruments used—are essential points that affect student achievement success.

REVIEW: IMPORTANT CONTENT COVERAGE PRACTICES TO INCREASE STUDENT ACHIEVEMENT

Appropriateness of Material

1. Check on the instruction level of the materials used.
2. Analyze the content in relation to required background knowledge.
3. Give a pretest to check on necessary background knowledge.
4. Give a skill diagnostic test to students.
5. Administer a cognitive assessment test to check on students' level of mental operations.

Appropriateness of the Test

1. Compose tests from objectives covered.
2. Cover content assessed by achievement tests utilized in the district.
3. Individualize testing materials when possible to match the student's learning level.

TOPIC 3: PERFORMANCE SUCCESS

RESEARCH AND THEORETICAL BASE

The third effective teaching practice emerging from the research that influences student achievement is student success. As the saying goes, ''Nothing succeeds like success.'' It is not surprising that student success is considered to be one of the most important instructional variables (Bloom, 1976; Skinner, 1968). This section of effective teaching practices will examine the importance of student success and the ways teachers can promote success.

Performance success refers to the extent to which students can accurately complete their assignments (Squires, Huitt, & Segars, 1983). Completing a high percentage of items correctly contributes to the students' positive feelings toward their ability to learn the content. The more positively the students' view their capabilities in a subject, the better chance they have to be successful learners. Success rates in seatwork activities should be completed with 90% to 100% range. Such success is especially important in the early grades, when students are learning basic knowledge and skills (Brophy & Good, 1986).

Again, as experienced teachers realize, the range of success within a class can be considerable. The Beginning Teacher Evaluation Study (Fisher et al., 1978) examined success rates in second-grade classrooms that varied from students who had only 9% of their reading tasks correct or mostly correct to students who had 88% or higher. Math ranges in second grade were similar with a spread of from 2% to 92% (Squires, Huitt, & Segars, 1983).

Brookover and others (1981) have stressed that a student success factor needs to be built into the lessons. Teachers need to plan so that the material is at a level whereby all children can experience a generous measure of success. Teachers need to provide rewards for this success. The level of success appropriate to encourage each student's achievement may vary according to individual student characteristics (Crawford, 1978). Complete mastery of the content at the 100% level is not necessary. A lower optimal level of success can be reached at which achievement continues to improve.

SUMMARY POINT

The point to remember from this information is that the success students experience with their learning tasks is an important factor in influencing student achievement.

APPLICATION TO PRACTICE

Returning to the Laura Trilby scenario at the beginning of the chapter, one can note Laura's acknowledging the importance of success with tasks by changing Bill's questions to simpler comprehension level ones and reducing their number. She was also concerned about three other students' inability to read the material analytically. She may have to consider less complex material for them so that they can practice the skills and encounter success. She collected the classwork so that she could observe the success each student had with the assignment. She seemed well aware of the need for each student to experience success.

The practices described in this section are suggestions teachers can use when making decisions about ensuring success for each student.

Individualizing Learning Tasks

Steps that the teacher can take to ensure more student success include analyzing the student's ability to handle the material and, if necessary, making necessary adjustments in the assignment as Mrs. Trilby did. Gearing all assignments and activities to the middle ability range of children in the class is setting the stage for a wide variance in performance success. Keeping the range of abilities in mind, the teacher should plan some learning tasks that all students can handle with success. For students who experience difficulty with learning activities, teachers should plan activities that differ from the rest of the class's activities but which enable those students to achieve success at the 75% level.

In order to provide a variety of materials and experiences on the individual level, the teacher will need to develop a file of alternative activities and exercises on different difficulty levels that can be used for supplementary work. Old textbooks and workbooks with practice pages can be helpful. Each student should have a mixture of items that are difficult and items that are easily handled correctly. Imagine the defeat Bill, who is in Mrs. Trilby's room, feels if she does not make decisions that will help him experience success. How long will he want to continue trying if he cannot get through reading and his papers are marked −45, or −50, or 38% on a 100-point scale? Mrs. Trilby must structure the materials and assignments so that he can succeed, and will continue to keep on trying. If she does not, because of lack of time or lack of knowledge about individualizing, Bill may be condemned to a −45 or 38% forever.

Setting Performance Standards

Another factor in assuring students success concerns performance standards set by the teacher. Setting high standards is an important practice that was discussed in Chapter 2; however, standards cannot be set so high that they become impossible for some students to reach. Remember that it is not necessary for teachers to push for perfect performance. High standards alone will not produce better grades. The point is that the teacher needs to know the level at which students will experience difficulty, then plan that only 20% of the items will be at that difficulty level or beyond. This goal allows for success at the 70% to 75% level and still encourages more able students who want a challenge. Establishing appropriate standards for individual students is a demanding task for the teacher. However, the alternative—preordaining student failure—is unacceptable.

Reviewing

Planning review lessons occasionally, perhaps once or twice a month, helps the student retain the information and build on past successes with the content. Hunter (1983) suggested that new material needs to be remediated each day with short periods of practice, then reviewed once a week and then once a month. This approach to practice is mentioned here to remind teachers of the importance of review to improve retention and hence to improve the student's success through having an expanded knowledge foundation to build on.

Planned Catch-Up Day

Incorporating catch-up days into the calendar can be helpful for students to improve their chances of success. Students can get caught up on assignments, take makeup tests or retests, do more practice and drill work, enjoy enrichment activities, and receive more individual help. Success can take time and teachers must be willing to spend some time to help students experience it. A flexible calendar that can accommodate catch-up days will help promote success.

Rewarding Success

Other instructional practices that teachers may use to encourage student success involve the reward system. Giving appropriate rewards for success is important. Noting student progress both verbally and nonverbally can be done in many ways. Displaying successful papers in the room is rewarding. All students should have a successful paper on display sometime during the year. Sharing successful papers with the class by reading portions of student work emphasizes performance standards and rewards achievement. When handing back papers, the teacher can verbally acknowledge good work. Also, writing positive comments on all papers whenever possible is strong encouragement: "Excellent idea here"; "Paper shows considerable improvement because of correct spelling"; "Good try on that tough extra credit problem. You almost cracked it;" or "Super, Kim, you know your facts."

Giving Feedback

Giving consistent corrective feedback can encourage students because it does not reprimand but rather helps them see what is wrong and how it can be corrected. The student's response can be accepted positively and the incorrect information can be corrected with some probing help. For example, "Good job, Tom. Seven right this time. You're getting better each time. Reread the question for number eight and see if your answer corresponds to the question asked."

Monitoring daily work though checking homework and giving frequent quizzes and tests supplies students with feedback they need in order to see their progress. Teachers can plan conferences with their students. In this manner, each child knows the progress being made. The emphasis through using a self-referenced criterion is put on the student to compete with his own progress, not that of the class. During such a conference the teacher can ascertain the feelings the student has toward his or her progress, and plan additional measures to improve the success rate, if necessary.

SUMMARY POINT

Important variables that are linked to student achievement in schools classified as effective are those pertaining to the amount of time students spend on task; the coverage of materials in terms of their appropriateness for the learner and appropriateness for the testing instruments to be used; and the performance success of the students. Performance success refers to the extent to which students can accurately complete their assignments. Mastery of content at the 100% level is not necessary to ensure success. A lower optimal level of success at which achievement continues to improve can be reached.

REVIEW: IMPORTANT PRACTICES TO ENCOURAGE STUDENT SUCCESS

Planning

1. Plan learning tasks that make it possible for all students to achieve success.
2. Individualize learning tasks so that students can succeed.
3. Plan performance standards that are challenging but not defeating.
4. Plan periodic review lessons.

Feedback

5. Give appropriate rewards for success.
6. Recognize progress both verbally and nonverbally.
7. Give frequent progress reports.
8. Give corrective feedback, not negative feedback.
9. Monitor daily work.
10. Give frequent quizzes and tests.

TOPIC 4: FEEDBACK AND PRAISE

RESEARCH AND THEORETICAL BASE

The fourth key practice that influences student performance and achievement is teacher feedback. Teacher feedback is information given to students concerning the correctness, quality, and remediation of their performance.

Student feedback can provide the teacher with essential information that enables the teacher to adjust instruction. Teacher feedback is being examined in this fourth section. As Laura Trilby worked with her students during the practice phase of the lesson, she not only made decisions to keep students on task as much as was possible by her teacher behaviors, but she also made decisions to give feedback and recommend corrective procedures to as many students as possible. She decided to spend more time this period with those who needed special help such as Cindy (difficulty with interpreting reading material) and Bill and Mark (reading comprehension problems). She gave Bill a change in questions to accommodate his problems. She instructed four students who had completed the assignment to give feedback to others who were finished. She decided she would recheck all the papers later so that she could give everyone corrective feedback on this important phase of the content. She could hand back their papers before the quiz the next day so that they would have some time before the test to learn from the errors on their papers. As she moved around the room she could quickly spot problems, as she did with Joan, by helping her locate the source of the error so that Joan could make corrections.

Mrs. Trilby was making decisions about her teaching behaviors based on her understanding that feedback—and especially immediate feedback—was essential to the learning process. She also understood that identification of right and wrong items was not enough. Students must be able to see necessary corrective procedures. In many cases, Mrs. Trilby could give instructional cues through questioning so that students could locate errors themselves. With some students she would have to identify the problem for them and help them make corrections. Throughout the practice time she would be involved in the feedback process.

Bloom cited feedback as the teaching behavior most consistently related to student achievement. Feedback commonly means receiving knowledge of results (Bloom, 1976). However, knowing whether the response is right or wrong is not sufficient for learning. Levin with Long (1981) point out that many research studies demonstrate that knowledge of right and wrong answers alone has little or no effect on improving learning. In his theory of school learning, Bloom (1976) emphasized that the student needs to know the corrective procedures to be taken. When teachers are able to provide information about what is left to be learned and corrective measures for students' responses, instruction is more effective. Bloom stated that student learning is dependent on knowledge of results when that knowledge can be used for correction.

As Levin with Long (1981) detailed in *Effective Instruction*, effective feedback contains three components: (1) a definition of correctness or standard of performance to be met; (2) evidence indicating whether the standard was or was not achieved; (3) corrective procedures as to what must be relearned and how it is to be learned.

A study by Wentling (1973) supports the theory that students who receive feedback with corrective procedures reach higher levels of achievement. Another study by Levin (1979) provides similar substantiation for the importance of corrective feedback.

Since a major form of feedback teachers use is grades, it is important to realize that grades do not provide the student with all the feedback necessary for learning. Grades do indicate a standard of performance and the student's progress relative to that standard, but grades do not indicate the kinds of problems students are encountering or steps being taken to remediate those problems. Therefore, it is advisable at grading period times for the teacher to provide each student with corrective feedback as well as to help students increase learning.

APPLICATION TO PRACTICE

As the research literature and examined experience have confirmed, feedback is an essential practice for effective teaching. Anyone who has ever tried to learn a sport such as golf or tennis can identify the frustration one can experience as a learner if the teacher does not give feedback in the practice stage. The learner needs to know what he or she is doing correctly or incorrectly with the body when the results are hitting balls into the net, or missing the golf ball entirely. A person can be doomed to repeat the same errors unless one can learn how to make corrections. Feedback that announces that one has missed the golf ball or hit the tennis net is useless in helping a person achieve goals. One needs to know what corrective procedures to take. Similarly, the student who receives a test paper marked 55% knows that he or she has not done well, but what to do next remains a question. Meanwhile, some of the most useful functions of a test—to correct misunderstandings and guide future learning—are not realized. More informative feedback is necessary.

Three Parts of Effective Feedback

Effective feedback contains three pieces of information essential to the learner: (a) the standard of performance, (b) the student's progress toward meeting that standard; and (c) corrective procedures to be taken. Examples of effective feedback are the following: (Verbal) "John, your paper was graded a 65% because you missed so many of the problems with a decimal in the divisor. Let's go over the procedure for working with decimals in the divisor and then you can try this practice exercise to see if you understand it better." Example: (Written comments on student's paper) "Good work, Betty. B is a big improvement over your last paper. You show definite improvement in paragraph development. You were able to separate ideas and develop them into complete paragraphs. On your next paper work on supporting details for the topic sentence." Example: (Verbal) "Your quiz grade is 32%. Your problem seems to be that you didn't read the chapter carefully. Review your outline of the main ideas of the chapter, then reread the chapter. Let's try for a retest on Thursday."

It is important that students know the standards of performance prior to the evaluated activities. The teacher should write on the board the evaluation criteria for a project or examples of acceptable paragraphs or procedures to follow in writing up the lab report, as well as an indication of the level of achievement required for a passing mark.

A teacher using effective practice relates the student's score to the acceptable level of performance to be met. Some examples are: "John, 80% is expected; you received 65%." "The essay must have four complete paragraphs; you have only three, Betty." "70% is passing, Tony; you have a 75." Teachers generally provide this knowledge of results to their students. However, the next step is the critical one—indicating the problem areas and the practice steps to be taken. As an example: "Four errors in your paragraphs involved run-together sentences. I will give you some practice papers on writing and punctuating complete sentences that may help you with the problem." Now the feedback process is complete and provides the student with information that can promote learning.

Immediate Feedback

The effective teacher provides regular and immediate feedback. For example, teachers can give oral feedback during recitation and practice. "Everyone close your eyes. Now raise your hand if this response is correct." Madeline Hunter in her presentations on effective teaching techniques demonstrates an oral diagnostic technique that gives both the teacher and the students immediate feedback during a lesson. She asks the audience to raise one finger if they think the answer to a teacher question is *A* and two fingers if the answer is *B*. When over half the audience raised the wrong finger to answer a question, she remarked that she would have to give more practice on that phase of class instruction because they overlooked a key point. She knew they were confused. The audience knew that they had not interpreted correctly the point she was making and the situation they were examining on the screen. The immediate feedback let them know the technique they needed to re-examine.

Using a simple oral diagnostic tool such as Hunter's "raising fingers" response method is an example of effective and immediate feedback for both the students and the teacher. The teacher discovers whether the students are comprehending while also involving every student in the activity. Other examples include correcting all important assignments, suggesting corrective procedures, and returning papers promptly. Giving frequent quizzes and tests is an important feedback measure and should be used for remediation. Requiring students to make corrections on graded assignments and to return them to the teacher for correction verification can assure the teacher that the students have examined their problem spots and have made the appropriate modifications.

Peer and Self-Evaluation of Papers

All this feedback can mean mounds of paper for the teacher to examine. Using peer and self-evaluation of papers by the students can be an effective technique as long as the students understand the evaluation criteria. Putting students into small groups of two or three and encouraging them to evaluate each other's work can be valuable for all concerned if students have learned how to handle that responsibility. Teachers can teach their students the procedures for peer and self-evaluation. Students from the 4th grade upward should be able to handle this type of group learning experience well as long as the teacher has indicated precisely what is required of the group. Having a chance to examine each other's work and receive help from a peer can be beneficial. Teachers can use small groups for peer instruction as well as for feedback. Students can teach each other the main ideas or check each other on vocabulary words, compare responses with the teacher's answer sheet, and help each other with corrections and remediation practice. Student feedback and instruction can be effective teaching tools.

The teacher plays a facilitator role during this experience in which he or she moves among the groups keeping them on-task, assessing how productively the groups are working, answering questions, and giving judgments when the group is confused and requests a teacher judgment.

Allowing students to self-check their papers is a good device to promote independence in the student and free the teacher to work with individuals. The teacher must learn quickly by observation which students abuse the privilege of marking their own papers and which ones can handle the task responsibly. Self-checking supplies the student with immediate feedback from which the student can decide whether to proceed or to continue on the current topic or skill.

Student checking does not relieve the teacher entirely from the responsibility of examining student papers. The teacher will need to check student papers in order to learn where errors are occurring. With that information the teacher then makes decisions concerning reteaching, regrouping, or moving the class along to the next unit.

Reinforcement, Praise and Criticism

Other forms of feedback used by teachers are praise and reinforcement—the rewarding of desired student performance—and criticism—the reprimanding or correcting of student performance. The use of praise and criticism should be considered carefully by the teacher as factors having an effect on the climate of the classroom and the self-concept of the individual student. The amount of praise used by the average teacher is between 1% and 2% of total classroom interaction time. Criticism is used twice as much as praise (Amidon & Flanders, 1967). Reinforced feedback is important for the development of student self-confidence and motivation. Criticism is linked negatively to these learning factors. Studies describe criticism as impairing learning because it decreases motivation and damages self-esteem (Levin with Long, 1981). Brookover (1979) found that teachers in effective classrooms used more positive reinforcement to encourage student achievement and used it on a consistent basis. In summarizing the research on effective schools, the *Encyclopedia of Educational Research* (Mitzel, 1982) pointed out that in the more effective classrooms pupils received more praise and fewer criticisms.

Brophy and Good (1986) in summarizing research on academic praise found weak but positive correlations tying praise to achievement, particularly for younger and lower ability students. A caution needs to be raised here because researchers have discovered that teachers can use reinforcement and praise to control students' behavior. Students can be made to feel insecure and dependent on the teachers' feedback if the praise becomes necessary for every student action to ensure the student that he is progressing satisfactorily. Therefore, the teacher should understand his or her use of reinforcement and its intended result. Also, if teachers can reinforce by praising every student response, participation is rewarded but encouragement for quality of response is neglected.

Two major points that come from the literature concerning reinforcement and/or criticism emphasize that students should understand the reason for any given reinforcement and that students should know when and how to modify behavior where appropriate (Levin with Long, 1981). Stallings' (1983) research showed that effective teaching behaviors are those that acknowledge or praise correct responses and probe to help the students examine incorrect responses. Another point from the research is that praise is not necessarily beneficial and more is not necessarily better. It may even be intrusive. Judicious and informed use of praise is recommended (Brophy & Good, 1986).

Effective Practice With Praise and Criticism

When giving feedback to students, teachers are likely to include words of praise and reinforcement or criticism. Both are important psychological tools and must be used carefully by the effective teacher. Praise can encourage the development of a positive self-concept which should increase a student's motivation to learn, to participate, and to become more self-directed. Reinforcement can take many forms. It can range from praise using one word such as "good" or "great," to using student ideas, to nonverbal types such as a smile or pats on the back. Similarly, criticism can range from verbal chastisement because of failure to perform well to nonverbal looks of disgust and annoyance. Suggestions on how to use both reinforcers and criticism more effectively to encourage student progress are offered below.

Reinforcement Praise. Reinforcement and praise that benefit the student the most are referenced specifically to the condition or product of merit. Example: "Good work in our discussion today, Jim. Your comments related very well to last night's reading assignment to the international trade question I asked today. You provided a good model for the other students to follow in the way you handled the question." And, "Sally has an excellent picture here because she kept the outline of the tree but within the tree drew a number of different scenes telling a story. She was very creative." The other characteristic of effective praise is that the praise includes use of the student's ideas. This type of reinforcement acknowledges that the student's contribution is important, thus encouraging more student involvement, acceptance by the teacher, and a stronger feeling of self-worth. Example: "Good idea, Carlos. Carlos calls our attention to the fact that Mrs. Bennett may not have wanted to accept the money at first. Is there any evidence of her reluctance that you can find in the story, class?"

Using Student Ideas

A powerful reinforcer that Flanders (1970) brought to our attention through his Analysis of Classroom Behavior instrument is his third category, acknowledging the use of student ideas. This reinforcer indicates to the student that his ideas are important enough to be mentioned and studied. The impact is greater than the perfunctory use of a one-word reinforcer such as "good." Rosenshine and Furst (1971) indicated five ways teachers can use student ideas when verbal interaction is taking place in class.

1. *Acknowledging* a student's contribution by repeating the response aloud to the class with the student's name. Example: "Sue said the number is brought to the right-hand side."

2. *Modifying* a student's contribution by putting it into different words to make it more understandable without changing the student's ideas. Example: "I believe you implied, Barry, that the gross national product is not an accurate measure of the economy's health. Is that right?"

3. *Applying* the student's response to some situation; or using it as an explanation for some event. Example: "Remember when Carmen told us that Jack's decision to leave before Todd came home with the news could get Jack into some trouble? Well, here is the trouble."

4. *Comparing* the student's response to something in the text or the lesson, or to a similar event. Example: "Julie said the word was used as an adverb. Let's look in our books on page 37 to see how an adverb can be used and see if we agree with Julie."

5. *Summarizing* a student's contributions and using them to make a point. Example: "After examining the comments that Jack, Della, and Carlos just made, I think they may be saying essentially the same thing—that nuclear disarmament plans are meaningless unless they include all nations with nuclear capabilities. This is an important point to consider. Let's examine what it means."

Using Verbal and Nonverbal Reinforcers

Teachers need to guard against the overuse of certain words for praise, which thereby lose their impact. Teachers need to plan a list of reinforcement words they can use, and also plan nonverbal reinforcers such as displaying student work, smiling, nodding, and patting on the back. Both aspects of praise, verbal and nonverbal, need to be used purposefully by teachers.

REINFORCEMENT WORDS	NONVERBAL REINFORCERS
"Well done. You have . . . "	smile and eye contact
"Excellent idea or response.	nod
Let's see how that fits	pat on back
into what we have said . . ."	paper displayed in room
"Good work"	choosing student for important job
"Bravo"	
"Fine"	using student's work as model
"Outstanding"	finger signal—O for OK
"Right on target."	putting student response on the board
"Let's examine the idea Tim	
just gave us to see . . . "	nodding head and listening
"Rosa's answer was correct.	with direct eye contact
Can you add more information to it?"	symbols of approval—stickers, stars, etc.
"Good point—that is the key idea."	

A note of warning is in order concerning nonverbal feedback. Many studies of nonverbal behavior have substantiated that nonverbal communication "speaks" louder than verbal. A student will acknowledge messages from a teacher's facial expressions over any spoken messages the teacher may send verbally. Therefore, it is important for teachers to be aware of the use of nonverbal feedback for praise or criticism because a teacher's "body language" is sending out evaluative nonverbal messages much of the time. Examples of nonverbal behavior that send negative messages to students can include ones such as the teacher's unwillingness to touch a student of a different race; teacher not making eye contact with certain students; teacher only sending scowling messages to selected students; teacher seldom calling on certain students; teacher not bending over a desk or moving to a student's desk to offer help.

Cautions Regarding the Use of Praise

Praise also needs to be used discriminately. All students need some praise; some students need more praise and encouragement than others. Better academic students need less praise, slower achieving students need more.

Less well understood is the fact that praise can be detrimental as well. Teachers need to scrutinize their use of praise as a controlling device to be sure that they are not limiting students by praising only those behaviors that reflect the teacher's thinking and ideas. Reinforcement also needs to be given to those students who, at times, display creativity and challenge conventional thinking. Furthermore, praise that is given too quickly or routinely can block the development of student ideas and critical thinking. In short, praise needs to be individualized and adjusted for the situation. The teacher must try to learn the acceptance and encouragement needs of each student and respond to each student accordingly.

Effective Praise

A useful set of guidelines for effective praise was developed by Jere Brophy (1981). It is especially helpful because it contrasts effective and ineffective praise.

EFFECTIVE PRAISE

1. is delivered contingently

2. specifies the particulars of the accomplishment
3. shows spontaneity, variety, and other signs of credibility; suggests clear attention to the student's accomplishment
4. rewards attainment of specified performance criteria (which can include effort criteria, however)

INEFFECTIVE PRAISE

1. is delivered randomly or unsystematically
2. is restricted to global positive reactions
3. shows a bland uniformity that suggests a conditioned response made with minimal attention
4. rewards mere participation without consideration of performance processes or outcomes

5. provides information to students about their competence or the value of their accomplishments

6. orients students toward better appreciation of their own task-related behavior and thinking about problem solving

7. uses students' own prior accomplishments as the context for describing present accomplishments

8. is given recognition of noteworthy effort or success at difficult (for this student) tasks

9. attributes success to effort and ability, implying that similar successes can be expected in the future

10. fosters endogenous attributions (students believe that they enjoy the task and/or want to develop task-relevant skills)

11. focuses students' attention on their own task-relevant behavior

12. fosters appreciation of, and desirable attributions about, task-relevant behavior after the process is completed

5. provides no information at all or gives students information about their status

6. orients students toward comparing themselves with others and thinking about competing

7. uses the accomplishments of peers as the context for describing students' present accomplishments

8. is given recognition without regard to the effort expended or the meaning of the accomplishment

9. attributes success to ability alone or to external factors such as luck or (easy) task difficulty

10. fosters exogenous attributions (students believe that they expend effort on the task for external reasons—to please the teacher, win a competition or reward, etc.)

11. focuses students' attention on the teacher as an external authority who is manipulating them

12. intrudes into the ongoing process, distracting attention from task-relevant behavior

Written comments on papers are an important form of feedback and can offer praise or criticism. Using comments to establish communication with individuals can be a valuable technique for the teacher. They communicate to the student that the teacher is concerned enough to write a message. After surveying a number of studies on the effects of written comments, Levin with Long (1981) emphasize the importance of making comments specific so that students know which response to continue and which areas need to be improved or relearned. Example: ''This is not one of your better tests, Rosy. You must have been tired. Notice that you missed four questions because you copied the numbers wrong. You did not appear to know the main points of the chapter. See me and let's schedule a retest.''

Using Criticism

Criticism as feedback does need to be considered. There are times when criticism may be appropriate to change the behavior of a student. However, if the criticism is continually repeated, it loses its impact and creates negative feelings. Some points to remember concerning the use of criticism are:

1. Reference it to the action or product that is not acceptable.
2. State the reason it is not acceptable.
3. Indicate what the student can do about it.
4. Get back to a pleasant tone with that student as soon as possible.
5. Never criticize the student, only the action. Example: "Combing your hair during class is unacceptable, Shirley. It disrupts the people around you and I suspect you aren't getting much done, either. Please keep your comb in your purse while you are here. Now, I see you have a good topic sentence written. Do you need any help to proceed with the paragraph?" Example of ineffective criticism: "You are always stirring up trouble in that corner, Peter. I am sick and tired of your disturbance. Get to work!" Such statements may release tension for the teacher but do not help the student because they do not contain any of the recommendations for constructive criticism.

SUMMARY POINT

Effective feedback regardless of its form (grades, verbal criticism, or written comments) includes reference to the standard or objective to be met, the results the student achieved in meeting the standard, and the corrective steps to be taken and the practice to be used. Reinforcement that most benefits the student references specifically to the condition or product of merit, and, when appropriate, includes the use of the student's ideas.

REVIEW: IMPORTANT FEEDBACK PRACTICES

1. Inform students of performance and specified criteria.
2. Provide various types of criteria for different students with varying abilities.
3. Provide both feedback and corrective procedures.
4. Provide constant and immediate feedback.
5. Provide oral feedback during practice and reaction segments.
6. Provide additional materials and sources for further study.

REINFORCEMENT AND IMPORTANT PRAISE PRACTICES

1. Use positive reinforcement to encourage students.
2. Use praise that is referenced to the condition of merit.
3. Use praise that includes student's ideas.
4. Use a variety of reinforcers.
5. Recognize that all students need some praise—some more than others.

ACTIVITIES FOR PRESERVICE TEACHERS

ACTIVITY I: FEEDBACK

1. Observe amount of feedback a teacher gives students. Keep a feedback record over two or three visits. Record the following:

Feedback Incidents	Type: Verbal or Nonverbal/Written	Corrective Procedures Given	Support Established
1. recitation	1. verbal-incorrect answers	1. none	1. listened to John's answer
2. individual practice	2. verbal	2. yes	2. provided help
3.	3.	3.	
4.	4.	4.	
5.	5.	5.	
6.	6.	6.	
7.	7.	7.	
8.	8.	8.	

Analysis: Explain what you have learned about the teacher's feedback behaviors from doing this analysis.

2. Interview two students from a class to discover the following:
   a. What papers were returned from the teacher over the last 2 weeks?
   b. Were corrective procedures indicated on papers as well as a grade?
   c. Did the papers contain comments?
   d. What kinds of feedback comments are helpful to students?

3. Write or explain the feedback you would give students on the following responses:

   a. Situation: Spelling test segment

Sample from Student's Paper	Student Grade	Teacher Feedback
receive	55%	
tomatos		
mans		
deers		

   b. Situation: Produce an outline for a composition on careers

Student Response	Student Grade	Teacher Feedback
military	unsatisfactory	
engineer		
computers		

Student Response	Student Grade	Teacher Feedback
doctors		
art field		
programmers		
health care		
creative work		
graduate school		

c. Situation: Exercises on adding whole numbers, mixed numbers, and fractions

Student Response	Student Grade	Teacher Feedback

$$
\begin{array}{ll}
2\ 5/6 & = 40/48 \\
+\ 10\ 1/8 & = \ \ 6/48 \\
\hline
12 & 46/48 = 12\ 23/24
\end{array}
$$

30%

$$
\begin{array}{ll}
13\ 3/5 & = 21/35 \\
+\ \ 5\ 2/7 & = 10/35 \\
\hline
18 & 31/35
\end{array}
$$

$$
\begin{array}{ll}
13\ 3/4 & = 30/40 \\
+\ \ 1\ 3/10 & = 12/40 \\
\hline
14 & 42/40 = 21/20
\end{array}
$$

ACTIVITY II: FEEDBACK ANALYSIS

To become more aware of feedback that you give, keep a feedback record over several days. Audiotape or videotape a practice or recitation session. In playback focus on your feedback using these criteria:

Tape Analysis Criteria	Tally Each Time Heard or Observed
Standard of performance mentioned	_____
Oral feedback given	_____
Corrective procedures discussed	_____
Supportive and/or encouraging tone used	_____
Student receiving feedback	_____
Nonverbal feedback given (video)	_____
Time for Practice Session: _____	_____

Analysis: Are you satisfied with amount of feedback given? Are you satisfied that you are giving corrective procedures along with feedback? What steps will you take to improve feedback?

ACTIVITY III: COVERAGE

This activity provides the learner the experience of analyzing content relating to the skills required to reach an objective and the knowledge needed to achieve the objective.

Example

Objective: To write paragraphs using correct form.

Skills Required	Knowledge Required	Diagnostic Test to be Used
Write complete sentence	Understanding of sentence	Write one paragraph on "What I Like About Me"
Use punctuation marks		
Group items according to topics	Topic sentence	
Pick out main idea	Punctuation marks	
Pick out supporting ideas	Main and supporting ideas and details	
Write supporting ideas and details		
Spelling and dictionary skills		

Practice Exercise, Skills and Knowledge Required for Unit

Unit Topic:

Main Objectives:

Skills Required	Knowledge Required	Diagnostic Tests

ACTIVITY IV: PERFORMANCE

1. Compute an average for each of your three lowest students in one subject level to determine each student's success level. (Average all grades in that subject for one student.) Make plans to increase each student's success level by at least ten percentage points within the next two weeks by changing the level of difficulty of material, by changing the amount of feedback and individual assistance, or by changing the amount of time the student spends on the subject.
2. List below the practices you have used to encourage students during the last two weeks.

APPENDIX: SELF-EVALUATION AND CHECKLIST FOR EFFECTIVE TEACHING PRACTICES

This rating sheet can be used to assess the extent to which the teacher is using effective teaching practices. It is designed for both supervisory use and self-examination.

TIME-ON-TASK

Directions:

Circle the appropriate number reflecting what was observed during the lesson. (1) Never, (2) Seldom, (3) Half the time, (4) Most of the time, (5) Always.

a. Teacher is aware of amount of time spent each period by students being actively involved.   1 2 3 4 5

b. Teacher actively monitors practice portion of lesson.   1 2 3 4 5

c. Teacher starts class promptly and uses time fully for learning activities.   1 2 3 4 5

d. Teacher is aware of verbal and nonverbal feedback that indicates students are off-task.   1 2 3 4 5

e. Teacher organizes class procedures so that they can be accomplished quickly and efficiently   1 2 3 4 5

f. Teacher uses a variety of practices to increase student participation.   1 2 3 4 5

g. Teacher studies those students who have difficulty staying on-task to determine measures that can be taken to help them.   1 2 3 4 5

APPROPRIATE CONTENT COVERAGE

a. Teacher knows the ability levels of the students.   1 2 3 4 5

b. Teacher knows the instruction level of materials being used.   1 2 3 4 5

c. Teacher is able to identify the skills and information needed to be successful with the content.   1 2 3 4 5

d. Teacher knows if students' prior learning is sufficient to learn new content.   1 2 3 4 5

e. Teacher's tests cover objectives taught.   1 2 3 4 5

f. Teacher is able to individualize content to fit students' differences in learning and cognitive development.   1 2 3 4 5

PERFORMANCE SUCCESS

a. Teacher plans learning tasks in which all students can encounter some success.   1 2 3 4 5

b. Teacher allows students time to become successful.   1 2 3 4 5

c. Teacher gives corrective feedback.	1	2	3	4	5
d. Teacher gives consistent rewards for success.	1	2	3	4	5
e. Teacher gives frequent progress reports obtained from tests and quizzes.	1	2	3	4	5

FEEDBACK

a. Teacher provides constant and immediate feedback on written work, oral discussion, and recitation.	1	2	3	4	5
b. Teacher encourages students to provide feedback.	1	2	3	4	5
c. Teacher lets students know what the standard of performance is, how student fared in trying to meet the standard, what corrective procedures are to be taken.	1	2	3	4	5
d. Teacher uses a variety of verbal and nonverbal behaviors for praise.	1	2	3	4	5
e. Teacher specifically references the student response being praised to the reasons why it is appropriate; inappropriate responses are handled similarly.	1	2	3	4	5
f. Teacher specifically references the student behavior being criticized to the reasons why it is inappropriate and what student needs to do to change it.	1	2	3	4	5
g. Teacher establishes a positive feeling tone with criticized student later.	1	2	3	4	5
h. Teacher includes use of student ideas as a reinforcement technique.	1	2	3	4	5

Total practices observed ______________________

APPENDIX: INTERACTION INSTRUMENT

DIRECTIONS

This data on the seating chart are to be collected throughout the selected class period. The seating chart on page 189 may be redrawn to fit the chair arrangement in the room. Each time a student or the teacher speaks to an individual student, a mark is placed on that student's seat block.

STUDENT VERBAL BEHAVIOR

↓ Student responds to teacher's interaction: "The answer is right."

⊖↓ Student does not respond or doesn't know: "I don't know."

↑ Student initiates, or asks a question or expands on an answer beyond more than is expected, "I think Mark Twain meant something different there from what you pointed out, Mrs. Jones."

⊖↑ Student initiates an off-task question or statement.

These data can help teachers see to whom they are speaking and the nature of the interaction. It will also provide a frequency count of the questions asked, praise given, reprimands, etc. If the classroom seating takes a different form from the seating chart, or if, for example, the tables are arranged in a horseshoe formation instead of rows of desks, then the seating chart should be redrawn to conform to the actual classroom arrangement. The important thing is to get each student's name in the right place on the seating chart.

TEACHER INITIATES

?   Teacher asks a student a knowledge level question: "Johnny, what is the spelling of the word 'voyage'?"

↗   Teacher asks a higher-level cognitive question: "Eric, how would you compare those two responses to the situation?"

⊘   Teacher asks student an open-ended, thought-provoking question: "Ursula, what do you think will happen next in this story?"

✓   Teacher checks for understanding: "Tell us in your words, Maria, what photosynthesis means."

TEACHER RESPONDS

+   Teacher praises or supports a response: "Very good, Jose, 42 is the correct answer."

C   Teacher corrects a student's response: "No, Barbara, that is wrong."; or "The correct answer should have been 'Mark Twain'."

G   Teacher corrects *and guides* a response: "Janice, try spelling the word one letter at a time, according to how it sounds, and see if you can figure it out."

—   Teacher reprimands behavior: "Martin, be quiet!"

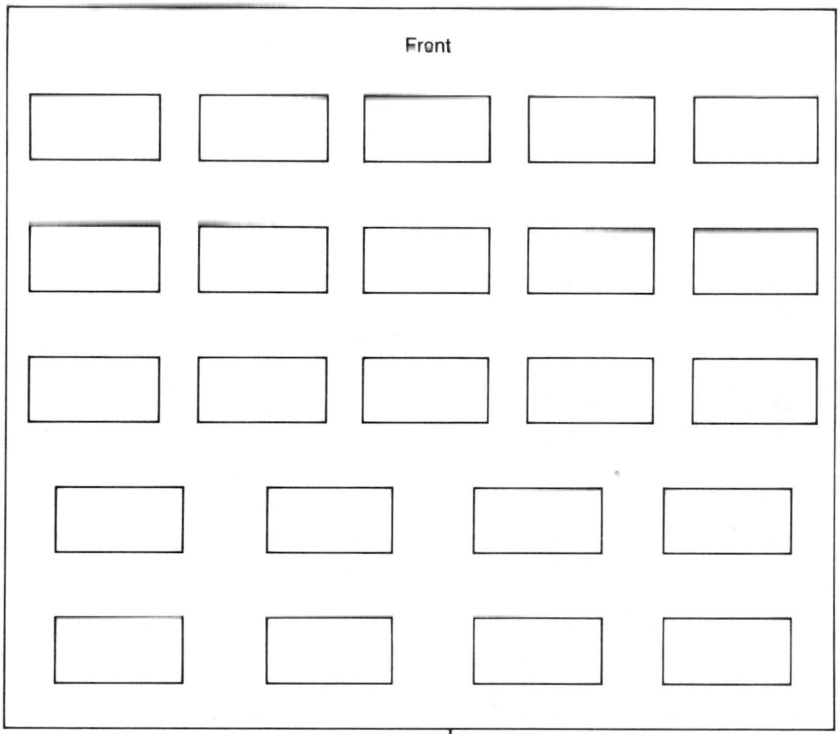

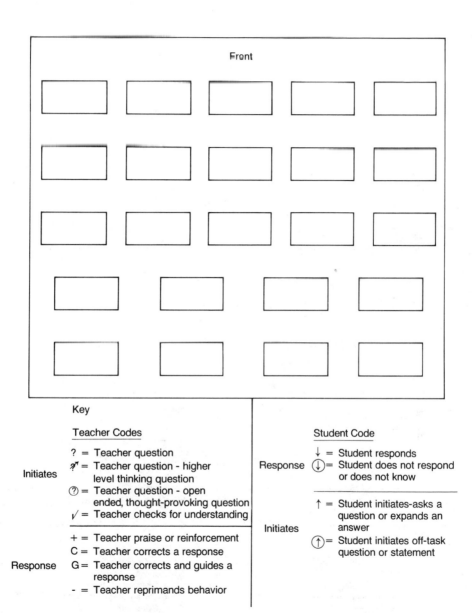

Key

Teacher Codes

Initiates
- ? = Teacher question
- ?↗ = Teacher question - higher level thinking question
- ⓘ(?) = Teacher question - open ended, thought-provoking question
- √ = Teacher checks for understanding

Response
- + = Teacher praise or reinforcement
- C = Teacher corrects a response
- G = Teacher corrects and guides a response
- - = Teacher reprimands behavior

Student Code

Response
- ↓ = Student responds
- (↓) = Student does not respond or does not know

Initiates
- ↑ = Student initiates-asks a question or expands an answer
- (↑) = Student initiates off-task question or statement

APPENDIX: STUDENTS OFF-TASK SEATING CHART
(Adapted from Stallings-Teaching Learning Institute)

Directions:

Observe entire class every 5 minutes. Code all off-task behavior in seat blocks. Then make a slash mark and show what the student was supposed to be doing.

Count number of times you sweep (observe) class. A summary of the percent of students off-task can be found by using this formula:

$$\frac{\text{the sum of the number of students off-task for each observation}}{\text{the number of students} \times \text{the number of sweeps}}$$

Teacher ——————   Date ————————

Grade ————————   Time ——————

Number of Sweeps: ——————

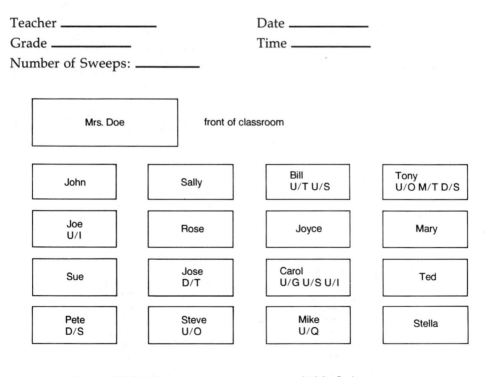

Mrs. Doe	front of classroom

John	Sally	Bill U/T U/S	Tony U/O M/T D/S
Joe U/I	Rose	Joyce	Mary
Sue	Jose D/T	Carol U/G U/S U/I	Ted
Pete D/S	Steve U/O	Mike U/Q	Stella

Students Off-Task key

S = Socializing
U = Uninvolved or Waiting
D = Disruptive
M = Moving Around Room
P = Personal Needs

Activity Codes

I = Instruction
O = Organizing, Directions
S = Seatwork
O = Oral Reading
G = Group Work
Q = Question, Answer
T = Transition - Changing to
    Another Activity

APPENDIX: ''P'' RATIO GRID

Directions: Take 10 samples of behavior from the same 10 students at fairly close intervals. Compute P ratio from these samples. In the course of a week cover all students. In the example, notice that Suzy was participating 6 out of 10 times. Dividing 6/10, her P ratio is 60%.

School _____   Date _____

Observer _____   Time _____

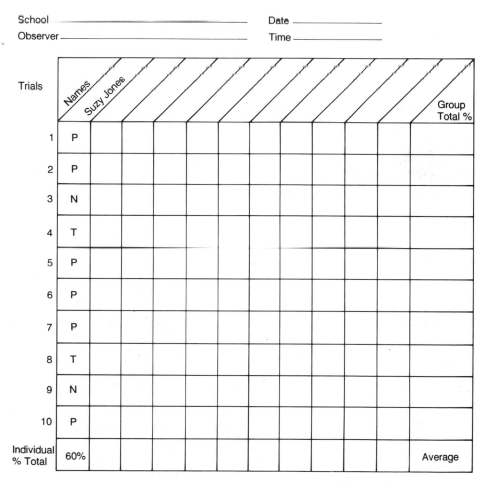

Trials	Names Suzy Jones										Group Total %
1	P										
2	P										
3	N										
4	T										
5	P										
6	P										
7	P										
8	T										
9	N										
10	P										
Individual % Total	60%										Average

P = Participating (actively involved in learning)
N = Not participating (talking, dawdling)
T = Transient (getting new materials, answer keys, etc.)
P ratio is P/10

APPENDIX: VIDEOTAPE OBSERVATION

DIRECTIONS: Check the criteria listed below with an X from your observation of the videotape. 1 is unsatisfactory; 2 below average; 3 average; 4 above average; 5 outstanding.

	1	2	3	4	5
1. Voice	—	—	—	—	—
2. Speech	—	—	—	—	—
3. Energy and vitality	—	—	—	—	—
4. Eye contact with all students	—	—	—	—	—
5. Use of teaching aids (maps, board, etc.)	—	—	—	—	—
6. Class participation	—	—	—	—	—
7. Ability to hold interest of class	—	—	—	—	—
8. Amount of time teacher talked	—	—	—	—	—
9. Use of praise or encouragement	—	—	—	—	—
10. Use of student ideas	—	—	—	—	—
11. Variety of questions asked (memory, convergent, divergent, evaluative)	—	—	—	—	—
12. Efforts to make lesson concrete	—	—	—	—	—
13. Use of directions or orders	—	—	—	—	—
14. Amount of criticism used	—	—	—	—	—
15. Amount of pupil response to teacher questions	—	—	—	—	—
16. Amount of pupil initiated talk	—	—	—	—	—
17. Class discipline	—	—	—	—	—
18. Class climate	—	—	—	—	—
19. Objective of lesson clear	—	—	—	—	—
20. Evaluation of class on the basis	—	—	—	—	—

REFERENCES

Alschuler, A., Dacus, J., & Atkins, S. (1975). Discipline, justice, and social literacy in the junior high school. *Meforum, 2,* 48–51.

Amidon, E. & Flanders, N. (1967). *The role of the teacher in the classroom.* Minneapolis, MN: Association for Productive Teaching.

Anderson, L. (1973). *Time and school learning.* Unpublished doctoral dissertation, University of Chicago.

Anderson, L, & Scott, C. (1978). The relationship among teaching methods, student characteristics, and student involvement in learning. *Journal of Teacher Education, 29.*

Block, J. (1970). *The effects of various levels of performance on selected cognitive, affective and time variables.* Doctoral dissertation, University of Chicago.

Bloom, B. (1976). *Human characteristics and student learning.* New York: McGraw-Hill.

Brady, M., Clinton, D., Sweeney, J., Peterson, M., & Poynor, H. (1977). *Instructional dimensions study.* Washington, D.C.: Kirschner Associates.

Brookover, W., Beady, C., Flood, P., Schweitzer, J., & Wisenbaker, J. (1979). *School social systems and student achievement: Schools can make a difference.* New York: Praeger.

Brophy, J. (1981). Teacher praise: A functional analysis. [Review of Educational research]. American Educational Research Association, 5–32.

Brophy, J. & Good, T. (1986). Teacher behavior and student achievement. In M. Wittrock (Ed.), *Handbook of Research on Teaching* (3rd ed.) New York: Macmillan.

Bushnell, D., Wrobel, P., & Michael, M. (1968). Applying 'group' contingencies to the classroom study behavior of preschool children. *Journal of Applied Behavioral Analysis, 1,* 56–61.

Chadwick, B. & Day, R. (1971). Systematic reinforcement: Academic performance of underachieving students. *Journal of Applied Behavioral Analysis, 4,* 311–319.

Conant, E. (1973). *Teacher paraprofessional work productivity.* Lexington, MA: Heath.

Crawford, J. (1978). Interactions of learner characteristics with the difficulty level of instruction. *Journal of Educational Psychology, 70*(4), 523–531.

Cusick, P. (1973). *Inside high school: The students' world.* New York: Holt, Rinehart and Winston.

Dishaw, M. (1977). *Descriptions of allocated time to content areas for the A-B period.* BTES Technical Note Series. (Technical Note IV-2a). San Francisco: Far West Laboratory for Educational Research and Development.

Fisher, C. W., Felby, W., Marliane, R., Cahen, L., Dishaw, M., Moore, J., & Berliner, D. (1978). Teaching behaviors, academic learning time and student achievement: Final report of phase 111-13. *Beginning teacher evaluation study.* San Francisco: Far West Laboratory for Educational Research and Development.

Flanders, N. (1970). *Analyzing teaching behavior.* Reading, MA: Addison-Wesley.

Good, T. & Beckerman, T. (1978). Time on task: A naturalistic study in sixth-grade classroom. *The Elementary School Journal, 78,* 193–201.

Hecht, L. (1977). *Isolation from learning supports and the processing of group instruction.* Unpublished doctoral dissertation, University of Chicago.

Hops, H. & Cobb, J. (1972). *Survival behaviors in the educational setting: Their implications for research and intervention.* Eugene, OR: Department of Special Education, University of Oregon.

Hunter, M. (1983). *Improved instruction.* El Segundo, CA: TIP Publications.

Kounin, J. & Gump, P. (1974). Signal systems of lesson settings and the task-related behavior of preschool children. *Journal of Educational Psychology, 66*(4), 554–562.

Lahaderne, H. (1968). Attitudinal and intellectual correlates of attention: A study of four classrooms. *Journal of Educational Psychology, 59*(5), 320–324.

Levin, T. (1979). Instruction which enables students to develop higher mental processes. In Choppin, B. and Postlesthwaite, N. (eds.), *Evaluation in education: An international review series.* Elmsford, NY: Pergamon Press.

Levin, T. with Long, R. (1981). *Effective instruction.* Alexandria, VA: Association for Supervision and Curriculum Development.

McGreal, T. (1983). *Effective schools and effective teachers.* Speech given at national meeting of the Association for Supervision and Curriculum Development. (Tape No. 612-20322).

Mitzel, H. (ed.). (1982). *Encyclopedia of Educational Research* (5th ed.). New York: Free Press (Division of Macmillan), American Educational Research Association.

Perkins, H. (1965). Classroom behavior and underachievement. *American Educational Research Journal, 2,* 1–12.

Rosenshine, B. & Furst, N. (1971). Research on teacher performance criteria. In B. O. Smith (Ed.), *Research in teacher education: A symposium.* Englewood Cliffs, NJ: Prentice-Hall.

Skinner, B. (1968). *The technology of teaching.* New York: Appleton-Century-Crofts.

Smith, B. O. (1984, September). *Research bases for teacher education.* Paper presented at Hearing of National Commission on Excellence in Teacher Education, Minneapolis, MN.

Squires, D., Huitt, W., & Segars, J. (1983). *Effective schools & classrooms; A research-based perspective.* Alexandria, VA: Association for Supervision and Curriculum Development.

Squires, D., Huitt, W., & Segars, J. (1981). Improving classroom and schools: What's important. *Educational Leadership, 39*(3), 174–179.

Stallings, J. (1983, June). Findings from the research on teaching: What we have learned. West Virginia Department of Education.

Stallings, J. & Kaskowitz, D. (1974). *Follow through classroom observation evaluation, 1972–1973.* Menlo Park, CA: Stanford Research Institute.

Stallings, J. & Mohlman, G. (1981). School policy, leadership style, teacher change and student behavior in eight schools. (Final Report, Grant No. NIE-G-80-66101). Washington, DC: National Institute of Education.

Wentling, T. (1973). Mastery versus nonmastery instruction with varying test item feedback treatment. *Journal of Educational Psychology, 65,* 50–58.

Wright, C. & Nuthall, G. (1970). Relationships between teacher behaviors and pupil achievement in three experimental elementary science lessons. *American Educational Research Journal, 7,* 477–491.

CHAPTER 6

Primary Instructional Methods

The focus in the previous two chapters has been on teaching skills and the conditions of effective teaching. In this chapter we present a synthesis of teaching techniques into instructional methods.

In its most general sense, an instructional method is a pattern of teaching actions designed to achieve student learning outcomes. Central to this definition is the term "pattern," which suggests a planned and sequential arrangement of actions. Actions refer to the variety of techniques available to teachers as they plan for lessons. Six techniques that are common to all methods are described in Chapter 4. A method can be applied in its essential form to many subject areas, and can be used by different teachers recurrently. We are also reminded that there are an indeterminant number of variations of procedure and style as teachers make decisions and plan for the implementation of any one particular method, or for a combination of methods. This within-method variability should be perceived as a strength (Gage & Berliner, 1984).

OVERVIEW

The focus of this chapter is on the presentation of three primary instructional methods representing a wide range of subject areas that can be used by teachers at the middle and high school levels. These methods are discussion, lecture, and inquiry. Several specific forms of each are presented. Each method is designed to achieve a particular kind of learning outcome and is generally flexible enough to be adapted to the range of student abilities and interests. Each form of the three primary methods will be described in terms of the instructional techniques essential for successful implementation. Patterns of sequential phases for the three primary methods are presented to assist teachers in applying them in a practical way in the classrooms. Experienced teachers accumulate a repertoire of methods and make conscientious decisions on a regular basis about how these methods might be effectively employed to achieve lesson objectives and unit goals. Analysis forms for the discussion, lecture, and inquiry methods are included at the end of the chapter to summarize the major features of each method, and to aid in your observation and analysis of their use.

SCENARIO

Robert Carl realized that one advantage of getting to school early was that he did not have to wait in line for the copying machine.

This morning he was making a transparency of a map (see Figure 6.1). If all went as well as Mr. Carl had planned, the map would serve as a springboard into a new unit. It was intended to stimulate higher level thinking in his 2nd-period Economics class. Although the students were bright, he thought they would probably not immediately guess that the reason why the countries on the map were shaped and sized so unusually was that they were drawn to depict the countries' gross national product rather than their physical size. As he started back to his room, he smiled at the thought of successfully challenging their critical thinking abilities.

"Today we start a new unit, one that will require you to apply what you have learned for the past 2 months. We have been studying the separate parts of the economy—the role of the consumer, producer, worker, government, corporation, and labor unions—and how each contributes to the big picture. Now we are going to change our focus from microeconomics to macroeconomics and begin a study of the interrelationships among the sectors of the economy and its performance."

"I would like to introduce some new ideas that contain a kind of puzzle for you to try to solve." Mr. Carl noticed two students toward the rear of the room glance up from their desks upon the mention of a puzzle. He placed the transparency of a miniature world map on the overhead projector. "What do you see?"

The first response was, "it's a map of the world with all of the countries. But the countries are shaped differently, with no rounded edges like on a real map."

Another student jumped in, "China's a lot larger than the United States but not on this map. It doesn't make any sense."

"The map is divided into northern and southern hemispheres," added another.

At this point Mr. Carl thought the stage was set to formally begin the inquiry. "The map does make sense if you know the key to the puzzle. I would like you to try to discover it by asking me questions. But there is a hitch. I will only answer 'yes' or 'no' to your questions, so you will have to think carefully as you phrase them."

"Why is the United States the largest country on this map?

"You will need to rephrase your question so I can answer 'yes' or 'no.'

"Okay. (pause) Could the map measure something other than size?"

"What do you mean by size?"

"Size. How big the United States is physically."

"Yes. The map is measuring something else."

One student pointed out the size of Japan in relation to the other countries. Another wondered why Denmark was almost as large as

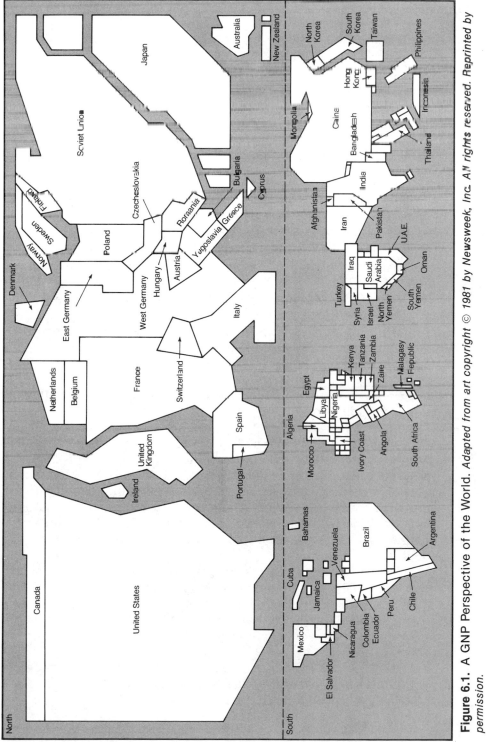

Figure 6.1. A GNP Perspective of the World. *Adapted from art copyright © 1981 by Newsweek, Inc. All rights reserved. Reprinted by permission.*

197

Australia. Another asked why Australia was part of the northern hemisphere and India a part of the southern hemisphere on this map. Still another wanted to know if the map was drawn by a computer.

After more discussion a hypothesis was offered. "Does the map measure the number of cars in the world?"

"Our first proposed solution to the puzzle. A good idea! Rather than answering you, what further questions could you ask me to test your guess?"

"What do you mean?" Someone asked with a puzzled look.

"Remember that when we use inquiry you have to gather information related to your proposed solutions to a problem. Here we have the same idea, only different in that your questions try to get from me the necessary information to test your hypotheses. Think about the relationships of the countries. How about a 'What if . . .' question?"

(Pause.) "If Mexico doubled its production of cars, would its size on the map double?"

"No. But its size would increase." Several other students offered hypotheses that also centered around products such as steel, computers and wheat. Eventually one student hypothesized money as the basis for each country's size, and this quickly led to wealth and GNP. After each hypothesis was tested with more student questions, the solution to the puzzle—the depiction of GNP—was confirmed.

After discussing what clues led a student to discover that GNP was the answer, Mr. Carl complimented the students on their perseverance and perceptiveness. He then defined GNP, gave examples of goods and services included in the computation of GNP, and provided statistics to support the size of some of the countries in both halves on the map. He also explained that the North/South line on the map was not meant to be the Equator but rather roughly 30 degrees north latitude.

"We are going to be spending the next several weeks on the concept of GNP because it is the most important indicator of economic growth in the United States, or a thermometer of our economic health, in a sense. It is also directly related to our standard of living. In other words, how well we live, what we can buy, and the services available to us."

"Let's take a look at our map again. Why do you suppose the countries roughly south of the 30-degrees-north latitude line are smaller than those in the north?"

"They have smaller GNPs."

"Right. But why are so many of the small GNP nations located south of the United States?"

One student suggested it might have something to do with climate because it is hotter in the southern hemisphere. He jokingly followed up with a comment about people taking siestas every day. Another thought that the northern countries have more technology. After further discussion, one student commented that some of the most heavily populated countries such as China and India are south of the line.

"You have come up with some fine ideas and possible explanations for this problem, and we will have an opportunity to pursue our inquiry further when we learn more about GNP. I have some excellent sources for you to consult and have made arrangements for a guest speaker to visit us on Monday. He is a graduate student from Brazil majoring in economics at the university. I think he will be an excellent source of information and that we will learn a lot about those factors that influence economic growth, particularly in those countries to the south of us."

Noticing that class time was almost over, Mr. Carl reviewed the lesson by asking the students what they had learned about GNP today. He gave Chapter 9 as the reading assignment in the text. "I also want you to watch the news tonight on television or read the paper to find out the latest quarter's GNP figures that are reported today. We will use them tomorrow as we begin formalizing some possible explanations and start our search for data. Depending on the number of hypotheses we can come up with, perhaps we can form into small groups for the investigation. So long!"

RESEARCH AND THEORETICAL BASE

Very little research has been conducted on instructional methods, especially that which attempts to determine the effectiveness of various methods in terms of increasing students' learning gains. Most of the research has focused on comparing one method with another. This avenue has not been fruitful because the general finding has been that for most students the use of different teaching methods does not seem to make a difference in learning. Different methods have yielded similar average results when the criterion measured has been achievement. Another conclusion that has been drawn based on a review of available research is that students with varying aptitudes will probably be affected differently by particular methods. This is only one of several factors, including instructional costs, time, and student attitude, that will need to be considered when choosing among different methods and strategies and making other decisions about instruction (Berliner & Gage, 1976).

Another generalized research finding is that using a variety of methods increases the probability that student interest will be maintained and that higher achievement gains will be made. Based on their review of research, Good and Brophy (1984) found that the "systematic use of a variety of techniques produces better results than heavy reliance on any one technique, even a good one" (p. 342).

Although research literature suggests that different instructional approaches should be used with low- and high-achieving students, Evertson (1982) found that this does not occur in practice. Her study investigated the differences in instructional methods and activities in higher and lower achieving urban junior high school English and mathematics classes. Each teacher selected for the study had higher and lower ability sections of students. After a year of observation she found that the teachers did not vary their activity patterns for the different sections of students. In other words, these teachers did not instruct their high- and low-achieving students differently. Furthermore, she found definite instructional patterns for English and mathematics teachers. For example, mathematics teachers consistently followed a five-phase lesson: (1) opening, (2) checking/grading, (3) lecture/discussion, (4) seatwork, and (5) closing. An additional finding was that the time allocation patterns for each of these phases were also generally consistent with all the math teachers.

What are teachers' preferences for various teaching methods and strategies? Thompson (1981) used a rating form to get at urban and suburban elementary and secondary teachers' preferences for Joyce and Weil's (1980) teaching models. Their choices indicated that secondary teachers placed more emphasis on strategies stimulating intellectual skills and growth than elementary teachers, who emphasized the social growth of students.

Along with lecture and recitation, discussion has been one of the most used instructional methods at all levels. Today, however, there is some debate about how extensively teachers actually use discussion, primarily because of the way the term is defined. In their review of descriptive studies on interaction patterns, Gall and Gall (1976) suggest that discussion is used infrequently. They characterize discussions by "student-to-student interaction and educational objectives related to complex thinking processes and attitude change." In his more recent review, Dillon (1984) indicated that the problem is that almost all teacher-student interaction sessions are labelled "discussions," when most should be labelled recitations because of the emphasis on memorization of knowledge.

Research on questioning behaviors since the turn of the century strongly supports teachers' use of predominantly low cognitive-level questions requiring the recall of information characteristic of recitations (Gall, 1984). Furthermore, two independent analyses of the same audiotapes of a group of secondary teachers involving their students in discussions across several subject areas reached the same conclusion: the teachers displayed a lack of discussion skills. Teachers and their students needed more training (Francis, 1987; Klinzing & Klinzing-Eurich, 1987).

Based on their extensive review of literature on the discussion method, particularly in the area of group dynamics, Gall and Gall (1976) made several recommendations related to the effective use of discussions in the classroom setting. Class size is critical, with the optimal group size being five students. To accommodate the reality of the school classroom, it was suggested that dividing classes into small groups might be a useful instructional approach. Another recommendation was that heterogeneous groups might be best for group discussions because of the potential input from a variety of perspectives represented in a diverse group of students. Moderate cohesiveness should be fostered by the teacher so that minority points of view are respected. Communication could be enhanced by ensuring that eye contact between students and teacher be established within the group setting. The final recommendation was that teachers should consistently model a democratic leadership style rather than an authoritarian one to encourage student thinking and involvement.

Research indicates that the discussion method is as effective as other approaches in learning subject-matter content. It may be even more effective than other methods, including the lecture, if achieving higher cognitive level outcomes is the goal (Gall & Gall, 1976). Gage (1969) suggests that research emphasis should not be put on comparing methods, such as lecture and discussion, but rather on determining which methods are most effective in achieving specific objectives.

The instructional method most associated with higher education is the lecture, and it is within this setting that most of the research on it has been conducted (McLeish, 1976). In their review of the research literature on lecturing across all levels, Gage and Berliner (1984) concluded that it is as effective as other methods. Furthermore, they suggested that the lecture was superior to other methods when ''(a) the basic purpose is to disseminate information; (b) the material is not available elsewhere; (c) the material must be organized and presented in a particular way for a specific group; (d) it is necessary to arouse interest in the subject; (e) the material need be remembered for only a short time; and (f) it is necessary to provide an introduction to an area or directions for learning tasks to be pursued through some other teaching method'' (p. 457).

Several studies compared the lecture with a variety of diverse methods. In one study three methods were compared in lessons with 9th-grade social studies students. The lecture-recitation approach was found to be superior over inquiry and public issues discussion in terms of student achievement. However, the relative effectiveness of the three methods was dependent, in part, on student ability (Peterson, 1979). In a study focusing on the training of paraprofessional reading tutors in seven skills using three different methods, role playing and modeling were found to be more effective than lecture (with discussion) (Willis & Gueldenpfenning, 1981). When comparing experience-based with lecture-based discussion approaches in a study involving undergraduate business students, Specht (1985) found that students' active involvement in learning enhanced comprehension and retention over their passive involvement.

The findings of several other research studies have implications for the use of the lecture method in secondary classrooms. The use of ''advance organizers'' has been advocated as a means to organize and structure students' thoughts in preparation for receiving information through a lecture (Ausubel, 1968). Several researchers reviewed the research conducted using advance organizers and found that their use only slightly increased learning and retention (Luiten, Ames, & Ackerson, 1980). In another review one of the qualities of an effective lecturer agreed upon by both lecturer and listerners is the ability to capture and hold attention. In addition, the reviewers found that a lecturer's nonverbal expressiveness may enhance learning (Cooper & Galvin, 1984). In their review of the literature, Michael and Weaver (1984) also found that a lecturer's expressiveness is important, and greatly affects students' ratings of lecturers.

Inquiry is a generic term, also referred to as *discovery,* that applies to methods with which teachers engage students' critical thinking skills to analyze and solve problems in a systematic fashion. Whereas lecture and recitation are used extensively by teachers, inquiry is used sparingly. Most of the research literature on inquiry centers on comparing it with other methods. One dissertation surveyed studies comparing discovery and expository approaches from 1908–1975 and could not conclude one was superior to the other (Weimer, 1974). Since then, Ponder and Davis (1982) in their review of research found a tendency in students taught by methods requiring students' critical thinking skills, such as inquiry, to perform as well as students taught by other methods of factual learning.

Two other studies conducted since 1975 favored inquiry over expository approaches, and one found that inquiry was more effective than a direct instruction strategy on some measures. Working with university students teaching chemistry concepts, Andrews (1984) found that groups of independent and dependent students taught by discovery performed better than those taught by an expository approach. Selim and Shrigley (1983) involved 5th-grade Egyptian students in science learning and found that the students taught by discovery scored higher on achievement tests emphasizing recall and retention. The discovery students also scored higher in science attitude. In another study groups of high school social studies students were taught a two-week unit by the tightly structured direct instruction strategy and the inquiry strategy which emphasized more open-ended inventive thinking. The direct instruction students performed better on objective and subjective tests requiring application of knowledge, whereas the inquiry students performed better on tests requiring evaluative judgments. Students also found the inquiry strategy more challenging on an attitude measure (Fielding, Kameenui, & Gersten, 1983).

Although the research is diverse and few conclusions are clear-cut, teachers can be aware of several generalizations that are supported by the research:

1. Many factors need to be considered in choosing a particular strategy or method.
2. No one method can be totally relied upon.
3. If a method is to be used effectively, the teacher needs to become proficient in its use.
4. The most effective teachers potentially are those who use several modes effectively.

5. The teachers' choice of methods has been less often a rational decision than defaulting to a comfortable pattern.
6. Making instructional choices based on instructional purposes is a potential approach to improving instructional effectiveness.
7. Specific methods are effective for particular sorts of learning outcomes; compatibility is the key factor.

APPLICATION TO PRACTICE: DISCUSSION METHOD

In its most basic form, a discussion is a purposeful group conversation through which a teacher may achieve a wide range of objectives. The discussion method involves groups ranging from several students in a small group situation to 20 or 30 students, which is more typical of secondary classrooms. A meaningful discussion can be conducted with a large classroom group, but not as effectively as with a small group of five to eight students that is generally recommended by research. Because a classroom discussion typically involves interaction about subject matter between a teacher and students, it is conducted as a businesslike conversation. However, discussion is a flexible method and is readily adapted to a variety of classroom situations. This characteristic, no doubt, helps account for its popularity as an instructional method.

Although the discussion method is widely employed, it has been criticized. Many have found classroom discussions to be "frequently boring, aimless, and even threatening to some participants" (Gall & Gall, 1976). One of the problems is that teachers and students are assumed to know the full range of discussion skills necessary for effective application of the method (Bridges, 1979). Although teachers have generally been acquainted with the questioning techniques necessary to conduct discussions, many have not been trained in their use. Teachers have tended to default to recitation involving primarily lower-level thinking as their preferred form of discussion. However, several other forms are designed to stimulate higher levels of student thinking and involvement.

Four types of discussions are regularly used by teachers: recitation, guided discussion, reflective discussion, and small group discussion. They share a common thread requiring the teacher and students to interact verbally in order for learning to occur. Each differs in terms of purpose, structure, interaction pattern, and levels of student thinking stimulated.

Recitation

A teacher uses a recitation primarily to ascertain the extent to which students have memorized pertinent facts. The interaction pattern typically is teacher question, student response and teacher reaction, a pattern Bellack (1966) found very common in his studies over 20 years ago. The pace of the interaction is fairly rapid. Level I Low Order Convergent questions are the primary ones asked by the teacher to stimulate recall of knowledge. Questions at this level are "who-what-when-where questions." (See Chapter 4 for a description of the four types of questions.) The intent of the teacher using recitation is to engage students in what Hudgins (1971) termed "reproductive thinking," as opposed to productive thinking, in which students demonstrate understanding or ability to apply learning. An important questioning technique teachers need to consistently use during a recitation is directing questions to both volunteering and nonvolunteering students in order to get all of the students involved.

Recitation is highly structured with the teacher clearly in control and directing the learning. Roby (1987) referred to this form of discussion as "quiz show" because students try to discover the right answers to topic-oriented teacher questions. If, for example, the students have been diligent in reading the chapter from the literature text, observing the history film or physics demonstration, practicing the pronunciations of French vocabulary, and memorizing the spelling words or mathematics formulas, the teacher will be able to cover the content quickly. Recitation is generally efficient in terms of time demands, which is one reason why it is the most widely used form of discussion. Furthermore, only brief planning or preparation time is required. Teachers can conveniently fit it into practically any part of a lesson. The primary drawback is that teachers tend to rely on it too much. Recitation should, ideally, serve as a means to diagnose student progress in learning basic information and their readiness to use that information to proceed with higher level reflective thinking.

Guided Discussion

The purpose of guided discussion is to promote understanding of important concepts. The interaction pattern of the guided discussion is similar to recitation in that the teacher asks questions, students respond, and the teacher reacts. Differences are apparent, though, because of the emphasis on higher level thinking. When a teacher asks a question, more than one student may respond, particularly if differences in opinion are expressed. In addition to the possibility of more students responding to each question, some interaction among students may occur. This is certainly not common during recitations, but is more prevalent during reflective discussions (explained in the next section) and is an absolute necessity during small group discussions. We should also expect some students to begin asking questions for the purpose of explanation and clarification.

The cognitive levels of a teacher's questions appropriate to achieve the goals of a guided discussion generally are Level II High Order Convergent and Level III Low Order Divergent. Convergent questions might, for example, request students to make comparisons between country and bluegrass music, explain South Africa's policy of apartheid, describe how safety is a critical consideration in an industrial arts laboratory, or interpret a political cartoon. Divergent questions might involve students in contriving a solution to a hypothetical community pollution problem or drawing conclusions to a difficult chemistry laboratory experiment. During a guided discussion, a teacher may probe some students' responses because clarification is needed or to extend thinking. Wait time becomes more important as students need time to think of responses to higher level questions. The teacher will also want to encourage students to begin asking questions.

A guided discussion is moderately structured in that the teacher still assumes the major role of directing learning. As one might surmise, it is not as structured as a recitation, but more structured than a reflective discussion. The discussion is guided because the teacher wants to lead students to predetermined higher level understandings. Students have more freedom, though, to present, explore, and test their ideas. Guided discussions still focus primarily on the cognitive dimension of subject matter content in contrast to reflective discussions that also involve affective learnings.

Reflective Discussion

The reflective discussion is potentially the highest level of discussion in terms of stimulated student thinking. It is also the least structured, has the potential to generate the most student-student interaction, and generally requires a greater investment of time than the other modes of discussion. It is probably the most difficult form of discussion to conduct, and, in any case, is the discussion format least used by teachers.

The purpose of a reflective discussion is to require students to engage in high-level critical and creative thinking as they solve problems, clarify values, explore controversial issues, and form and defend positions. In many ways it is the most exciting of the discussion strategies because of its potential to push students to the highest levels of cognition. In order for students to respond reflectively to a teacher's questions, they must have a solid understanding of the subject matter that serves as a basis of the discussion. If not, the discussion may turn into what Roby (1987) referred to as a "bull session" in which both teachers and students think they have the right answers, freely shared without any supportive data. Reflective thinking requires students to learn the facts, perhaps through class recitations, and to develop understandings, perhaps through teacher-guided discussions. Without knowledge and understanding, opinions cannot be supported and, therefore, are useless in achieving the goals of a reflective discussion.

The interaction pattern is flexible and can range from a traditional approach characteristic of guided discussions to one in which a student, or several students, have assumed leadership and guide the discussion and inquiry themselves. This is the most open form of a reflective discussion. It permits students considerable freedom for direction and expression. This situation will more likely result if the group is smaller than regular class size and the students are particularly responsible and motivated to learn and participate. Another factor influencing the effectiveness of a reflective discussion is that too much teacher questioning may forestall and frustrate student participation, primarily because of the control the teacher may exercise over the discussion (Dillon, 1983). There are several interaction patterns that a teacher needs to consider when employing discussion. The decision will probably depend on the size of the group and capability of the students.

Openness is a key component that a teacher attempts to achieve in a reflective discussion. Divergent questions help provide a key to intellectual freedom. Bridges (1979) spoke about the characteristic of discussion openness: "(a) the matter is open for discussion, (b) the discussants are open-minded; (c) the discussion is open to all arguments; (d) the discussion is open to any person; (e) the time limit is open; (f) the learning outcomes are open, not predictable; (g) the purposes and practices of the discussion are out in the open, not covert; and (h) the discussion is open-ended, not required to come to a single conclusion."

Levels III and IV Low and High Order Divergent questions are the most appropriate to achieve the objectives of a reflective discussion. At Level III students draw conclusions, make inferences, form generalizations, and analyze information, among other intellectual behaviors. Level IV questions require students to engage in original and evaluative thinking, such as predicting the future in terms of technological advances given current trends and research findings; speculating on how history might have changed if a particular vice-president, given his political beliefs, had become president; defining their stands on abortion; or evaluating the impact a famous conductor/composer had on his musical era.

As teachers conduct reflective discussions they must keep in mind a variety of questioning techniques that will increase the probability that their objectives will be attained. Implementing a recitation requires only basic communication skills, with the most important questioning technique being to involve the widest possible number of students in reviewing factual material. Wide participation is not necessarily important in a reflective discussion since some students may feel uncomfortable sharing their opinions, views, or ideas. The content in reflective discussions often involves students' feelings, attitudes, and values. Because the questions are on a higher level and therefore are more complex, question clarity is critical. Teachers will need to consistently use ample wait time with higher level questions during a reflective discussion to provide students enough time to think of responses. Probing is necessary to encourage students to clarify, expand, and support their responses. Finally the teacher will need to encourage students to formulate questions as an alternative means to stimulate thinking.

The structure of a reflective discussion can range from moderate to very low depending on several factors. The most important is the ability and interest level of the students. If students are not stimulated, and are not mature enough or capable of assuming responsibility for their own learning, the most open form would be difficult to implement. Reflective discussions focusing on problem solving have similar outcomes to the inquiry method presented below. Both require teachers to assume a stronger role as facilitator than instructor in the traditional sense. A facilitator guides, advises, and keeps students directed toward the goals established, and often serves as a resource person for the group. As the structure the teacher normally provides the discussion decreases and students assume more responsibility, a more democratic atmosphere develops. Students are involved in more decision making as they use the "power" delegated by the teacher. This characteristic is particularly evident in the inquiry method and also in small groups.

Small Group Discussion

Dividing the large classroom into small groups of students to achieve specific objectives permits students to assume more responsibility for their own learning, develop social and leadership skills, and become involved in an alternative instructional approach. The small group approach does not have a specific place within the hierarchy of discussion approaches because it is flexible enough to be used to attain the objectives generally associated with guided and reflective discussions, and even recitation.

Although small groups are most appropriate for promoting problem solving, attitudinal change, and critical and creative thinking that coincides with the purposes of reflective discussions, they can also promote the understanding of subject matter and the learning of facts. To illustrate how reflection about a controversial issue might be stimulated, a government teacher could organize students into groups based on their points of view regarding the need for the Equal Rights Amendment to the Constitution. Each group might be charged with determining how they would gather evidence to support their point of view, collecting and organizing the evidence, and presenting it to the class in the form of a panel presentation. A variety of critical thinking skills would be developed as the students reflectively gathered and organized information and supported a point of view. This process is similar to the inquiry method.

In order to teach subject matter understandings, a teacher could have students in a general science class explore the advantages and disadvantages of several forms of energy: gas, solar, nuclear, wind, and coal. The class could be divided into small groups—each assigned to investigate one energy source—to gather information in the library, draw conclusions about its effectiveness, and report on it in written form. A teacher interested in teaching basic facts using an alternative instructional approach arranges the class into small groups of 5 or 6 students and challenges them, in a gaming fashion, to use their textbooks to accurately complete a worksheet in the shortest time possible. Another approach to "teaching" a test or using it as a learning activity is to permit small groups to review their texts or search other sources in order to correct answers they missed. In these cases small groups would be formed for only the limited period of time necessary to complete the task.

The structure a teacher establishes for small group instruction depends primarily on the maturity level of the students. If students are to be involved in problem solving they need freedom to determine direction and make decisions. The teacher monitors group progress and serves as a resource person to assist them in accomplishing their task. More structure may be needed when the objectives center on developing subject matter understandings and learning facts.

Mature students will be able to work without extensive teacher supervision. A problem may occur with less mature students who will need a more structured atmosphere in order to accomplish a task. Because these students handle freedom ineptly, they should not be involved in small group activities requiring considerable freedom of decision making.

Discussion Method Phases

Although there are different kinds of discussions that encompass a wide range of purposes, a sequence of phases can be generalized. They are Entry, Clarification, Investigation, and Closure. The intention in providing a sequence of phases is to describe the discussion strategy "in action." This provides for a better understanding of its application in the classroom under differing circumstances, and presents a flexible step-by-step approach to implementation. Our intent is not to prescribe the "only" way to conduct discussions. The discussion strategy is probably the most flexible of all the strategies presented in this chapter. Therefore teachers should feel free to modify the sequence of phases but maintain the integrity of the method to suit their own classroom situations, students, subject matter, and course goals.

Phase I. Entry: Identification of Problem, Issue or Topic

    A. Springboard and/or attention-getter used
    B. Identify problem, issue, or topic
    C. State objectives and rationale

As a teacher begins the lesson and introduces the discussion, the entry is important. There are many ways to enter a discussion depending on the nature of the students and their previous learnings, the topic, issue or problem, and size of the group. The purpose of the entry is to inform students what is to be accomplished and why it is important. The most straightforward way to do this is to inform students of the objective(s) and rationale. This basic approach would be most appropriate for a recitation, and could also be used for the other forms of discussion. A more stimulating way to enter a discussion is to use a springboard to arouse student interest. In a guided discussion, for example, an industrial arts teacher could use a brief series of national statistics related to accidents in school shops—what kind and how many—to lead into a discussion on safety. A more dramatic approach would be to show slides of actual shop accidents or to graphically describe an accident that may have occurred in the classroom in the past. Springboards and attention-getters are also very appropriate for reflective discussions. As an illustration, a home economics teacher could role-play a fortune teller and have students ask questions about what the home of the future might be like. The answers the teacher gives could be based on a recent article, made up at the moment, or a combination of both. This would serve as an attention-getting lead-in to a reflective discussion on future technology. The entry to a small group activity could range from the basic introduction specifying the objective and a rationale to a dramatic entry, depending on the imagination and inclination of the teacher.

Phase II. Clarification

    A. Establish procedures
    B. Define terms and concepts related to the problem, issue, or topic

Informing students of the procedures for a discussion may only be necessary at the beginning of the year or if a particular discussion the teacher has in mind requires specific guidelines. Common rules, of which students may need to be reminded, are that they respect the opinions of others and are not allowed to talk when the teacher or another student is talking. This is particularly appropriate for a reflective discussion. If a controversial issue is to be discussed, the teacher may have other guidelines. A teacher may wish to provide more structure in cases involving less mature students who require more supervision. Small group discussions may need more structure, especially when first initiated, because students may attempt to take advantage of the social dynamics created by small groups. It is important to keep in mind that too much structure and control will stifle student participation and initiative. This is particularly self-defeating for a reflective discussion in which the emphasis is on encouraging student freedom. Another factor influencing the extent of rules is the size of the group, which determines whether or not more structure may be necessary.

Clarification of the problem, topic or issue may be necessary if the subject to be discussed is particularly complex and difficult for some students to understand. This becomes critical if the text or other material students have read in preparation for a discussion is ambiguous and confusing. In such a case definitions of terms, clarification of concepts, and elaboration of ideas may be all that is necessary to increase the probability that most of the students will participate and understand. For example, clarification may be necessary at the beginning of a reflective discussion on abortion because of the conflict between legal definitions and the many interpretations by special-interest groups. On the other hand, the teacher may consider clarification of these positions to be an objective of the discussion.

Phase III. Investigation

    A. Ask levels of questions appropriate to achieve desired levels of student thinking.
    B. Use questioning techniques to maintain discussion and stimulate student involvement and thinking.
    C. Encourage student initiative and leadership.

  D. Request that students support opinions offered.
  E. Ensure sufficient coverage of the problem, issue, or topic being dis-
     cussed.

The Investigation is the main body of any discussion because the teacher
uses questions and questioning techniques during this phase to interact with
students in order to achieve the objectives of the discussion. The teacher will
ask questions congruent with the levels of student thinking desired: predominantly lower convergent questions (Level I) during a recitation, predominantly
upper convergent and lower divergent questions (Levels II and III) during a
guided discussion, and lower and upper divergent questions (Levels III and IV)
during a reflective discussion. The levels of questions specified here are only
suggestive because of the need to be flexible. For example, a teacher may have
as an objective that the students will compare and contrast the views of citizens
representing various economic and social groups on the U.S. Constitution during the time it was being ratified. If students had not read the assignment they
would not know what the various groups were and how they felt. In this case,
after having the students read the chapter section, the teacher will conduct a
recitation before having them engage in higher level thinking involving comparisons and conclusions.
  The use of appropriate questioning techniques is critical to conducting effective discussions. Misuse can defeat the purpose of most discussions. This
particularly applies to reflective discussions. On the other hand, recitations require a minimal application of questioning techniques. During a recitation a
teacher is concerned, for example, with determining what students know about
the important facts of a reading assignment. Questions are used to diagnose
students' knowledge. In order for this to be accomplished, all students should
ideally be called on several times. This is obviously not the case in the schools
since only a maximum of 40% to 50% of the students are called on to recite, on
the average, and most of them are volunteering students who usually get most
of the attention. However, another contributing factor is that recitation rarely
occurs in its pure form with all teacher questions categorized at Level I Low
Convergent. More often teachers incorporate Level II High Convergent questions to encourage students to display understanding of the facts. In this case
the recitation has assumed some of the characteristics of the guided discussion.
  The guided discussion requires an emphasis on other techniques to achieve
its goals. Phrasing, balance, and sequence become more important because the
questions are at differing and generally higher cognitive levels. Also, adapting
questions to the language and ability levels of the students, particularly in a
heterogeneous class, becomes important. Pausing after asking questions and using probing questions to encourage students to complete, clarify, and expand
their responses may also be necessary, particularly at the Low Divergent level
(Level III). Furthermore, student questions can be encouraged.
  When the teacher involves students in reflective discussions all questioning
techniques need to be conscientiously and consistently employed. Because the

emphasis is on developing critical and creative thinking, probing students' responses in order to expand their thinking and provide support for points of view will be necessary. Another crucial technique is wait time. Because the majority of questions generally asked in reflective discussions are at the Low and High Divergent levels (Levels III and IV), teachers need to pause at least 3 seconds after asking questions in order to give all the students time to think. Pausing several seconds after a student gives a response will also increase the probability that the response will be extended with higher level thinking involved. Students should be encouraged to ask questions during a reflective discussion. For example, in a discussion dealing with issues related to abortion, a teacher may ask students to pause and come up with some questions they would ask a convicted abortion clinic bomber if he or she was in class. Also, what responses might this person give to the questions? High-level divergent thinking can be accomplished by having students devise questions.

A note of caution about the use of questions and questioning, particularly in reflective discussions, needs to be given. As has been previously mentioned, students' participation in discussions can be diminished if teachers misuse questioning techniques. Reflective discussions characterized by too many questions, too rapid a pace, too little attention paid to listening, and too little support for students' contributions will regress to an inappropriate recitation or even a lecture. The sign that this is happening is that the teacher begins to answer his or her own questions.

Effective discussions may also involve nonquestion alternatives to stimulate student thinking and participation. In his analysis of several tapes of high school classes, Dillon (1985) found that students spoke more extensively, exhibited more complex thought, and became more personally involved in discussions when the teacher used alternative approaches. Examples of nonquestion alternatives include use of declarative statements, reflective restatements of what students have said, invitations for students to elaborate on what they have just said, deliberate silence, particularly after a student's response, and the encouragement of students' questions (Dillon, 1983). Teachers might attempt to integrate some of these techniques into their overall questioning approach to provide variety and depth to their practice.

During the Investigation phase of a small group discussion, the students serve as the principal questioners and respondents as they search for information or attempt to propose solutions to a problem. As a facilitator, the teacher may ask questions in working with individual groups to help guide their inquiry and keep them on target. The teacher assumes a secondary role as a questioner in most small group discussions.

Phase IV. Closure: Summary, Integration, Application

    A. Summary in the form of consensus, solutions, insights achieved in relation to topic covered, issue explored, or problem investigated.

B. Integrate lesson with goals and previous learning.
C. Apply discussion outcomes to other stituations.

Closure is least important in a recitation and most important in reflective and small group discussions. In a recitation closure may center on reviewing those areas in which students displayed the least understanding. Because guided discussions involve higher level thinking, the teacher needs to use closures to help students summarize important points and integrate understanding with previous learning. Transitions to the lessons following up recitations and guided discussions are also appropriate to prepare students for upcoming activities.

Closures are extremely important to reflective discussions because for many students this is where ideas, points of view, generalizations, and conclusions are summarized and synthesized, and where important learning occurs. Syntheses can ''bring it all together'' for students who may have been confused during the discussion. Application and transition are also very appropriate within the closure because it is often at this point that decisions students reached in connection with a course of action, for example, might be further examined and evaluated in the real world. Suppose that after reflective discussion students reached the decision to actively support a nuclear freeze bill being considered in Congress. At this point near the end of the lesson the teacher could suggest some of the problems students will face as they become actively involved, focusing on cost in terms of time and money or opposition from fellow students, parents, and so on. This would be an ideal problem for further investigation that could be the focus of the next day's class. More than likely the teacher has the inquiry method in mind as a means to involve students in dealing with this reality.

The closure of a small group discussion is the point where students generally present what they have found as a result of their ''investigations.'' If the students were guided by higher level thinking questions and activities, each group might report, for example, the benefits and disadvantages of the energy source it investigated or support for their positions on the ERA. At the end of the lesson we would expect the teacher to follow up with a summary and integration of the various points of view, and perhaps a consensus if it was the objective. In the case where the teacher ''taught the test'' using small groups of students to search out the answers to the objective test items, the closure could simply be a review of the test with the right answers based on students' findings. The closure is important because it provides the teacher with a final opportunity at the end of a lesson to ensure that objectives have been achieved, learning has occurred and that students will be prepared for the next lesson.

Scenario Analysis

In the introductory scenario, Mr. Carl engaged in considerable interaction with the students, but the students did most of the questioning. He was using guided inquiry. After the students discovered the solution to the ''puzzle,'' Mr. Carl engaged them in another form of the inquiry method that required him to conduct a mini-discussion to get students to hypothesize reasons why countries of the world generally to the south of the United States have lower GNPs. At two other points Mr. Carl had "discussions," but they were, in essence, simply short episodes of interaction facilitating inquiry.

The lesson could have been easily conducted as a guided discussion. Instead of having the students question him, Mr. Carl could have used Levels II and III High Convergent and Low Divergent questions to stimulate thinking about what the map depicted. For example, "What do you think is the reason why the countries are shaped the way they are?" (key entry level question) "How do the sizes of the United States and India compare on a real map?" "Why is the United States the largest country on this map?" "If GNP increases by 10% this year what will that do to the size of the U.S. on this map?" "How can we summarize what this map is trying to show us?" "Why is GNP important?" (key closing question). A recitation would have been appropriate if the objective was for students to recall the countries with the largest GNPs and other characteristics that distinguish them from one another. As a natural follow-up to the inquiry lesson, Mr. Carl could have as his objective for a reflective discussion that the students evaluate United States' foreign policy toward several developing nations in terms of the approaches we are using to help these countries raise their standard of living.

SUMMARY POINT

Discussion is one of the most useful instructional methods because of its potential to stimulate students' active involvement in learning at a variety of levels of thinking. Four types of discussion have been presented. The recitation has as its purpose the diagnosis of student knowledge of basic facts. The guided discussion aims to promote student understanding through processing information. The goal of the reflective discussion is to stimulate students' critical thinking about issues and problems. Finally, use of small group discussions is an alternative to large group discussion. It encourages students to assume more responsibility for their own learning. The basis for making decisions about which form of discussion to use when planning will depend on the level of student thinking desired. And this, of course, will be reflected in the teachers' objectives for the lesson.

A Discussion Method Analysis Form is included at the end of the chapter to aid in your observation and analysis.

REVIEW: IMPORTANT PRACTICES—PHASES OF A GENERALIZED DISCUSSION METHOD

Entry: Identification of Problem, Issue, or Topic

A. Springboard and/or attention-getter used
B. Identify problem, issue, or topic
C. State objectives and rationale

Clarification

A. Establish procedures
B. Define terms and concepts related to the problem, issue, or topic

Investigation

A. Ask levels of questions appropriate to achieve desired levels of student thinking
B. Use questioning techniques to maintain discussion and stimulate student involvement and thinking
C. Encourage student initiative and leadership
D. Request that students support opinions offered
E. Attempt to ensure sufficient coverage of problem, issue, or topic

Closure: Summary, Integration, Application

A. Summary in the form of consensus, solution, insights achieved in relation to topic, issue explored, or problem investigated
B. Integrate lesson with goals and previous learnings
C. Apply discussion outcomes to other situations

APPLICATION TO PRACTICE: LECTURE METHOD

The lecture method is essentially a teacher-centered, one-way presentation of information and ideas. This method, like the discussion method, consists of a generalized sequence of phases easily adaptable to several varieties of lecture that are commonly used by teachers in secondary level classrooms. Information-giving, a technique presented in the previous chapter, was described as a mini-lecture, or shortened and informal form of the lecture. These primarily spontaneous introductions, explanations, and demonstrations can last from less than a minute when responding to a student's question to 5 to 10 minutes that a teacher might devote to introducing a guest speaker or simulation game. The lecture method is generally reserved for more formal presentations of subject matter and demonstrations lasting for as long as a full class period. It is appropriate for more extensive and complex one-way communication.

The research has indicated the lecture method is as effective as other methods in achieving its intended goals. Compared to other methods, lecturing is particularly effective when the purpose is presenting information that is not readily available elsewhere. It is also effective when information presentation needs to be tailored to a particular group and there is an intended follow-up using other methods. Furthermore, it is useful when long-term retention of the information presented is not the major consideration (Gage & Berliner, 1984). A lecture has its strengths and limitations that are consistent with the objectives for which it is intended.

Although all teachers need to be able to give information effectively in the classroom, not all teachers can lecture effectively nor should they be expected to. Critical to the success of presenting a lecture is the effective application of communication skills. Another related factor is the personality of the presenter. The ideal lecturer is dynamic, and presents material in a well organized and convincing manner. In order to be effective, teachers need to make a thoughtful selection of those skills which help hold students' interest and attention and stimulate their mental involvement. Particular attention needs to be paid to those motivating behaviors and skills presented in the previous chapter: physical movement, nonverbal behaviors, voice, lesson pace, and instructional mode. Each contributes to the creation of an enthusiastic teaching image. The application of these qualities is desirable whenever a teacher is instructing. They seem most pertinent and necessary, however, when a teacher is presenting information over extended periods of time. When communication is two way, such as during discussions, students' attention is not directly focused on the teacher every minute. The teacher's ability to induce motivation seems to be more critical during one-way communication.

The most important quality of a good lecturer is the ability to present material in an organized manner so that it is well understood by the listeners. A teacher delivering a lecture will obviously need to be well prepared on the topic. The most dramatic and flamboyant lecturers will be ineffective if they do not deal with matters of substance! Some lecturers rely on planned notes to deliver a talk. The well-planned teacher will incorporate visual aids to assist in the presentation of the content. They may range from a single transparency of a lecture outline to an elaborate demonstration involving numerous materials and artifacts. Styles of lecturers will vary as widely as their personalities and mannerisms; the effectiveness of a presentation is better measured in terms of outcomes rather than delivery style.

Three of the most common forms of the lecture method will be presented: formal lecture, interactive lecture, and demonstration. They have in common the primary emphasis on one-way communication over an extended period of time (more than 10 minutes), and they differ with respect to the degree of student interactive involvement.

Formal Lecture

The formal lecture at the secondary school level is the least used form of the lecture method. It is the most common strategy at the university level. An average student's attention span at the secondary school level is not extensive. After approximately 20 minutes students' minds even at the high school level wander. Younger students have even shorter attention spans. The exception is noticed in advanced placement, honors, and college preparatory classes where coverage of content is emphasized and many teachers feel obligated to prepare their students for teaching and learning in the typical university classroom.

The formal lecture is sometimes noticed in schools that have flexible scheduling and emphasize other instructional approaches that complement lectures well. Scheduled small group classes are arranged to discuss the material presented in large group sessions and independent study projects fulfill the needs of the more capable and motivated students who want to pursue topics, problems, and issues in depth. In these cases, large group lectures are sometimes presented by guest speakers who have a particular field of expertise such as a local historian, president of the Chamber of Commerce, a labor union official, or a politician. The large-group lecture, in which students are, for the most part, passively involved, would not be effective if it was not supported by a variety of other instructional approaches to encourage and stimulate students' active involvement in learning (Trump, 1961).

Interactive Lecture

This is the most common form of the lecture method in secondary schools. When teachers describe themselves as lecturers, they usually mean that they teach using interactive lectures. Teachers realize that students' attention spans are not long. Therefore, they attempt to involve students through the use of questioning by encouraging them to ask questions at various points during the presentation. Although some may wait until the presentation is completed before entertaining questions and comments, most lecturers encourage their students to contribute their thoughts and questions during the lecture.

The objectives a teacher has for the interactive lecture will primarily determine the level of questions he/she will ask during or after the presentation. It is common to hear all four levels of questions asked during an interactive lecture. For example a world history teacher in an interactive lecture on the Protestant secession might pause to review key facts and ask students the names of the six popes who ignored calls for reform during the Renaissance and brought the Papacy into disrepute (Level I). At another point the teacher might ask students to compare the reigns of Leo X and Clement VII in terms of acts that inadvertently helped pave the way for the secession (Level II). In order to stimulate some higher level thinking near the end of the lecture, the teacher might ask students for some principles that future Popes might have learned from the six decades of Papal misrule (Level III). At the end of the lecture, time permitting, a final high divergent question might be asked: Which Pope do they think could have had the greatest influence and opportunity to avert the Protestant secession? Questions judiciously interspersed throughout a lecture can successfully stimulate students' active involvement and increase the probability of longer term learning.

Demonstration

Demonstrations, as typically used by teachers at the middle, junior and high school levels, are basically formal or interactive lectures depending on the extent that student involvement is encouraged. Although many demonstrations are brief, and do not extend beyond ten minutes, others are complex and attempt to provide students with more information. Demonstrations provide teachers with an opportunity to show students a procedure, process or illustration from which they will be able to learn. For example, a physics teacher performs a demonstration using the Van de Graaff generator to show the effects of static electricity to the students. In an art class, the teacher demonstrates the technique of the Pointillists by creating a painting in their once-popular style. The teacher's intention in this case is not for the students to learn the technique but to appreciate and understand more about this school of painters, especially Georges Seurat and his devotees. The demonstration has the potential to contribute substance and immediacy to a lecture, to breathe life into it!

Teachers more commonly use demonstrations to model particular skills that students are expected to learn. Very often specific levels of performance are demonstrated. Examples include a basketball lay-up shot in a physical education class, computation of compound interest within a consumer mathematics unit, or turning wood on a lathe in a technology class. If students are expected to practice and perform the skill the teacher has demonstrated, the teacher is training students using the demonstration as a model.

Lecture Method Phases

Phase I. Entry: Preparation for Learning

    A. State objectives and rationale
    B. Provide a context for the new material to be presented.
    C. Focus attention on a key concept, generalization or principle that encompasses the lecture.

The purpose of the entry to a lecture or a demonstration is to inform students what the teacher intends to accomplish, why it is important, and to prepare students to understand what will be presented. The objectives could be verbally stated very generally or more formally in specific terms. They might even be listed on a handout or transparency. In this way the students will know what the teacher expects them to learn as a result of the presentation.

A rationale provides students with a purpose for the presentation and how it fits into the unit being studied. This generally satisfies students' urge to know why they are studying something. Teachers often overlook this component of a lesson because they assume it should be obvious to students. Following a rationale could be a brief summary of what has been covered up to a certain point in order to provide a learning context for students. Another approach to providing a learning context is to preview or give an overview of what will be covered in the presentation. The order of lecture-entry components is flexible, and depends on the level of structure of the presentation.

Preparation for students to assimilate information to be presented in a lecture would not be complete without an organizer. The purpose of the organizer is to focus students' attention on and help them understand the ''big idea'' of the lecture. In many respects the organizer is the common thread weaving through all the information presented. Ausubel (1968) stated that ''organizers are introduced in advance of the learning material itself and are also presented at a higher level of abstraction, generality, and inclusiveness.'' The purpose of the organizer, Ausubel continues, ''is to bridge the gap between what the learner already knows and what he needs to know before he can successfully learn the task at hand.'' In short, it is the glue that holds together in a meaningful pattern the information that is presented; or, stated another way, it is a hook on which to hang ideas.

The key to the effective use of organizers is to identify a central concept, generalization, term, or principle that encompasses the material to be presented and then relate it to what students already know or have experienced. Research confirms that organizers can increase students' comprehension of new learning material. It is logical that the more difficult the learning material, the more useful and necessary an organizer. In order to prepare students for a formal lecture on the Romantic period of poetry, a teacher might use the organizer ''love'' to help students understand the works of Keats, Shelley, and Byron. The teacher could start off with formally defining it from the dictionary and including some other diverse definitions from several other sources, including some teenagers' definitions. This would help relate the concept to students' lives. If the teacher was using an interactive lecture approach, he or she might ask students what love means to them. Going a step further might involve comparing and contrasting the love students have for parents, pets, and friends. The interactive approach increases significantly the chance that students will understand the concept and, therefore, the subsequent information on the Romantic period.

Another illustration of an organizer applies in a middle school science class. A science teacher wants to use an interactive lecture to demonstrate the principle of air pressure. An organizer can be used to ensure that students understand what pressure is. The teacher might explain the concept and use examples of pressure within the realm of students' experiences such as tires on a bicycle, a shaken can of soda or blood pressure. Once the teacher is sure the students understand what pressure is, several planned demonstrations may proceed.

Phase II. Presentation

    A. Sequence content from simpler to complex understandings
    B. Enhance presentation with visual aids
    C. Stimulate attention with verbal and nonverbal behaviors

During the presentation phase the main body of the lecture is presented or the demonstration occurs. Comprehension will be enhanced if the learning material is sequenced from simple to complex understandings and visual aids are used to illustrate key and/or difficult concepts, processes, or other content. For example, in a formal or interactive lecture on the Constitutional Convention's ''Great Compromise,'' an American history teacher might use as an organizer the principle that a compromise results when one gives up something to get something else. The teacher could easily relate it to students' lives by describing a conflict between a brother and sister over watching television at a particular time. An even more effective and appropriate question for an interactive lecture, would be to ask students about their conflicts with brothers and sisters and how they were resolved. After presentation of the organizer, the teacher would need to logically present the differing views on a plan of government of the large and small states. The Virginia and New Jersey plans could be compared by analyzing their strengths and weaknesses from the perceptions of the delegates to the Convention and, perhaps, by consideration of current political scientists' views on that episode in history. Finally, the formation, presentation, and acceptance of the Connecticut Plan, or "Great Compromise," would need to be explained, and the process of compromise analyzed.

In this illustration, the teacher progressed from the presentation of basic facts and information related to the Virginia and New Jersey plans to the more complex analysis of the role of compromise in resolving the conflict. The ability of the students to comprehend the lecture is increased because of the logical development and presentation of content. We can also imagine the teacher using several colorful transparencies detailing the provisions of each of the two plans, another of the Connecticut Plan that was finally accepted, and one on the process of compromise.

Phase III. Closure: Review of Learning

    A. Integrate with students' knowledge and experiences
    B. Transition to next lesson or activity

A teacher has the opportunity during the closure of a formal lecture to reinforce what has been presented with a review of key points, concepts and ideas. Students should also be able to raise questions and make comments, all of which will help the teacher determine how effective he or she was in presenting the lecture. In the case of the interactive lecture, the teacher might use questions to have the students examine the process of compromise they have used with friends and parents to get what they want, and compare it with the one that led to the formation of our legislative branch of government. In this way the teacher can diagnose the students' understanding of the content in the lecture by having them apply it to their own lives. This is a powerful approach to integration. The same approach could be applied to the closure of a demonstration.

The last component of the lecture, whether it be formal, interactive, or a demonstration, is the transition during which the teacher bridges the gap to the next lesson. Because the lecture is primarily one-way communication, students' higher levels of thinking are generally not being stimulated directly through questions. This, of course, is a major advantage the interactive lecture has over the formal lecture. In the case of a formal lecture or an interactive lecture in which little high level thinking has been encouraged, the transition is the ideal time to challenge students with a problem or assignment that will serve as the basis for the next lesson. This follow-up should be aimed at engaging students in divergent thinking (Levels III and IV). For example, the American history teacher might have students attempt to locate in the newspaper at least one instance of a compromise that was reached at any level of government over any issue, and evaluate the decision reached based on their perceptions of the criteria for a compromise. Several goals are accomplished through such transition. The bridge to the next lesson is made, students are applying what they have learned in the lecture, and students' higher level divergent thinking is involved. The closure provides teachers with an opportunity to directly evaluate students' understanding of the information presented and to encourage their application of what has been learned. Student performance during the closure and during the next class session is, indirectly, an evaluation of the teacher's effectiveness in applying the lecture method.

Scenario Analysis

Mr. Carl used the inquiry method that incorporated guided discussion in the hypothetical teaching situation. After the students had discovered the solution to the map "puzzle," he provided some background information on the concept of GNP—definition, examples of goods and services, and statistics comparing the GNP of different countries. His instructional approach could be classified as *information-giving* rather than *lecture*, primarily because of the brevity of the explanation.

The lesson could have been a formal or interactive lecture. The entry might have focused on the organizer "standard of living," with Mr. Carl giving illustrations of families with different living standards. He then could have related it to students' lives by asking them to examine their own and family members' needs now and in the future. The lecture would naturally be on several aspects of GNP intended to be covered, supplemented, perhaps, with transparencies illustrating some of the more complex concepts and processes: circular flow of money and products, categories of spending, and leading economic indicators. During the presentation Mr. Carl could use the transparency of the map depicting countries, each with a different size GNP. Another possibility would be to use it in the closure for the purpose of summarizing and reviewing.

SUMMARY POINT

The lecture method is the most straightforward instructional approach. It is the most effective way to convey large amounts of information not readily available to students. It also presents an opportunity for teachers to lay the groundwork for higher level thinking during follow-up class sessions.

Three closely related forms of the lecture method have been presented: formal lecture, interactive lecture, and demonstration. They all have as their primary purpose the presentation of content using a one-way communications approach. The interactive lecture is the most familiar. An important aspect is that teachers purposely incorporate questions at several levels to stimulate student involvement and thinking during the lecture. The formal lecture is the noninteractive form of the lecture method. Demonstration is essentially an interactive lecture, featuring display or performance, and explanation. Teacher decision making in relation to the lecture during the planning stage involves selecting which form to use to achieve the lesson's objectives. Selection of the form will primarily depend on the amount of content to be covered, the ability level of the students, and the extent of interaction desired.

A Lecture Method Analysis Form is included at the end of the chapter to aid in your observation and analysis.

REVIEW: IMPORTANT PRACTICES: PHASES OF A GENERALIZED
        LECTURE STRATEGY

Entry: Preparation for Learning

A. State objectives and rationale.
B. Provide a context for the new material to be presented.
C. Focus attention on key concept, generalization or principle that encompasses the lecture.

Presentation

A. Sequence content from simpler to complex understandings.
B. Enhance presentation with visual aids.
C. Stimulate attention with verbal and nonverbal behaviors.

Closure: Review of Learning

A. Integrate with students' knowledge and experiences.
B. Transition to next lesson or activity.

APPLICATION TO PRACTICE: THE INQUIRY METHOD

Inquiry is an extremely versatile instructional method because it can be used to teach content, problem solving, critical thinking skills, and decision making. Many consider inquiry to be synonymous with discovery, inductive teaching, reflective teaching, and problem solving. Writers vary somewhat in their interpretation of what it is. In its most general form, inquiry is the analysis of a problem in a systematic fashion. Several key words help us to understand more about inquiry. A problem is central to inquiry, and it can take many forms. It could be academic problem solving, such as mathematics students attempting to discover the process by which an answer was obtained. The problem could occur in social studies, such as, what can the students of a government class do to help get a particular candidate they support elected to the city council? Or the problem could be personal, such as a student's attempt to decide what to do to help a friend in a personal crisis. The word *analysis* suggests that the problem will be dissected into parts and studied; *systematic* means that the problem will be methodically studied through a step-by-step procedure. Inquiry is a process that students can learn and experience as they solve problems through reflective thinking.

Although the steps of inquiry vary depending on the specific objectives the teacher intends to achieve, there is agreement on a basic form. That form is John Dewey's model of reflective thinking (1910). An adaptation is presented here:

1. Identify and clarify the problem.
2. Form hypotheses.
3. Collect data.
4. Analyze and interpret the data to test hypotheses.
5. Draw conclusions.

The problem is created out of a discrepancy in perceptions of data. The more puzzlement involved and the more personal attachment the students have toward the problem, the better the potential for inquiry. Hypotheses are the students' proposed solutions to the problem based on experiences and information they have related to the problem. Data collection requires consulting resources for information related to the hypotheses. Once data have been collected, they need to be analyzed and interpreted to select promising hypotheses. As a result of this process, a conclusion will be drawn that reflects an acceptance, rejection, or modification of a hypothesis. Depending on the problem, the conclusion could be a solution, generalization, or explanation.

One of the strengths of the inquiry method is that both content and process are taught at the same time. Whether content or process is more important and therefore emphasized will depend on the objectives for the lesson and the teacher's judgment. Research confirms that inquiry is as effective as other methods in teaching content and may be better than most in teaching other learnings, especially the process of inquiry.

Teaching the process of inquiry is an opportunity for students to learn and practice skills associated with critical thinking. Helping students develop the ability to think is receiving increased emphasis because of the realization that students will benefit from being independent and reflective thinkers in the real social world (Paul, 1984). For example, in the area of social studies particularly, there is major concern that as much emphasis needs to be placed on the ''4th R''—reasoning—as on ''reading, 'riting, and 'rithmetic.'' The rationale is that responsible citizens are those who are aware of and approach societal issues, concerns, and problems rationally, and are active in working toward their resolution (NCSS, 1979). Mindlessness occurs when citizens act without reflective thinking, and being able to think critically increases the potential for effective citizenship.

Byer (1984) has proposed a series of critical thinking skills and several practical approaches to teaching these skills sequentially within a K-12 curriculum. The skills include: ''(1) distinguishing between verifiable facts and value claims; (2) determining the reliability of a claim or source; (3) determining the accuracy of a statement; (4) distinguishing between warranted or unwarranted claims; (5) distinguishing between relevant and irrelevant information, claims, or reasons; (6) detecting bias; (7) identifying stated and unstated assumptions; (8) identifying ambiguous or equivocal claims or arguments; (9) recognizing logical inconsistencies in a line of reasoning; and (10) determining the strength of an argument'' (p. 557). Most of these skills can be taught and practiced as students engage in inquiry in connection with analyzing and solving social issues and problems. In this case the process taught would be inquiry, with the content being information related to a current social issue such as updating immigration laws, corruption in law enforcement, increase in teenage suicides, star wars defense system, violence in movies, and the growing influence of political action committees. Critical thinking skills could also be thought of as the content that is taught.

When we think about preparing students to deal with personal problems, the skills associated with decision making come to mind. It should be apparent that there is considerable similarity between the processes of inquiry and decison making. To a great extent, both are appropriate in solving problems, both social and personal. One major difference is that personal attitudes and values generally play a greater role in decision making. Personal values need to be considered along with information gathered from sources. Solutions can then be proposed for which the consequences of each need to be considered. Finally a decision is reached, implemented, and eventually evaluated to determine the appropriateness of that decision (Armstrong, 1980).

Three forms of the inquiry method are presented: guided inquiry, open inquiry, and the individualized inquiry investigation. Their commonality is that they are primarily subject-matter oriented and they have as their structure the process of inquiry. Their differences lie in the extent of guidance provided by the teacher, and in the case of the individualized form, the number of students involved.

Guided Inquiry

The extent of the teacher's involvement during the implementation of inquiry is the primary difference between the guided and open forms. As the teacher becomes more involved more structure is provided, and this results in less freedom for students to take initiative and direction for their own learning experiences. The teacher assumes these responsibilities. During guided inquiry the teacher provides the data and the students are questioned in order to help them inductively arrive at an answer, conclusion, generalization, or solution. Because the teacher generally has the ''right'' answer in mind, or a narrow range of acceptable answers, the students are led to the conclusion (Shulman & Tamir,

1973). In this case the teacher, being actively involved, is more a director of students' learning and thinking than a facilitator. The guided inquiry form of the method is especially appropriate as a way to introduce the inquiry process to students. The structure serves as security as they venture into a new area involving different kinds of thinking.

Because of the necessity to provide guidance, the teacher's questioning behavior becomes very important in the guided inquiry process. Although the questions asked by the teacher cover the full range of thinking levels, the most effective ones to stimulate inductive thinking are those classified at Levels II, III and IV—high convergent, and low and high divergent thinking. As a result of the direct involvement of the teacher in questioning students, the effective use of a full range of questioning skills becomes critical.

One illustration of guided inquiry takes place in an 8th-grade science classroom. The teacher shows the students three test tubes all half-filled with clear liquid. A few drops from the first test tube is poured into the second and the liquid turns bright purple. Some of the clear liquid from the third tube is poured into the second and the purple liquid becomes completely clear again. As the students stare in amazement, the teacher asks them, "What happened?" to start the inquiry with a review of the facts. Once the problem has been clarified, hypotheses are generated as tentative explanations for the unusual event. The most difficult part is using questions to lead them to test their ideas, such as "What is this liquid?" "Suppose we poured the liquid from the first tube into the third?" "What would happen if . . . ?" The teacher needs to probe students' responses to focus, clarify, extend, and expand their thinking as they are guided to discover that the first tube contained a base (ammonia), the second contained a small amount of phenolphthalein in water, and the third was an acid (white vinegar). Phenolphthalein is an indicator of a base and the acid served as a neutralizer. As the result of being guided by the teachers' questions, the students were able to inductively discover the explanation for the puzzling event.

Open Inquiry

Students' freedom to initiate and think is expanded in open inquiry. In essence, they assume more responsibility for their own learning and, as a result, lessen their dependence on the teacher. The inquiry process remains the same with the focus on inductive thinking as students propose solutions, gather data, and draw conclusions. A primary difference lies in the data collection phase. During guided inquiry the teacher provides the data to help students draw conclusions; during open inquiry the students gather the data (Shulman & Tamir, 1973). Student questioning becomes more important during open inquiry because they ask questions and search for the answers. Teacher questions generally guide structured inquiry. The teacher's role is to facilitate by assisting students within the phases of the process. As part of this role the teacher also serves as a resource person, suggesting sources students might consult such as the library, and helping arrange other sources such as people in the community. Although the teacher usually commences open inquiry with a problem related to what is being studied and assists students in hypothesis formation, the students assume responsibility for data collection and generalizing. This is an essential component in open inquiry.

An illustration for an open inquiry lesson centers around a class of U.S. government students interested in establishing a recycling center in their community. Assume the class has been studying environmental issues with a particular emphasis on what they perceive as their community's problems. Inquiry was initiated when students decided to focus on ascertaining the extent of community support for a recycling center. Naturally they were hopeful that this would lead to the development of a center. The teacher guided them as they proposed ideas about how they could get support. Some of their brainstormed approaches were interviewing city officials for their suggestions and their perceptions of problems and issues associated with building a center, conducting a survey of citizens, attending a city council meeting to propose the center, contacting a nearby community that has a center to find out how they got support, and writing to the state and federal governments to see what guidelines might exist. Clarification was achieved as their purpose was more sharply defined and the list of ideas was reduced to four. The data-gathering phase was initiated when it was decided that the class could be divided into small groups, each assuming responsibility for investigating one of the proposed approaches. For example, one group planned to formally present the idea of a recycling center to the city council to find out if it had been considered in the past, if they might give tentative support to the idea now, if they had suggestions for getting more support, or suggestions for proceeding to get their idea approved.

The data gathering could take several weeks, most of it being conducted by the groups outside of the regular class sessions. After the information is gathered and analyzed by the groups, a class session will need to be set aside for the presentation of the group findings. The culminating activity of the inquiry process is drawing a conclusion and, in this case, finding out the extent the community supports the construction of a recycling center. In the open form of the inquiry method, the students are more involved in determining the direction of the learning process as they start with a problem of concern to them, propose solutions, gather and analyze the data, and draw conclusions.

Individualized Inquiry Investigation

The individualized inquiry investigation method (Wilen & McKenrick, 1987) involves identifying able and interested students who will benefit from engaging in independent study. This interpretation of the inquiry method most closely approximates the format of the open inquiry form because of the freedom given to students. The issue or problem devised should naturally relate to the unit currently under study and, most importantly, have personal meaning for the student. Examples are an American literature student who, after reading several of Ernest Hemingway's novels and short stories for a class assignment, wants to find out more about how his work has influenced other writers, or an American history student who wants to find out more about how the Japanese treated

American prisoners during World War II because his uncle survived the infamous Bataan "death march." Once a willing student has been identified, and preliminary research has yielded a general issue or problem area, a contract should be drawn up in order to specify the conditions of the inquiry investigation. The contract could be formal or informal, written or verbal, depending on the needs of the teacher and student. Important questions need to be directly answered: How much time should the student devote to the investigation? Under what conditions should the student be excused from class sessions to pursue the inquiry? Should he or she take the tests with other students? What is to be the method of reporting the investigation? How will the student's effort be evaluated? How will this grade influence the marking period grade? The contract needs to be designed to clarify mutual expectations

Once the contract has been agreed upon, the investigation should continue with a formal statement of the problem in question form. This will help ensure specific direction. The teacher then needs to assist the student to reflect on tentative explanations or solutions to the problem in order to guide the inquiry. It is important for the teacher to be supportive and nonjudgmental to encourage intellectual freedom. After assistance from the teacher in identifying key sources, the student should be left alone to pursue the inquiry. The role of the teacher is to encourage and facilitate, offering assistance when necessary. The individualization of inquiry investigations provides teachers with an opportunity to encourage responsible students to pursue their own interests within a structure agreed upon by the teacher and student.

Inquiry Method Phases

The phases of the inquiry method basically have their roots in the steps of reflective thinking as conceived by Dewey (1910). Although there is flexibility, the sequence of phases is considered more important than in the other methods presented in this chapter because inquiry is designed to teach an investigative process as well as content.

Phase I. Entry: Presentation and Clarification of a problem, issue or query

    A. Statement of objectives; provide rationale
    B. Identification of a problem, issue or query
    C. Relation to students' experiences and lives
    D. Clarification of the problem

The nature of the problem or issue selected as the basis for the inquiry investigation is important for motivational purposes. Although it probably will be at least indirectly related to the unit currently under study, students' attachment to the problem can be greatly enhanced if it in some way relates to their lives. Another motivational approach is to select a problem that causes a discrepancy between what students expect to happen and what actually does happen. A way to accomplish this is to present statistics that can be interpreted differently. The diverse interpretations can serve as a springboard to an inquiry problem. Statistics related to drug usage and abuse might stimulate inquiry in a health class, for example.

The objectives and rationale can be presented before or after the problem is presented, depending on a teacher's preference for an entry format. A problem may evolve naturally out of lesson content and be suggested by a student or a small group. Student initiation is a powerful motivator, particularly if a majority of students express an interest. The teacher generally plans for the investigation. Although a teacher-selected problem can be presented conveniently during the rationale, it should be presented in an interesting way in order to grab students' attention. For example, a vivid description of the final days of the Jonestown mass suicide in 1978 would be an interesting way to lead sociology students into investigating why and how people can be brainwashed into committing themselves so completely, and sometimes tragically, to religious cults.

How the problem, issue, or query is presented in the entry is equally important to all forms of the inquiry method. The opportunity for students to explore problems with which they feel close attachment probably occurs more often with the individualized approach because the student has a choice, and therefore would not be engaging in inquiry without interest. Open inquiry should also be a stimulus to some extent because of the freedom students have in gathering data. In the case of the guided inquiry approach, teachers tend to control students' involvement more directly because it is more highly structured.

Phase II. Formation of hypotheses

   A. Encourage the formation of tentative explanations or solutions
   B. Clarify hypotheses

A hypothesis is a plausible but tentative explanation for a discrepancy in information or student beliefs, or a proposed solution to the problem. They are considered tentative until they have been tested by data that will be gathered in the next phase. The teacher initially wants to encourage as many solutions as possible. In some cases few solutions may be offered because students are unfamiliar with the inquiry process so the teacher will have to encourage them. Creativity may even be one of the teacher's objectives during this phase, and the students are therefore expected to brainstorm solutions. In this case quantity is the primary emphasis, with the quality of proposed solutions being the focus later as the hypotheses are clarified.

The teacher can encourage hypotheses to be generated in the large group situation or in small groups, or in the case of the individualized approach, in a one-to-one meeting. Using small groups to form hypotheses may take somewhat more time than in the large group, but students may not feel as inhibited and may therefore contribute more. Once the students have generated hypotheses in their small groups, they need to be reconvened in the large group to share solutions and devise a list reflecting their collective thinking. While the hypotheses are being discussed for inclusion on the final list, terms are defined and assumptions clarified. The result should be a list of tentative solutions clearly understood by the students.

Phase III. Collection of Data

A. Facilitate the identification of sources for evidence
B. Assist in the evaluation of the evidence

The purpose of the data collection phase is to accept or reject each hypothesis. By this stage the students have shared some information about the problem by virtue of the fact that the problem was clarified and tentative solutions were formed. Sharing common knowledge and experiences is important in the initial phases of inquiry, but at some point information needs to be gathered from a greater diversity of sources and from more authoritative sources outside the classroom. Sources may range from references in the school library to interviewing experts in the field. If information is unavailable, students may need to order it by mail, which naturally takes time. Students may also wish to create the data themselves, as in the case of a survey form to be administered to parents or a sample of community members. In other cases, students may need to generate data through observation and experimentation in a science laboratory. The quality of generalizations students reach at the end of an inquiry investigation can often be directly related to the quantity and quality of sources consulted.

The teacher's role is to assist students in their identification of sources for evidence and to facilitate the collection and evaluation of the data. This interpretation of the teacher's role applies primarily to the open inquiry form of the strategy. Thoughts about sources might have been shared immediately after the hypotheses are clarified. Of course the range of sources will be limited by the problem under investigation. The teacher will have to take a more active role in acquainting students with possibilities for sources, particularly if they are neophytes to the inquiry process. The rich possibility of finding evidence to support hypotheses from nonprint sources such as films and videotapes, filmstrips, records and audiotapes, and computer data bases is often forgotten. The teacher's responsibility during this phase is to serve as a resource person who continually encourages students to consult and explore a variety of sources.

The teacher also needs to help students evaluate the quality of the sources from which they are gathering information. All sources consulted should not be given equal weight when deciding their influence on validating students' hypotheses. Students will need to know the differences between primary and secondary sources, how a writer's frame of reference influences the work, and how to detect a writer's biases and prejudices, for example. Standards for judging sources should apply to all sources including nonwritten ones.

A major difference between the three forms of the inquiry method is noticed in the data gathering phase. In guided inquiry the teacher provides the data and structures how students will use them to support or refute their hypotheses. In the case of the open and individualized forms, the students gather the data with the assistance of the teacher, whose role is to facilitate rather than direct. As an illustration, in Suchman's (1962) interpretation of the inquiry method, the teacher provides a science-related discrepant event and the students inductively proceed through the stages by asking questions to which the teacher responds ''yes'' or ''no.'' During the hypothesis formation and data gathering phases the teacher structures the inquiry so that students' questions are focused on the variables and conditions of the event. This knowledge is used to hypothesize and test relationships within the data. The formation of causal relationships leads to an explanation for the event. In essence, the students first hypothesize then collect and analyze the data through their questions, as guided by the high structure provided by the teacher. Suchman's inquiry training form of the method is essentially guided inquiry. It becomes more open as students gather data themselves as, for example, in the case when they literally test their hypotheses by performing experiments in a laboratory situation.

Phase IV. Testing Hypotheses

   A. Assist in organizing the data
   B. Assist in the analysis and evaluation of the data

The purpose of this phase is to examine the evidence that has been gathered to determine the extent it validates or invalidates the hypotheses. In essence, the students are testing the hypotheses. As the information is gathered and recorded, students will need to be concerned with how to handle the quantity of data, some of which might be incomplete and conflicting. Organization and presentation of the data are particularly important for the beginner in the inquiry process. Armstrong (1980) suggests that the data be recorded and categorized in chart form in order that students might analyze and evaluate them more easily. For example each proposed solution or explanation might be placed on a separate large piece of paper or transparency. Three columns might be set up labelled: ''Evidence Supporting,'' ''Evidence Not Supporting'' and ''Evidence Neutral.'' Students can then categorize the evidence they have found based on its worth in supporting or refuting each hypothesis. This structure will make it easier for students to evaluate the data.

This phase is similar for the guided, open, and individualized forms of the inquiry method. The structure the teacher provides for the process will depend on the capacity of the students to pursue inquiry. This is another reason for selecting a particularly capable and responsible student for individualized inquiry investigations. Once students have analyzed and evaluated the evidence they are ready to draw a conclusion.

Phase V. Closure: Drawing Conclusions

    A. Develop a generalization, explanation or solution
    B. Integrate into the unit of study

    The final stage of inquiry is the acceptance, rejection, or modification of the hypotheses. Drawing a conclusion is the natural follow-up to analyzing and evaluating the data that have been gathered. In fact, these phases often run together, depending on the nature of the problem being investigated and how the teacher structures the hypothesis testing. Although the data may strongly suggest that a particular hypothesis be accepted over others, the teacher should encourage students to support their view by reexamining the evidence. Questions that may need consideration are: Have enough data been gathered to arrive at a conclusion? Does the evidence support only one conclusion or could others be considered? or How final is the conclusion?

    The conclusion reached, whether it be a generalization drawn from a collection of data, an explanation of a phenomenon or observations, or a solution to a problem, should be considered tentative. Students may tend to accept a conclusion, particularly to a major investigation, that involves the opinions of experts as the final answer or the truth. Reality suggests that any conclusions drawn should be considered tentative because all the evidence related to any issue, topic or problem can never be available at one time. Students and teacher may have missed several key and influential sources. Furthermore, a conclusion reached may have to be rejected completely if new evidence is reported that refutes it.

    This final stage of the inquiry method is basically the same for the three forms discussed in this section. In the case of the individualized approach the teacher may meet with the students doing the investigation to review the conclusions drawn before writing the paper, if this is to be the means for reporting findings from the inquiry. The review made and questions raised during this final phase will increase the chances the student will arrive at a conclusion consistent with the evidence gathered.

Scenario Analysis

Mr. Carl used guided and open inquiry to achieve his objectives. The first part of the lesson centered on applying an adaptation of Suchman's (1962) inquiry training approach to stimulate students to explain the discrepant event as represented by the puzzling world map. Clarification was achieved as the students responded to "What do you see?" The inquiry was formally begun after Mr. Carl explained the procedure of student questioning as the means to gather data from the teacher. The second phase began after a series of student questions related to specifics about the map, and a tentative solution was offered. At that point Mr. Carl asked the student to test his hypothesis by gathering more evidence with more questions. He wanted the student to begin forming causal relationships (''Think about the relationships of the countries. How about a 'What if . . . ' question?'').

After several other student questions yielded other hypotheses and more data, one student eventually came up with the correct explanation that the map depicted countries' GNP. Mr. Carl rounded out this part of the lesson with a brief discussion on the clues, or pieces of evidence, that led to the discovery of the explanation. Guided inquiry was used effectively by the teacher to initially grab students' attention through the use of a discrepant event. Student questioning was structured to stimulate inductive thinking that eventually led to the explanation for the event.

After providing some information on GNP, Mr. Carl initiated the final phase of the lesson with a shift to open inquiry. He referred students back to the map and asked why there was a tendency for the smaller GNP countries to be located south of approximately 30-degrees-north latitude. Students responded with several tentative explanations and then he suggested that inquiry would be pursued in the next class period. We can envision him beginning the next class period with a review and clarification of the hypotheses offered so far. One indication of a data source was a guest speaker from one of the lower GNP countries to the south. The suggestion was also made that small groups might be formed for the investigation based, perhaps, on the hypotheses formed. If Mr. Carl continues with open inquiry we can expect the students will assume the major responsibility for gathering the data. Although time consuming, open inquiry provides students with the opportunity to examine significant issues and problems in-depth, using a process practiced by both physical and social scientists.

SUMMARY POINT

Inquiry is a versatile instructional method that is used to involve students in a process to analyze a problem or issue in a logical and systematic way. The problem is defined very generally and can be identified within subject matter content, societal issues, or personal situations. The process of inquiry begins with the problem, issue, or query for which an explanation or solution is desired. Students propose hypotheses, gather data, analyze and evaluate the data, test hypotheses, and draw conclusions. A key consideration teachers need to take into account when deciding if the inquiry method is appropriate is the extent to which inductive thinking and learning the inquiry process itself are among the objectives. The inquiry method teaches content, but its unique strength lies in its ability to teach an investigative process.

Three forms of the inquiry method have been presented with their commonality being the process itself. Their differences lie in the extent the teacher structures the students' inquiry by directing or facilitating the collection of data. With the guided and open forms, whole classes of students are generally involved, and in the case of the individualized approach, one or more responsible students are usually encouraged.

An Inquiry Method Analysis Form is included at the end of this chapter to aid in your observation and analysis.

Phase I —Entry: Presentation and Clarification of a Problem, Issue or Query

A. State objectives; provide rationale
B. Identify a problem, issue, or query
C. Relate to students' experiences and lives
D. Clarify the problem

Phase II —Formation of Hypotheses

A. Encourage the formation of tentative explanations or solutions
B. Clarify hypotheses

Phase III —Collection of Data

A. Facilitate the identification of sources for evidence
B. Assist in the evaluation of the evidence

Phase IV —Test Hypotheses

A. Assist in organizing the data
B. Assist in the analysis and evaluation of the data

Phase V —Closure: Draw Conclusions

A. Facilitate the reaching of a generalization, explanation, or solution
B. Integration and transition

APPLICATION TO PRACTICE: ADDITIONAL METHODS

Ten instructional forms of the discussion, lecture, and inquiry methods have been presented. These represent the approaches most commonly presented in the literature and most typically and regularly used by teachers in secondary classrooms. Many other instructional methods exist for which information is readily available to teachers. These secondary methods are more highly specialized and as such are used less frequently by the majority of teachers. Some are especially appropriate for attaining objectives of an affective and psychomotor nature. Since research clearly supports teachers' use of instructional variety and flexibility as means to maintain students' attention and increase achievement, consideration of the use of additional methods seems essential to increase the probability of effectiveness. The critical factor for selecting any method should be, of course, its potential to achieve the intended objectives.

Several other instructional methods are presented in definitional form for teachers to consider as they make decisions about matching objectives and methods:

Role Playing—designed to help students understand the perspectives and feelings of other people regarding a wide range of personal and social issues. This is accomplished by having several students act out, or dramatize, situations in which people are in conflict or faced with a dilemma of some sort. The majority of the class will be involved in observing and analyzing the enactment(s). The teacher's role is to structure and facilitate the role playing, and conduct the follow-up discussion(s).

Simulation—designed to help students study and analyze a social situation or process while being active participants within it. Simulations are abstractions of reality that have been simplified for classroom use. As students are involved in simulations, they role play, make decisions, and experience the consequences of their decisions. Many simulations have been commercially prepared as simulation games and therefore include the element of competition. The teacher's role is the same as in role playing—to structure and facilitate the simulation, and to conduct the debriefing discussion.

Game—designed to involve students in competition as the primary means to achieve a learning goal. An instructional game has rules, a structure for playing the game, and a method for determining the winners and losers. Games are ideally suited for a change of pace when reviewing for a quiz or test, for example. In this case the questions would be primarily Level I Low Convergent as a result of the necessity for students' answers to be right or wrong. The teacher's role is to structure the setting, facilitate by conducting the game, and manage the students.

Panel and Debate—designed to help students understand several points of view related to a topic or issue. The panel is more informally made up of a group of students who discuss an issue among themselves, based on their preparation, with a chairperson facilitating the discussion. The debate is more formal, with two small teams of students addressing opposite sides of an issue. Timed speeches and rebuttals are an important part of the debate structure. Panels and debates are conducted for the benefit of the whole class, which becomes involved through question and answer sessions upon the panel's completion. The teacher's role is to structure and facilitate, and perhaps conduct discussion to clarify and consolidate learning.

Laboratory—designed to involve students in actual experience or experimentation with social, psychological, or physical phenomena. This method is adaptable to a wide range of laboratory situations such as the gymnasium, home economics, art rooms, technical education shops, and, of course, all the science areas. In these settings, students are directly involved with materials associated with the task as individuals or in small groups. The teacher's role is to structure, facilitate, and manage.

Field Trip—designed to involve students in learning experiences in the community. It is appropriate for many subject areas and can easily be adapted in many forms. The advantage of this method is that students are exposed to and learn about the real world they cannot directly experience in the classroom. The teacher's role is to plan the logistics of the trip, facilitate the visit, and conduct the debriefing after the return to the classroom.

Computer-Assisted Instruction—as instruction's newest "method," CAI is designed to help students learn—generally on an individual basis—basic facts, skills, and concepts related to the subject. Although the majority of CAI programs are tutorial, increasing numbers involve students in higher level thinking. Simulation games involving students' decision making represent a growing body of software. In the case of the tutoring function, the teacher's role is to diagnose students' learning deficiencies, to prescribe an appropriate program to enhance learning and skill development, and to evaluate students' progress.

Central to the idea of instruction is that it is the means for "turning knowledge into learning" (Jones, Bagford & Wallen, 1979). Without a knowledge of and practical experience with a variety of instructional techniques and methods, Mr. Carl would not have been able to accomplish what he had intended in his lesson. The implementation of a planned sequence of instructional approaches brought the concept of GNP to life. The probability is high that the knowledge the students gained from reading was turned into learning by the teacher as a result of decisions he made while planning the lesson. Effective decision making is basic to effective teaching.

ACTIVITIES (ANALYSIS FORMS FOLLOW)

ACTIVITY I: DISCUSSION METHOD

Observe a videotape of a teacher conducting a discussion. Analyze and evaluate the performance using the analysis form for the discussion method. Devise a series of questions that you would ask the teacher to find out why he or she engaged in certain discussion-related behaviors. If the teacher asked you for your opinion about how to improve the performance, what suggestions would you offer?

ACTIVITY II: DISCUSSION METHOD

Prepare a 10-minute guided or reflective discussion on a topic agreeable to a small group of your peers in class. Base your discussion on a sequence of approximately ten Levels II, III, and IV questions. Incorporate them into a lesson plan that also includes an objective and means of evaluation. Make notes at several places in the plan to remind you to use specific questioning techniques such as wait time after high level questions, calling on nonvolunteers, and having students form questions. Conduct the discussion with an audiotape recording your performance and analyze it using the analysis form. Evaluate your effectiveness in attaining your objective.

ACTIVITY III: LECTURE METHOD

Observe teachers and college instructors using the lecture method and categorize them as a formal lecture, interactive lecture, or demonstration. Consider how they might be improved using the analysis form.

ACTIVITY IV: LECTURE METHOD

Plan a 20-minute lecture in lesson plan form structuring it around the three phases of the generalized lecture method. Be sure to build an organizer into the entry, develop an outline of the content sequencing simple to complex understandings, incorporate visual aids, and build a means to integrate the learnings in the closure. If you have an opportunity to teach it, be sure to audio-record it and evaluate your performance using the analysis form.

ACTIVITY V: INQUIRY METHOD

Use the inquiry method analysis form to evaluate an inquiry lesson you observed. An alternative is to observe a reflective discussion and suggest how it might be naturally extended into an open or individualized inquiry. As you design the modification, be sure to consider all the phases.

ACTIVITY VI: INQUIRY METHOD

Assuming you have been placed in a school as part of a teacher education field experience, discuss with a teacher the individualized inquiry investigation as presented in this chapter. Encourage him/her to be realistic in terms of its potential to motivate above-average students to pursue an independent study project. Interview the teacher in terms of its perceived strengths and weaknesses.

ANALYSIS FORM   *DISCUSSION METHOD*

ANALYSIS SCALES

TEACHER _____

OBSERVER _____

CLASS _____

DATE _____

OCCURRENCE	EFFECTIVENESS
1. Not evident	1. Not effective
2. Slightly evident	2. Slightly effective
3. Moderately evident	3. Moderately effective
4. Quite evident	4. Quite effective
N Not applicable	N Not applicable

CATEGORIES (Parts A–B Correspond to Occurrence and Effectiveness in the Analysis Scale)	A. OCCURRENCE	B. EFFECTIVENESS
PHASE I: ENTRY: IDENTIFICATION OF PROBLEM, ISSUE, OR TOPIC		
A. Springboard and/or attention-getter used		
B. Identify problem, issue, or topic		
C. State objective and rationale		
PHASE II: CLARIFICATION		
A. Establish procedures		
B. Define terms and concepts related to the problem, issue, or topic		
PHASE III: INVESTIGATION		
A. Ask levels of questions appropriate to achieve desired levels of student thinking		
B. Use questioning techniques to maintain discussion, and stimulate student involvement and thinking		
C. Encourage student initiative and leadership		
D. Request that students support opinions offered		
E. Ensure sufficient coverage of problem, issue or topic		

continued

Analysis Form: Discussion Method, *continued*

PHASE IV: CLOSURE; SUMMARY, INTEGRATION, APPLICATION A. Summary in the form of consensus, solutions, insights achieved in relation to topic covered, issue explored, or problem investigated		
B. Integrate lesson with goals and previous learning		
C. Apply discussion outcomes to other situations		

ANALYSIS FORM   LECTURE METHOD

ANALYSIS SCALES

TEACHER _____

OBSERVER _____

CLASS _____

DATE _____

OCCURRENCE	EFFECTIVENESS
1. Not evident	1. Not effective
2. Slightly evident	2. Slightly effective
3. Moderately evident	3. Moderately effective
4. Quite evident	4. Quite effective
N Not applicable	N Not applicable

CATEGORIES (Parts A–B Correspond to Occurrence and Effectiveness in the Analysis Scale)	A. OCCURRENCE	B. EFFECTIVENESS
PHASE I: ENTRY: PREPARATION FOR LEARNING		
A. State objectives and rationale		
B. Provide a context for the new material to be presented		
C. Focus attention on a key concept, generalization, or principle that encompasses the lecture		
PHASE II: PRESENTATION		
A. Sequence content from simpler to complex understandings		
B. Enhance presentation with visual aids		
C. Stimulate attention with verbal and non-verbal behaviors		
PHASE III: CLOSURE: REVIEW OF LEARNING		
A. Integrate with students' knowledge and experiences		
B. Transition to next lesson or activity		

ANALYSIS FORM   INQUIRY METHOD

ANALYSIS SCALES

TEACHER _____

OBSERVER _____

CLASS _____

DATE _____

	OCCURRENCE	EFFECTIVENESS
	1. Not evident	1. Not effective
	2. Slightly evident	2. Slightly effective
	3. Moderately evident	3. Moderately effective
	4. Quite evident	4. Quite effective
	N Not applicable	N Not applicable

CATEGORIES (Parts A–B Correspond to Occurrence and Effectiveness in the Analysis Scale)	A. OCCURRENCE	B. EFFECTIVENESS
PHASE I: ENTRY: PRESENTATION AND CLARIFICATION OF A PROBLEM, ISSUE, OR QUERY		
A. State objective; provide rationale		
B. Identification of a problem, issue, or query		
C. Relate to students' experiences and lives		
D. Clarification of the problem		
PHASE II: FORMATION OF HYPOTHESES		
A. Encourage tentative explanations or solutions		
B. Clarify hypotheses		
PHASE III: COLLECTION OF DATA		
A. Facilitate the identification of sources for evidence		
B. Assist in the evaluation of the evidence		
PHASE IV: TEST HYPOTHESES		
A. Assist in organizing the data		
B. Assist in analysis and evaluation of data		

continued

Analysis Form: Inquiry Methods, *continued*

PHASE V: CLOSURE: DRAWING CONCLUSIONS A. Facilitate the reaching of a generalization, explanation, or solution		
B. Integration and transition		

REFERENCES

Andrews, J. D. W. (1984). Discovery and expository learning compared: their effects on independent and dependent students. *Journal of Educational Research, 28,* 80–89.

Armstrong, D. (1980). *Social studies in secondary education.* New York: Macmillan.

Ausubel, D. P. (1968). *Educational psychology: a cognitive view.* New York: Holt, Rinehart and Winston.

Bellack, A., Kliebard, H. M., Hyman, R. T., & Smith, F. L. (1966). *The language of the classroom.* New York: Columbia University.

Berliner, D. C. & Gage, N. L. (1976). The psychology of teaching methods. In N. L. Gage (Ed.), *75th Yearbook of NSSE.* Chicago: University of Chicago Press.

Bridges, D. (1979). *Education, democracy and discussion.* Berks, England: NFER Publishing.

Byer, B. K. (April, 1984). Improving thinking skills. *Phi Delta Kappan,* 556–560.

Cooper, P. & Galvin, K. (1984). *What do we know about research in teacher training in instructional strategies?* Paper presented at the annual meeting of the Central State Speech Association, ERIC, Chicago.

Dewey, J. (1910). *How we think.* Lexington, MA: Heath.

Dillon, J. T. (1984). Research on questioning and discussion. *Educational Leadership,* 50–60.

Dillon, J. T. (1983). *Teaching and the art of questioning.* Bloomington, IN: Phi Delta Kappa.

Dillon, J. T. (1985). Using questions to foil discussion. *Teaching and Teacher Education.* 109–121.

Evertson, C. M. (1982). Differences in instructional activities in higher and lower achieving junior high English and math classes. *Elementary School Journal, 82,* 329–350.

Fielding, G. D., Kameenui, E., & Gersten, R. (1983). A comparison of an inquiry and direct instruction approach to teaching legal concepts and application to secondary schools. *Journal of Educational Research, 76,* 287–293.

Francis, E. (1987). The application of group analysis to classroom discussion. In J. T. Dillon (Ed.), *Classroom questions and discussion.* Norwood, NJ: Ablex.

Gage, N. L. (1969). Teaching methods. In R. L. Ebel, (Ed.), *Encyclopedia of educational research.* London: Macmillan.

Gage, N. L. & Berliner, D. C. (1984). *Educational psychology.* Boston: Houghton Mifflin.

Gall, M. (1984). Synthesis of research on teachers' questioning. *Educational Leadership*, 40–47.

Gall, M. D. & Gall, J. P. (1976). The discussion method. In N. L. Gage (Ed.), *The psychology of teaching methods. 75th Yearbook of the NSSE*. Chicago: University of Chicago Press.

Good, T. L. & Brophy, J. E. (1984). *Looking in classrooms*. New York: Harper & Row.

Hudgins, B. (1971). *The instructional process*. Chicago: Rand McNally.

Jones, A. S., Bagford, L. W., & Wallen, E. A. (1979). *Strategies for Teaching*. Metuchen, NJ: Scarecrow Press.

Joyce, B. & Weil, J. (1980). *Models of teaching*. Englewood Cliffs, NJ: Prentice-Hall.

Klinzing, H. G. & Klinzing-Eurich, G. (1987). Teacher questions, student utterances, and teacher reactions in classroom discussions. In J. T. Dillon (Ed.), *Classroom questions and discussion*. Norwood, NJ: Ablex.

Luiten, J., Ames, W. & Ackerson, G. (1980). A meta-analysis of the effects of advance organizers on learning and retention. *AERA Journal, 17*, 211–218.

McLeish, J. (1976). The lecture method. In N. L. Gage (Ed.), *The psychology of teaching methods. 75th Yearbook of the NSSE*. Chicago: University of Chicago Press.

Michael, T. A. & Weaver, R. L. (1984). Lecturing: means for improvement. *Clearinghouse, 57*, 389–371.

National Council for the Social Studies (1979). NCSS Social Studies Curriculum Guidelines. *Social Education*, 261–278.

Paul, R. W. (1984). Critical thinking: Fundamental to education for a free society. *Educational Leadership*, 4–14.

Peterson, P. L. (1979). *Aptitude-treatment interaction effects of three teaching approaches: lecture-recitation, inquiry, and public issues discussion*. ED 186427.

Ponder, G. & Davis, O. L. (1982). Social studies education. In H. E. Mitzel (Ed.), *Encyclopedia of Educational Research*. New York: Free Press.

Roby, T. (1987). Commonplaces, questions and modes of discussion. In J. T. Dillon (Ed.), *Classroom questions and discussion*. Norwood, NJ: Ablex.

Selim, M. A. & Shrigley, R. L. (1983). Group dynamics approach: a sociopsychological approach for testing the effect of discovery and expository teaching on the science achievement and attitude of young Egyptian students. *Journal of Research in Science Teaching, 20*, 213–224.

Shulman, L. S. & Tamir, P. (1973). Research on teaching in the natural sciences. In R. M. W. Travers, (Ed.), *Second handbook of research on teaching*. Chicago: Rand McNally.

Specht, P. H. (1985). Experiential learning-based vs. lecture-based discussion: the impact of degrees of participation and student characteristics of comprehension and retention. *Journal of Business Education, 60*, 283–287.

Suchman, J. R. (1962). *The elementary school training program in scientific inquiry*. NDEA Project 216. Urbana, IL: University of Illinois.

Thompson, B. (1981). Teachers' preferences for various teaching methods. *NASSP Bulletin, 65*, 96–100.

Trump, J. L. & Baynham, D. (1961). *Focus on change—guide to better schools*. Chicago: Rand McNally.

Weimer, R. C. (1974). *A critical analysis of the discovery versus expository research studies investigating retention or transfer within the areas of science, mathematics, vocational education, language, and geography from 1908 to the present* (Doctoral dissertation, University of Illinois, 1975) Dissertation Abstracts International, Vol. 35.

Wilen, W. & McKenrick, P. (1987). *Exploring issues related to the bicentennial documents using the I.I.I. approach*. Paper presented at the NCSS Great Lakes Regional Conference, Columbus, OH.

Willis, J. & Gueldenpfenning, J. (1981). Relative effectiveness of lecturing, modeling, and role playing in training paraprofessional reading tutors. *Psychology in the Schools, 18*, 323–329.

7   Teaching Strategies
for Promoting Achievement

The preceding chapters have discussed teaching techniques verified by effective teaching research and basic teaching methods that are essential to every teacher's practice. A strategy for the purpose of this chapter is a general approach to instruction. It subsumes a variety of methods such as were described in the previous chapter. A strategy serves as an organizer for the delivery of instruction by guiding decision making about the teacher's role, the students' role, the selection of methods, and instructional materials. A strategy helps the teacher make optimal use of methods and resources in achieving particular goals.

A distinguishing characteristic of the strategies presented in this chapter is that they emerge from the effective teaching research (Roberts & Kenney, 1985). Their resource is the compensatory education programs initiated in the late 1960s for the purpose of improving the achievement of pre-kindergarten and primary children. Since that time, use of the strategies from these programs has spread to secondary and college levels. The commonality of these strategies is that they utilize many of the effective teaching practices and emphasize as their purpose higher student achievement. They link relevant research and exemplary practice (Roberts & Kenney, 1985). These strategies are direct teaching, mastery learning, and cooperative learning.

As Joyce and Weil point out in their influential work, *Models of Teaching* (1980), there is not one single teaching strategy that is the best approach. Teachers need a variety of approaches to address their many instructional purposes and students' varied learning styles. Teachers will have a better command over their instructional decisions if they employ a variety of strategies and methods. Strategies provide teachers with an organizational pattern or plan with which to structure the curriculum, determine curriculum materials, and guide teacher behaviors with students. Strategies are the pedagogical arsenal to accommodate a wide range of instructional maneuvers.

OVERVIEW

This chapter describes three general strategies of teaching in sufficient detail to enable teachers to recognize their potential and initiate their use. The direct teaching strategy emphasizes structure and high teacher visibility, and is especially effective in promoting on-task student behavior. Mastery learning establishes minimum levels of performance that every student is expected to achieve. While traditional approaches consider time to be a constant and achievement a variable, mastery learning does just the opposite. The cooperative learning strategy takes advantage of students' natural inclination to sociability. After learning the skills of communication, group process, and leadership, students become an effective source of instruction for each other as they work together, primarily in small groups.

At the end of the chapter, analysis instruments are included to help the reader examine the strategies described in this chapter.

SCENARIO

Mrs. Blaine was reviewing her plan for tomorrow's lesson. She would be introducing a unit on composition in conjunction with a literature theme. The unit's purpose is to enable students to improve their written communication while exploring story elements and reacting to plot development. She had decided to structure this unit using the cooperative learning approach that she had learned about recently in an in-service workshop presented at the high school. She had made her decision about using the approach based on the following factors:

1. Her class includes seven weak academic students who have reading skills at the 4th-grade level and need much remediation and attention to motivate them to turn in any assignments.
2. Several students in the class have excellent writing skills but the majority of the students need more practice on fundamentals from paragraph instruction to punctuation usage.
3. Four students in the room are social isolates, ignored by the rest of the class. One of the four is a new student from Vietnam whose English fluency is weak.
4. The class is dominated by the "socials" and "jocks" who are quick to interact with the teacher by responding and asking questions while the rest of the class sits passively.
5. Ten students seldom turn in any homework. Six of these students received "Fs" for the last grading period.

Considering these factors, Mrs. Blaine felt it was time to try a different instructional approach that might address the difficulties of this class with its diverse, heterogeneous makeup and its high number of students receiving below-average grades.

The prospect of changing the class dynamics by mixing the extroverts and introverts, the academically able and the academically weak, the motivated students and the unmotivated students was exciting to her. But she knew that she would have to spend time over the next several days and weeks focusing the students on group and interpersonal communication skills, as well as on paragraph coherence and transitions. She had written the communication objectives into her unit.

Mrs. Blaine had decided that the group project would be a short story composed by each group, along with individual portfolios of compositions containing two short, critical essays on the assigned literature and one research essay on group dynamics. She had prepared a reading list of sources to help each group with background material and models for their essays.

Tomorrow she would introduce the new approach by involving them all in the group process game of putting together a puzzle in each group without talking. She decided to let the students experience this cooperative task, then at its completion they would talk about what happened and about their feelings during the experience. She would then organize them into their groups for the unit and outline their tasks and roles.

She had already decided that the isolates would each be assigned to a different group and would be in charge of the resource list of books. Everyone in the group would be given a certain responsibility.

On Wednesday much of the lesson would focus on group process skills that the students would have to utilize.

As Mrs. Blaine continued to review the structure of her unit and note where she needed to obtain more materials she felt considerable excitement about the learning experience ahead for her students and herself. She was glad that Mike Jones down the hall had been using the approach for a month with his general math students and would be able to give her advice on how to proceed. Tomorrow would start an adventure in learning for all of them.

In Mrs. Blaine's building, other teachers were trying varied approaches to instruction in order to raise achievement. Mr. Rosenberg had been using a mastery learning approach in his 9th-grade algebra class since the beginning of the semester. He had spent much of the summer organizing his curriculum with support materials in several units complete with pre- and posttests and specific instructional objectives that indicated the level of mastery the students must reach. He had arranged a file cabinet with numerous practice sheets and had also obtained some software packages on beginning algebra to use on the computer in the back of the room.

Mr. Rosenberg reported that the students were handling the individualized approach to instruction well. Several students were four to five units behind, but were working and progressing—even though their pace was slower than most of the rest of the class. Overall, he was pleased with the improved achievement of the students in the class.

Also, upstairs in the science lab Miss Fortunato, using the direct teaching approach, was ready to move from the presentation phase of the lesson in which she had conducted a demonstration on chemical bonding into the group practice stage. During the group practice she would review the concept using overheads and models, and would ask the students a number of questions to check on their understanding of the concept before they did their individual practice in the laboratory.

Miss Fortunato felt comfortable with the use of the six instructional functions to structure her chemistry lessons because they facilitated her lesson planning and helped her maintain much student involvement through comprehension checks and group practice. She was pleased with the achievement level of the class.

All three of these teachers were encouraged by their principal to examine and extend their instructional practices to accommodate strategies that were reported in educational research as increasing students' achievement. They had received information and an orientation to these strategies in a series of in-service meetings held in the district. Small summer stipends had been made available for curricular planning to implement the strategies. The school district was committed to focusing on the improvement of instruction to increase achievement.

RESEARCH AND THEORETICAL BASE

The first strategy to raise achievement to be examined is direct teaching. Direct teaching refers to the instructional approach emerging from the works of Berliner, Bloom, Harnischfiger, and Wiley (Peterson & Walberg, 1979) on the impact of time and content covered on student success. It is also based on the system of direct instruction developed by Good and Grouws (1983) on the teaching of mathematics following a structured approach that became identified as lesson functions. Although most of the research on direct teaching comes from studies of elementary classrooms, the strategy is presented here for secondary teachers so that it can be used at appropriate times and with the appropriate students, as explained on page 247.

Direct teaching refers to academically focused, teacher-directed classrooms using sequenced and structured materials. It also refers to teaching activities in which goals are clear to students, sufficient time is allowed for instruction, coverage of content is extensive, performance of students is monitored, and feedback is academically oriented (Rosenshine, 1979). In the past few years, Rosenshine has included the teaching functions from Good, Grouws, and Ebmeier's work (1983) to provide a six-stage sequenced structure to instruction (Sparks & Sparks, 1985).

Rosenshine (1986) in his report on direct teaching in the *Handbook of Research on Teaching* indicated that across a number of studies the more effective teachers in terms of promoting student achievement were those who maintained a strong academic focus and spent less time in nonacademic activities. Studies by Soar, Stallings, Kaskowitz, Solomon and Kendall (1970–1973) showed that teachers who most successfully stimulated gains in achievement played the role of a strong leader. Researchers found that classrooms organized so that children had a great deal of choice about the activities they would pursue had lower academically engaged time and achievement (Rosenshine, 1979). Rosenshine described the direct teacher as the more successful instructor in teaching content that is measured by achievement tests. This type of teacher structures and selects activities within a controlled classroom.

In the past, the picture of the direct teacher was that of a grim, didactic authority figure who instructed the class as a whole and dominated the class time with much teacher talk. This teacher made the instructional decisions and taught through lecture and drill for a high percentage of correct rote-memory responses. This picture caused many educators to question the negative side effects that this approach could produce. However, researchers confirmed to the contrary that direct teachers in more structured, formal classrooms with higher achievement results are warm, concerned, and flexible, and allow more freedom of movement (Rosenshine, 1979). These studies reported that direct teaching is effective in teaching skill subjects such as reading and mathematics, and does not produce a negative classroom climate. Other strategies may be more appropriate for achieving creative and expressive goals. As was stated in Chapter 5 (Elements of Effective Teaching), there is no *one* strategy for effective instruction, just as there is no *one* list of teaching behaviors that will guarantee achievement. These strategies and teaching behaviors need to be part of a teacher's information so that they can be tied to the accomplishment of certain goals, such as teaching basic skills to students who may react most positively to much teacher direction.

The teaching functions considered part of the direct teaching strategy reflect the information from researchers, working independently, who came up with similar findings on the systematic approach to instruction being used by teachers whose students had higher rankings on achievement tests (Rosenshine & Stevens, 1986). These studies were conducted mainly in elementary settings in which teachers implemented direct teaching behaviors and their students obtained higher achievement and/or higher academic engaged time than did students in classrooms where direct instruction was infrequently practiced.

Two noteworthy studies for secondary teachers using direct instruction need to be mentioned: The Texas Junior High School Study (Emmer et al., 1982) and Organizing and Instructing High School Classes (Fitzpatrick, 1982).

The second strategy for instructional variety and achievement improvement is the mastery learning model developed by Benjamin Bloom (1968) and James

Block (1971) and derived from the work of Carroll (1963). This strategy is based on the idea that learning depends largely on time—the time allowed for learning and the time needed for learning (Carroll, 1963).

Benjamin Bloom developed the mastery approach which maintains that all students in an ordinary classroom can master a subject given sufficient time. This instructional approach is an individualized, diagnostic one in which students receive immediate remediation if they cannot pass the formative test at the prescribed level. They continue to study and test until they have reached that prescribed mastery level.

The research base of mastery learning is less well established because it has been used in single school districts where rigorous research evaluation has not been applied to it, whereas the direct teaching approach has been examined in a number of national studies including the National Follow Through Evaluations (Stallings & Stipek, 1986). The main studies on mastery learning from a decade ago were reported in Block and Burns (1976) in their findings of seventeen studies comparing mastery and nonmastery groups. They found that mastery-taught students scored significantly higher 61% of the time on standardized tests. Students' interest in and attitude toward the subject, positive self-concept, and academic self-concept also ranked higher.

Since students are given more control over the amount of time for learning the content, their success rate is expected to be higher. This expectation that success can be achieved through effort has been shown by achievement theorists to affect motivation positively (Dweck & Goetz, 1978) (See Chapter 2). Many advocates of mastery learning recognize this expectation for success from the teacher and the student as the strongest feature of this model.

Bloom's Learning for Mastery strategy has been widely used around the United States and in 20 other countries (Block, 1979). It is used more often in elementary schools, but is included in this text because of the extent to which competency-based education is popular in this country. In competency-based instruction, students at various levels in their schooling must pass a competency test on selected performance objectives in a basic skill area such as reading, math, and/or composition. Using the mastery learning approach to remediation with students in a competency-based program, whether they be elementary or secondary, would be helpful for raising students' skill levels.

Mastery learning has its critics because of its possible effects of limiting teacher time with brighter students, its narrow view of the curriculum in terms of defined sets of skills, and its too structured and mechanistic approach to instruction (Stallings & Stipek, 1986). However, mastery-based educational programs have been reasonably successful in increasing the number of elementary students who have learned the basic curriculum (Stallings & Stipek, 1986), and is, therefore, an important instructional strategy for secondary teachers to consider when mastery of information is essential.

The third instructional strategy for promoting achievement is the cooperative learning approach that uses peer tutoring and team cooperation to encourage student learning. It emphasizes motivation, as does mastery learning, and like the other two models it can be implemented by teachers in both elementary and secondary classrooms using the instructional materials of that system. The key components of the strategy are peer interaction, cooperation, and communication (Roberts & Kenney, 1985).

Cooperative learning strategies are used to accomplish at least four purposes: (1) to raise the value of academic achievement among students and encourage students to help each other learn; (2) to use cooperation and peer instruction to benefit both high and low ability students; (3) to provide an alternative cooperative model to the competitive model most used in schools; and (4) to improve human relations among races and ethnic groups in a school.

One approach to cooperative learning developed from the work of Robert Slaven (1978) and staff at Johns Hopkins University is called Student-Team Achievement Divisions and Teams-Games-Tournaments. Another approach is Jigsaw, a cooperative program started at the University of California at Santa Cruz (Roberts & Kenney, 1985). A number of studies on these approaches were cited by Stallings and Stipek (1986) in the *Handbook of Research on Teaching*. Studies by Johnson, Johnson and Scott (1978), Webb (1982), DeVries et al. (1975); and Slavin (1983) report the effects of cooperative learning on student learning and attitudes. The studies show positive outcomes from cooperative learning on achievement and attitudinal variables; however, academic superiority was not clearly identified. The incentive structure used in cooperative learning was found to be an essential part of the model. Group rewards appeared to increase achievement in cooperative learning. Research reviews suggest that perhaps the key outcome of cooperative learning is in the affective domain, with more positive relations and peer support produced for students from varying ethnic and racial backgrounds.

APPLICATION TO PRACTICE

Each of these three achievement improvement strategies—direct teaching, mastery learning, and cooperative learning—will be examined regarding how they fulfill the following aspects of their instructional design:

> Purpose
>
> Focus
>
> Role of teacher
>
> Method
>
> Role of learner
>
> Structure
>
> Evaluation
>
> Appropriate content and types of learners

Direct Teaching

This strategy also may be called systematic teaching or active teaching. The information for this strategy was obtained mainly from the following authors: Rosenshine (1979); Barnes (1981); Good (1982); Rosenshine and Stevens (1986); and Stallings and Stipek (1986). For more detail on this instructional approach, readers are urged to examine these key sources, as well as the work of Madeline Hunter (1981).

Purpose. The purpose of direct teaching is to increase achievement by the teacher's attention to specific, analytical, academic objectives, by coverage of objectives to be tested, and by engagement of the student in academic tasks. Attention is to be given to promoting student success through a variety of means such as those described in Chapter 2. The teacher takes charge of the classroom in order to provide a climate for learning.

Focus. The focus of the strategy is academic and teacher-centered with a structured curriculum of sequenced materials useful for teaching skills and new information. Within this focus the teacher conveys that the business of the classroom is learning.

Role of the Teacher. This is a teacher-directed strategy which means that the teacher chooses the activities and controls the time spent on the phases of the lesson. There is much interaction of the teacher with the students in all phases of the lesson. The teacher's immediate, corrective feedback is very important for student learning. When the teacher is not involved in the presentation, or leading group practice, he or she is monitoring students' progress by moving around the room, keeping students on-task, giving feedback, and working with individuals.

The teaching practices described in Chapters 5 and 6 of this book are those appropriate for direct instruction.

Student. A teacher planning to use direct teaching would want to divide the curriculum into small segments or steps through such curriculum techniques as using skill analysis and conceptual mapping. After skills, processes, and concepts are identified and arranged in a meaningful order, they can be presented in small steps after which students are provided with classroom time for practice and feedback. Therefore, the basic elements of direct or systematic instruction include (1) preparing students for the lesson; (2) presenting the lesson; (3) students' practicing the lesson; (4) evaluating and providing feedback on student learning (Barnes, 1981).

The structuring of the lesson is very important in this model. Rosenshine (1983) and Rosenshine and Stevens (1986) put together from a number of research sources a list of six instructional functions which are essential to the structure of direct teaching. These functions include review, structuring and presentation, guided practice, feedback and correctives, independent student practice, and weekly and monthly reviews. The functions are presented below in more detail:

Instructional Functions (Rosenshine & Stevens, 1986)

1. Daily Review and Checking Homework
   Checking homework (routines for students to check each other's papers)
   Reteaching when necessary
   Reviewing relevant past learning (may include questioning)
   Review prerequisite skills (if applicable)
2. Presentation
   Provide short statement of objectives
   Provide overview and structuring
   Proceed in small steps but at a rapid pace
   Intersperse questions within the demonstration to check for understanding
   Highlight main points
   Provide sufficient illustrations and concrete examples
   Provide demonstrations and models
   When necessary, give detailed and redundant instructions and examples
3. Guided Practice
   Initial student practice takes place with teacher guidance
   High frequency of questions and overt student practice (from teacher and/or materials)
   Questions are directly relevant to the new content or skill
   Teacher checks for understanding (CFU) by evaluating student responses
   During CFU teacher gives additional explanation, process feedback, or repeats explanation—where necessary
   All students have a chance to respond and receive feedback; teacher insures that all students participate
   Prompts are provided during guided practice (where appropriate)
   Initial student practice is *sufficient* so that students can work independently
   Guided practice continues until students are firm
   Guided practice is continued (usually) until a success rate of 80% is achieved
4. Correctives and Feedback
   Quick, firm, and correct responses can be followed by another question or a short acknowledgment of correctness (i.e., ''That's right'')
   Hesitant correct answers might be followed by process feedback (i.e., ''Yes, Linda, that's right because . . .'')

Student errors indicate a need for more practice
Monitor students for systematic errors
Try to obtain a substantive response to each question
Corrections can include sustaining feedback (i.e., simplifying the question, giving clues), explaining or reviewing steps, giving process feedback, or reteaching the last steps
Try to elicit an improved response when the first one is incorrect
Guided practice and corrections continue until the teacher feels that the group can meet the objectives of the lesson
Praise should be used in moderation, and specific praise is more effective than general praise

5. Independent Practice (Seatwork)
Sufficient practice
Practice is directly relevant to skills/content taught
Practice to overlearning
Practice until responses are firm, quick, and automatic
Ninety-five precent correct rate during independent practice
Students alerted that seatwork will be checked
Students held accountable for seatwork
Actively supervise students, when possible

6. Weekly and Monthly Reviews
Systematic review of previously learned material
Include review in homework
Frequent tests
Reteaching of material missed in tests

Methodology. The instructional functions need not be present in every lesson, nor do they limit instructional methods to the lecture mode. Within the function phases a variety of methodology may be used. For example, in the presentation stage the teacher may use an interactive lecture or modeling with a demonstration, or a simulation. Even guided inquiry can be part of a presentation phase. Guided practice could involve a guided large or small group discussion on a focused topic related to the concept presented. Role playing in which students follow through the steps of a process to be learned also could be used as a method. Both independent and guided practice could be conducted in three ways: students working alone using written materials or computer materials; students working with others; and the teacher leading the practice. Certainly all the techniques including entry, closure, and motivation must be used, as well as the skills of informing, supporting, questioning, managing, and listening.

To summarize, the methodology of direct teaching needs to be varied and should include many methods with a systematic approach to instruction.

Role of Learner. Within this academically focused classroom, the role of the learner is to follow, stay on-task, and perform. If this structure appears to be stifling the creativity of the learner, the teacher can provide opportunities for the learner to use divergent and creative thinking in some of the learning experiences planned for the independent and review functions. For example, the student could demonstrate knowledge of the problem-solving process by describing a situation and the different steps groups of people might use to solve a problem (i.e., solving the problem of dealing with a class bully in an 8th grade gym class).

Evaluation. The direct teaching strategy includes both formative (during instruction) and summative (conclusion of instruction) evaluation. The teacher giving corrective feedback during guided practice and independent practice is a key to students' achievement. Frequent tests are given during the weekly and monthly reviews so that reteaching of key material can take place as needed.

Appropriate Subjects and Types of Learners. This direct instruction strategy is reported from the research to work best with teaching skill subjects such as reading and mathematics, grammar, and factual parts of science and history (Rosenshine & Stevens, 1986). Those bodies of knowledge that are hierarchical in structure with step-by-step progression can best be taught with the direct instruction model.

As to which types of learners benefit most from this systematic approach, research tells us that it is helpful for young children, slower learners, and students of all ages and abilities during the first stages of learning informative material or material difficult to learn (Berliner, 1982). Opportunities are provided for students to have considerable feedback and practice. Teachers can make adaptations in the model by shortening the time spent on guided practice and independent practice for more mature learners and increasing the presentation time for new material.

Another Model Using Direct Teaching. Madeline Hunter's Instructional Skill program contains many of the features of the direct teaching strategy and is being implemented via in-service workshops in many parts of the country. The program includes identifying clear instructional objectives, structuring instruction with lesson functions almost identical to those named by Rosenshine, and emphasizing the importance of comprehension checks. Although the Hunter approach has promise in the authors' view, the total strategy is not included with these instructional improvement strategies in this chapter because its research base is in the process of being established. Studies are currently being conducted in Pittsburgh by the Learning Research and Development Center, and in Napa and Marin counties in California (Stallings & Stipek, 1986) on the impact of this approach on student learning.

Mastery Learning

The next strategy to be examined for improving student achievement has been implemented in a number of large city districts such as Atlanta and Chicago to improve basic skills acquisition. This strategy is considered an individualized instruction approach using a structured curriculum divided into small groups of knowledge and skills to be learned. It is diagnostic/prescriptive instruction taught with the belief that all students can reach reasonable instructional objectives. Many of the components of direct instruction are included in this strategy with these important differences: it emphasizes flexible, structured time with the content, diagnostic/prescriptive teaching, and successful completion of all objectives by all students.

Purpose. The purpose of mastery learning is the accomplishment of a specific learning task at a designated performance level by all the students. The intent is that through this approach learning can be improved, and the variability in what students learn can be decreased. The assumption evidenced in this purpose is that all children without learning handicaps can master learning tasks, given the necessary amount of time and instruction needed to learn the task.

Focus. The focus of mastery learning is an academic one concentrating on the individual's acquiring specified skills and knowledge within a flexible time frame. The complete model developed by Carroll (1963) includes the following equation for learning (Gage & Berliner, 1984):

$$\text{Degree of learning} = \frac{\text{time allowed for learning} \times \text{motivation}}{\substack{\text{time needed to learn} \times \text{quality of instructor} \\ \times \text{ability to understand instructor}}}$$

Role of Teacher. This strategy is teacher intensive with considerable responsibility on the teacher to promote student success. The teacher starts by breaking down the curriculum into units with prerequisite skills and identified knowledge. Objectives are arranged according to the scope and sequence of the units. During instruction, the teacher presents the material in a variety of forms, monitors students' work, and tests students' progress in mastering the objectives. Using diagnostic/prescriptive techniques the teacher identifies the areas that need remediation. Whole class instruction, lecturing, and inquiry strategies can be used if the amount of time for individual students to achieve mastery remains flexible. In addition, the teacher must be able to provide alternative learning strategies for students when they encounter difficulties. Recording student progress and success in meeting defined performance objectives is an important part of the teacher's role. Students need to know how they are progressing in accomplishing goals.

The role of the teacher differs in two approaches to mastery learning—Bloom's Learning for Mastery and Keller's Personalized System of Instruction

(Stallings & Stipek, 1986). In Bloom's Learning for Mastery, the teacher uses interactive verbal instruction with the whole group as well as in monitoring individuals, whereas in the Personalized System of Instruction, the teacher monitors the curriculum as instruction proceeds through the self paced instructional materials. One approach that is similar to the direct teaching strategy relies on teacher interaction with students, and the other has students interacting more with materials.

Method. The diagnostic/prescriptive approach is used in this strategy in which the teacher identifies prerequisites, assesses students' present knowledge, and formulates testing to determine students' progress in reaching objectives. The emphasis of instruction is usually on the individualized approach with the teacher-to-student relationship being the key. Peer instruction and small group work also can be used. Indeed, the entire variety of instructional methods may be used with the total class or with a small group when the teacher covers the same part of the curriculum with everyone together. Supplemented alternative approaches must be used to accommodate different learning styles if students have not learned the content. However, methodology relies heavily on tutorial approaches with small group sessions, one-to-one tutoring, programmed instruction, alternative workbooks, games, and computer-based instruction.

In Keller's Personalized System of Instruction (PSI) the method is tutorial, with students moving through the structured curriculum via sequenced learning materials. "Thus a visitor to a PSI classroom would see students working independently at their desks with a teacher and possibly several aides moving from student to student to offer assistance" (Stallings & Stipek, 1986).

Role of Learner. The learner in mastery learning has more control than in direct instruction by determining the amount of practice time needed. This means that the student is given considerable freedom in deciding how fast he or she moves through the objectives. In Bloom's (1980) Learning for Mastery approach, the students take responsibility for mastering the task by working on their own, even though the class may be moving on to the next unit. In PSI classrooms, the students control their rate of progress by working through structured materials at their own speed throughout the course. The progress of the students rests heavily on individual effort and perseverance.

Structure.
Phase I. The structuring of a course or a unit for mastery learning can be considered in five phases (Bloom, 1984). The first phase involves breaking down the content into small units of learning in order for students to be able to learn and be evaluated on each incremental step. These units are arranged hierarchically with clear instructional objectives, and component skills and concepts are identified. Bloom (1984) recommends breaking the unit down into a number

of elements ranging from specific terms or facts, to more complex and abstract ideas such as concepts and principles, and a hierarchy of learning tasks.

Phase II. Phase II involves decisions concerning the use of appropriate instruction to enable students to accomplish the objectives. The methods of instruction are not prescribed in this model and are open to any number of strategies that accommodate the teacher's teaching style and students' learning style.

Phase III. In Phase III, the teacher designs and administers formative diagnostic tests which can be scored by the students to give themselves feedback on their progress. A formative test is administered after each learning unit is completed.

Phase IV. Students who have not achieved mastery are provided in Phase IV with additional materials and/or individualized instruction such as teacher or peer tutoring, or small group instruction to help the students learn the information. Students who have achieved mastery are provided with enrichment materials until the class is ready to move on to the next unit. In Bloom's LFM model the student is to relearn the material on his/her own time if mastery has not been reached when the class moves on to the next unit. In Keller's PSI model students work individually through these phases at their own pace throughout the course.

Phase V. The final phase involves summative testing to determine mastery. Students receive an Incomplete until they have reached the mastery level.

Student progress is rewarded in terms of individual mastery of specific objectives. Mastery is defined by the school system and is usually at the 80% level for the objectives in a unit (Roberts & Kenney, 1985).

Evaluation. As has been mentioned throughout the discussion of the strategy, formative diagnostic testing is critical to the program. Students may self-score the tests in order to identify the areas of difficulty immediately. These errors are targeted in subsequent instruction. Finally, summative tests are administered at the end of a unit or several units to determine grades. Most students are expected to reach mastery level; therefore, it is essential that realistic mastery levels are carefully set by each school or district.

Since this grading system is criterion-referenced (based on reaching objectives at a specified level), it is essential that the principal be informed of the teacher's use of mastery learning. This approach is accommodated best in an ungraded school where students move through the entire curriculum at their own rate.

Appropriate Subjects and Types of Learners. Bloom (1984) points out that mastery learning works best for subjects that can be sequenced with hierarchical objectives such as mathematics or reading in the lower grades. In secondary schools, subjects that have no prerequisites such as algebra and science work best. Obtaining mastery with students who have a history of difficulties with a subject such as 8th-grade arithmetic may necessitate too much time to make this approach feasible for them.

Keller's Personalized System of Instruction (PSI) is used more often in secondary and college classrooms (Stallings & Stipek, 1986). This approach that enables students to work through materials at their own pace works better with more mature students who have more intrinsic motivation.

Low-ability students or students with learning difficulties would be expected to benefit from the Mastery Strategy (Stallings & Stipek, 1986) since time is available for practice and remediation. Certainly students who have poor self-concepts in terms of their learning ability could benefit from this approach with its emphasis on success within the student's own time frame. Students' errors are considered an expected happening in the learning process; therefore, students' fear of failure can be eliminated. It is this positive motivational thrust that may be the strongest feature of mastery learning in promoting achievement.

Cooperative Learning

For the third achievement strategy, one can recall Mrs. Blaine's classroom in the scenario in which she was planning to implement a cooperative learning approach for her next unit. She had considered carefully the heterogeneous makeup of the class and decided that this cooperative strategy could benefit her students. She anticipated increases in both achievement and positive attitudes for her students due to their working together. Mrs. Blaine knows that this third instructional improvement strategy—cooperative learning—uses a noncompetitive, student-centered approach to learning, as did the Mastery Teaching Strategy. However, this model emphasizes students' working together in cooperative learning projects, engaging in peer tutoring, and receiving a grade based on the group's performance.

Purpose. The purpose of this strategy is (1) to increase achievement through group collaboration that enables students to learn from each other; (2) to provide an alternative to the competitive structure of most classrooms today that discourages the poorer student; and (3) to improve human relations in the classroom by promoting interdependent activities that teach collaborative skills.

A number of cooperative learning programs are in operation around the country, and the impact of several of these programs has been evaluated (Stallings & Stipek, 1986). Cited were Teams-Games-Tournaments, Student Teams and Achievement Divisions, and Jigsaw; other programs include Learning Together, Group Investigation, and Team-Assisted Instruction.

Focus. The focus of cooperative learning is both academic and affective, with emphasis on achievement of shared goals through cooperative efforts. To accomplish this focus, four basic elements must be included (Johnson et al., 1984):

1. establishment of positive interdependence;
2. promotion of interpersonal and small group skills;

3. maintenance of individual accountability for mastering learning tasks; and

4. promotion of face-to-face interaction among students.

Role of the Teacher. The teacher role differs considerably in this strategy from the other two strategies examined. Teachers act as facilitators in cooperative learning by establishing groups to work together on shared goals.

In the planning stage the teacher's responsibilities include (1) structuring the curriculum into units with objectives that can be achieved cooperatively and (2) establishing groups to work together on reaching shared objectives. These objectives must be clearly specified with both cognitive objectives and collaborative skill objectives.

In the instructional stage, the teacher's role involves (Johnson et al., 1984): (1) clearly explaining the task, goal structure, and learning activity to the students; (2) monitoring the effectiveness of the cooperative learning groups, providing assistance as needed, and giving feedback on students' work with content and group skills; then (3) evaluating students' achievement and encouraging their self-evaluation.

Methodology. The major methodology used is the small group approach. Within that approach, discussion, inquiry and modeling methods may be used by the teacher. Certainly the strategy of cooperative learning would not be used exclusively for all class work. Students need to experience independent work and some competitive experiences as well. At times the teacher will teach the whole class, using a range of instructional methods. However, the methodology utilized most frequently will include methods which accommodate group process skills and cooperative learning skills.

Role of the Learner. This strategy gives students much control within the group structure. They become both teachers and learners and are taught communication and group process skills, as well as leadership skills. Each student is expected to utilize these skills in order to promote group success. The reward structure promotes group importance. In most cooperative learning models, the students work in small groups of four or five students and receive a group grade or reward for their efforts. Their grade may be contingent upon a group project or the average of each student's progress toward meeting group objectives. Having to share the same grade encourages students to provide support for those members who are having trouble reaching goals, be they academic goals or the performance of cooperative learning skills. However, individual accountability may be maintained to meet specified objectives.

The students are held responsible for determining whether cooperative skills are practiced within the group. They are encouraged to analyze the progress of the group in light of each member's role. Peer feedback and self-evaluation are solicited. Therefore, the student's role involves responsibility to the group as well as to oneself for academic progress.

Structure. As one can observe in the scenario describing Mrs. Blaine's planning for a unit, cooperative learning is structured around a curriculum designed to be learned through cooperative groups of students who have shared responsibilities for accomplishing their goals. Specific lesson objectives are established within a group task. Much time must be spent in planning how to implement the curriculum and prepare students for this cooperative approach to instruction.

The following 18 steps for implementing cooperative learning are from Johnson et al. (1984), *Circles of Learning* and provide a brief outline of the procedure to use in structuring this model. Note the number of steps in the planning and preparation phases.

Phase I: Planning
1. Specification of instructional objectives—both academic objectives and collaborative skills objectives
2. Decisions on the size of the group
3. Assignment of students to groups—heterogeneity recommended
4. Arrangement of room to accommodate working groups
5. Arrangement of instructional materials to promote interdependence— all given same materials or each given different resources

Phase II: Preparing Students
6. Assignment of roles to ensure interdependence—each member given a responsibility
7. Explanation of the academic task
8. Communication of group's interdependency—reward structure explained
9. Communication of individual's accountability—each individual will be assessed as well as the group
10. Promotion of intergroup cooperation—encouragement of groups working together
11. Explanation of criteria for success
12. Specification of described behaviors

Phase III: Monitoring & Intervening
13. Monitoring students' behavior
14. Assistance provided, where needed
15. Intervention to teach collaborative skill

Phase IV: Evaluation & Processing
16. Providing closure to the learner—both teacher and students can summarize
17. Evaluation of quality and quantity of student's learning
18. Assessment of how well group functioned

Evaluation. Evaluation does not play as critical a role in this strategy as it does in mastery learning. Summative evaluation remains important, as does group and self-evaluation of the progress being made toward reaching individual and group objectives. A criterion-referenced approach may be used to assess that the specified objectives within the assigned concepts and information were accomplished. Students generally receive a group grade. They may also receive a grade as to their individual ability in functioning within the group.

Appropriate Subjects and Types of Learners. The cooperative learning approach can be used with most learning tasks, especially concept attainment, verbal problem solving, categorizing tasks, skill attainment, and judging tasks. Any lesson can be structured into a group learning situation that promotes collaborative skills. Cooperative learning has been used in such diverse subject areas as business classes and computer training (Johnson, et al., 1984). The approach has been used with kindergarten students up through adults in college. In Johnson et al., (1984), a list of schools and teachers around the country that use cooperative learning was printed. This listing included teachers in all grade levels, as well as in higher and continuing education classes.

It appears that low-achieving students can benefit considerably by cooperative learning because they are coached and helped to achieve objectives through group support. The effect on their self-image and motivation can be very positive. High-achievers can benefit also because they are working toward group success rather than their individual achievement, and hence feel less isolated. They also can find challenges in the opportunity to learn decision making, leadership role, and conflict management skills.

Although student achievement is improved because students help each other, it is in the area of human relations that the strength of this strategy appears to lie. Students develop interpersonal and group skills that encourage students to work well with others and accept each other's differences. Students from a variety of racial and ethnic backgrounds may be perceived more positively in cooperative learning situations.

SUMMARY POINT

This chapter has focused on three strategies—direct teaching, mastery learning, and cooperative learning—whose positive effects on achievement have been studied and documented. These approaches developed from compensatory education programs in the late sixties and early seventies for urban school elementary children but have since been used throughout the country in all school settings and with students of all ages.

Both direct teaching and mastery learning are structured approaches and require sequenced curriculum materials. Students are continually tested to see if they have learned the material, then recycled and/or retaught until objectives are reached.

Mastery learning allows students time flexibility in attaining the mastery level. In comparison, direct instruction moves the class along as a group, but allows for individual differences in learning through individual practice activities and group work. Cooperative learning emphasizes improved achievement through collaborative learning with positive group identity.

None of these three should be used as the sole approach to instruction. There is no one model for effective instruction. Each has much to offer in presenting strategies for accomplishing particular learning objectives. Teachers' decision making enters in when determining which parts of the curriculum can be accomplished most effectively by using a particular strategy. Beginning teachers need opportunities to instruct various units of the curriculum using these strategies and others in order to develop a varied teaching repertoire. Also, teachers need to assess the effect instructional strategies have on all different types of students.

REVIEW: IMPORTANT PRACTICES FOR ACHIEVEMENT STRATEGIES

Direct Teaching

1. is academically focused and teacher-directed;
2. uses sequenced and structured materials;
3. uses designated teaching functions to provide a sequenced structure for instruction;
4. emphasizes effective use of class time and coverage of content; and
5. is recommended for teaching skill subjects

Mastery Learning

1. is an individualized, diagnostic/prescriptive approach;
2. involves the student controlling the time needed for obtaining mastery;
3. uses pre- and posttesting and recycling with remediation; and
4. is recommended when mastery of information is essential

Cooperative Learning

1. is a noncompetitive student-centered approach;
2. uses peer interaction and cooperation to accomplish group learning projects and receive group award;
3. involves teacher structuring the curriculum into units with objectives that can be achieved cooperatively; and
4. is most effective in teaching collaborative skills and promoting group identity

ACTIVITIES FOR PRESERVICE TEACHERS
(ANALYSIS FORMS FOLLOW)

ACTIVITY 1:

Observe a teacher's classroom or see a videotape in which one of the three strategies described in the chapter is being used. Critique the instructional dimensions of the strategies by using the appropriate Analysis Form.

ACTIVITY 2:

Devise a series of questions that you would ask the teacher who uses one of the strategies. Ask questions concerning the effectiveness of the strategy on student achievement and attitudes toward school. Also question the impact of the strategy on the teacher.

ACTIVITY 3:

Prepare one lesson plan using the direct teaching strategy. Describe the teacher's role when engaged in this lesson.

ACTIVITY 4:

Using the same lesson plan as devised for Activity 3, modify the plan for a mastery learning lesson.

ACTIVITY 5:

Plan an overview to a cooperative learning unit that includes description of the following:

1. Main obectives to be accomplished
2. Role of teacher
3. Structuring of the groups (deciding which students are in which groups)
4. Group tasks
5. Individual responsibilities within the group
6. Evaluation procedures
7. List of possible group skills to be taught

ACTIVITY 6:

Participate in a role-playing situation in which you are trying to convince another teacher in your building to plan some units using one of the three strategies discussed in this chapter.

ANALYSIS FORM	ACTIVITIES FOR OBSERVATION DIRECT TEACHING

ANALYSIS SCALES

TEACHER _____

OBSERVER _____

CLASS _____

DATE _____

OCCURRENCE	EFFECTIVENESS
1. Not evident	1. Not effective
2. Slightly evident	2. Slightly effective
3. Moderately evident	3. Moderately effective
4. Quite evident	4. Quite effective
N Not applicable	N Not applicable

CATEGORIES (Parts A–B Correspond to Occurrence and Effectiveness in the Analysis Scale)	A. OCCURRENCE	B. EFFECTIVENESS
1. Is this a teacher-directed classroom in which the teacher makes decisions about activities and materials and teacher controls students' time in the classroom?		
2. Does the instruction have a stated academic purpose?		
3. Is there considerable interaction between teachers and students?		
4. Is the amount of off-task time for students kept to a minimum?		
5. Does the teacher have the curriculum divided into small units with skills, process, and concepts identified?		
6. Has the teacher prepared the students for the lesson with review and overview?		
7. Do the students know the objective of the lesson and how it fits in with the unit being studied?		
8. Does the teacher use a variety of approaches to presenting lessons including a. presenting material in small steps? b. presenting outlines when material is complex?		
9. Does the teacher provide time for guided practice with teacher and students working together as a group?		

continued

Analysis Form: Activities for Observation, *continued*

10. Is there a high frequency of questions and overt student practice?		
11. Does the teacher conduct comprehension checks while involved in the presentation and group practice phase?		
12. Does the teacher give immediate corrective feedback?		
13. Does the teacher reteach when necessary?		
14. Does the teacher provide time for individual practice with evaluation and feedback?		
15. Does the teacher monitor the class during the group practice and independent practice phases?		
16. Does the teacher plan weekly and monthly reviews?		

ANALYSIS FORM

MASTERY LEARNING

TEACHER _____

OBSERVER _____

CLASS _____

DATE _____

ANALYSIS SCALES _____

OCCURRENCE	EFFECTIVENESS
1. Not evident	1. Not effective
2. Slightly evident	2. Slightly effective
3. Moderately evident	3. Moderately effective
4. Quite evident	4. Quite effective
N Not applicable	N Not applicable

CATEGORIES (Parts A B Correspond to Occurrence and Effectiveness in the Analysis Scale)	A. OCCURRENCE	B. EFFECTIVENESS
1. Is the curriculum structured into small hierarchical units with prerequisite skills and knowledge identified?		
2. Are specific objectives with a designated mastery level identified?		
3. Are a variety of instructional techniques used to instruct students?		
4. Are students working independently as the teacher provides input where needed?		
5. Does the teacher administer formative tests to give students feedback on their progress?		
6. Are students given additional instruction and study materials if they have not reached the mastery level?		
7. Is ample time provided for student to accomplish the unit objectives at mastery level?		
8. Is student progress recorded in terms of individual mastery of specific objectives?		
9. Are realistic mastery levels set for the abilities of students in the class?		
10. Are students given corrective feedback as well as scores on tests?		
11. Is the student permitted to move to the next unit without mastering the previous unit?		
12. Do the class grades reflect success with mastery objectives?		

ANALYSIS FORM   *COOPERATIVE LEARNING*

ANALYSIS SCALES

TEACHER ——————————— OCCURRENCE   EFFECTIVENESS

OBSERVER ——————————— 1. Not evident   1. Not effective
                                      2. Slightly evident 2. Slightly effective
CLASS ——————————————— 3. Moderately evident 3. Moderately effective
                                      4. Quite evident   4. Quite effective
DATE ———————————————— N Not applicable   N Not applicable

CATEGORIES (Parts A–B Correspond to Occurrence and Effectiveness in the Analysis Scale)	A. OCCURRENCE	B. EFFECTIVENESS
1. Has the teacher structured the curriculum into units with objectives that can be achieved cooperatively?		
2. Is group collaboration evident in the classroom?		
3. Are students encouraged to learn from one another?		
4. Is there an emphasis in the room on the use of communication and group process skills?		
5. Is it evident from observing the groups that the following elements have been addressed: a. positive interdependence? b. cooperative learning skills? c. individual accountability for completing tasks? d. promotion of face-to-face interaction?		
6. Does the teacher give feedback on students' progress with group skills as well as progress with academic objectives?		
7. Are students encouraged to self-evaluate their academic and group success?		

REFERENCES

Barnes, S. (1981). *Synthesis of selected research on teaching findings.* Austin, TX: Research and Development Center for Teacher Education, University of Texas.

Berliner, D. (1982). Should teachers be expected to learn and use direct instruction? AECD *Update, 24,* 5.

Block, J. (Ed.) (1971). *Mastery learning.* New York: Holt, Rinehart and Winston.

Block, J. (1979). Mastery learning: The current state of the craft. *Educational Leadership, 37,* 114–117.

Block, J. & Burns, R. (1976). Mastery learning. In L. S. Shulman, (Ed.), *Review of research in education, 4,* Itasca, IL.: F. E. Peacock.

Bloom, B. (1980). Learning for mastery. In K. Ryan & J. Cooper (Eds.), *Kaleidoscope, Readings in Education.* Boston: Houghton Mifflin.

Carroll, J (1963). A model of school learning. *Teachers College Record, 64,* 723–733.

DeVries, D., Mescon, I., & Shackman, S. (1975). *Teams-games-tournaments (TGT) effects on reading skills in the elementary grades* (Rep. No. 200). Baltimore: Johns Hopkins University, Center for Social Organization of Schools.

DeVries, D. & Slavin, R. (1978). Team-games-tournaments (TGT). Review of ten classroom experiments. *Journal of Research and Development in Education, 12,* 28–38.

Dweck, C. & Goetz, T. (1978). Attributes and learned helplessness. In J. Harvey, W. Ickes, & R. Kidd (Eds.), *New directions in attribution research.* Hillsdale, NJ: Erlbaum.

Emmer, E., Evertson, C., Sanford, J., Clements, B. & Worsham, M. (1982). *Organizing and managing the junior high classroom.* Austin, TX: Research and Development Center for Teacher Education, University of Texas.

Fitzpatrick, K. (1982). *The effect of a secondary classroom management training program on teacher and student behavior.* Paper presented at the annual meeting of the American Educational Research Association, New York.

Gage, N. & Berliner, D. (1984). *Educational psychology* (3rd ed.). Boston: Houghton Mifflin.

Good, T. (1982). *Classroom research: What we know and what we need to know.* Austin, TX: Research and Development Center for Teacher Education, University of Texas.

Good, T., Grouws, D., & Ebmeier H. (1983). *Active mathematics teaching.* White Plains, NY: Longman.

Hunter, M. & Russell, D. (1981). Planning for effective instruction: Lesson design. In *Increasing your teaching effectiveness.* Palo Alto, CA: The Learning Institute.

Johnson, D., Johnson, R., Holubec, E., & Roy, P. (1984). *Circles of learning: Cooperation in the Classroom.* Association for Supervision and Curriculum Development.

Johnson, D., Johnson, R., & Scott, L. (1978). The effects of cooperative and individualized instruction on student attitudes and achievement. *Journal of Social Psychology, 104,* 207–216.

Joyce, B. & Weil, M. (1980). *Models of teaching* (2nd ed.). Englewood Cliffs, NJ: Prentice-Hall.

Peterson, P. & Walberg, H. (Eds.). (1979). *Research on teaching: Concepts, findings and implications.* Berkeley, CA: McCutchan.

Roberts, J. & Kenney, J. (1985). *Implementing four models of instructional improvement. Research for Better Schools, Philadelphia, Pa.* Paper presented at Annual Meeting of American Educational Research Association, Chicago. (ERIC Document Reproduction Service No. ED 256-742.)

Rosenshine, B. (1979). Content, time, and direct instruction. In P. Peterson & Walberg, H. (Eds.), *Research on teaching: Concepts, findings and implications.* Berkeley, CA: McCutchan.

Rosenshine, B. (1983). Teaching functions in instructional programs. *The Elementary School Journal, 83,* 4, 335–351.

Rosenshine, B. & Stevens, R. (1986). Teaching functions. In M. Wittrock (Ed.), *Handbook of research on teaching.* New York: Macmillan.

Slavin, R. E. (1978) Student teams and comparison among equals. Effects on academic performance and student attitudes. *Journal of Educational Psychology, 70,* 532–538.

Slavin, R. (1983). *Cooperative learning.* White Plains, NY: Longman.

Soar, R. (1970–1971). Follow through classroom process measurement and pupil growth; Stallings, J. & Kaskowitz, D. (1972–1973). Follow through classroom observation evaluation; Solomon, D. & Kendall, A. (1973). Individual characteristics and children's performance in varied education settings; Final Report, Gainesville, FL: College of Education, University of Florida. In M. Wittrock (Ed.), *Handbook of research on teaching.* New York: Macmillan.

Sparks, D. & Sparks, G. (1984). *Effective teaching for higher achievement.* Association for Supervision and Curriculum Development.

Stallings, J. & Stipek, D. (1986). Research on early childhood and elementary school teaching programs. In M. Wittrock (Ed.), *Handbook of research on teaching.* New York: Macmillan.

Webb, N. (1982). Peer interaction and learning in cooperative small groups. *Journal of Educational Psychology, 74,* 642–655.

Discipline typically has an ominous connotation for the teacher. The term conjures up an image of misbehaving students frustrating the teacher's sincere instructional efforts. One may be left with the impression that teaching would be more appealing if it were not for discipline. However, this perception takes into account only a narrow—but highly visible—band within the wide spectrum of discipline.

In a more dispassionate and broad-based perspective, discipline is neither good nor bad. It is a necessary and pervasive dimension of every classroom. Within that setting, discipline refers to the inclination of students to comply with the teacher's expectations. Discipline, then, is understood to be a condition that is in an important way internal to each student, respectively, for each student determines the extent of his or her own compliance. Taken collectively, the level of compliance is imparted to the classroom climate in terms of positiveness and negativeness.

When collective student behavior is "good" (i.e., when students are acceptably compliant), discipline is taken for granted. Classroom activities proceed in a manner that is satisfying to the teacher. Little overt attention is given to the subtle factors that result in the compliant behavior. But when "bad" behavior occurs, it calls attention to itself. Dealing with it becomes a matter of urgency on the teacher's part. At the very least it is annoying; it may even be threatening to the teacher and precipitate an uncomfortable emotional state. Impulsive or irrational discipline-related decisions are likely to occur when a teacher experiences this condition.

When teachers think of discipline, usually this uncomfortable "bad" condition comes to mind. Yet the "good" condition, during which students behave within the limits of teacher expectations, is also a part of discipline. Establishing in the classroom those conditions to which students respond positively is as much a part of discipline as the monitoring, controlling, and intervening behaviors more commonly associated with it. Discipline, in this teacher-oriented sense, refers both to the structure—especially the explicit limits placed on student behavior—intended to produce an optimum learning setting, and to the manner in which the teacher's authority will be used.

OVERVIEW

An informed belief system is the basis for sound teaching decisions, including discipline-related decisions. A commonsense or conventional wisdom basis for addressing the concerns of discipline is not adequate in the modern secondary classroom. The first step in developing a personal plan for classroom discipline is becoming informed regarding pedagogically endorsed principles. The second step is developing a comprehensive set of practices that attends to all four phases of discipline: prevention, maintenance, intervention, and adjustment. Finally, acquiring an understanding of teacher power in the classroom will be useful in implementing the intended practices.

The ideas previously presented on classroom climate, planning, and the elements of effective teaching (Chapters 2, 3, and 5) focus on producing the conditions of productive learning. Essentially they form the foundation of sound discipline. The thrust of this chapter is to help new teachers acquire a framework for decision making about discipline. It stops short of providing prescriptions, since these are situational and would require more elaboration than space allows. Many sources in the literature describe practices in detail, and the reader is encouraged to seek those which are pertinent to individual needs.

An analysis instrument is included at the end of the chapter to help the reader summarize important components of discipline, and observe discipline-related teacher behaviors.

SCENARIO

Jane DiFederico—"Mrs. D" to her students—was trying some new ideas in managing her general science class this third year of her teaching. Her first two years had not been all that bad, but she felt that the class could have accomplished much more if she had not had to spend so much time and energy maintaining a reasonable semblance of order. She had attended a course on discipline during the summer and had written a term paper describing a personal discipline strategy based on her new understandings. She would find out whether "theory" was helpful in addressing her concerns.

She had done some things the first few days of class that she had not done in the past. She established a seating arrangement that provided ready access to all the students, but that gave special consideration to students who might need the greatest attention. Expectations, just a few in number and positively stated, had been written on the board, discussed at length, and left there as a continuing reminder. Students were given the opportunity to express what they expected from her. Class routines and signals had been established and practiced. And, importantly, she had installed a system of "behavior adjustment notices"—written communication that created an ongoing record—to address chronic and flagrant misbehavior. With these things done, she felt more comfortable and in control.

Now the class was in the third week, and Mrs. D was beginning a unit on chemistry. As the bell rang, she stood at the front of the classroom affecting a businesslike demeanor. To her satisfaction, the class came quickly to order. As an advance organizer for the day's lesson she was using the concept of bonding. The class was asked to think of instances that involved an attraction between two things.

Claire called out almost immediately upon hearing the activity described, "My mom and dad."

Mrs. D moved a few steps to the board and tapped purposefully on Rule #3 referring to raising one's hand to be called on by the teacher. Claire raised her hand somewhat sheepishly. "All right, Claire, that certainly is one kind of bond. What are some more, class?" Several hands went up. Mrs. D pointed to Anita.

"People and dogs," answered Anita.

"Well, yes, bonds often exist between people and animals; emotional bonds I suppose we would call them. Why do these kinds of bonds exist?" Several hands that had been up went down as this higher level question was posed. As hands began to go up tentatively once again, Mrs. D called on Susan.

"They are attracted to each other." Mrs. D gave an encouraging nod and Susan continued. "Each one gives the other something it wants."

As Susan was answering the question, Mrs. D noticed Andrew and Leslie on the opposite side of the room begin a whispered conversation. She looked in their direction as she continued the discussion. "Yes, that is a key idea, Susan. And it applies to things other than people and animals, class. Leslie, can you think of an example of inanimate things?"

Leslie's attention was quickly drawn back to the class discussion and she remarked, "Magnets stick to our refrigerator door at home. That seems like a bond."

In response to Leslie's example, Ronnie exclaimed in a low but audible voice, "That's dumb." Mrs. D acknowledged Leslie's answer and called on Jeremy for his idea. Meanwhile she arrived at Ronnie's seat and looked sternly at him for a few moments until his eyes dropped. He had gotten the message. The discussion in the class proceeded for several minutes as many examples were given. Finally Aaron observed that it seemed as though bonding was everywhere.

"Exactly," Mrs. D responded enthusiastically, "and that is just the point. Now we're going to be studying chemistry for the next two weeks. What sort of bonds do you think we are going to be especially thinking about?"

"Mrs. D, my pencil is broken. Can I sharpen it?" interjected

Renee as she raised her hand but did not wait to be called upon. Mrs. D placed her left hand on her hip and gave Renee a brief, sharp look. Renee put her hand over her mouth and drew in her breath in the realization that her impulsive comment was inappropriate. But throughout the class Mrs. D recognized that there was some fidgeting and straying of attention. She had hoped to continue the discussion for a few more minutes, but realized now that a change of pace and activity was in order to regain students' attention and avoid further possible disruptions such as Renee's, or worse. She proceeded to answer her own question about the bonds they would be thinking about, then pulled down a periodic table chart as a reference for the class. A more direct teaching mode would help, she reasoned; they need some information about the elements so they can begin to understand how chemical bonding creates all the kinds of matter we know. She began a mini-lecture about the electrical charges associated with protons and electrons which establish the basis for bonding.

This brief glimpse into Jane DiFederico's classroom illustrates her informed systematic approach to discipline. Jane had been helped by having written a term paper in which we may assume her design for discipline was carefully thought out, the underlying principles were identified, and it had been shared with and critiqued by other knowledgeable educators. She quickly implemented her plan at the beginning of the year by conducting several activities intended to clarify expectations and reduce the students' need to "test the teacher." When inevitable misbehavior did occur, she was ready to respond. Meanwhile, she would do what she could within the instructional mode to prevent most of the incidental misbehavior.

Jane indicated that she was realistic in her expectations for student behavior and was willing to accommodate as necessary. As a sensitive teacher she became aware during this episode that the class was nearing the end of its tolerance for the discussion mode, even though her plan had been for further use of discussion. A likely response to students' waning attention might have been an expression of dissatisfaction with their off-task behavior. Jane's more enlightened response was to change the pace and shift to a more promising mode. Her informed belief system served her well in this instance of mid-lesson decision making.

When minor lapses in student compliance occurred, Jane took immediate but judicious action. In each case the lesson proceeded smoothly while Jane dealt unobtrusively with the target student or students. The tacit message the students received is that learning is important in this classroom, but that students' dignity is important, too. Students have probably begun to sense by this third week of class that Mrs. D "has her act together." No serious problem occurred in this episode, and this classroom seems to be an unlikely place to expect it. It could happen, of course, but Jane DiFederico seems prepared to deal competently with it if and when she must.

RESEARCH AND THEORETICAL BASE

Discipline, as a general aspect of every classroom, is difficult to study as such. Discipline does not exist as a discrete entity, but rather as a collection of many factors. Much of the research which is helpful in understanding discipline is more specifically focused on such factors as reinforcement, span of attention, or teacher transitions. Furthermore, this sort of research has as much implication for instruction as it does for discipline.

Clarification of the relationship between instruction and discipline is helpful in understanding the research in areas which affect both. Many of the teacher strategies and behavior that are intended as effective instruction operate simultaneously, but tacitly, to diminish misbehavior. Some teacher behaviors are specifically instructional; others are specifically disciplinary. Between these two extremes is an overlapping area which is referred to as classroom management, as is depicted by Figure 4.2. Prevention strategies and maintenance of order strategies such as clearly stating expectations and establishing efficient classroom routines fall within this area. In Chapter 2, these strategies are addressed as they relate to classroom climate.

Since 1970, over a dozen discipline-related strategies of varying degrees of structure have been developed. These so-called models are not based directly on research as such, but they employ generally accepted social and psychological principles. Wolfgang and Glickman (1980) arrange them along a continuum from those that are predominantly student-centered and use psychotherapeutic and communications principles to those that are decidedly teacher-centered and are based on behavioral psychology.

Gordon's (1974) *Teacher Effectiveness Training* is an example of a student-centered strategy. Discipline for Gordon is a matter of developing positive interpersonal relationships. He stresses the use of ''I messages'' to communicate one's feelings, and the necessity of avoiding winners and losers in resolving conflicts. Teacher authority is minimized as much as possible. While this approach, based largely on Carl Rogers' nondirective counseling, requires an unusual degree of learned behavior, aspects of it are useful for any teacher.

Glasser's (1969) *Reality Therapy* approach is an example of a mid-continuum strategy. His position is that students must find ways to deal with the world as it really is. Students' misbehavior signals their need to make a plan to deal more effectively with the conditions they encounter. Glasser's model describes a straightforward approach for the teacher, but its full implementation tends to be time consuming. Glasser also promoted the class meeting approach to provide students with a role in decision making within the classroom.

Perhaps the best known of the discipline strategies is Canter's (1976) *Assertive Discipline*. The bases for the model are the teacher-centered premises that the teacher must be in charge in the classroom and that no student has the right to interfere with the classroom instruction. Assertive discipline provides for predetermined rewards for compliant behavior and penalties for misbehavior. This model is popular with teachers because it presents a definitive set of procedures that the teacher controls.

Kounin (1970), in a series of landmark studies on effective classroom management, developed several key concepts in the area of group dynamics. His studies were conducted with videotapes in elementary classrooms, but the implications clearly extend into the secondary level. While scholarly work on discipline was published prior to 1970, Kounin's studies at that time marked the beginning of a more intensive scientific approach to discipline. In order to describe what he observed in classrooms, he applied terms to discipline in ways that had not been done before, most notably "ripple effect," "withitness," and "overlapping." Ripple effect refers to the influence that a control measure applied to one student has on the others in the group. Withitness describes teachers' awareness of what is happening throughout the classroom, staying one jump ahead of the students, and thereby averting potential misbehavior. Overlapping is associated with withitness in that it describes teachers' ability to attend to more than one activity at a time. Kounin also found that both more effective and less effective classroom managers tended to use similar intervention techniques. Prevention, one may conclude, more so than intervention, is the key to effective discipline.

Commendable efforts were made by the National Education Association through its "What Research Says to the Teacher" series to translate research and scholarly writing into suggested classroom practices. The first of three booklets was written by Gnagey (1965). In his opening section of the monograph, he lamented the limited amount of published scientific research on discipline. At the time of the writing of this booklet, works on mental hygiene, behavioral psychology, and group dynamics were recognized to have implications for classroom discipline. The second monograph (Davis, 1974) reflects the emergence of certain identifiable approaches to handling misbehavior: teacher dominant, analytic, behavioristic, student-centered, and teacher-student. By this time, a fairly extensive body of literature had accumulated. The most recent monograph (Swick, 1980) presents descriptions of "promising practices." This monograph, like the two previous ones, cites informed opinion and descriptive research as the primary bases for its recommended approaches. No experimental research is cited in any of the research-base monographs. This is, perhaps, not so much an indictment of the professional literature as it is a commentary on the manner in which research is translated into practice.

Weber (1981) examined experienced teachers' discipline-related strategies in order to determine empirically those practices which teachers perceive to be most effective. He found a surprisingly high degree of agreement among these teachers as they identified six approaches as being especially effective: using positive reinforcement, applying logical consequences, establishing and maintaining group cohesiveness, establishing and maintaining productive group norms, exhibiting unconditional positive regard, and using time out and extinction. Just as surprising is the fact that administering punishment was the approach least selected by respondents, even though this is the approach most commonly associated with disciplinary practice. Weber made the point from his survey that teachers tend to be eclectic in the selection of practices they employ, rather than conforming to any specific model.

Attribution of the causes of misbehavior was the topic of a study by Brophy and Rohrkemper (1981). They found that teachers tend to assign cause to factors outside themselves, often targeting the students directly. While many factors affect students' behavior, teachers' reluctance to recognize their own culpability diminishes the likelihood that they will make useful adjustments in their classroom practices.

Brophy (1982) reviewed the research on classroom organization and management to determine its implications for effective practice. He affirms Kounin's finding that conducting class in an alert, smooth fashion does indeed substantially diminish the occurrence of misbehavior. He further commented on the value of getting off to a good start, modeling correct procedures, and conveying purposefulness. The research he reported on, including his own, was conducted at the elementary level. While this research has clear implications for secondary level students, the fact remains that far less research has been done with secondary level students than secondary educators prefer.

The first weeks of school are especially important, according to findings from a study of junior high classrooms. Sanford and Evertson (1981) found from case studies in a low socioeconomic status junior high school of three teachers that teaching rules beginning on the first day, being realistic about the students' abilities, keeping students occupied, and enforcing rules consistently resulted in generally compliant student behavior. A good beginning is a necessary but not sufficient condition for a productive classroom; the teacher must continue to employ these effective measures to avoid deterioration of classroom order and productivity.

A research synthesis of literature on student discipline and motivation by Cotton and Savard (1982) included as a major conclusion that tangible rewards tend to have a temporary positive effect but often a long-range negative effect. On the other hand, classroom conditions that provide students with academic and social success experiences tend to reduce discipline-related problems. Furthermore, the authors assert that punishment in and of itself is ineffective. Only when punishment is clearly related to misbehavior and is recognized as such by the student does it have the intended effect.

Richmond and McCroskey (1983) examined the teacher power construct in the classroom. Five types of power are available to teachers: referent (personality), expert, legitimate, coercive, and reward (these terms are defined in the Teacher Power in the Classroom section of this chapter). These categories were originally defined by French and Raven (1968) in their research on supervisor style. Of these power types, referent power has the greatest impact on cognitive and affective learning, but expert power also has a favorable effect. Legitimate power and coercive power tend to retard both aspects of learning. Reward power is unrelated to either. The investigators conclude that teachers should attempt to employ referent and expert power, but to use reward power in preference to either legitimate or coercive power when possible.

Emmer, Evertson, Sanford, Clements, and Worsham (1984) used the research on classroom management extensively in writing their book on that topic for secondary teachers. The book presents practical suggestions based primarily on the authors' interpretations from descriptive research. The emphasis tends to focus on management techniques presented more or less discretely rather than in terms of a broad, cohesive plan.

Until quite recently, virtually none of the research was directly translatable into prescriptions for teacher practice. Even now, they represent only a small part of the literature on discipline. This gives rise to the misconception that research on discipline is not a very useful source of information for the teacher. In fact, research as it is initially reported serves to reinforce at the general level certain principles of discipline, and clarifies effective patterns of teacher behavior. Knowledge of these principles or patterns is then available to be incorporated into a teacher's belief system. The extent to which this knowledge actually is acquired by a teacher, the priority assigned it, and the extent to which it is reflected in practice remains an individual matter. In this sense, informed teacher decision making must be considered the most basic aspect of effective discipline. Research is a necessary but indirect part of it.

The literature on discipline is far too extensive to present a representative sampling in this brief review. However, the authors have selected certain works that they hope will convey some sense of its content. On the whole, the literature on discipline includes a great deal of expository commentary relating to theory, principles, and practices. Research is less abundant, and it is mostly descriptive in nature. Almost no experimental research involving manipulation of variables is available. Even with its shortcomings, the literature is the basis for the science of discipline. It is an invaluable resource for a teacher's informed belief system.

APPLICATION TO PRACTICE

Classrooms characterized by a positive climate and academically motivated students are those in which misbehavior of consequence occurs infrequently. Realizing this, however, is of little help to those preservice or in-service teachers who feel the need to understand the dynamics of discipline and who want to acquire confidence in their ability to establish order and decorum, and want to deal effectively with misbehavior when it occurs. An important purpose of this chapter is to contribute to the understanding of discipline and to make realistic suggestions regarding discipline-related approaches.

One may wonder why concern with discipline should still be prevalent after so many years of being recognized as a school problem? Writings from ancient

Egyptian, Greek, and Roman societies inform us of the recalcitrant nature of students from those eras. For example, an elderly Socrates wrote in the fourth century B.C.:

> From the day your baby is born you must teach him to do things. Children today love luxury too much. They have detestable manners, flout authority, have no respect for their elders. They no longer rise when their parents and teachers enter the room. What kind of awful creatures will they be when they grow up?

The question regarding the concern with discipline has no easy response, or it would have been answered long ago. The nature of discipline is such that a final solution is not even possible. Only the sound principles of discipline will remain constant; the application of those principles will vary as the factors and conditions in classrooms vary. The commentary in this chapter is essentially a rationale for this statement.

Discipline is not a neat, discrete concept. It is comprised of a rather wide assortment of more specific concepts. Addressing the topic of discipline is a multifaceted, complex task. The perennial efforts of educators to oversimplify discipline have led to the emergence of many widely accepted but suspect beliefs about discipline. Raywid (1976) astutely observes that "the most tyrannical of all our beliefs are those which are persistently unexamined—precisely because they appear so patently reasonable as to be mandated by common sense and impervious to question" (p. 37).

The professional literature presents a rather wide array of definitions of discipline, which may in itself be testimony to the misunderstanding often attending it. As was previously stated, discipline for the purposes of this book refers to the inclination of the students to comply with the teacher's expectations for behavior. Discipline, therefore, is a dynamic set of conditions that exists within students, individually and collectively, the effect of which is revealed in the classroom in terms of order and decorum. Direct implications for the structure established in the classroom and the use of teacher authority stem from these conditions. Discipline is not something a teacher does in the sense that a teacher "disciplines" students. To use discipline as a verb is to confuse it with a teacher's controlling or punishing acts. Discipline recognized as a dynamic set of conditions affecting the pertinent conditions, not just the visible symptoms, is clearly the basis for an informed approach.

Addressing the conditions related to discipline greatly complicates the task of the teacher in achieving a desirable level of classroom decorum. It is one thing to tell the class to be quiet, or to confiscate a squirt gun, or to intercept a surreptitiously passed note; it is quite another to create conditions within which these behaviors are neither attractive nor feasible alternatives in the students' view. The relationship of climate and motivation to discipline becomes clearer when one considers that student behavior is in large measure influenced by the quality of the climate and the level of their motivation.

The educational practices that are associated with effective classroom management are sophisticated. This fact has not been fully appreciated by educators. As a result, personal experience and intuition—sometimes generally referred to as "common sense"—are the basis of many teachers' discipline-related practices. For example, while one must be careful in generalizing out of context, the widespread use of punishment, when defined as retribution involving physical pain or mental discomfiture, is not defensible in a democratically oriented environment. Yet new teachers entering the classroom are socialized very compellingly into the use of retributive punishment. (Consider the frequent use of detention.)

A further implication of the sophisticated nature of discipline is addressed by Gage (1978) as he comments on the effect of multiple variables on teacher decision making:

> Scientific method (straightforward application of principles or "laws") can contribute relationships between variables taken two at a time and even, in the form of interactions, three or perhaps four or more at a time. Beyond say four, the usefulness of what science can give the teacher begins to weaken, because teachers cannot apply, at least not without help and not on the run, the more complex interactions. At this point, the teacher as artist must step in or make clinical or artistic judgments about the best ways to teach. In short, the scientific base for the art of teaching will consist of two-variable relationships and lower order interactions. The higher-order interactions between four and more variables must be handled by the teacher as artist (p. 20).

Discipline commonly involves decision making of the "four and more" variable type as described above. In a classroom of 20 to 30 students, each a separate personality with unique perceptions and needs, all involved with the many academic, social, and psychological factors indigenous to that setting, the complexity of achieving and maintaining order is apparent. Gage has pointed to the futility of depending upon preconceived prescriptions such as often are included in lists of "teacher shoulds." He contends that effective functioning at this level requires an artist dimension, or a level of performance that transcends routine or mechanistic applications. Redl (1966) has recognized this same phenomenon when he states that "for the job of establishing good discipline and maintaining it . . . the personality of the teacher is the most essential factor" (p. 254). This is not to say that teachers do not have much to learn from the professional literature about discipline, but in fact just the opposite. An informed belief system is essential for being aware of—let alone achieving—the desirable outcomes of effective discipline. Prospective teachers should recognize the value of being well-informed, but realize that their own personal interactive style and level of social development are critical factors as well. "Withitness," in other words, is a matter both of possessing social competence and of being well-informed.

Dealing with discipline is further complicated by its emotional aspects, especially in the case of teacher interventions with noncompliant students. When students misbehave in classrooms in obvious violation of the teacher's expectation, it may be sensed as an affront by the teacher. A teacher's self-esteem is in large measure a function of his or her own perceived competence, students' misbehavior signals the teacher's impotence at that given moment. By undermining a teacher's perception of personal competence, students trigger what psychologically are instinctive acts of self-preservation by the teacher (i.e., preservation of the self-concept). Meanwhile, those pedagogical principles that are relevant to such situations are likely to be ignored in the urgency to restore psychological comfort. The teacher is swept up in a tide of events of which he or she has only tenuous control and limited understanding—fertile conditions for nurturing a mystique. A succession of these events in the classroom can be devastating to a teacher.

The Myths of Discipline

The mystique of discipline resulting from the conditions described above has deterred teachers from seeking rational—or pedagogical, if you will— approaches. Some of the expedient approaches that have been devised deserve to be considered as the myths of discipline. The myths are widely accepted and form the basis for many teachers' discipline-related decisions. But these myths simply do not stand up to scrutiny; they are not pedagogically valid. Taken collectively they violate several generally accepted, virtually self-evident classroom principles: that students' worth and dignity must be respected in accordance with democratic ideals; that teachers should structure classrooms with the needs and natural inclinations of students clearly in mind; that teachers should use authority judiciously in the classrooms; and that teachers have a major responsibility for students' motivation. Recognizing the myths for what they are and rejecting them as the basis for one's discipline decisions is necessary for the development of a defensible approach to discipline. Eight of the more common myths are listed below.[1] These may be helpful in screening new ideas encountered about discipline or in purging already held ideas that are not sound.

Myth 1. Any student noncompliant behavior is self-evidently the fault of the student.

Myth 2. Discipline implies an adversarial situation which involves a power struggle between the teacher and students.

Myth 3. Good control depends on finding the right gimmick.

Myth 4. Every teacher can become highly competent in creating the conditions of good discipline.

Myth 5. The best teachers are those in whose classrooms students do not dare misbehave.

Myth 6. Punishment is educational.

Myth 7. The teacher should not smile until Thanksgiving.

Myth 8. Being consistent should take precedence over all other considerations.

Teachers have the responsibility to provide every student with the realistic opportunity for emotional comfort and personal success. It is unrealistic, possibly unethical, to force students to fit the school without regard for any other concerns, for to do so is not only self-serving, but also the discipline problems that result from this approach underscore its inadequacy.

In the scenario at the beginning of the chapter, Jane DiFederico was depicted as using appropriate approaches to address the disciplinary aspects of her classroom. If she had subscribed to Myth Number 1 (misbehavior is self-evidently the fault of the students), she may simply have proceeded with her lesson as originally planned even as students grew restive. Then, when misbehavior occurred on the part of students whose attention spans had been exceeded, she may have acted in terms of Myth Number 3 (good control depends on finding the right gimmick) and Myth Number 7 (punishment is educational). In so doing, she could have assigned a detention to offending students with the rationalization that they deserved it and would know better next time. One does not need to proceed very far with this type of scenario to realize what sort of climate is being created in such a classroom, and that a self-serving teacher is exploiting teacher authority.

Students should be expected to cope with reasonable conditions and responsibilities and be dealt with firmly when they do not conform with the necessary expectations of a democratic institution. But even more importantly, children need the guidance of enlightened teachers who are free of the shackles of the myths of discipline and who employ practices which reflect the best of both the art and science of teaching.

Principles of Discipline

Discipline is sometimes thought of essentially as reacting to misbehavior and restoring classroom order. When this is the case, the ends may be considered to justify the means, which gives rise to misguided and punitive control techniques. However, an educationally sound approach to discipline has its basis in humane, democratically oriented principles. They function both as a guide and a check in the teachers' discipline-related decisions. As examples, therefore, teachers' discipline approaches should:

1. be conceived on the basis of pedagogical and human relations principles and in all cases preserve the dignity and personal integrity of the students.
2. have a developmental thrust that produces important personal and social learning outcomes.
3. reflect the belief that promoting self-control in students is at least as important as procuring their compliance.

4. have the intent of doing something *for* students more so than doing something *to* them.
5. avoid aggravating the problem of an already troubled student.

SUMMARY POINT

Teachers' discipline-related decisions are influenced by philosophical considerations, pedagogical principles, and teacher personality. Purposeful reference to each of these sources is necessary for each teacher in the development of his or her informed approach to discipline.

REVIEW: IMPORTANT CONSIDERATIONS REGARDING DISCIPLINE

1. Discipline is usefully considered to be the inclination of students to comply with the teacher's expectations.
2. Refer to the myths of discipline as an aid in scrutinizing current ideas and selecting new practices.
3. Keep the faith; expedients may seem to serve the moment but they undermine the quality of discipline.

The Phases of Discipline

While becoming aware of the myths and developing an informed belief system, teachers must also acquire a clear understanding of the concept of discipline. As was implied by the definition of discipline in terms of student predispositions, it is a neutral concept, a means of categorizing certain factors related to interaction in the classroom. Realistically, however, discipline often has a negative connotation for practitioners because it conjures images of misbehavior, the primary source of teachers' apprehension. Developing an informed, practical approach to discipline requires that one transcend the intuitive, often negative and simplistic view, that frequently exists and acquire a comprehensive awareness of the several interrelated components. A straightforward approach to acquiring a comprehensive view of discipline is to consider in order the nature and implications of its four phases: prevention, maintenance, intervention, and adjustment.

Prevention. This phase is first, both logically and intuitively, in the process. The chapters on classroom climate, planning, and instruction addressed this phase of discipline in important ways. The climate that is developed over time through the cumulative interactions of teacher and students establishes the social norms that both define and limit appropriate student behavior. The motivation, especially intrinsic motivation, that is associated with the learning activities energizes both the substance and direction of students' behavior. When this motivation is strong, students' immediate basic drives are satisfied, or at least sublimated, and misbehavior is not an attractive alternative. Thus it is obvious that teachers need to be well prepared, to try to make the topic somehow relevant (otherwise why teach it?), to provide for variety and individual differences, and to be enthusiastic, fair-minded, and good-humored. Complying with these conditions is the most crucial aspect of discipline; paradoxically, these conditions do not readily come to teachers' minds when concerns about discipline arise. Rather, teachers are more likely to think of discipline in terms of authority and control.

Motivation is so important to prevention, and therefore to positive discipline, that it is again being given attention in this section. Ardrey's (1970) theory of motivation provides a useful perspective on the role of the teacher in establishing positive conditions for learning. He postulated that human beings have three basic psychological needs: identity, stimulation, and security. We have extended this list to include the need for power. When these needs are not sufficiently met, deficiency conditions occur, respectively: anonymity, boredom, anxiety, and impotence. If one were to design a situation in which the deficiency conditions were the intention, it is likely that something that looks like a classroom would result! Consider the possibilities for relative anonymity in a classroom of 20 to 30 students; for boredom when physically and socially active adolescents are rendered mostly passive and quiet for extended periods of time while they study material about which they have limited innate interest; for anxiety in a setting in which their academic achievement is incessantly tested and their social status is tentative; and for impotence as they are manipulated without personal recourse by the whim of the teacher.

This obviously is a pessimistic view of the classroom, and yet Silberman (1970) and Goodlad (1983) have reported through their research that these conditions—characterized as "mindlessness" and "monotonous sameness"—are all too common in American classrooms. That is the bad news; the good news is that teachers can do much to provide for the basic needs of students in the classroom setting in the four critical areas of identity, stimulation, security, and power. In the organization of secondary schools teachers are inclined to view themselves as purveyors of their disciplines. Teachers need to sense what lies beyond that narrow interpretation of their role. Preferably, they should conceive of themselves as agents for enriching their students' lives in many dimensions.

Teachers can give straightforward help to students in the area of identity by knowing their names and using them outside as well as inside the classroom. A greeting by name from the teacher is very satisfying to a student. Beyond that, knowing students more personally provides opportunities to refer to them in the course of learning activities: Bill is an avid birdwatcher; Jennie is a fine pianist; Danny, who is disfigured from a childhood burn accident, skydives on weekends; Allison has lived in seven different states. Teachers may make special efforts to talk with students, especially shy or unpopular ones. Eating lunch with students occasionally may be appropriate. By using praise judiciously, a teacher can make a student's day. Supportive notes on students' papers are also helpful. As these suggestions indicate, providing students with evidence of their worth as human beings basically involves the application of effective human relations principles.

Stimulation is the need factor that is most readily associated with motivation. Teaching approaches in achieving it make up much of the commentary on effective teaching. In a sense, one can consider the instructional ideas in Chapter 2 through Chapter 7, and in particular Chapter 5, as the basis for promoting compliant student behavior. More specifically, teacher enthusiasm and liveliness contribute to stimulation. Providing students with a credible rationale for learning activities and convincing students of the relevance of a topic is helpful. In the course of instruction, teachers should plan for "peak experiences" that will be remembered when the Compromise of 1820, quadratic equations, gerunds, and sporophytes are forgotten. These might include dinner at an ethnic restaurant, a three-day backpacking expedition, being a quasi-official city or county officeholder for a day, or developing a mural for the cafeteria wall.

Finally, the teacher gains credibility by modeling his or her academic discipline for students: the math teacher who is a computer specialist; the English teacher who publishes poetry; or the technology teacher who flies an aircraft of her own design. Being a showman in the classroom helps, but over time being a scholar of substance may account for more for the purpose of stimulating students to achieve academically.

Students' needs for security essentially require that the teacher help them feel confident that they will be able to cope sufficiently with the tasks and challenges of schooling. Providing every student with the reasonable opportunity for success is most important in this regard. This involves recognizing individual differences among students and accommodating them in appropriate—even creative—ways. Such strategies as variable grouping, differentiated expectations and assignments, individual projects and independent learning, peer tutoring and cooperative learning arrangements, and grade contracts with stress on personal goals and personal improvement may be employed. A formative approach to testing that de-emphasizes the competitive aspects of grades and stresses feedback and corrective measures is recommended. Tests then become learning aids instead of simply the basis for grades. Teaching study skills to the students and monitoring their use is a straightforward means of contributing to students' confidence in coping with class assignments. The strategies for promoting a sense of security have an effect on students' self-concept and identity, as well. These categories are not mutually exclusive.

Power, like security, is a need which has implications throughout the needs categories, but it has a particular focus that is useful for teachers. By power we mean that everyone has the need to exert reasonable control over his or her own life and have influence among associates. Two strategies cited above regarding the security need, independent learning and grade contracts, are pertinent to satisfying the power need as well. Students' perceptions and opinions should be sought when feasible and acted upon when possible. The classroom should be established as a participatory democracy, but with the necessary limitations imposed by the school organization. Classroom meetings are a common and useful mode for addressing classroom concerns. Within this setting the students are encouraged to "own" the learning objectives established within the class. Having access to power through these means diminishes students' needs to seek power in less desirable, possibly disruptive, ways; or worse, to experience anxiety from feelings of frustration and develop increasingly negative attitudes over time.

The commentary regarding the four basic needs makes little reference to discipline as such. However, in the classroom, as in a football game, the best defence is a good offense. The teacher who maintains an effective discipline offensive based on the motivation that results from effective instructional practices will engage infrequently in defensive reactions to student noncompliance.

In the scenario we find Jane—Mrs. D—attending to prevention by developing a comprehensive approach to discipline and clearly establishing regularities to facilitate the classroom operation. However, the effect of prevention measures tends to be pervasive rather than specific, and establishes the norm of compliant behavior within the classroom. We can infer from the quality of the interaction that prevention, as defined in terms of classroom climate and student compliance, was acceptably evident, yet it did not totally prevent instances of minor deviation.

While preventive approaches to discipline occur continuously, they are most essential at the beginning of the year. Based on extensive research, Emmer et al. (1984) suggest four principles as being especially pertinent in guiding planning for the first week: (1) Resolve student uncertainties—the basic rules and expectations for the routine operation of the class should be explained; (2) Help students be successful by planning uncomplicated lessons—the students' immediate success in the academic aspect of the class contributes to a positive attitude about the class; (3) Keep an entire class focus—conduct learning activities during the first week that engage the class as a whole group while students become accustomed to the class operation; and (4) Be available, visible, and in charge—during the first week as you establish yourself as the group leader, keep students alert to your presence, your influence, and your willingness to help.

Because of its special importance, the concern for clear expectations deserves elaboration. Classroom order depends upon clear, explicit rules. The students may be involved as much as possible in developing these rules in order to promote "ownership" of them. Most recommendations in the literature are for a few general rules stated in a positive way rather than a lengthy list. Such rules might include: Respect the property of others; Help maintain a quiet and orderly classroom; and Be responsible for keeping your own workspace tidy. Once developed the rules should be displayed continuously where they may be referred to as necessary. Most importantly, perhaps, students should be taught what the implications of the rules are for their behavior in an initial discussion, and in later discussions as behavior warrants. When all this has been done, the teacher must be consistent in enforcing compliance and dealing with noncompliance.

Management routines are closely associated with rules. These involve establishing early and clearly procedures for such things as accomplishing routine tasks, speaking to the teacher or other students, going to the rest room or library, sharpening pencils, using learning centers, and whatever else is appropriate, then carefully monitoring the implementation of the procedures. Students' awareness of guidelines for doing most of the things that are necessary for efficient classroom operation contributes to their sense of well-being.

Maintenance. The line of demarcation between prevention of misbehavior and maintenance of acceptable behavior is hazy at best. However, maintenance behaviors of the teacher are generally those things a teacher does that are concomitant with instructional behaviors and which are intended to keep students on task. As a first order of concern, this requires having a businesslike, purposeful (although certainly not humorless) approach to learning activities. Furthermore, it involves moving around the room during the course of the lesson, maintaining eye contact with students, noting any occurrences of incipient misbehavior, citing instances of exemplary behavior, actively involving as many students as possible in the learning activity, and stating expectations as appropriate. These behaviors reflect the teacher's "withitness." Monitoring students' behaviors and conducting classroom meetings, referred to as prevention practices, would in some instances be more appropriately considered as maintenance activities.

A major concern regarding the maintenance phase is that teachers tend to take students' behavior for granted by shifting the major responsibility for behavior to the students. Students should be responsible up to a reasonable point and should be given as much responsibility (and corresponding freedom) as they can manage. However, the students deserve the teachers' systematic attention to maintenance tasks to diminish the temptation of and opportunity for misbehavior. Therefore, teachers should develop complementary instructional and managerial strategies designed to promote a smooth-running, orderly, productive classroom. For example, teachers should move about the classroom and have intermittent eye contact with every student while they lecture or conduct instruction. The teacher should move to a distant part of the room as a student responds or comments so the student will speak loudly and the teacher will be able to view most of the class. If the teacher is incompetent in this regard, should students nevertheless be expected to remain continuously forgiving and compliant? Only if they are zombies!

The most important day of class in terms of its potential impact is the first day of school. Students acquire their first impressions at this meeting, the tenor of the class is established, and momentum is initiated. This day should be more carefully and purposefully planned than any other. Although no formula exists for conducting this meeting, a likely sequence of events might be:

1. introductions, beginning with the teacher's, in which an appropriate bit of personal information is shared;
2. presentation of a course overview and rationale, highlighting interesting and relevant activities;
3. presentation of academic expectations and grading policy, accompanied by a rationale;
4. presentation of behavioral policies, expectations, and conventions;
5. opportunity for the students to express their expectations for the teacher, with the possibility of some mutual verbal contracting.

Along with these activities, matters such as making seating plans, handing out textbooks, and making assignments must be attended to. More than one period may be needed to complete the entire agenda, but it will be well worth whatever time it takes.

In Mrs. D's room, the maintenance phase of discipline was readily evident. She commenced class in a businesslike away as she assumed a posture that clearly communicated her expectation. Students' participation was encouraged and supported so that they would stay with the lesson. Through alert monitoring, two instances of incipient misbehavior were detected and quickly defused. Meanwhile she enforced the rule about the raising hands to be recognized. She changed the mode when restlessness occurred but did not chide the students about it. She displayed the all-important quality of "withitness" to an admirable degree.

Intervention. This is the phase generally associated with discipline by teachers. New teachers frequently ask: What can I do when these kids won't be quiet, or are insolent, or are always fooling around? Seasoned colleagues respond with their favorite approaches, although sometimes these have a basis in conventional wisdom. Experts in the scholarly aspects of discipline tend to hedge their answers, realizing that there are no guaranteed effective approaches. They leave the new teacher not only frustrated but questioning the credibility of pedagogy in the area of discipline. The problem does not necessarily lie in the colleagues' practices, which seem to work for them, nor in the pedagogy. The problem is in the question itself, for it essentially addresses symptoms rather than causes. A more appropriate question, at least to begin what could be an extended process, is: What are the conditions, internal and external, that are causing this situation? When the question is thus posed productive problem solving can begin.

More than a score of books and many dozens of articles have been written focusing on this particular phase of discipline. We could hardly do justice to the topic if it were our intention to pass along all the sound advice and suggestions included in literature. A few important considerations will be considered here, but wider reading on the topic will be necessary to supplement this commentary for the reader who has a special interest in this area.

When the indirect and tacit techniques of the prevention and maintenance phases are insufficient to preserve order, intervention is necessary. One of the reasons that preservice teachers have difficulty in learning about appropriate interventions from effective teachers is that effective teachers only occasionally need to use them. The teachers who need to use them frequently, on the other hand, are not the preferable role models. Therein lies a paradox: Intervention, or overt teacher intrusions, are least well-learned from the most effective practitioners. Furthermore, some research indicates that less effective classroom managers cannot be reliably distinguished from more effective ones by the nature of their intervention practices (Kounin, 1970, Emmer et al., 1980). So while judiciously selected intervention techniques should be part of every teacher's repertoire, they are always expedients, and not the definitive aspects of a teacher's style.

Since interventions, or teachers' efforts to stop disruptive behavior, are by definition expedients, they should be used frugally and with discretion. An important consideration should be to initially use the mildest form of intervention that is likely to be effective, and resort to more stringent forms only as necessary. It is useful to consider the more seriously misbehaving student to be a troubled child exhibiting the symptoms of a personal problem rather than a "bad kid" who needs to be straightened out. The teacher then approaches the situation as a "therapist" rather than a "disciplinarian," and uses as a matter of personal style the science and art of pedagogy instead of the raw power with which the teacher role is endowed. Teachers in these circumstances might share the motto of the practitioners of emergency medicine: *Primum non nocere*, or, "As a first concern, do not further injure the patient." We affirm, however, that firmness is an essential quality for effective discipline.

Teachers need to have skill in applying a graduated set of interventions. The preferable approach to dealing with a nonattentive or mildly disruptive student is to use a question or some other instructional approach to enlist the student's active involvement in the lesson. This may be considered as much a maintenance activity as an intervention. If this is not possible, and the teacher notices incipient misbehavior, nonverbal interventions such as eye contact and a "teacher look" should be used. If a look doesn't suffice, then moving to the target area in the room provides a stronger signal. The proximity of the teacher to restive students is usually sufficient to quell a minor disturbance. When these means have not been sufficient the teacher may catch the student's eye and gesture with the head or hand, indicating that a particular behavior is inappropriate. Or, if the teacher is in the immediate vicinity of the misbehavior, touching the student lightly but meaningfully, or opening the book on the student's desk, send unmistakable signals.

When these unobtrusive, nonverbal approaches fail or are not feasible, a verbal reminder is necessary. Initially, just saying the student's name, perhaps accompanied by shaking the head, should be employed. If the misbehavior is moderately disruptive or persistent, using the student's name followed by a statement redirecting him or her to the appropriate task is the next order of rigor. If these approaches do not restore order, the teacher should approach the student purposefully and quietly but firmly direct him or her to another seat, a time-out site, or whatever else is appropriate under the circumstances. This is the point where the teacher may feel anger and affronted by the student. Resist it! Remain calm and in control. Above all, avoid a confrontation of any sort. It is a no-win situation for the teacher.

Teachers' responses to student misbehavior must qualify as reasonable consequences related to the behavior. Arbitrary punishments such as remaining standing, writing a phrase repeatedly, serving a detention, or receiving an angry reprimand, rarely if ever meet the test. They tend to be retributive, and have no redeeming social or educational value. Despite teachers' common belief, research shows that they are largely ineffective as deterrents of future misbehavior. On the other hand, reasonable consequences sometimes appear superficially to be similar to a punishment (i.e., mild reproval may be appropriate or a student may be directed to take another seat). The difference lies in whether the student recognizes the consequence as being directly and logically related to the misbehavior, and whether it is a potential learning experience for the student. Furthermore, punishment tends to satisfy the needs of the teacher but a reasonable consequence attends to the needs—at least the predicated needs—of the student.

Many kinds of misbehavior obviously have no readily conceivable direct and reasonable consequence. For example, a student may have a habit of calling out, using profanity, or intimidating other students. A more generalized and systematic teacher response is useful for such behavior. A program which uses behavior adjustment notices (BANs) might be established. Such notices serve as a record of the incident and incorporate a graduated set of consequences. The first might involve a brief conference in which the teacher tries to help the student develop insight into his or her behavior and make a commitment to more appropriate conduct. The second BAN would repeat the procedure and intent of the first, but involve a more extensive conference and possibly a written contract as well. A third BAN would build on the first two, and perhaps involve a third party—parent, administrator, counselor—as appropriate. A fourth BAN would signal a serious behavior problem and involve referral to a specialist. If this approach is adopted schoolwide, especially at the secondary level, it should involve in-school suspension, but with counseling available to the student as an integral aspect of that suspension. Any teacher—or school—that adopts a program based on these general guidelines has to work out the specifics accordingly. The major advantages are that it does qualify as a reasonable set of consequences of misbehavior, it emphasizes the developmental thrust of enlightened discipline, and it is consistent with the humane, democratic principles that are espoused by modern thinking educators.

Mrs. D had generally compliant students in her classroom, better this year than in her first two years because of her new, well-planned approach to discipline. Nevertheless she did utilize several nonverbal interventions. When Claire called out an answer, Mrs. D tapped rule Number 3 on the board specifying that students should seek permission by raising a hand. A question addressed to Leslie on the topic was, in fact, an intervention into Leslie's whispered conversation. Ronnie received a "visit" from Mrs. D as she strategically positioned herself at his desk and caught his eye. And Renee, who asked impulsively to sharpen her pencil, elicited the teacher's assertive posture and sharp look. All of these unobtrusive interventions occurred without missing an academic beat. Mrs. D had become proficient in using nonverbal measures. Inevitably, verbal reminders will be required on occasion, and sometimes even stronger measures. Hopefully, she will employ these with the same measured restraint and judicious judgment.

Adjustment. The purpose of behavior adjustment is to diminish—and ideally eliminate—student's disposition to noncompliance. As is noted above, it may begin as an extension of the teacher's intervention and incorporate follow-up as the consequences of the BANs are applied. This is the phase of discipline within which important student learning outcomes may occur. Teachers are not trained therapists, and they must recognize their limitations in dealing with pathologically induced behavior. Nevertheless, as well-informed, compassionate adults, teachers have the potential to affect students' attitudes and behaviors in beneficial ways. Teachers can help students realize that behaviors have reasonable consequences. They may also help students gain insights into the underlying reasons for their behavior, and thus be better able to control their own lives. Furthermore, as the remedial aspect of the BAN contracts, teachers can help students consider alternative behaviors and monitor their compliance to the contract. How much time can a teacher spend in this sort of activity? It is a matter each teacher must work out individually. But it is a means of effective change, possibly even dramatic change, in the lives of some students who greatly need to change.

Teacher Power in the Classroom

The commentary in the previous section described classroom conditions and teacher behaviors associated with a comprehensive approach to discipline. The final section of this chapter presents another perspective on teachers' discipline-related behaviors. In any social situation in which a leader exerts influence on the other members of the group, power is involved. As noted in the research section, five kinds of power are possible: referent (personality), expert, legitimate, coercive, and reward (French & Raven, 1968). Each of these dimensions of power has implications for the teacher (Richmond & McCroskey, 1983). Students' behavior can be related to their perception of the teacher's use of these different types of power. The teacher who is aware of the uses and possible pitfalls in the application of each type of power has, therefore, a cogent decision-making rationale for selecting appropriate discipline-related practices.

The concept of power does not itself constitute an approach to discipline. Rather, power is a dynamic within the process. Understanding its role and effect helps the teacher acquire a more in-depth understanding of discipline. With this understanding, the teacher can more knowledgeably recognize optimum and inferior modes of discipline-related interaction and establish teacher behavior goals accordingly. Any approach to discipline will be enhanced when the teacher refines discipline decisions by using insights into the power dynamic.

Referent power is probably more readily understood if it is thought of as the influence one has through personality. Referent power is especially related to the interpersonal and communication dimensions of the classroom. A teacher who is endowed with or acquires a generous measure of referent power may be expected to have a high degree of social poise, exhibit a healthy sense of humor, maintain a respect for the feelings and rights of students, and be reasonably stable and consistent in demeanor. The teacher remains aware of the impact of each verbal interchange and demonstrates to the students sincere concern for their best interests. The outcome of these characteristics is a classroom climate that is comfortable and students who perceive the teacher as a person with whom they identify, and even sincerely want to "be good for."

In the scenario Mrs. D can be assumed to have relied to some extent on referent power as she took a position at the front of the room to begin the class session. The students' respect is implied as they quickly come to order. As we get a sense of the kind of teacher she is in the remainder of the scenario, there is no hint that other kinds of power are necessary. Referent power, however, is often subtle in its effect.

Expert power refers to the competence of the teacher in conducting the tasks of managing the classroom and guiding learning. The teacher, therefore, must be a sound scholar who is an advocate of the subject and is able to select aspects of it that are appropriate for the students in order to bring it alive, flesh it out, and help students recognize its relevance and possibilities.

Other aspects of expertise are manifest in the teacher's classroom management practices. Systematic approaches are evident in much of what routinely occurs, such as making seating arrangements, establishing expectations, keeping records, marking and evaluating students' work, and passing out papers. The teacher's instruction is characterized by variety and student involvement. Students sense a certain "ownership" in the learning objectives and activities. In addition to the typical teacher-dominated presentations, one might also expect to find role playing and simulations, projects, learning centers, hands-on opportunities, and independent study. Higher level thinking will occur as students reflect on important ideas. The concept of individualization will be applied as special purpose groups form and disband, and enrichment and remediation are available to students as needed. Motivation will be an overriding concern of the teacher, who realizes that instruction without motivation is bankrupt.

In describing expert power, we are, in effect, describing effective instruction. The implication is not that a teacher must be unusually talented to be reasonably successful. We do believe, however, that a mediocre teacher cannot depend on control measures to compensate for an inability or unwillingness to provide effective instruction.

Mrs. D displayed her expertise in the instructional dimension as she began the chemistry unit with an advance organizer, then proceeded to develop the topic using the students' ideas. Later in the class she changed instructional modes as some students' span of attention was expended. These are expert instructional behaviors that have a positive impact on students' behavior as well. As a competent classroom manager, she attended to seating arrangements, classroom expectations, class routines, and a systematic plan to cope with serious misbehavior. Her students undoubtedly—albeit tacitly—recognize Mrs. D's competence and consider her acceptable in the teacher role. This positive attitude, in turn, inclines them to generally compliant behavior.

Referent power and expert power together create a charisma that endows the teacher with virtually all the power that is needed to manage very successfully in the classroom. Achieving some degree of charisma might well be a goal of every teacher and, in this fashion, to operate as a general guide for the teacher's professional growth.

As far as misbehavior is concerned, charisma operates primarily as a preventive influence. Realistically, however, the teacher must expect that misbehavior will occur and that intervention will be necessary. In such cases, other types of power are available. One of these is legitimate power. This power is inherent in the teacher role, just as it is for a police officer, lifeguard, or military officer, and it is the basis for their authority.

Students ordinarily submit to legitimate power and respond to it readily. For this reason legitimate power is attractive to people with a special need to wield power. It could become, in effect, an end in itself and result in abuse of power. The existence of this condition may be inferred from an inordinate number of rules, unreasonable expectations for decorum, rigid classroom structure, gimmicky means of control, or teacher nagging about student behavior.

Legitimate power used appropriately involves establishing reasonable, minimal expectations for order and procedure, monitoring student behavior, and keeping students on-task through the use of nonverbal cues and mild verbal reminders or restraint. In cases of serious misbehavior or persistent disruptive behavior, the wise use of legitimate power involves follow up in determining causes and using soundly conceived behavior-adjustment techniques with the student.

Mrs. D used legitimate power when the indirect influence of referent and expert powers was not a sufficient deterrent. She did monitor the classroom diligently and used unobtrusive reminders as appropriate. On the other hand, she was careful not to use legitimate power injudiciously. She seemed to recognize the point at which its use was counterproductive.

The point where legitimate power ends and coercive power begins is not clearly discernible. In practice it can be the point at which the teacher's voice rises from normal volume to louder than normal, when the teacher asks the class in an exasperated tone for the third time to be more quiet. If the teacher makes direct reference to his or her authority or threatens or uses punishment, coercive power is clearly being used.

Coercive power is necessary on rare occasions in the classroom. When students are fighting, are openly defiant, or are endangering themselves or others, the teacher must certainly take appropriate coercive action since the time for reason and mild authoritarian action has passed. The intervention should employ the minimum force necessary to restore normal conditions: causing the fighting students to be separated; requesting that a defiant student go to a designated place; insisting that firecrackers be relinquished.

Coercive power, as an extension of legitimate power, is highly subject to abuse in the hands of teachers with personalities that incline them to its use. Punishment is the means such teachers use to attempt to gain control over students' behavior. But coercive power, in general, and punishment, in particular, is far less effective than conventional wisdom would suggest. Teachers who are routinely dependent on punishment to achieve a semblance of order are essentially failing in their instructional and/or managerial performance. On the other hand, when students do misbehave they should expect to confront the reasonable consequences of their behavior. The astute teacher recognizes the difference, which is sometimes subtle, between punishment and reasonable consequences, and between measures which are merely self-serving and those which are educationally sound.

The use of rewards is the final application of power. Rewards are actually an integral part of expert or referent power as a teacher approves students' commendable performance. Reward in the form of deserved praise or other appropriate recognition of achievement has a positive overall effect and, in fact, is probably necessary for optimum teaching effectiveness.

Although rewards properly employed are recommended, incentives—rewards not intrinsically related to performance—should be used with discretion. They may serve to initiate student efforts toward achieving some performance goal, but at some point internal sources of motivation should supersede. Otherwise, the performance remains only a means toward an end and learning is incidental rather than purposeful. The use of grades as incentives is probably the most common form of this type of suspect practice.

Rewards can take the form of a bribe or bargain, particularly in regard to discipline. For example, a teacher might offer to let students go to lunch early if they are quiet during the lesson. In this case, they are being quiet for the wrong reason, and a reward is used as a substitute for effective teaching. The insecure teacher who "runs a popularity contest" with students is especially prone to misuse rewards. In general, when rewards are used to manipulate students, or for any other ulterior motives, it is a misuse of this type of power. Furthermore, incentives diminish in effectiveness over time, and ultimately impede learning.

Mrs. D limited her use of reward power in the scenario to praising the ideas presented by two students. In each case the praise was low-keyed and emerged as a natural part of the interaction in the class. These instances are examples of the appropriate use of extrinsic reward. Such thoughtful use of reward power contributes over time to students' inclination to be active participants and contributors.

SUMMARY POINT

The complex nature of discipline is readily inferred from the commentary in this chapter. Some teachers have a naturally occurring, mature interaction style that serves them well in the disciplinary aspects of teaching. Although these teachers may acquire useful insights and skills from experience, much remains to be learned about discipline by any teacher. Anti-intellectualism, more pervasive within discipline than any other aspect of teaching, has inhibited the attainment of a norm condition characterized by fully professional practices. The ideas presented in this chapter can be helpful in transcending the paraprofessional level that is characteristic of current practice and in convincing educators that discipline is not a dirty word.

An analysis instrument is included at the end of this chapter to help the reader observe discipline-related behaviors in the classroom.

REVIEW: IMPORTANT CONSIDERATIONS REGARDING DISCIPLINE

1. Effective discipline and effective instruction are inseparable.
2. Plan a comprehensive, pedagogically sound approach to discipline addressing, in particular, the four phases: prevention, maintenance, intervention, and behavior adjustment.
3. Utilize the five types of teacher power as a means to select appropriate behavior modes within the broad strategies employed.
4. Nothing is so strong as gentleness; nothing so gentle as real strength. (Indian proverb)

NOTE

1. See Kindsvatter and Levine (1980) for a fuller discussion on the specious nature of the myths of discipline.

ACTIVITIES (ANALYSIS FORMS FOLLOW)

ACTIVITY I

In the following discipline-related incidents,
    a. ascertain the source of the disruption;
    b. critique the teacher's approach; and
    c. cite the approach you would recommend, including your rationale. Include in your rationale reference to principles discussed in this chapter.

Incident Number 1

Our school has approximately an equal mixture of black and white students. Some racial tension exists and as a result there are occasional flare-ups.

My 2nd-period 7th-grade English class had a representative student population. I had tried to establish an open climate in the class in order to help the students feel as comfortable as possible. I tried not to be too "picky" with the students regarding minor infractions. This resulted in talking out both in response to teacher questions and to other students. Also, students got up during class and sharpened pencils rather noisily, and frequently requested the use of the rest room pass. On the other hand, the students did reasonably good classwork.

This morning on the way to school a fight broke out between a black student and a white student. It escalated until a dozen or so boys were involved, and it had to be restrained by police. As the students came into class they were still talking about it loudly. Some taunting and adolescent threats were exchanged even as I tried to conduct class. My insistence that the students refrain from this sort of behavior were unheeded. When I made an especially strong effort to quiet one boy, he accused me of showing favoritism. "You're as bad as they are," he shouted emotionally.

The frustration and sense of impotence I had initially felt turned to rage. I virtually shouted, "OK, the next kid to open his mouth in here will get it personally closed by me." The class became quiet and we proceeded with the lesson.

Incident Number 2

Last year those teachers who had Jessie in their classes often referred to her in their lounge gossip as a tramp. I privately considered that rather unprofessional, but now that she is in my class this year, I'm tempted to do the same.

In class Jessie does as little as possible to get by. She won't do any outside assignments. She and the girls in her group are a constant source of disruption in the classroom. Jessie often arrives a few moments after the bell and while in class engages in combing her hair, passing notes, and taunting the boys.

Today I don't know whether Jessie was worse than usual or my tolerance level was lower, but she got to me as I tried to help the kids understand something about the Reconstruction period. After having arrived late, she was up to her usual antics. I spoke to her several times; it didn't help. Finally, I said, "Jessie, for the love of Pete, what is your problem today?" "I'm bored," she replied. "This stuff is so dry. Who cares what happened a hundred years ago. Why don't we talk about Bruce Springsteen or something interesting?" When I told her that I didn't think it was my job to entertain her she said, "Maybe you ought to go back to college and learn to teach. You don't know nothin' about kids."

Incident Number 3

It was one of those groups! They came to class without pencils, paper, or completed assignments. They seemed to have no interest in science. I found I spent most sessions pretty much talking to myself, because getting them to respond to questions or engage in a discussion was very difficult. Meanwhile, their restlessness in the classroom resulted in talking and "playing around" to the point that I spent as much time controlling behavior as teaching science.

After some weeks of cajoling, I told the class that they would lose three points on their grade point accumulation for every day they came unprepared, and would get a detention after three occasions of being unprepared. I then found myself spending a considerable amount of time keeping accurate records of students' punishments. They resented it, often arguing that my records were incorrect. Meanwhile, there was a slightly higher incidence of preparedness but no appreciable difference in their test performance.

ACTIVITY II

Given the opportunity to observe a teacher over several periods of instruction with a given class, use the Classroom Discipline Analysis Form to analyze the teacher's discipline-related approach and behaviors.

ANALYSIS FORM

CLASSROOM DISCIPLINE

TEACHER _____

OBSERVER _____

CLASS _____

DATE _____

	OCCURRENCE	EFFECTIVENESS
1.	Not evident	Not effective
2.	Slightly evident	Slightly effective
3.	Moderately evident	Moderately effective
4.	Quite evident	Quite effective
N	Not applicable	Not applicable

CATEGORIES (Parts A–B Correspond to Occurrence and Effectiveness in the Analysis Scale)	A. OCCURRENCE	B. EFFECTIVENESS
1. PREVENTION: The teacher makes provision for a smoothly run class and on-task student behavior. 　Teacher preparaton for instructon is thorough 　Addresses concerns for students' identity, stimulation, security and power 　Rules are displayed or readily accessible 　Procedures are established		
2. MAINTENANCE: The teacher exhibits leadership qualities. 　Teacher affects a businesslike demeanor 　Keeps students continuously occupied and interested 　Is alert to students' behavior 　Defuses incipient noncompliance		
3. INTERVENTION: The teacher has a self-controlled, appropriately modulated style of intervention. 　Teacher relies on teacher authority at the lowest effective level 　Uses nonverbal, unobtrusive interventions insofar as possible 　Maintains calm but firm demeanor in addressing noncompliance 　Avoids confrontations with students during class 　Uses reasonable consequences rather than punishment		

continued

4. BEHAVIOR ADJUSTMENT: Teacher follows up discipline-related problems. Teacher has a plan for behavior remediation Conferences are conducted with students as needed Developmental and attitudinal outcomes are emphasized		
5. TEACHER POWER: Teacher displays discretionary use of teacher power. Referent (personality) and expert power are the basis for classroom discipline Legitimate power is used only as needed and then in the form of enforcing rules and mild reproval Reward is used judiciously to recognize commendable achievement Use of coercive power is avoided		

REFERENCES

Ardrey, R. (1970). *The social contract.* New York: Atheneum.

Brophy, J. (1984). Classroom organization and management. (Occasional paper #54, Institute for Research on Teaching, Michigan State University, May 1982). In *Effective Classroom Management.* Bloomington, IN: Phi Delta Kappa.

Brophy, J. & Rohrkemper, M. (1981). The influence of problem-ownership on teacher perceptions. *Journal of Educational Psychology, 73,* 295–311.

Canter, L. (1976). *Assertive discipline: A take charge approach for today's educator.* Seal Beach, CA: Canter and Associates.

Cotton, K. & Savard, W. (1984). Student discipline and motivation: research synthesis. (Prepared for Northeast Regional Educational Laboratory, April 1982). In *Discipline.* Bloomington, IN: Phi Delta Kappa.

Davis, J. (1974). *Coping with disruptive behavior.* Washington, D.C.: National Education Association.

Emmer, E., Evertson, C., Sanford, J., Clements, B., & Worsham, M. (1984). *Classroom management for secondary teachers.* Englewood Cliffs, NJ: Prentice-Hall.

Emmer, E., Evertson, C., & Anderson, L. (1980). Effective classroom management at the beginning of the school year. *Elementary School Journal, 80,* 219–231.

French, J. & Raven, B. (1968). The bases of social power. In D. Cartwright & A. F. Zander (Eds.), *Group dynamics: Research and theory* (2nd ed.). Evanston, IL: Row Peterson.

Gage, N. L. (1978). *The scientific basis of the art of teaching.* New York: Teachers College Press.

Glasser, W. (1969). *Schools without failure.* New York: Harper & Row.

Gnagey, W. (1965). *Controlling classroom misbehavior.* Washington, D.C.: National Education Association.

Goodlad, J. I. (1983). *A place called school.* New York: McGraw-Hill.

Gordon, T. (1974). *Teacher effectiveness training.* New York: McKay.

Kindsvatter, R. & Levine, M. A. (1980). *The myths of discipline.* Phi Delta Kappan, *61,* 690–693.

Kounin, J. (1970). *Discipline and group management.* New York: Holt, Rinehart and Winston.

Raywid, M. A. (1976). The democratic classroom: mistake or misnomer? *Theory into Practice 15*(1), 37–46.

Redl, F. (1966). *When we deal with children.* New York: Free Press.

Richmond, V. & McCroskey, J. (1983). *Power in the classroom: Two studies.* Paper presented at the annual meeting of the Association for Teacher Education, Orlando, FL.

Sanford, J. & Evertson, C. (1981). Classroom management in a low SES junior high: three case studies. *Journal of Teacher Education, 32,* 34–38.

Silberman, C. (1970). *Crisis in the classroom.* New York: Random House.

Swick, K. (1980). *Disruptive student behavior in the classroom.* Washington, D.C.: National Education Association.

Weber, W. (1984). Teacher perceptions of effective classroom management strategies. Paper presented at the annual meeting of the AERA, Los Angeles, 1981. In *Effective classroom management.* Bloomington, IN: Phi Delta Kappa.

Wolfgang, C. & Glickman, C. (1980). *Solving discipline problems.* Boston: Allyn & Bacon.

CHAPTER 9

Evaluation of Pupil
Performance

Evaluation is one of the three major components of teaching, along with planning and instruction. Yet in the informal view of teachers, evaluation is often perceived as the stepchild of teaching. Writing tests, grading them—especially essay tests—and reporting students' grades are grudgingly executed as onerous chores of teaching. Very few teachers are attracted to teaching by this aspect of the job. It is not surprisingly, then, that evaluation is probably the major aspect of teaching that receives the least professional attention from teachers, and so is an area in which many teachers can substantially improve. This chapter is designed to initiate thinking toward the development of a sound concept and effective practices of evaluation.

Although evaluation is described above as one component of teaching, it is not mutually exclusive from the other parts. Evaluation occurs in planning in the selection of particular topics and strategies. As objectives are being written, the implication is that they will become the basis for subsequent evaluation. On a daily basis, teachers need to plan for collecting data on student progress. And during instruction, evaluation occurs as teachers observe student behaviors, consider student responses, provide feedback and correction to students, and judge the extent to which instruction has been effective. At the completion of a unit of work written tests and other demonstrations of achievement typically occur. When teachers think of evaluation, this latter aspect is generally what comes to mind. However, the many aspects of evaluation deserve thoughtful consideration by teachers if evaluation principles and practices are to contribute optimally to the effectiveness of teaching.

In a very fundamental sense, evaluation means placing a value on some entity, thus expressing an indication of its worth. Implied within the process is a standard, usually in the form of a criterion or a comparison, and a decision. Evaluation as decision making should conform to the principles of decision making described in Chapter 1. Evaluation should be made on the basis of the best information/evidence available and should be insofar as is possible a rational process.

OVERVIEW

This chapter describes the role and process of teacher classroom evaluation. This broad perspective will serve as a framework for the teacher's continuing development of an informed comprehensive approach to this component of the teacher role. Brief commentary on two major components of teacher classroom evaluation is also presented: grading and test writing.

This limited treatment of the topic is intended to help the reader understand evaluation as a pervasive and integral part of teaching. It does not make a pretense at being comprehensive. Many fine texts devoted entirely to measurement and evaluation are readily available to provide in-depth information on specific practices and statistical measurement.

SCENARIO

The end of the second 6-week grading period at Jofferoon County Local High School was approaching. John Sykes, the school's art teacher, remembered clearly the end of the first grading period. As a teacher with several years' experience, he had proceeded to assign the first 6-weeks' grades in his Art I class much the same as in the past years. Art was not considered to be one of the difficult courses in the school but this particular class had less apparent ability than any John remembered. He had assigned quite a few C grades as well as two Ds and an F.

John's approach to assigning grades had always been rather casual. He examined the art work each student turned in and made an overall judgment of its quality. He prided himself on his connoisseurship approach, including the critique he wrote on every project, but he also tempered his evaluation with compassion when he thought students deserved it. In the academic aspect of the course dealing with art principles and art history, he examined the numerical scores, looked for natural breaks throughout the range of scores, and assigned letter grades by inspection.

After grades had gone out John got calls or visits from four of his students' parents from that class, in his experience a surprisingly large number. The parents did not understand why their child had gotten a grade as much as two letters below expectation. He explained the basis for the grade as best he could and tried to enlist parents' cooperation in urging students to take their art work seriously and conscientiously. Mrs. DeTano, a parent and herself a teacher in another district, was one of the parents to visit. Her daughter, Lynn, had gotten a D, and Mrs. DeTano was not satisfied with John's explanation of how he determined the grade. She pointedly referred to the explanation as "unconvincing," and asked John to produce his explicit standards. Her Lynn, she said, had been unable to produce a copy of any such standards or inform her of any that had ever been communicated to the class.

John spent an uncomfortable half-hour with Mrs. DeTano. She was obviously knowledgeable, but she was rather self-righteous, he thought. He was shaken and had therefore responded defensively in the conference, but in later reflection he was willing to grant that she might have a point. He felt she was being condescending when she insisted on sending him a copy of the approach she used to assign grades, but nevertheless he examined it when it arrived. He also talked with several fellow teachers whose judgment he respected. Then he set about rethinking his approach to evaluation.

Art, he reasoned, is not only for artists. But as he examined the grade distribution for the first 6 weeks, he realized that the students who had a knack for art had been rewarded with the high grades. He intended to encourage these students, but he wondered if it had been at the expense of some of the others. What, in fact, is important in a beginning art course? Is it the same for everyone? Can individual differences be accommodated without abandoning reasonable standards? His implicit answers to these questions were reflected in the new grading criteria he established after a week of thoughtful consideration. Three categories for evaluation were included:

Artistic rendition
   Technical skill
   Creativity
Attitude and effort
   Attendance and punctuality
   Work habits
   Preparation and initiative
Academic achievement
   Quality of participation
   Test scores

John Sykes was especially pleased with the final touch to his system. The categories were weighted 2-1-1, but students would individually select which category was to be given the highest weight. This would be considerably more fair to students with only moderate talent. When he initiated the new system he spent a whole period describing it to the class and inviting their comments. He was encouraged by their enthusiasm.

The following day, after making minor modifications based on the students' feedback, he provided a copy of the system to each student. He asked them to share it with their parents and to decide which weighting alternative they each preferred. He also set up a system whereby he would keep anecdotal notes on each student that would be useful for evaluating attitude and effort. It would be more work, he realized, but if 50% of some of the students' grades was to be determined by this sort of information, he would need credible documentation; enough, he thought, to satisfy Mrs. De-Tano.

As John talked with his colleagues prior to setting up his own new system, one of them impressed him with the idea that evaluation should be an integral part of instruction, and that students needed thoughtful feedback and correction to contribute to the learning process. "I certainly do this as they are doing their projects," John thought, "but not while we are focusing on principles and history." He decided, therefore, to occasionally use quizzes in class that would include several objective items and a short essay item. In most cases, John did not collect the quizzes. The correct answers to the objective items were given immediately, then the papers were passed on to another student to critique the essay. Following this phase, they were passed on once more and both the essay and the first critiquer's comments were critiqued. When the papers were returned to the writer, questions about the essay and the critiques were invited. On the several occasions he had done this over the past 5 weeks, animated discussions which featured thoughtful insights occurred. Using these "teaching quizzes," both he and his students had the opportunity to engage in feedback and correction. At first he thought the students might object to their peers reading their papers, but they actually enjoyed this approach. When John Sykes did plan to collect quizzes and grade them himself, he announced it a day ahead.

Now, as grades were about to be assigned for the second 6 weeks, John felt reasonably comfortable with this new, more accountable approach. But one student, Ricky, still concerned him. Ricky had missed school sporadically throughout the term due to complications following a summer bout with mononucleosis. Ricky was an average student, but a wholly undistinguished artist. Now he had fallen behind considerably in all aspects of his work. His grade for this period, based on the established criteria, was clearly an F.

Mr. Sykes called Ricky in and informed him of the situation. Almost in tears, Ricky nodded his understanding. "But, Ricky," said Mr. Sykes, "suppose I assign you a C grade because I'm sure you could have made it if your health had been up to par. However it would be conditional. I will ask you to sign a contract specifying what you'll need to make up from this past several weeks in addition to the regular work for the next grading period. And we will need to see improvement over your work so far. By the way, how is your health now? Are you up to it?"

Ricky's eyes had lit up. "Oh, yeah. You bet, Mr. Sykes. I sure appreciate the chance. I just can't afford to get any Fs in high school. I won't disappoint you—or myself."

As a delighted Ricky retreated down the hall, John thought, "So what's a grade for after all? I feel better about grades this grading period than I ever have before." Then he smiled as he uttered half aloud to himself, "Thank you, Mrs. DeTano."

RESEARCH AND THEORETICAL BASE

Although research has accumulated at a rapid rate in education as a total enterprise throughout this century, the attention has been uneven from area to area. One of the areas about which the available research is limited is teachers' classroom evaluation practices (Lazar Morris, Polin, May & Burry, 1980; Stiggins, Conklin & Bridgeford, 1986). The relative effects of various evaluation approaches and the effect of particular student testing and grading practices are not well documented in literature. On the other hand, the treatment of the principles of evaluation and measurement is extensive. Excellent texts provide comprehensive coverage of this area (Gage & Berliner, 1984; Ebel, 1979; Bloom et al., 1971; Gronlund, 1974; & Popham, 1975).

Teachers tend to feel comfortable in the testing aspect of evaluation (Gullickson, 1984). They generally feel confident with and rely heavily on their own judgment (Lazar-Morris et al., 1984). On the other hand, grading is a painful responsibility (Gage & Berliner, 1984). This apparent paradox is at least partly explained by the findings that teachers are often not well prepared to conduct classroom evaluation and that their formal training is minimal and narrow in scope (Rudman, Kelly, Wanous, Mehrens, Clark & Porter, 1980; Stiggins et al., 1986). Furthermore, teachers learn their evaluation techniques primarily from their colleagues as well as from personal experience (Stiggins, 1985). As the findings indicate, teachers tend to employ intuitive and expedient practices in evaluation. They express little concern about the mechanical aspects of test writing and grading. Yet they do not, as a rule, have a well-developed, pedagogically defensible system of evaluation that they trust. Dealing with the affective implications of evaluation is thus often emotionally stressful.

The area of standardized testing has been given a disproportionate amount of attention in the evaluation literature as compared to other areas (Stiggins & Bridgeford, 1985). A substantial body of literature describes large-scale standardized testing for accountability; however, teachers consider standardized tests to be of little importance (Stiggins et al., 1986; Salmon-Cox, 1981). Standardized testing has had limited impact in the classroom. It does not lead to higher achievement, nor do test results influence subsequent teacher practice (Kellaghan, Madaus, & Airasian, 1982). In fact, standardized test results and teachers' ratings produce very similar information on student performance for teachers (Pedulla, Airasian, & Madaus, 1980). Standardized tests clearly have their greatest influence outside the classroom and are primarily useful for administrative and public relations purposes. They constitute an essentially neutral factor in classrooms (Stiggins, 1985). If teachers are to find ways to exploit the potential of standardized tests in their classrooms, they will probably need to take individual initiatives; their colleagues are likely to be of little or no help in this task.

Evaluation is a complex—perhaps deceptively complex—aspect of teaching. In addressing this concern, Stiggins et al. (1986) state that, "We begin to comprehend the complexity of classroom assessment as we explore the range and frequency of teachers' decisions and the plethora of student characteristics they must consider in making those decisions" (p. 10). They go on to report that a review of several studies produced 66 student characteristics used by the sample teachers in evaluation-related decision making. One may conclude from this report that evaluation can no more be a totally rational process than instruction. Teachers' sensitivity and values are inevitable factors in the effectiveness of their evaluation.

Teacher-made tests are a staple in most teachers' approach to assessment of student progress. Rudman et al. (1980) found that teachers prefer norm-referenced tests (i.e., graded on an in-class comparative basis) over criterion-referenced tests (i.e., graded on the basis of a predetermined absolute standard). However, Lazar-Morris et al. (1980) reported that norm-referenced tests are considered by most experts to be characterized by narrowness of focus, bias, and unreliability. The preferred alternative is the criterion-referenced test because of its diagnostic, placement, and remediation uses, and its ease of interpretation. Except in those instances in which ranking of students' performance is necessary, criterion-based measures are recommended.

One effect of tests that works to teachers' and, in a sense, to students' advantage is that by their very nature they are an incentive to students. Halpin and Halpin (1982) report that students increase their study efforts when they know a test is imminent. Every experienced teacher knows this, for teachers commonly exhort students with the reminder that certain material will be on a test. In some cases it is virtually posed as a threat. Nungester and Duchastel (1982) found in their study that students' retention of learned material was enhanced if they were tested on it. Tests, therefore, are useful in serving both instructional and evaluative purposes.

A clear similarity is apparent between teachers' verbal questioning and the items they write for classroom tests: both tend to emphasize factual recall. Fleming and Chambers (1983) found that teachers preferred matching questions and used very few essay questions. Carter (1984) reported both from her own study and a review of the literature that teachers had a limited repertoire of test writing skills and found it difficult to write items for testing higher order thinking skills, in particular inference and prediction. One may conclude that, to a large extent, teacher-made tests are superficial. If teachers are, in fact, concerned about students' higher order thinking skills, it isn't always apparent from their tests.

The variability of school marks was a concern as long ago as the early part of this century. Kindsvatter (1966) found that variability exists to a much greater degree than most educators suspect. Starch (1913; 1918) determined that the factor that contributed most to variability was teachers' inability to distinguish reliably between close levels of performance. As a result of his influence, the ABCDF system has largely replaced the use of a hundred-point scale. That was the last major change in school marks in this century, although many reforms have since been attempted and abandoned. Although the ABCDF scale is often criticized, it apparently is here to stay for the foreseeable future (Agnew, 1983).

The grading system affects the curriculum in the view of teachers (Agnew, 1983). They feel that it "trivializes" learning because it establishes a predisposition for readily assessed low cognitive-level learning; the curriculum is "covered" rather than "uncovered." Furthermore, from the students' viewpoint grades as the measure of achievement replace achievement itself as the prized outcome of classroom learning activities. Grades become the hidden—but not very well hidden—curriculum.

From the research on classroom evaluation, we discern that the problems affecting evaluation practices in the classroom tend to involve human complexity and diversity more than mechanical or technical issues. The philosophical and emotional aspects of assessment are more difficult to deal with than matters of form or measurement. We realize that we search in vain for final solutions to the most vexing problems of evaluation. In the final analysis, ongoing judicious decision making based on a sound understanding of the principles of evaluation holds the greatest promise. In this aspect of teaching, as in planning, instruction, and discipline, there is simply no substitute for informed teacher judgment.

APPLICATION TO PRACTICE

Role of Evaluation in the Classroom

Why evaluate? A good question. The simplest answer a teacher might give is, "Because I am required to assign grades to students." That answer expresses an unassailable fact of teaching. But there is much more to it. Would teachers evaluate if it were not for the necessity of assigning a grade? Certainly teachers committed to excellent instruction would use evaluation in several ways: to diagnose students' readiness; to individualize learning; to ascertain the interim progress of students; to decide when tutoring or reteaching is advisable; and to assess the effectiveness and the outcomes of instruction.

Evaluation is sometimes considered to be an add-on to the instructional process, or something that occurs only after a unit of study in order to assign a grade to a student. This is a decidedly myopic view. As is implied in the opening section of this chapter and the subsequent comments, evaluation is an integral part of the teaching process. Evaluation is an important aspect of planning as content is selected, objectives are written, and remediation and enrichment are considered. During a unit of study evaluation provides continuing feedback to the teacher and students and is an important information source for making adjustments.

At the completion of a unit of study, evaluation focuses on assessing the level of learning students have attained, assigning grades, and obtaining evidence of instructional effectiveness. In one sense, some of these aspects of evaluation tacitly occur regardless of teacher intentions. The point is that purposeful attention to evaluation enhances the several kinds of contributions that evaluation potentially makes to classroom outcomes.

The Process of Classroom Evaluation

Goals and Objectives. Written goals and objectives serve nominally as the beginning of the evaluation process. However, because evaluation is cyclical (i.e., the evaluation from one unit of study may affect planning for the next), there may be no absolute starting point. Care must be taken during the writing of objectives, especially at the unit and specific outcomes levels, that they lend themselves to evaluation. Improperly or vaguely written objectives seriously impede evaluation of learning. John Sykes, in his art course, may have had as a program goal:

Students will understand the contribution of color to the intent of an artwork.

Obviously, there is no way that Mr. Sykes could see inside the students' minds to assess the level of understanding of this concept. Therefore, he would need to have at least one—and probably more—specific objectives, the attainment of which he would accept as evidence of probable understanding. Such specific objectives might be:

Students will match a list of color tones to a set of possible intents.

Students will explain Klee's use of color to emphasize the graphic dimension of his art.

Students will produce a colored-pencil sketch in which they use color tone to express a feeling level.

If teachers are to evaluate learning at the various levels of thinking (6 levels were presented in the planning chapter), then objectives must be written at the respective levels. The various levels of objectives, if used as guides to direct instruction, result in developing learning activities conceived at those levels. However, evaluation would have to occur in terms of the objectives at those levels to determine the actual learning outcomes.

Goals and objectives are also used as the basis for building tests with a table of specifications. In its simplest form, each goal that the test covers is listed and assigned a percent weighting. Within each goal, each objective is assigned a percent. In writing or selecting items to be included on the test, the appropriate number of items may then be included for each objective and goal to assure a sampling of subject matter. Table 9.1 is a general example.

Table 9.1 Generalized Table of Specifications

GOAL 1	60%	
Objective 1.1		30%
Objective 1.2		15%
Objective 1.3		15%
GOAL 2	40%	
Objective 2.1		25%
Objective 2.2		15%
		100%

Content Selection. The selection of content and the development of learning objectives occurs more or less simultaneously, each complementing the other. From the curricular point of view, courses are essentially a body of content; from an instructional point of view, courses are a sequence of learning activities.

John Sykes probably views his art course both in terms of knowledge to be learned and activities to engage in, and each becomes very much a part of the other. For this group of students, basic information about art will have to be presented, including principles of form, balance, perspective, and medium. He will also want students to be aware of the role of art in our cultural setting, and the contribution of art in the practical and aesthetic dimensions. Finally, of course, he will want students to create works of art at the level at which they are capable.

A variety of levels of learning are implied by the content this teacher intends to teach, as are several different sorts of learning outcomes. He must make two kinds of decisions: what content in what sequence is most pertinent for this group of students, and what learning activities are most appropriate to achieve the objectives related to that content? By knowing his content well, making reference to the course syllabus, and becoming increasingly familiar with his students, Mr. Sykes will correlate content and activities. However, continuing evaluation of achievement and instructional effectiveness will be used to redirect and ''fine tune'' teaching as necessary.

Data Collection. Evaluation has two components: information on achievement or performance and a standard which provides a base for measuring. Information on achievement is obtained in a variety of ways. Informally, teachers make evaluations continuously as they observe students. Students' willingness to attend class, ability to respond, and demonstration of interest and initiative provide the teacher with a sense of how things are going and what adjustments are expedient. Teachers also notice patterns of behavior in individual students and begin to determine where extra help may need to be given, where enrichment is possible, and where additional monitoring is required. John Sykes had noticed that Ricky had a unique problem, and he devised a unique approach in the form of a conditional grade and a contract to accommodate him.

More formally, teachers use instruments to collect data useful for evaluation. They may be in the form of checklists and various kinds of tests. Also, data collection may involve such assignments as homework papers, journals and notebooks, reports, and creative projects. During the course of a unit, evaluation based on these sources should be used to assess students progress, diagnose students' problems, and provide continuous valuable feedback to students. The intention of teachers should be that students are well-informed about their progress through the systematic use of feedback and correction procedures, and that no student's learning and achievement problems go unattended for very long.

In John Sykes' class we observe him using "teaching quizzes" as a means of providing useful interim evaluation to students and the opportunity for immediate correction. In this regard, the most important consideration was student learning, not assigning grades.

Establishing a standard against which data are compared is the second aspect of evaluation. Teachers' astute judgment is required for this task. In some cases, teachers allow their standards to remain implicit, as John Sykes initially did. This may lead to difficulty, as is illustrated in the scenario. Standards must be clearly stated to be as useful as possible, and they must be communicated to the students. Students are thus provided with a goal and a sense of direction in their learning.

Applying Standards. Teachers sometimes think of their grading scales as standards, such as 65% or a D mark is passing. These are only a part of the standards. It still leaves open the questions, 65% of what? Or, a D based on what? A teacher's well-written course and program goals provide the basis for establishing the "what" part of the standard. However, the teacher must still determine how the level of compliance with the standard is to be measured and the appropriate scale to express the level of compliance.

In the case of John Sykes, a program objective is, as we cited: "Students will understand the contribution of color to the intent of an art work." He may establish, according to the specific objectives related to this goal, that (1) students must match with at least 70% accuracy color tone with possible intent; (2) students must describe in a brief paragraph that they are aware of the concept "graphic dimension" and how color may contribute to it; and (3) students will render a sketch that in his practiced view expresses (marginally at least) feeling through the use of color tone. This is about as explicit as standards for performance can be for this type of learning. Students who do not achieve the minimums stated will have to be retaught until they do. If Mr. Sykes is using the ABCDF scale, then the correct number of matching items, the extent of students' understanding of Klee's use of color tone, and the quality of the sketch will all have to be translated into grade symbols. He will have to depend on his judgment to do this. Experience will be helpful to him in making these judgments. New teachers will find this to be one of the more difficult aspects of teaching.

Reporting and Using the Results of Evaluation. The implication in the foregoing commentary is that evaluation is useful only if it is communicated to concerned parties. Teachers, of course, immediately use the results of evaluation for making decisions about appropriate strategies, pacing, individualizing, and assessing instructional effectiveness. Students need to know the results of evaluation to guide them in their ongoing work and to provide incentive for their continued efforts. Others who are indirectly involved with classroom learning—counselors, administrators, and parents—also have the need to be informed at least periodically about students' classroom achievement.

The results of evaluation procedures are reported to students both informally and formally. Casual comments by the teacher in class in response to students' answers or during a supervised study period constitute a useful kind of feedback. Marks and comments on homework papers provide a somewhat more structured means for assessment reporting. Conferences with students to attend to exceptional situations are useful, as was John Sykes' conference with Ricky. Quizzes administered in class, the results of which may or may not be recorded as a grade in the gradebook, constitute an even more structured form of evaluation. Formal evaluations usually occur in the form of weekly or unit tests, or assessments of some type of performance such as timed athletic events or the quality of a creative effort. In Chapter 5, which deals with the elements of effective teaching, a section is devoted to describing effective feedback and corrective practices that the teacher uses as a component of instruction.

All the separate evaluations that occur during a grading period, usually 6 to 9 weeks in duration, are accumulated, processed according to the teacher's predetermined plan, and entered on a report form as the official grade assigned to the student. These grading period grades are averaged again at the end of the semester and at the end of the year so that ultimately all the student's academic achievement in a course is reported as a single mark.

When grades are viewed in this perspective, their possible shortcomings are apparent. Are they reliable? Are they valid? Do they really convey meaning? Generally speaking, they are, in fact, as reliable as any other predictor of future academic achievement. They are also useful in that they have become the basis of a convention of communication that is widely understood among the many parties who ultimately make use of them. Finally, there are simply no currently available alternatives to grades as the symbols that summarize the results of teacher evaluation.

Test Writing

In the course of comprehensive classroom evaluation, both formal and informal data will be obtained in several ways. Observation of students provides a continuing series of impressions. Anecdotal records, checklists, and rating scales are used to collect and record more substantive information. But, on the whole, paper-and-pencil tests are the source of most of the formal evaluation-related information that teachers obtain.

Paper-and-pencil tests are made up of essay and objective items. The essay items may be short-answer questions that require a sentence or two, or they may be extended to involve several paragraphs. The most common types of objective items are true-false, completion, matching, and multiple choice.

Essay Items. These are especially useful for measuring higher order thinking, including analysis, synthesis, and evaluation. Because they take a relatively long time to answer, compared to objective items, only a limited sample of learning can be measured with essay items. Factual information and basic comprehension are much more efficiently measured with objective test items.

Essay items may be written rather quickly since they are in the form of a question to which students respond or a suggested topic about which students are asked to write. However, care must be taken to write the items clearly and specify precisely what the response should address. Since an essay item can cover only a relatively limited range of information, items should be judiciously selected, based on a priority of objectives. In other words, sampling is a prime concern.

In John Sykes' class, we can imagine as a test item: "What is the contribution of art to our culture?" Obviously, entire books have been written on the topic and whole courses are devoted to investigating certain aspects of it. Although he may want students to begin to appreciate the contribution of art in his course, we can imagine students' frustration in attempting to respond to such a broad question. We also wonder how a teacher would grade their responses.

A more limited question in this class might be: "What was Paul Klee's contribution to the art of the first half of this century?" Here again, however, we recognize some problems. Did Paul Klee make only one contribution? Should the students simply name the contribution in a brief phrase or sentence, or should they provide a context, some description, and the impact? How much should the student write? The item does not meet the criteria of clearness and preciseness.

Consider one more example: "In a one-page essay (approximately 150 words) describe the single most identifiable characteristic of Paul Klee's painting in the 1920's and 1930's, and give an example of how his work influenced other artists of his time." In this item, three things are made clear to the students: the length of the essay, the expectation that they will describe the single-most identifiable characteristic of Klee's painting, and that they can produce evidence supporting the assertion that Klee had professional influence. Although writing essay items may be done more quickly than writing most objective items, much care must still be taken to write with optimal effectiveness. The time spent writing such items will pay off when teachers grade them. It is so much easier when teachers know exactly what to look for!

The art course that has been used as a setting for the examples above is not a language arts course, and this presents another concern. To what extent does a student's word comprehension skills related to reading and interpreting an item and his or her expressive skills related to responding to an item become factors in the evaluation of a student response? In other words, teachers may find themselves grading students' language skills as much as their acquisition of understandings in the art course. This is a dilemma without an immediate solution. At the very least, students should be made aware of the extent to which expression will count as a factor in grading—if it counts at all. Also, every effort should be made to use clear, basic language in writing test items. Finally, students who are known to have limited comprehension and expressive skills should be given whatever consideration is helpful and fair. Within the context of these considerations, informed teacher decision making that focuses on the students' best interest should be the goal.

Objective Items.   Most tests are made up primarily or entirely of objective items. They have the advantage of covering a lot of material efficiently, of being easy to score, and of being easy to translate into students' grades. On the other hand, they are most commonly used to test at the lower thinking levels, primarily recall and comprehension, although it is possible to have objective items at all levels of thinking. Because of the attractiveness of objective items, teachers incline toward their use, with the possible effect of trivializing the evaluation of learning outcomes. Objective means of measuring learning are necessary but not sufficient as a comprehensive approach to evaluation.

Matching, completion, and true-false items are the usual means of measuring students' recall. To the extent that some information is very important to students' understanding and becomes the "raw material" for subsequent information processing, these types of measurement are useful. However, one of the clear findings from research is that these items are used with disproportionate frequency, or at the very least they are not supplemented by a sufficient number of items that test at the higher levels of thinking.

Although these three kinds of objective test items are straightforward in form, they nevertheless must be carefully written. True-false items, for example, deal in absolutes. However, absolutes that are also not self-evident are rather difficult to find. Students become testwise and realize that an absolute or specific determiner such as "always" or "never" usually signifies a false answer. Ambiguity is a problem as well. For example, a true-false statement might be: Michelangelo was a 16th-century artist. A knowledgeable student would realize that Michelangelo produced one of his greatest sculptures, the *Pieta*, in the last years of the 15th century, and in the absolute sense the statement is false. Yet the teacher would probably intend this as a true statement. In writing any objective test item, a teacher must constantly keep in mind the concern for avoiding ambiguity.

The multiple choice form is the most difficult to write but the most useful objective test item. It involves producing a stem which describes the substance of the item and from 3 to 5 possible answers from which to select. This type of item can potentially measure all the levels of thinking, but it is most useful for measuring recall, comprehension, application, and analysis.

The best approach to writing a multiple choice item is to write a stem and correct response that deals with a pertinent and important aspect of the unit of study and is directly related to a unit goal. Then write at least two, but preferably three or four so-called distractors, or possible responses that would be attractive to a person who was insufficiently informed. This latter task is the most difficult, and the effectiveness of the item is especially dependent on the finesse with which the distractors are written. Because plausible distractors are so difficult to write, most multiple choice items include four instead of five possible responses from which the student picks one. In some cases, only three possible responses are included, but the chances of guessing right reduces the discriminating power considerably.

Some examples of multiple choice questions provide a basis for examining their qualities.

1. Michelangelo is associated most closely with which Italian city?
   a. Bologna   c. Milan
   b. Rome   d. Florence

This is a straightforward example of a recall level item. Of course, one might have used a true-false item to test for the same knowledge. One might also have embedded this bit of information in a format which requires matching artists with locales.

2. Michelangelo's greatest art work is
   a. David   c. Pieta
   b. Mona Lisa   d. Sistine Chapel

This item has at least two flaws. First, one will probably encounter more argument than agreement about which was the greatest work of art. There is clearly no best response, and ambiguity results. Second, Mona Lisa is a "ringer" in this list, since another artist painted it. Students might very likely form unintended impressions if Mona Lisa is included as a distractor. In a more general sense, Mona Lisa lies outside the range from which appropriate distractors should be selected; it is of a different genre.

3. The "power" in Michelangelo's art lies primarily in his ability to
   a. give embodiment to a transcendent level of human experience.
   b. create a perfect mirror image of reality in both sculpture and painting.
   c. use line and perspective to produce unusual spatial relationships.
   d. represent common and familiar objects in unique, emotionally charged images.

This analysis level item may be appropriate for a college level course in art history or art appreciation. However, if this were a question asked in Mr. Sykes' 9th-grade class or in any level high school class, students could not handle the language level. It would be as much a test of reading comprehension as of art knowledge.

4. Michelangelo can appropriately be formally considered a "Renaissance Man" primarily because
   a. he lived in the 15th and 16th centuries.
   b. he was a master of several forms of art.
   c. he was a friend of powerful people in his time.
   d. his art was not limited to the traditions of his time.

This example of an analysis level item meets the criteria presented below for writing effective multiple choice items.

Writing multiple choice test items, according to Gage and Berliner (1984), is "a kind of art form" (p. 719). This should not discourage teachers from writing them. Rather, it advises teachers not to take the skill for granted and to work at developing it. The above examples begin to give a sense of the intellectual task involved in producing these items. A set of suggestions will help to guide the writing of such items. Practice in developing a "feel" for them will contribute to improving the skill.

1. Keep the language at the students' level; use good grammatical form.
2. Write the stem and correct response first, then add three or four plausible distractors.
3. Express as much of the substance of the item as possible in the stem.
4. Avoid ambiguity; be certain that one response is clearly the best response.
5. Keep the responses in an item consistent in type and length.
6. Avoid specific determiner words and absolutes such as every, none, always, and never.
7. Avoid the use of negative words (no, not) in the stem if possible; always avoid a double negative, or a word used both in the stem and in the response.
8. Do not use "all of the above" as a distractor.

Purposes of Evaluation

Diagnostic Evaluation. Students in a typical secondary classroom present teachers with a staggering range of individual differences. In an ungrouped 9th grade class, reading comprehension levels alone may span up to 8 years. Especially in classes in which cumulative learning is a factor (mathematics and language), diagnostic tests provide the teacher with useful information about students' level of previous achievement. Involving students in studies for which they have insufficient background is self-defeating; teaching student material that they have already mastered is equally self-defeating.

Diagnostic tests may be of two sorts. Standardized tests may be used to determine how a particular student or entire class compares with typical students at that level (a norm group). Also, standardized tests are available that measure students' learning skills (reasoning and computational). The *Mental Measurements Yearbook* (Buros, 1978) is a standard reference for teachers in this area.

The second sort of diagnostic test is sometimes referred to as a pretest. This teacher-made test is written to reflect the goals/objectives of an imminent unit of study. It may be quite similar to the test intended to be administered at the completion of a unit of study. Students' scores and success rate on these diagnostic tests will provide valuable information for planning learning activities within the unit and individualizing learning to the extent it is feasible. If, for example, grading contracts are used, diagnostic test information provides the basis for specifying the terms of the contract. Parenthetically it should be noted here that a separate and unique contract for each student (which could involve over 100 contracts per teacher!) is unrealistic, although separate contracts may be developed for occasional exceptional situations. However, contracts written at three levels of student learning within a course of study is manageable for most teachers and will help the teacher avoid teaching only the mythical average student.

Formative Evaluation. This aspect of evaluation asks the question, ''How am I doing?'' It is not particularly different in form from the other tests, although it may be somewhat informal. These are tests or other approaches to evaluation which are administered at opportune times to provide feedback to the teacher and students regarding achievement. They serve a diagnostic function within a course of study. They serve as a basis for the teacher in ascertaining instructional effectiveness, making mid-unit curricular decisions, determining the impact of instructional innovations, and deciding whether reteaching should occur. They serve as a means for the student to gauge progress at any point and identify gaps or weaknesses in the mastery of the unit goals.

For example, during a unit on painting in John Sykes' art course, a particular student may have been found to be quite adept in sketching in the outlines of an intended painting. This student would be introduced to the next phase involving mixing colors, while other students continued to improve their sketches. In the scenario, another sort of formative evaluation occurred as John Sykes used ''teaching quizzes.'' These not only gave the students information on the extent to which they were meeting the teacher's expectations, but were also an incentive to study efforts.

Summative Evaluation. When most people—especially nonteachers—think of evaluation, summative evaluation is what they have in mind. Summative evaluation occurs at the completion of a unit of study, and its primary purpose is to determine the extent to which each student has achieved the unit goals/objectives. Summative evaluation can occur in a variety of forms (including timed performances, written reports, or presentations to the group), but usually it occurs as a written test. The scores derived from summative evaluation exercises are usually the primary source for determining students' grades.

If evaluation is considered to be a cyclical process, summative evaluation may also serve a diagnostic function. The end-of-unit test indicates to the teacher the extent to which students have benefitted from a unit of instruction. Some students in an algebra class, for example, simply may not be ready to proceed to second order equations if they have not mastered simple linear equations. Remediation may be prescribed based on diagnosis from the summative evaluation outcome.

Classroom Tests

Teacher-made tests are a traditional and indispensable part of evaluation. They serve several functions, including, of course, measuring achievement. The items on a test provide the teacher with the opportunity to select for the student those aspects of the unit of study that are most important, and thus reinforce learning of the material one last time during the study of the unit. Furthermore, students' attention is entirely devoted to the test for the duration of the time. Perhaps the most intense learning that occurs in a classroom is that which involves test-taking, a strong rationale for writing powerful tests.

A test score has no meaning until it is compared to a referent. Three types of referents are presented below. The teacher's purposeful choice of the appropriate referent is an important evaluation-related decision.

Norm-Referenced Tests. The referent for norm-referenced tests is the average of the students' scores on that particular test. It is an attractive approach to teachers because it "lets them off the hook" regarding making prior decisions about levels of achievement. Either by "eyeballing" a set of scores after the fact and assigning letter grades using break points in the range, or even by using a more sophisticated approach involving normal curve statistics, teachers establish norm-referenced student grades. It has the effect of neutralizing the teacher's possible shortcomings as an instructor because "the highest score made is the highest score possible."

Many standardized tests are norm-referenced, using what Gage and Berliner (1984) refer to as the distant peer group. Teachers or administrators often wish to know how their students compare with their cohort group districtwide, statewide, or nationwide. Teachers may make curriculum decisions or revise expectation levels based on the results of such tests.

Also, students may wish to know their standing within a certain population. The Student Achievement Test (SAT) and American College Test (ACT) are examples of norm-referenced standardized tests that provide college-bound students with important information about their current relative levels of achievement, which in turn are a predictor of future academic achievement.

The use of norm-referencing is widely criticized in the literature. The major problem associated with it is that teachers, in their evaluation-related decisions, tend to default to norm-referencing even when it is not the pedagogically recommended approach. However, norm-referencing is a useful—in fact, indispensable—means of addressing the evaluation purposes for which it is intended.

In cases in which it is useful to rank students in the class, to cite achievement in terms of percentiles, or to usefully employ a competitive approach, norm-referenced grading is appropriate. However, it does allow the teacher to get by with unclear objectives and expectations and with marginally effective instruction. In general, teachers should think very carefully before using norm-referenced tests in the classroom.

Criterion-Referenced Tests. As the term implies, students are required to meet a predetermined level of performance in order to be assigned a particular grade. Establishing the appropriate level, or criterion, may be a difficult task for the teacher, especially an inexperienced teacher. A criterion set too low results in unreasonably high grades and little grade dispersal. At the other extreme, a criterion set too high dooms a disproportionate number of students to low grades. This results in disappointed students and a grim teacher who is shaken by the specter of personal failure. Setting appropriate criteria is an important but risky part of evaluation.

Although the major disadvantage of criterion-referenced testing is the difficulty of establishing appropriate standards, the advantages far outweigh this disadvantage. The criterion-referenced approach allows teachers to establish, in their judgment, reasonable targets for student performance. If a target is not met, the teacher may need to analyze the possible causes and perhaps revise expectations, but it is not a reason to abandon the use of the approach. Criterion-referenced testing also allows the teacher to set a level of mastery which determines when reteaching should occur. Because this approach is based upon an absolute referent, each student's level of competence is clearly represented.

The objectives within a unit of study may, in fact, be written in terms of criteria. In an art class, the teacher may set as an expectation: ''Students will mix three shades of each of the secondary colors within the ranges displayed on the classroom chart.'' This statement clearly establishes what students are to accomplish and further specifies the criterion against which it is to be compared. Other objectives in Chapter 3 on planning are examples of the relationship of objectives to criterion-referenced approaches to evaluation.

Self-Referenced Tests. For some students under particular conditions, the only evaluation approach that is appropriate is an assessment based on past performance. In a typing class, a criterion of 60 words-per-minute may be established to get an A grade. However, a student with poor motor skills could never hope to attain anything close to that. A more reasonable approach is to determine through several trials the student's current speed level, then establish a reasonable target, such as a weekly increase of 2 words-per-minute for the next 6 weeks. A subsequent dilemma arises: should a student who achieves only 32 words-per-minute get a higher grade than one who may type 45 words-per-minute? It can be resolved only in terms of the teacher's philosophy as it relates to evaluation: what, in fact, is the purpose of grades?

Students' Grades

Grades (the term *marks* is also used) have been called the coin of the students' realm. They are the object of the students' ardent desire. Getting high marks is a satisfying experience for students; getting low marks may be devastating. School marks are an important factor in students' determination of their self-images.

In the most basic sense, school marks are symbols with which the teacher communicates to students and other interested parties an estimate of each student's academic performance. From an academic point of view, grades convey pertinent and useful information. But grades are so highly emotionally charged that the academic uses of grades are frequently overshadowed.

The academic functions of grades are straightforward. Wrinkle (1947) and Adams and Torgerson (1964) have identified four functions: (1) administrative, for determining such things as promotion, transfer, class standing, and eligibility for honors; (2) guidance, for identifying characteristics of strength and weakness, advising on enrollment in particular programs, and planning for careers; (3) informing, for communicating the results of evaluation to interested parties, primarily students and parents; and (4) motivation, for providing an incentive for students when innate interest in learning is minimal. On the other hand, grades have certain suspect qualities. Kindsvatter (1969), after reviewing the literature, concluded that school marks may have these shortcomings:

(1) Marks are variable, subjective, contaminated, even capricious.

(2) Marks create a condition of unfair competition.

(3) Marks reflect an aristocratic rather than democratic attitude.

(4) Marks preoccupy students and their parents.

(5) Marking practices deny the psychological principle of individual differences.

(6) Marking practices tend to influence teaching in the direction of memorization and regurgitation at the expense of concept formation and creativity.

(7) Marking practices encourage student dependency. (p. 331)

Although there is general agreement that grades are necessary (some might say a necessary evil), an informed and sensitive approach to evaluation can attenuate some of the negative outcomes of grading. A teacher who takes an arbitrary, self-righteous approach to grading will almost certainly hurt some students unnecessarily. On the other hand, a teacher who uses a positive, developmental approach to determining grades, as Mr. Sykes did in the case of Ricky, can take advantage of the contribution that grades can make to promoting classroom achievement while minimizing contingent negative effects.

The Teacher's Personal Grading System. The system by which the teacher arrives at a student's grade is, by and large, a personal invention. Although the teacher must operate within the school's grading policy, which at the very least specifies what is marked (e.g., achievement, effort, citizenship, attitude), what scale and symbols are used, and the length of grading periods, the teacher generally has a wide range of freedom in selecting/devising personal marking practices. No one system is recognized as the best.

One factor in determining a grading system is the nature of a particular course. In a case in which grades are accumulated from a series of periodically administered, objectively scored tests, straightforward averaging is sufficient. If a variety of sources of evaluation is involved, matters of accumulating and weighting add complexity to grading. Three general criteria apply for any system: it should be functional, fair, and clear.

Informing the students early and clearly regarding the teacher's approach to grading is more important than what approach is used. The students deserve to know what factors are taken into consideration, what relative weight is assigned to each factor, and the minimum expectations for achieving each grade. Describing this information in writing and delivering it to students with explicit directions on the sheet that it is to be shared with parents is the best approach; no student or parent can claim not to have been informed insofar as the teacher is culpable.

SUMMARY POINT

Classroom evaluation is an inevitable component of teaching. However, it is underused as a contributor to teaching effectiveness. Potential will be realized through a comprehensive understanding of the several dimensions of classroom evaluation and the discerning and imaginative application of its pertinent principles. This potential includes greater scope in planning, more informed decision making during instruction, and an increased base of information for assessing achievement.

REVIEW: IMPORTANT PRACTICES FOR EVALUATION

1. Write incisive, unambiguous unit goals and objectives that are both guides for instruction/learning and the bases for standards of achievement.
2. Gather evaluative data from as wide a range of sources as is feasible, both formal and informal.
3. Write tests which reflect the objectives at all the levels of thinking and which become powerful teaching tools as well as well-designed data gathering instruments.

4. Develop a comprehensive approach to evaluation incorporating its diagnostic, formative, and summative functions.
5. Use a criterion-referenced approach for interpreting test results unless there is a specific reason to use another approach.
6. Develop a personal grading system that is functional, fair, and clear.

ACTIVITIES

ACTIVITY I

John Sykes, at the close of the scenario, asked the rhetorical question, "So what's a grade for after all?" Your own philosophical approach to grading can be brought to the level of explicit awareness by writing a paragraph in response to John Sykes' question.

ACTIVITY II

Reference has been made in this chapter to the importance of an informed belief system for making evaluation-related decisions. What are the key principles that serve as the basis for your approach to evaluation?

ACTIVITY III

Textbooks serve as useful tools for planning, instruction, and evaluation. Examine and compare several texts in your teaching area. Which ones best serve the evaluation function, and why? How might texts be better designed to serve this function (e.g., including statements of objectives that are useful as the basis for measuring learning outcomes)?

ACTIVITY IV

Develop an evaluation design for a typical unit that is taught in your subject area. How will you accommodate the diagnostic, formative, and summative phases? What sources of evaluative data will you use?

ACTIVITY V

Develop a grading system for your future classroom that is functional, fair, and clear. What factors will be considered in grading? What weighting will be assigned to each? How will grades be accumulated, and 6 (or 9) weeks grades be calculated? What, if any, is the role of grading contracts in your system?

ACTIVITY VI

How would you deal with the evaluation implications of the following cases?

a. A student has been placed in your class who clearly is unable to function at what you consider to be a minimum level of accomplishment.

b. A student is found to be cheating on an important unit test.

c. Both knowledge and performance (or creative) outcomes are included in the course, yet only one final mark is given.

d. A student has a poor attendance record, completed only about half the homework assignments, was consistently late turning in work, but scored well on the unit test.

e. Describe at least two other dilemmas that have evaluation implications in your classroom.

REFERENCES

Adams, G. & Torgerson, T. (1964). *Measurement and evaluation in education, psychology, and guidance.* New York: Holt, Rinehart, and Winston.

Agnew, E. J. (1983, April). *A study of the letter grade system and its effect on the curriculum.* Paper presented at the annual meeting of the AERA, Montreal. (ERIC ED 238143)

Bloom, B., Hastings, J. T., & Madaus, G. (1971). *Handbook on formative and summative evaluation of student learning.* New York: McGraw-Hill.

Buros, O. (1978). *Mental measurements yearbook.* Lincoln, NE: Buros Institute of Mental Measurement.

Carter, K. (1984). Do teachers understand the principles for writing tests? *Journal of Teacher Education, 35*(6), 57–60.

Ebel, R. L. (1979). *The essentials of educational measurement* (3rd ed.). Englewood Cliffs, NJ: Prentice-Hall.

Fleming, M. & Chambers, B. (1983). Teacher made tests: windows on the classroom. In W. E. Hathaway (Ed.), *Testing in the schools: New directions for testing and measurement, No. 19* (pp. 29–38). San Francisco: Jossey-Bass.

Gage, H. & Berliner, D. (1984). *Educational psychology* (3rd ed.). Boston: Houghton Mifflin.

Gronlund, N. (1974). *Improving marking and reporting in classroom instruction.* New York: Macmillan.

Gullickson, A. B. (1984). Teacher perspectives of their instructional use of tests. *Journal of Educational Research, 77*(4), 244–248.

Halpin, G. & Halpin, G. (1982). Experimental investigations of the effects of study and testing on student learning. *Journal of Educational Psychology, 72,* 32–38.

Kellaghan, T., Madaus, G. & Airasian, P. (1982). *The effects of standardized testing.* Boston: Kluwer-Nijhoff.

Kindsvatter, R. (1966). *The dynamics of change in marking systems in selected innovative and non-innovative high schools in Ohio.* Unpublished dissertation, The Ohio State University.

Kindsvatter, R. (1969). Guidelines for better grading. *Clearinghouse, 43*(6), 331–334.

Lazar-Morris, C., Polin, L., May, R., & Burry, J. (1980). A review of the literature in test use. (Report No. 144). Center for the Study of Evaluation, University of California.

Nungester, R. J. & Duchastel, P. C. (1982). Testing versus review: effects on retention. *Journal of Educational Psychology, 74,* 18–22.

Pedulla, J. J., Airasian, P. W. & Madaus, G. F. (1980). Do teacher ratings and standardized test results of students yield the same information? *American Educational Research Journal 17*(3), 303–307.

Popham, W. J. (1975). *Educational evaluation.* Englewood Cliffs, NJ: Prentice-Hall.

Rudman, H. C., Kelly, J. L., Wanous, D. S., Mehrens, W. A., Clark, C. M., & Porter, A. C. (1980). Integrating assessment with instruction. (Research series No. 75). The Institute for Research on Teaching, Michigan State University.

Salmon-Cox, L. (1981). Teachers and standardized achievement tests: what's really happening? *Phi Delta Kappan 62*(8), 631–634.

Starch, D. (1913, October). Reliability and distribution of grades. *Science 38,* pp. 630–636.

Starch, D. (1918). *Educational measurements.* New York: Macmillan.

Stiggins, R. J. (1985). Improving assessment where it means the most: in the classroom. *Educational Leadership 43*(2), 69–74.

Stiggins, R. J., & Bridgeford, N. J. (1985). The ecology of classroom assessment. *Journal of Educational Measurement 22*(4), 271–286.

Stiggins, R. J., Conklin, N. F. & Bridgeford, N. J. (1986). Classroom assessment: a key to effective education. *Educational Measurement: Issues and Practice 5*(2), 5–17.

Wrinkle, W. (1947). *Improving marking and reporting practices in secondary schools.* New York: Rinehart.

CHAPTER 10

Toward Effective Teaching

This book has presented hundreds of ideas about teaching, and especially about instruction. No reader could or should remember them all separately. What the reader should have acquired as a synthesis of the book's content is a sense of what a mature and professional teacher is; the respect this teacher has for the science of teaching; the approach this teacher takes to decision making; the model this teacher provides for students as a scholar and a leader; the skill with which this teacher employs a range of teaching methods; and the tolerance this teacher has for conditions that cannot be directly controlled.

The challenge to the new teacher, as is perhaps now clear, is not to emulate precisely some expert model, but rather it is to be an effective decision maker. Training is most useful in situations that are highly predictable and repetitious. Teaching is not like that. At any moment the situation in the classroom occurs as the interplay of numerous dynamic variables. Conditions change quickly within a classroom and vary markedly from class to class. The task of the teacher is to control as many variables as possible and be able to react with assurance to those that are not directly controllable. Teachers, therefore, depend much more on knowledge and judgment than on training to be effective decision makers. The fact that the answers are not ''out there'' to be found is at first difficult to accept. The fact is that the answers—or at least the decisions—come from within. This sometimes makes teaching a lonely job, and not a job for the faint-hearted or the insecure.

The effective teacher is not a single, readily described entity. Effective teachers share some common general traits, but in practice those traits are exhibited in unique and personal ways. In a real sense, each aspiring teacher must reinvent the effective teacher based on his or her knowledge, beliefs, perceptions, personality, and interaction with students at various contexts. Assistance with this task is available from this book, from teacher educators, and from practicing teachers. However, the responsibility for ultimately acquiring identity in the teacher role and integrity as a professional educator lies with each prospective teacher.

We presume that the reader has by now considered the many ideas in this book and that the image of the effective teacher has begun to take shape. The next likely step is to develop one's teaching skills through extensive teaching. This phase usually occurs as student teaching or the internship. This book was designed for teacher education students, student teachers, and first year teachers to provide direction in applying instructional skills. Activities were devised to aid beginning teachers and supervisors in obtaining data to help measure the effectiveness of these skills on students and in turn influence instructional decisions. The data collection instruments included in Chapters 2 through 8 are intended for this purpose. We suggest, therefore, that this book's contribution, more than one of informing per se, has the potential to contribute to one's actual entry into teaching.

STUDENT TEACHING AND INTERNSHIP

Student teaching and/or an internship is the usual culmination of the teacher-education program. In the view of student teachers or interns, it is the most important phase because they finally encounter the real demands of the teacher role. It is typically approached with some anxiety and perceived to be a trial-by-fire or a sink-or-swim proposition. Realistically the possibility of this exists, but students who have been reasonably successful in preparation experiences prior to student teaching have little rational basis for fear. It is essentially a very special time for learning in ways that have been previously unavailable because of the limited definition of teacher preparation programs. Now as the training responsibility for the development of preservice teachers is carried over into the first years of in-service teaching, more technical assistance is available to the beginner through and beyond student teaching. The profession is acknowledging that an optimally effective teacher develops only after a substantial period of study and practice. This support approach should make the beginner feel more secure.

A number of teacher preparation institutions, including members of the Holmes Group (1986), have adopted models which extend practice teaching to a full year internship within a school district. This influential group of teacher preparation institutions promotes a year-long internship for prospective teachers, with pedagogical studies to start upon the completion of a four-year liberal arts program. This approach to graduate teacher training is also endorsed by the Carnegie Task Force (1986). Nine states already require entry year assistance programs for their beginning teachers and many other states are considering tying in completion of an entry year program to initial certification or renewal of certificates. The need for guidance and support of the beginning teacher through student teaching and into the first year of in-service teaching is now recognized around the country as essential to attracting quality teachers and retaining them in the profession.

Meanwhile, as a student teacher or intern adjusts to these first intensive periods of teaching, his or her focus shifts from the cognitive, or intellectual, preparation to experiential engagement. This shift presents a new set of demands to the student teacher or intern about which he or she will feel some measure of stress. This stress can cause a beginning teacher to abandon newly acquired, pedagogically endorsed ideas and revert to more comfortable intuitive ones. This is a time for tough-minded decision making on the part of the student teacher or intern. Student teaching and the internship will be a more valuable experience if deliberate efforts are made to employ approaches and practices as they are described in this book. Resisting the temptation to practice without consideration of effective teaching techniques will diminish the extent of necessary relearning later in order to function as an optimally effective teacher. Those who play golf by first using a flawed swing and then learning a proper swing will appreciate the logic of this suggestion.

Student teaching and the internship enlist the services of a successful practicing teacher, variously referred to as the cooperating, support, or host teacher, to supervise the beginner. The function of the cooperating teacher is far more than simply making a classroom available to the student teacher. An important contribution made by this person is in observing the student teacher's or beginning teacher's performance to provide descriptive and evaluative feedback. Receiving impressions and advice from a perceptive observer is valuable. To the extent that the data provided is focused, systematically obtained, carefully analyzed, and thoughtfully interpreted, it is especially valuable. The entire process that is referred to as *systematic analysis* and *clinical supervision* in the literature is facilitated by the instruments provided in this book.

SCENARIO

Denton Coleman had been student teaching in a Spanish III class for 6 weeks. He had gotten by the initial jitters and uncertainty and was beginning to establish his own teaching style. He realized he tended not to be as structured in his approach as his cooperating teacher, Kay Obrock; however, she did not insist on more structure. She was willing to let Denton experiment and find his own most comfortable and effective way.

Denton had felt a sense of relief after the first 3 weeks, when he realized he was able to manage acceptably well as a teacher. With the relief came a surge of confidence and exhilaration about teaching. Now, however, at the 6-weeks point, he experienced some self-doubt and a decided letdown. The students in his Spanish III class seemed complacent. They had not been well prepared for class nor had they been as enthusiastic in their participation as he remembered they were for Ms. Obrock.

When he shared his concern with his cooperating teacher, she responded, "I've noticed it, Denton. Part of it, I guess, is that the honeymoon is over. When you are a new face and a different personality the kids are naturally curious and interested. Every teacher experiences that, and it usually works to your advantage at first. When you don't have that going for you any more you have to look more carefully at what is happening." They talked for a few more minutes, but he still felt uneasy and didn't have any clear notion of what to do about it. Then something Kay Obrock had said came to mind: ". . . look more carefully at what is happening." He remembered the text he had used in his principles and methods course that Included a series of instruments for analyzing instruction.

Denton took the book from the bookshelf when he got home and began to look through it. As he revisited the familiar pages he thought it just might be what he needed. The next day, in their first period conference, Denton showed the book to Kay   especially the analysis instruments. "We didn't have anything like this when I was in college," she said, "but it looks interesting." She spent some time during the day looking through the book.

When they met again after school for their daily wrap-up, each had some ideas. Denton said, "The problem seems to be motivation. They aren't working very hard, and they are fooling around in class more and more. Isn't there something in the book about motivation?"

"Yes," Kay replied. "But motivation is a big topic. A lot of things contribute to motivation. As I see it, that is one of the advantages of the book, that it helps make you aware of the parts and gives you a way to examine them." After some discussion, Jay went on to say, "Look, there is an instrument in Chapter 4 called "Motivating Behaviors." It includes six different aspects of motivation. Why don't I use this in class tomorrow, and it will help us focus more specifically on something we can handle. The book suggests making a videotape so that you can do some analysis, too. Maybe I can get the VCR away from the football coach for a day or two. You know, maybe the coaches are on to a good thing with the VCR. I never thought about that."

Denton Coleman taught while Kay Obrock observed with the instrument before her. Then they both viewed the videotape later. Their analysis, done independently and then compared, revealed a similar pattern. Denton used his voice well enough, changed the instructional mode frequently, and controlled the pace appropriately. He did less well in displaying enthusiasm. However, moving about the classroom and using purposeful nonverbal behaviors were identified as the motivation areas of most need in both of their analyses.

They discussed the results of their analyses at some length. Then Kay said, "Denton, you can't change everything at once. Let's take one thing at a time. Suppose we concentrate on your movement about the class. We agree that you tend to plant yourself next to the desk too much of the time. We can get to nonverbal behavior later. OK?" Denton agreed. They examined what was involved in moving about the class, including the monitoring that was facilitated by that movement. "Why don't I make a diagram of the room and chart your movements for a whole period. I'll also identify situations that should be monitored and see if you respond by moving there."

"Sounds good to me," Denton agreed enthusiastically. "Now maybe I should give some thought to just how I can move effectively. You know, maybe I'll start class from the back of the room tomorrow. I wonder what they'll think about doing the warm-up drill that way?"

APPLICATION TO PRACTICE

Systematic Analysis

The most common approach to instructional improvement, whether in a self-analysis or supervisor-teacher mode, relies on the biases and impressions of the observer. That is, the teaching episode is viewed either directly or by recording, and the observer's reaction is based on his or her particular frame of reference. The information obtained is often highly inferential, but it may be helpful if the observer is perceptive. A more direct approach, however, is to deal with discrete, manageable components of instruction in a methodical manner.

The most powerful approach to instructional improvement is referred to as self-confrontation, or the use of video- or audiotapes. However, a recording alone is largely ineffectual. Teachers hearing/viewing themselves tend to get caught up in the cosmetic aspects of the playback. Research confirms that three elements are required to produce the strongest influence for change: a recording, particularly a videotape; a focus, usually provided with a selected instrument; and the presence of another knowledgeable person to provide a dispassionate perspective, usually a cooperating teacher in the case of a student teacher or support teacher in the case of an intern (Fuller & Manning, 1973; Peck & Tucker, 1973). Self-analysis without a third party is less effective but is still sufficiently effective to be well worth using.

Systematic analysis of instruction is conducted as a straightforward process of quantifying discrete segments of teacher behavior for the purpose of analyzing that behavior. The steps are listed and explained below.

Step 1. Determine what aspect of instruction on which to focus. The many instruments in this book suggest a range of possibilities, but any discrete aspect of teaching about which objective data may be obtained may be selected. Obviously, the choice will be determined by the perceived need for improvement in that skill or method. Denton Coleman and Kay Obrock recognized motivation as an area that deserved attention.

Step 2. Select (or develop) an instrument that focuses on the targeted skill or method. This book provides many appropriate instruments, but doesn't nearly exhaust the possibilities. Teachers can readily develop personally tailored instruments, often in the form of straightforward checklists or tallying forms, to obtain quantitative data on performance. For example, a very simple kind of form is a set of tallies indicating the number of times a teacher uses a verbal reinforcer. Kay Obrock devised a room diagram to serve this purpose.

Step 3. Teach a lesson and make an audio- or videotape of it. The instrument selected may be used during the lesson if an observer is available. Otherwise, the tape playback will provide the means for obtaining data. The optimum situation occurs if data can be obtained during the performance by an observer and later from the tape by the student teacher. Comparison of the two sets of data obtained is an especially fruitful basis for discussion and analysis. The teacher and student teacher in the scenario used this approach.

Step 4. Tabulate and examine the data obtained. This is the data base that provides an indication of the current status of that particular factor of instruction.

Step 5. From analysis of the data, evaluate the effectiveness of the target teacher behavior. (Data on student behavior might also be collected for some purposes, but it would only indirectly relate to teacher behavior, e.g., students' time on-task.) Decide what teaching improvements are desirable, especially in quantifiable terms according to the instrument used. For example, a teacher may establish a goal to increase by 50% the number of higher level questions asked. On other occasions the intended outcome may not be so readily quantifiable, as was the case in the scenario.

Step 6. On the next appropriate occasion, repeat the data collection process and the subsequent analysis. Compare the data from the latter episode to the data base established in the first and to the goal established for the second.

Step 7. Repeat the cycle as many times as seems useful until the goal in Step 5 has been achieved. Meanwhile, as further experience is acquired the original goal may need to be adjusted.

The process of systematic analysis has the particular advantage of describing teaching factors in measurable terms. Determining change in any factor is not dependent on only impression or perception; it is a matter verified by data. While connoisseurship (i.e., informed impression) can be a valuable source of information for making decisions about teaching, data-based sources should probably be used where they are applicable. The two approaches, qualitative and quantitative, are mutually complementary as sources of useful information.

Clinical Supervision

Clinical supervision is the highly structured and intensive means with which the cooperating teacher contributes to the process of systematic analysis. Goldhammer (1969) and Cogan (1972) originally described clinical supervision, and numerous authors have written more recently on the topic (Bryan & Copeland,

1978; Goldhammer, Anderson, & Krajewski, 1980; McFaul & Cooper, 1984; Snyder, 1981; Sullivan, 1980).

In a regular in-service setting, clinical supervision tends to be somewhat unwieldy because of the extensive amount of time that is required of the supervisor unless it is part of an assistance program for beginning and marginal teachers. With a designated mentor or support teacher to give the beginning teacher feedback on teacher behaviors and their effect on student behaviors, the clinical supervision model can be a valuable tool to promote informed decision making for the beginning teacher. Clinical supervision is ideally suited for the internship and the student teaching phases since the student teacher and cooperating teacher or support teacher necessarily work in a close relationship over a considerable period of time. The time the cooperating teacher or support teacher spends observing the beginning teacher will be used to maximum advantage if clinical supervision is implemented.

Clinical supervision varies in its number of steps from author to author, but in essence the process is the same. The following four steps describe the process in its simplest form using the student teacher-cooperating teacher titles, but the process is the same for intern-support teacher, and beginning teacher-supervisor.

Step 1—Preobservation Conference. The student teacher and cooperating teacher decide together what aspect of the student teacher's performance will be targeted. This area is then behaviorally defined in terms of its discrete components. An instrument comprised of a series of components such as those in this book provides such a definition. Next, a criterion or goal stated in measurable terms is established. Finally, if an instrument is not already available for collecting pertinent data, one will have to be devised.

Step 2—Observation and Data Collection. The cooperating teacher may actually use the instrument to collect data during the student teaching episode. However, the cooperating teacher might more usefully operate a videotape recorder in order to assure that the episode is expertly taped. The tape can then be used later for obtaining data. Ideally, both the student teacher and cooperating teacher will tabulate and analyze data independently for later comparison, discussion, and evaluation.

Step 3—Analysis of Data. Whatever the situation is regarding data collection, the most essential aspect is that the cooperating teacher use the data collection instrument. Examination of the data, either independently or cooperatively, should reveal patterns which in turn suggest underlying meanings. The cooperating teacher needs to be certain that thorough analysis does occur and that the implications are translated into appropriate teaching strategies.

Step 4—Postobservation Conference. The cooperating teacher and student teacher compare their respective analyses and implications. Considerable attention should be given to probing underlying meanings together and discussing promising strategies. A new target or goal should be agreed upon and the student teacher should be made responsible for developing a plan to reach it. This initiates a new cycle of clinical supervision, and the cycle continues as long as it is productive in any area of teaching improvement. In the scenario we find Denton Coleman and Kay Obruck beginning the processes of systematic analysis and clinical supervision that have the potential to help Denton make measurable improvement in his teaching.

SUMMARY POINT

Effective teacher decision making about instructional improvement or any other aspect of teaching requires an informed belief system. While a popular aphorism postulates experience as the best teacher, teaching experience alone provides no guarantee of instructional improvement over time. However, decisions made in the interest of improving instruction that are based on self-confrontation and an understanding of systematic analysis are virtually certain to produce targeted gains.

REFERENCES

Bryan, N. & Copeland, W. (1978). *Instructional supervision training program.* New York: Merrill.

Carnegie Task Force on Teaching as a Profession (1986). *A nation prepared: Teachers for the 21st century.* New York: Carnegie Forum on Education and the Economy.

Cogan, M. (1972). *Clinical supervision.* Boston: Houghton Mifflin.

Fuller, F. & Manning, B. (1973). Self-confrontation reviewed: a conceptualization for video playback in teacher education. *Review of Educational Research, 43,* 469–528.

Goldhammer, R. (1969). *Clinical supervision: Special methods for the supervision of teachers.* New York: Holt, Rinehart and Winston.

Goldhammer, R., Anderson, R. & Krajewski, R. (1980). *Clinical supervision.* New York: Holt, Rinehart and Winston.

Holmes Group (1986). *Tomorrow's teachers: A report of the homes group.* East Lansing: Michigan State University, The Holmes Group, Inc.

McFaul, S. & Cooper, J. (1984). Peer clinical supervision: theory vs. reality. *Educational Leadership, 41,* 4–9.

Peck, R. and Tucker, J. (1973). Research on teacher education. In R. Travers (Ed.), *Second handbook of research on teaching.* Chicago: Rand McNally.

Snyder, K. (1981). Clinical supervision in the 1980's. *Educational Leadership, 38,* 521–524.

Sullivan, C. (1980). *Clinical supervision: A state of the art review.* Alexandria, VA: Association for Supervision and Curriculum Development.

Index